Inclusive Child Care
for Infants and Toddlers

Inclusive Child Care
for Infants and Toddlers

Meeting Individual and Special Needs

by

Marion O'Brien, Ph.D.
University of Kansas at Lawrence

·P·A·U·L·H·
BROOKES
PUBLISHING CO®

Baltimore • London • Sydney

·P A U L·H·
BROOKES
PUBLISHING C°®

Paul H. Brookes Publishing Co.
Post Office Box 10624
Baltimore, Maryland 21285-0624
www.brookespublishing.com

Typeset by Barton Matheson Willse & Worthington, Baltimore, Maryland.
Manufactured in the United States of America by
Lightning Source, La Vergne, Tennessee.

The cases described in this book are based on the author's actual experiences. Names have been changed and identifying details have been altered to protect confidentiality.

Readers are granted permission to photocopy the Quality Checks and forms in the appendices of this volume for use in child care services.

Second printing, July 2000.
Third printing, May 2003.
Fourth printing, July 2007.

Library of Congress Cataloging-in-Publication Data

O'Brien, Marion.
    Inclusive child care for infants and toddlers : meeting individual and special needs /
  by Marion O'Brien.
      p.   cm.
    Includes bibliographical references and index.
    ISBN-13: 978-1-55766-296-5 (pbk.)
    ISBN-10: 1-55766-296-7 (pbk.)
    1. Infants—Care.   2. Infants—Development.   3. Toddlers—Care.   4. Child care.
  5. Child development.   I. Title.
  HQ774.0323   1997   97-12828
  649'. 122—DC21   CIP

British Library Cataloguing in Publication data are available from the British Library.

Contents

v

121718

About the Author

Marion O'Brien, Ph.D., is Associate Professor of Human Development and Family Life at the University of Kansas and Director of the Sunnyside Infant-Toddler Program there. She has been working with infants and toddlers and their families for more than 20 years, both in child care and research. Dr. O'Brien has written extensively about infant and toddler development and early intervention for professionals, practitioners, and families. She is a principal investigator for the National Institute of Child Health and Human Development (NICHD) Study of Early Child Care and a member of the Society for Research in Child Development and the National Association for the Education of Young Children.

Preface

This book is intended as a resource for all those who work tirelessly to provide high-quality care to our youngest children and as a training guide for students and beginning teachers. Although more than half of U.S. infants and toddlers are cared for by someone other than their parents for many hours each workday, there are still few comprehensive models for quality infant-toddler care. With an increasing emphasis on *inclusive* care, which is care for children with and without disabilities within the same setting, there is a greater need for tested and workable approaches to provision of such care.

The philosophy, ideas, and concrete suggestions included in this book have been developed, revised, tried, revised, tried again, revised again, and finally written down so that others can also try and revise them. Each classroom environment is different, each group of children has unique needs and preferences, and each effective teacher of infants and toddlers must have flexibility to develop relationships with children in his or her own way. Therefore, the approach taken in this book is not prescriptive. It is expected that readers will find some ideas more to their liking than others and will adapt the program model presented here to their own situations.

Nevertheless, the description of inclusive child care for infants and toddlers that is included here is comprehensive and practical. It is possible to take this book and use it as a blueprint for operating infant and toddler classrooms that serve all children. Too often, authors offer a general philosophy about infant and toddler care and early intervention but avoid the complex and difficult issues that surround implementation. Most people who work with young children already share a common philosophy and a set of core values. What is difficult is translating this philosophy into practice when our primary experience with the care of infants and toddlers is parental care at home. It is not intuitively obvious how to provide responsive and loving care when the babies or toddlers outnumber the adults. Most early childhood teachers are trained and experienced in educating children who can walk, talk, use the bathroom, and sit still to listen to verbal explanations; infants and toddlers do not fit this description. Thus, neither our usual approach to infant and toddler care practices nor our experiences with teaching in a classroom setting provide appropriate designs for inclusive care environments for infants and toddlers. It is, therefore, no wonder that high-quality infant and toddler child care is in short supply in the United States.

The model of care and early intervention on which this book is based is one that has been developed through direct experience with the operation of infant and toddler child care programs at the University of Kansas. Our current full-day inclusive child care center, the Sunnyside Infant-Toddler Program, is operated as part of the academic and service mission of the Department of Human Development and Family Life. My colleagues and friends Kathleen Zanolli and Gretchen Goodman have shared in all aspects of the management, planning, and program development at Sunnyside as well as in the joys and stresses that come with the territory. They are responsible for many good ideas and creative approaches that have found their way into this book but for none of the errors and less successful ideas. Working alongside Kathy and Gretchen has been a truly delightful and enriching experience.

Before our collaboration to create Sunnyside in 1995, I founded and for 5 years directed the EarlyCare Toddler Program, a half-day early intervention program for 1- and 2-year-old children. At both EarlyCare and Sunnyside, many graduate students made substantial contributions to the programs and to the lives of the children and families we served. Classroom supervisors and teaching assistants have included Michele Lausier, who infused our classroom with love and energy; Jo Fritts, who taught us to sign; Barbara Garland-Schwering, who provided us with a useful, general framework for organizing our curriculum; and Kere Hughes, Joy Herrera, Elizabeth Mulkey, Amy Anderson, Anabella Pavon, Gina Rideout, Ann Cook, Xiufen Bi, Virginia Gronwaldt, Lisa Sheik, and Jennifer Ryther. The family services coordinators who have worked to help us serve families along with their children include M. Patricia Robinson, who contributed an optimistic and positive outlook that has sustained us for many years; Laura Giusti, who first got us organized; Sarah Kirk; Jo Mullins; and Cynthia Pagenkopf. There have been too many undergraduate student teachers at EarlyCare and Sunnyside for me to name them all, but each one made his or her individual mark on the program—and, we hope, incorporates a bit of our philosophy into future work with children.

The genealogy of both EarlyCare and Sunnyside can be traced to my involvement as part of a team directed by Todd R. Risley that developed group care programs for infants and toddlers in the 1970s. It was at the Infant Center and Toddler Center that I was first involved in efforts to create quality child care programs. Many of the issues we grappled with then have been reformulated and altered in my work in the years since, but some of our solutions, especially those developed by Jan Porterfield, continue to be effective and are part of the programs described here.

Throughout this 25-year history of working with young children and families, either in child care or in research programs aimed at gaining a better understanding of children's development and families' contributions to that development, the people I have to thank most are the children and families themselves. There is nothing more enjoyable or more educational to me than watching children play or talking with parents about their children. The innumerable insights I have gained over the years from these activities served as the foundation for many of the ideas in this book and also the motivation to produce it.

I also wish to thank my family for their love and support. My husband, John, and my now adult children, Connor, Shay, and Lia, have provided inspiration for this work and tolerance during the many times when other children and families took first place.

This book has been greatly enhanced with the photographs taken by Wally Emerson of Wally Emerson Photography in Lawrence, Kansas, and by the work of the professional and editorial staff at Paul H. Brookes Publishing Co., especially Elaine Niefeld and Michelle Porter. Many thanks for your patience and skill.

Inclusive Child Care
for Infants and Toddlers

Part I
_____

An Introduction
to Inclusive Child Care
for Infants and Toddlers

The approach to inclusive child care for infants and toddlers described in this book incorporates a combination of developmental and ecological principles. All aspects of the program described here are linked to the capabilities of infants and toddlers and the developmental tasks important for them. In addition, this approach is founded on the belief that the physical and social environments of *all* children can and should be structured to support and enhance their development.

Infant care is difficult and demanding because babies are completely dependent on adults for physical care, intellectual stimulation, and emotional support. In a child care setting, teachers may sometimes feel frustrated because they are unable to provide one-to-one care all of the time. Nevertheless, it is important for teachers to remember that even young babies begin to develop the important ability to regulate their own emotions and behavior if they are appropriately challenged to wait briefly for adult attention and if they are provided with a great deal of love and affection along with that attention.

Toddlers are no longer babies who depend on adults to provide experiences for them. Instead, toddlers actively seek to experience the world for themselves. However, toddlers have not yet developed the strong desire, typical of preschoolers, to behave as adults do and in accordance with adults' expectations. Thus, to many adults, typical toddler behavior is unpredictable, frustrating, and, not infrequently, unacceptable.

Although there are challenges associated with teaching toddlers, there are also great rewards. When viewed from a developmental perspective, toddlerhood is the crucial bridge between infancy and childhood and is the time when most of an individual's temperamental characteristics, ways of behaving, and relationships with others coalesce into a stable "personality." As toddlers, children also begin to compare their own view of themselves, formed primarily within the family, with the image that is reflected back to them from the responses of other children and adults to their social overtures. These early social experiences are likely to have long-lasting influences on children's self-concept and social-emotional development.

It is easy to forget how much of each day's experience is *new* to a baby or a toddler and how quickly repeated patterns of behavior become ingrained habits. The philosophy of program design described in this book is based on developmental principles and

1

the idea that infants and toddlers are learning and developing new skills constantly. Thus, teaching and learning opportunities are incorporated into all aspects of the day. At the same time, teachers must have expectations for child behavior that are attainable by infants and toddlers. Teachers are encouraged to view the world through children's eyes and gently guide children in ways that promote positive development.

An ecological approach to program design involves using the physical and social environment to enhance development. An environment with many hazards from which children must be restricted can produce only frustration and an eventual decrease in children's interest, initiative, and involvement. By contrast, an environment that is completely safe and within which children are free to select their own activities encourages active exploration and the development of an intrinsic motivation to learn. In this book, environment is broadly defined to include people as well as toys and room arrangements. In infant and toddler care, it is important that the environment be specifically designed to promote the healthy development of all children, including those with developmental delays or disabilities.

Because the infant and toddler periods are characterized by considerable variability in development and because all infants and toddlers require adult help with daily living activities, children with delays or disabilities can be readily incorporated into an infant or toddler group. In addition, early intervention techniques developed for children with special needs are useful in enhancing the development of *all* children. Thus, high-quality child care for infants and toddlers is an ideal setting for both remedial and preventive intervention and is appropriate for all children.

The chapters in Part I address the general characteristics required for high-quality infant and toddler care in a setting that encourages inclusion of all children. In Chapter 1, the philosophical framework for quality infant-toddler care is presented, and the developmental tasks of the infant and toddler periods and how they translate into teaching approaches within a classroom-based program are described. Chapter 2 focuses on inclusion, the benefits of providing early intervention within a child care setting, and effective team approaches. Chapter 3 focuses on the family's role in child care and early intervention and the importance of parent–teacher relationships for the overall well-being of children. A plan for the organization of infant-toddler care, as it is experienced by children and by teachers, and the organization of space for infants and toddlers are outlined in Chapter 4. Together, these four chapters provide a comprehensive and theoretically based outline for a quality child care and early intervention program uniquely suited to the developmental needs of infants and toddlers.

Chapter 1

A Developmental-Ecological
Approach to Inclusive Infant-Toddler Care

The developmental-ecological approach taken in this book is based on two principles:

1. Infants and toddlers face unique developmental tasks that are different from those of older children.
2. Quality child care environments can be structured to help children achieve these tasks.

The first part of this chapter focuses on the developmental characteristics of infants and toddlers that set them apart from older children. The second section provides a general perspective on aspects of child care program design that are particularly appropriate for children from birth to 3 years of age.

ABOUT INFANTS AND TODDLERS

Taking a developmental approach to infant-toddler care involves defining the important tasks with which children are presented at particular points in their development and then identifying programmatic aspects that will help them master these tasks. This emphasis on development builds on and extends the concept of "developmental appropriateness" that has been widely discussed in both early childhood education and special education forums (Bredekamp, 1987; Wolery & Bredekamp, 1994; Wolery, Strain, & Bailey, 1992) by focusing on the psychological and emotional needs of infants and toddlers as well as on their "readiness" or competencies to perform particular tasks. The environment described here is designed to support infants' and toddlers' development of a secure sense of self, ability to communicate effectively, and trust in others—three psychological qualities that form the basis for learning and adaptation throughout life.

This section outlines the psychological tasks facing infants and toddlers and describes specific ways in which the developmental and ecological approach taken in this book is uniquely designed to help children with those tasks.

3

The Developmental Needs of Infants

Most people are familiar with babies and have an understanding of their needs. In general, babies demand a lot of physical care, and their schedules are determined internally—largely by their needs for food and sleep. In an infant classroom, it is also important to give babies many experiences with objects and people when they are not eating or sleeping. Infants thrive when they are given responsive, individual attention. Providing such attention should be the goal of quality infant care.

Many people have an image of infant care that is more similar to babysitting than to teaching, but responsive teachers of infants are expected to do a lot more than be babysitters. They must follow regular routines for feeding, diaper changing, and naps that involve high standards of care and cleanliness, and they must learn to use a wide range of toys and play activities to help babies explore and experience the world. Babies tend to cry a lot, often for no explainable reason, and this is stressful. It is tempting for teachers of infants to think that the work is done when all of the babies are fed, have clean diapers, and are happy, but that is not the case. Infants who are comfortable and alert are ready to learn, and so teachers must use these calm moments as opportunities for teaching. Overall, teachers of infants constantly work very hard providing responsive care and presenting interesting play activities.

Despite the hard work involved, it is very rewarding to care for infants. Every baby offers unlimited possibilities and gives us hope for the future. Babies smell good (most of the time), make sweet sounds, and have cute faces. Infants also develop rapidly, so that a baby who starts the year all curled up and with an inward focus will be an active, smiling,

interactive child by the end of the year. Babies are very interested in sounds, especially those made by people, and are beginning to learn about communication and conversation from the back-and-forth babbling teachers do with them. Motor achievements in infancy are truly amazing and fun to watch, as each week brings some new skill. By late in infancy, babies pick out the people they know from those they don't, and it is heartwarming to be recognized.

Although most people are familiar with babies, few have given thought to how best to care for a group of them together. This book is based on extensive experience in managing care for a group of babies, and the program design described here ensures that each baby receives individualized and responsive care.

Some of the developmental tasks of infancy that must be taken into consideration in designing an infant program are described in Table 1.1. Of crucial importance in program design is a recognition of the almost complete dependence of infants on their caregivers. Babies have very limited abilities to ask for care or seek out experiences for themselves. In fact, young infants cannot change positions without help. Furthermore, babies have so little experience with the social world that they do not understand the effects their behavior can have on others, nor can they anticipate the consequences of their actions on objects. These characteristics make it crucial that teachers of infants be loving, sensitive, mature, and dependable, and also that a program serving a group of infants be highly organized to anticipate needs and meet them quickly.

Infants' first memories are for regularly occurring events (Bauer & Mandler, 1992), and their earliest efforts to regulate their emotions come in situations that are harmonious, predictable, and consistent (Field, 1994; Thompson, 1991). Therefore, routine daily activities form the heart of an infant care program. Also of great importance is a focus on the individuality of children—their unique ways of responding to everyday care; their developing personalities; and their network of relationships with family, other babies, and teachers. Responsive teachers of infants do not treat every baby in the same way; rather, they adapt their behavior to match the preferences and personalities of each individual. In this way, strong and secure relationships are built between teachers and children.

The Developmental Needs of Toddlers

Toddlers are no longer babies, but they are not yet "little kids" either. The toddler stage is an in-between one that has often been overlooked in developmental research and also in practice. Most people's image of a toddler is based on the popular idea of the "terrible 2s." In fact, though, toddlers are delightful people whose behavior is very reasonable if you look at the world through their eyes instead of insisting they should be more (or less) competent than they are.

A successful toddler classroom must be organized and structured to meet the unique developmental needs of 1- and 2-year-old children. These needs are different from those of infants because they include independence, choice, and more complex social interaction. Toddlers' needs are also different from the needs of preschoolers, who can take care of

Table 1.1.   Meeting the needs of babies in group child care

Babies are:	Therefore, a program that meets babies' needs will:	And responsive teachers of babies will:
Completely reliant on others for care and stimulation	Be organized so that babies' needs for care can be met in a relaxed way, without stress or irritation Include routines of daily living as an important part of the curriculum Have the environment arranged to provide interesting things for babies to look at, listen to, and experience but that are not over-whelming to a baby	Provide care in a warm and responsive manner Respect babies' need for care and be able to provide care without expecting to get some-thing in return Make everyday care routines a focus of their teaching Pay careful attention to babies' interests in the things around them
Not able to anticipate their own needs and desires or communicate them until they become urgent	Anticipate the needs of babies by having a flex-ible and organized schedule that provides for individual needs and ensures that a teacher/caregiver will be available to provide care when it is needed	Be alert to babies' efforts to communicate and respond to them, thereby helping babies learn to communicate more effectively
Unaware that they can use their own behavior to achieve social goals, particularly in recruiting adult attention	Establish a schedule of activities that provides enough teacher time so all babies receive indi-vidual attention during routine caregiving and also when they are awake and happy and not in immediate need of care	Focus their full attention on the children at all times Not interpret fussiness or crying as efforts to gain adult attention but as attempts to communi-cate real needs or desires Show affection fre-quently and noncontin-gently to all children

(continued)

Table 1.1. (continued)

Babies are:	Therefore, a program that meets babies' needs will:	And responsive teachers of babies will:
Required to stay in one place unless someone moves them until they can move independently	Arrange the environment to allow children at all developmental levels to see and experience a variety of materials and events Minimize the use of "containers," such as infant seats, swings, cribs, and playpens, that restrict children's ability to move independently	Pay attention to individual children and present toys and materials in a way that is suited to their developmental level Reposition children who are unable to move independently on a frequent and regular schedule
Not able to remember much of what happened in the past	Provide a daily schedule that includes a lot of familiar routines and activities so babies have a maximum of opportunities to try out their developing memories	Not expect babies to respond in the same way to a similar event from day to day but notice and comment when they do
Not able to anticipate what is going to happen in the future	Establish regular daily routines for caregiving and a predictable daily schedule to help babies learn to anticipate and prepare themselves for what will happen next	Help babies accept sequences of events by following established procedures carefully and by describing each step in simple words, signs, and gestures just before it happens

(continued)

Table 1.1. (continued)

Babies are:	Therefore, a program that meets babies' needs will:	And responsive teachers of babies will:
Only beginning to become aware of themselves as individuals	Establish daily routines that are flexible enough to accommodate babies' individual likes and dislikes Have mirrors and pictures of babies and their families so babies can begin to truly "see" themselves	Respect children's temperamental differences and work to make each child feel valued and valuable as a person Respect the baby's individuality and encourage him or her to show preferences and dislikes for food, toys, and activities Call babies by name frequently and label themselves by name Behave affectionately with babies to make them feel loved and lovable

many of their own needs themselves, follow verbal directions, and amuse themselves without adult involvement. Some of the ways in which toddler classrooms must differ from programs geared toward infants are listed in Table 1.2, and the ways in which they must differ from preschool programs are listed in Table 1.3. These comparisons highlight what is unique about toddlers and about the approach to toddler care presented in this book.

Unlike infants, toddlers can effectively signal their needs to adults and will actively seek out stimulation for themselves—often in places where adults do not want them to be! Toddlers also are gaining a rudimentary understanding of just how effective they *can* be in attracting adult attention to themselves. Far from needing help to change positions, typically developing toddlers are so active that they appear to be in almost constant motion. All of these characteristics of toddlers require that teachers be willing to relinquish control in order to help children gain confidence and self-knowledge and that the child care environment be safe and secure but also challenging and interesting.

Toddlers live almost entirely in the moment. They want a teacher's attention *now*, a turn on the slide *now*, lunch *now*, but no nap, please, because going to sleep means giving up opportunities to play and explore. Toddlers also need a great deal of adult help in structuring their experiences. They cannot foresee the consequences of their own or others' actions, nor can they invent extended play scenarios with toys or other

children. Teachers of toddlers must be constantly vigilant—from a distance, consistently available—but not intrusive, and firm in their guidance—delivered with affection and love.

Toddlers get a bad press largely because they are making rapid strides toward independence at a time when parents and other adults have just learned to enjoy them as babies. It is true that toddlers learn and use the word "no" (particularly when it is used a lot by the adults around them), but it is also true that they are quite agreeable and willing to do almost anything *if* an enthusiastic adult will do it with them. Toddlers *are* possessive about toys and other belongings; in fact, so are most adults. Understanding possession is an important step toward understanding what *me* means, and objects must be possessed before they can be shared or given away. Toddlers *do* get "into everything" because they have limitless curiosity and desire to explore and experience the world. These are admirable traits that we should encourage and enjoy because they will develop into a lifelong motivation to learn.

In their second and third years, children learn many of the crucial skills they will need throughout their lives. They learn functional skills: to feed themselves, to use the toilet independently, to put on coats and shoes, to open drawers and doors, and to turn lights on and off. They learn to talk and to understand when others talk to them—fantastic achievements that we take for granted because most toddlers seem to

Table 1.2.   How toddlers differ from babies

Because toddlers are no longer babies, they are:	Therefore, a program that meets toddlers' needs will:	And responsive teachers of toddlers will:
Not completely reliant on others for care and stimulation	Give toddlers opportunities to choose their own activities and to select from more than one type of activity while playing Give toddlers some autonomy during daily living activities Plan individual rather than group transitions	Respect toddlers' choices and the decisions they make for themselves even when teachers think they are not the best choices, as long as toddlers are not endangering themselves or others or damaging materials
Able to signal their own needs and desires	Provide many opportunities throughout the daily schedule for children to indicate what they want and need, rather than either anticipating all toddlers' needs or insisting that toddlers fit into a rigid schedule	Be attuned to toddlers' efforts to communicate needs and desires by being aware of nonverbal communication attempts as well as sounds and single spoken words Help toddlers learn to signal their needs and desires by using a total communication approach that involves using basic signs along with words
Aware that they can use their own behavior to achieve social goals, particularly in recruiting adult attention	Foster an atmosphere of acceptance and caring through a teacher–child ratio of no less than 1:4 and a schedule of activities that provides for a lot of individual attention	Focus their full attention on the children at all times and work to keep children actively involved in play and daily living activities in which individual attention is provided for positive behavior Show affection frequently and noncontingently to all children

(continued)

Table 1.2. (continued)

Because toddlers are no longer babies, they are:	Therefore, a program that meets toddlers' needs will:	And responsive teachers of toddlers will:
Unwilling to stay in one place or be still for more than a few minutes at a time	Create an environment that is completely safe and appropriate for a toddler's size Arrange a schedule of activities that permits children to move freely from one activity to another as they choose, rather than having to fit into an adult-defined schedule	Fit their teaching into the child's ongoing activity and be constantly alert to naturally occurring opportunities to teach
Able to remember events and repeat them later	Provide a daily schedule that balances familiarity and novelty to give children a maximum number of opportunities to build more complex behaviors on a foundation of often-repeated actions and events	Realize that watching others is a useful activity for toddlers and respect toddlers' right to spend some of their time simply watching what others are doing Recognize that toddlers repeat undesirable as well as positive behavior and avoid doing things that they do not want toddlers to imitate
Able to anticipate events when they are part of a frequently repeated sequence	Establish and follow regular daily routines for caregiving and a predictable daily schedule so that toddlers learn to anticipate and prepare themselves for what will happen next, thus building their ability to self-regulate their emotions and behavior	Help toddlers understand sequences of events by following established procedures carefully and by describing each step in simple words, signs, and gestures

(continued)

Table 1.2. (continued)

Because toddlers are no longer babies, they are:	Therefore, a program that meets toddlers' needs will:	And responsive teachers of toddlers will:
Beginning to be aware of themselves as individuals and to exert their own needs for personal space and ownership of things	Provide adequate space for children and an organization of space and activities that gives children opportunities for solitary as well as social play Encourage children to use their own blankets or soft toys brought from home or provided in the classroom as sources of comfort in the early morning, at naptime, or during other periods of stress	Respect children's temperamental differences and growing sense of who they are and work to make each child feel valued and valuable as a person Avoid situations in which toddlers are crowded together in a small space Let children hold a favorite toy if they wish even when it is time to change activities, clean up, or move to a different area

learn language effortlessly. They go from taking a few steps to running, climbing, jumping, pedaling a tricycle, and steering a wagon. They learn how to make friends and how to be a friend.

Teachers of toddlers must help children learn such skills. Academic skills—colors, letters, numbers, sorting, and other teacher-invented tasks—are best saved for later. It is important for teachers of toddlers to focus on really important skills, namely life skills.

Toddlers can be frustrating, but they are also endlessly entertaining. They are a rich source of funny stories and joyful moments; and by looking at the world through their eyes, teachers can get a new and fresh perspective on everyday events that will enrich their own experiences in countless ways.

HOW INFANTS AND TODDLERS LEARN

It is sometimes difficult to realize how little experience infants and toddlers have had with the world and how much they have yet to learn. Events and objects that are commonplace to us—the feel of grass, the ringing of a bell, the taste of green beans—are adventures to babies. Everyday tasks that older children and adults take for granted—hand washing, drinking milk from a cup, putting on socks—are new and wondrous to toddlers.

Infants and toddlers also perceive the physical world differently from the rest of us. As adults, many of our perceptions and actions are guided by what we already know about objects and by what we have

Table 1.3. How toddlers differ from preschoolers

Because toddlers are not yet preschoolers, they are:	Therefore, a program that meets toddlers' needs will:	And responsive teachers of toddlers will:
Reliant on the support and comfort of familiar people who are consistent and loving	Establish policies that encourage long-term teacher employment Select teachers who are emotionally secure and able to establish positive and loving relationships with children Develop strong and supportive relationships with parents and other family members and encourage the direct involvement of extended family in the classroom program	Be emotionally invested in the children so they can establish meaningful relationships with each of them Interact with all children in an affectionate, caring, and responsive way View themselves as providing support to the children's families, rather than competing with them or supplanting their role with the children
Unable to organize and maintain extended social play or interaction	Organize the daily schedule so that teachers are always available to support toddlers' play Place increased emphasis on planning for transitions between activities so that toddlers are never expected to wait with nothing to do or to be without teacher involvement	Involve themselves actively in toddlers' play, beyond simple monitoring, to provide the structure that enables toddlers to expand their repertoire of skills and knowledge Be constantly alert to children's interactions with one another and intervene sensitively to maintain positive interactions and extend social play episodes

(continued)

Table 1.3.   (continued)

Because toddlers are not yet preschoolers, they are:	Therefore, a program that meets toddlers' needs will:	And responsive teachers of toddlers will:
More likely to behave in response to the immediate context surrounding them, rather than according to social expectations or in a goal-directed way	Create contexts that encourage toddlers to be as actively involved in play or daily living activities as possible Provide a physical environment that is safe and in which almost all of the things toddlers choose to do are acceptable	Avoid interpreting undesirable toddler behavior as intentional, motivated, or goal directed and especially avoid viewing toddlers' behavior as a challenge to teacher authority Maintain control over their own behavior at all times so that they can *respond* rather than *react* to toddler behavior. Be aware of the types of situations that often give rise to undesirable toddler behavior and intervene to avoid or interrupt them
Unable to fully understand such abstract concepts as *time* and *fairness*	Be structured so that expectations and rules are within reach of toddlers Follow regular, predictable routines throughout the day so toddlers can anticipate upcoming events and gain a rudimentary understanding of time Modify typical preschool classroom rules to suit toddlers' limited ability to take the perspective of another person	Gear their explanations and rationales to the level of understanding of toddlers Be aware that much of the behavior that would be described as aggressive in older children is simply instrumental in toddlers and does not require a negative consequence

(continued)

Table 1.3. *(continued)*

Because toddlers are not yet preschoolers, they are:	Therefore, a program that meets toddlers' needs will:	And responsive teachers of toddlers will:
Much more likely to be involved in play that is functional or exploratory than in play that is representational or constructive	Have a preplanned schedule of play activities that balance familiarity and novelty and have the primary goal of providing exposure to a wide range of materials for toddlers to explore and experience Use play activities that are open ended rather than goal oriented Focus play activities on objects and activities that are experienced by children at home and in other familiar contexts as well as in the classroom	Build on toddlers' individual interests in toys and play materials in ways that enhance their exploration and experience Use naturally occurring opportunities for teaching and shift the teaching focus of a play activity as needed to meet the interests of the children, rather than insisting that children learn what the teacher wants to teach
Largely unable to foresee the consequences of their own actions	Establish a safe environment that allows exploration and experimentation without danger	Expect toddlers to make a lot of mistakes, to use what adults would call bad judgment, and to fail more often than they succeed Find ways to make these experiences positive for the children through encouragement and by providing the support toddlers need to turn mistakes into successes Avoid characterizing accidents and errors of judgment as misbehavior or as intentional actions

(continued)

Table 1.3. *(continued)*

Because toddlers are not yet preschoolers, they are:	Therefore, a program that meets toddlers' needs will:	And responsive teachers of toddlers will:
Not aware of social expectations for behavior or use of toys	Set broad learning goals to encompass the unexpected	Enjoy the nonconventional behavior of toddlers and focus on their creativity and pleasure in experimentation, rather than focusing on teaching toddlers to fit into social expectations Respect the toddler stage as a unique developmental period with its own important tasks and not try to "prep" children for preschool

experienced. Very young children, however, are not so limited; they explore all of the properties of objects—including how objects feel, smell, sound, and taste. From the time they can actively manipulate objects, infants and toddlers put toys together in improbable combinations and use toys in unique and unpredictable ways. It is through this extensive exploration of objects that children acquire knowledge of the physical world, and it is through a similar exploration of people that they learn about the social world (Gibson, 1979). Thus, free exploration must be supported and extended, rather than discouraged because it doesn't meet adults' ideas about appropriate play. Teachers of infants and toddlers must constantly make an effort to look at the world through children's eyes so that they can provide the types of experience that infants and toddlers will find meaningful.

In addition, environments geared toward infants and toddlers must be based on the recognition that infants and toddlers are learning constantly, rather than just during the times teachers are thinking about teaching. Thus, all daily activities, including such routine events as diaper changes and feedings or mealtimes, are important learning times for infants and toddlers. In fact, some of the most effective teaching situations involve embedding something new into the midst of a familiar and often repeated activity or routine. Regular routines for care and play that follow a similar script from day to day allow infants and toddlers to anticipate events and thus be prepared for what will happen next. When a slight variation in the routine or script is introduced, the child will always notice. In that fleeting moment, teachers have children's complete attention and can use the opportunity for effective teaching.

Learning Self-Regulation

Consistency in everyday routines also allows young children to gain experience with self-regulation of their emotional states. By knowing in advance what is likely to happen, babies and toddlers can plan and think about what they will do. When routines are not established, children are constantly being surprised or challenged by events that they did not anticipate, and they cannot be expected to cooperate or maintain control over their emotional reactions.

Increased self-regulation is an important developmental task for young children, especially toddlers (Kopp, 1989). They must learn to focus their attention during play so that they can stay with a task long enough to extend their knowledge of objects and actions and also so they can experience success. In addition, toddlers must learn to regulate their social responses to other children in order to participate in more complex joint play and resolve conflicts without becoming upset and aggressive.

Coping with separation from parents and settling to sleep away from home can be particularly difficult aspects of self-regulation for some children. All infants and toddlers need a stable, consistent environment in which sensitive teachers recognize that everyone—even the youngest child—can truly experience distress and other negative emotions, and teachers must accept these as valid feelings. Rather than feeling pity when a child shows distress, responsive teachers empathize and offer emotional support. Through repeated experiences of successful self-regulation and the assistance of caring adults who respond with affection and concern, rather than irritation and anger, young children gain positive attitudes about themselves and learn to view themselves as valued by others (Barrett & Campos, 1987; Thompson, 1991). Ways to encourage the development of self-regulation and social behavior are described in Chapters 6 and 7.

Learning to Communicate

In their first 3 years of life, children acquire the basics of a communication system. During the early months, babies learn the essence of emotional communication through facial expressions and tone of voice (Nelson, 1987; Soken & Pick, 1992). By their first birthday, typically developing 1-year-olds say a few words and understand many more. Amazingly, less than 2 years later, children have extensive vocabularies and have mastered enough grammatical structure to use those words effectively in complex ways. During this infant-toddler period, the acquisition of communication skills, including language, is perhaps the most important developmental achievement, and it is the one achievement that changes children the most. With effective communication comes more efficient memory, the ability to pretend, greater flexibility in thinking and problem solving, and an enhanced ability to coordinate and extend social interchanges.

Young children's desire to communicate is evident in all that they do. At times infants will focus with great intensity on the lips of a person speaking to them, and typically developing toddlers will repeat and then retain almost every word spoken around them. A rich language environment is an important part of quality care for infants and toddlers (Hart & Risley, 1995). Responsive teachers give children many opportunities to communicate and work to understand children's body language as well as their vocal and gestural efforts to make themselves understood. Also, although language learning often appears to be effortless, some children do not acquire communication skills readily and are at risk for long-term social and educational difficulties if they are not identified and helped in these early years.

As children begin to talk, they must learn not only words and grammar but also how to move their lips, teeth, and tongue to make sounds that others can understand. Often, children's early attempts to say words are not understood by the adults around them. Children typically imitate the intonation patterns and cadences of others' speech before they can articulate single words clearly. Thus, infants and toddlers may appear to be talking in long sentences or having involved conversations, but the syllables and sounds they are using are not intelligible to anyone but themselves. Other children seem to wait until they can reliably make the sounds they intend before they say very much.

By listening carefully to children as soon as they begin to babble and croon, teachers can identify the sounds each one is able to use. Consultation with a speech-language specialist is needed if a child produces an unexpectedly small number of sounds or if a child is not saying more than a few words by 24 months of age.

Language differs from speech in that it involves comprehension of the meaning of words and sentences and the ability to communicate thoughts, feelings, and wishes. Language does not have to be spoken; infants and toddlers who are exposed to sign language are able to use signs to communicate before they can talk. Most children are able to understand what others are saying before they can make themselves understood. In specialists' terms, children develop *receptive* language prior to *expressive* language. Some specific techniques for encouraging communicative development in infants and toddlers are included in Chapter 6.

A PRACTICAL ECOLOGY FOR INCLUSIVE INFANT-TODDLER CARE

The ecological approach to program design used in this book is based on a broad definition of *environment* that encompasses people and how they spend their time as well as the physical arrangement of space and equipment. Like other ecologically based intervention approaches (e.g., Bricker & Cripe, 1992; Warren, 1992), the teaching and learning activities described here are embedded in child-focused play times. The approach presented goes further than most programs, however, in considering *every* activity in which a child is involved—whether it is planned or unplanned, guided or not—to be a learning activity. From this perspective, the environment must be carefully structured and teachers must be constantly attuned to what children are doing so that what they learn is positive and functional.

Focus on Exploration and Experience

Because the world is still so new to infants and toddlers, they are learning something from every experience they have. Many of these experiences will occur incidentally in the course of a day, as children and teachers go about the business of living together. Responsive teaching involves awareness of the learning potential of all experiences and recognition of the crucial role of adult reactions to unexpected events. When Kevin makes a face after touching his tongue to the soap, Heather surprises herself by rolling from her stomach to her back, or Delores's eyes widen in amazement after seeing the beanbag she has thrown hit the ceiling, responsive teachers of infants or toddlers know they have succeeded in providing opportunities for learning that day. By participating positively and enthusiastically in these unpredictable moments of experience, teachers can give meaning and importance to children's learning.

Crucial to exploration is the chance for children to *select* what they want to explore. When children choose what they want to do, they have an intrinsic interest in that activity and the motivation to continue toward a self-determined goal (McWilliam & Bailey, 1992). In a successful program for infants and toddlers, teachers yield much of the control over the day's activities to the children and then support and extend learning by stepping in with a comment, suggestion, or demonstration at just the right moment. Of course, adults must help structure the learning environment through selection and presentation of toys and other materials and through their own involvement in play with the children.

This approach is in contrast to many preschool-based and early intervention approaches that focus on adult-selected and adult-led activities geared toward specific learning goals defined as important by teachers or therapists. In most such models, the teacher's role is a directive, rather than supportive or responsive, one. Teachers plan a lesson, gather a group of children together, and present the task to them, assisting as needed to keep children's attention focused on the predefined goal. When individual attention is necessary, the teacher circulates from child to child, presenting a skill-based activity, assisting and directing the child's activity for a few minutes, and then moving on to the next child. In many programs, these few minutes of instruction are considered to be *the* most valuable teaching and learning times, and these are also, presumably, the highlight of the child's experience.

Within the ecologically oriented program described in this book, the child's entire day is considered learning time. Characteristics of such an approach are flexible teaching and intervention goals that are able to be adapted in creative ways to fit the ongoing activities of the children. Children have opportunities to choose among several different toys or activities. As they explore these materials, babies or toddlers suggest by their actions and by difficulties encountered the learning goal of the activity. The teacher's job is to be responsive to each individual child and situation, making use of teaching opportunities that arise in the context of the child's ongoing exploration and experience. Teachers must be prepared for some children to refuse participation in planned activities or to transform those activities into something altogether different from what the teacher intended.

Selection of activities by children is a teaching and intervention strategy that is effective only in a well-organized environment. The quantity and type of materials available at any one time must be planned with careful attention to the number of children who will be present and the range of their developmental levels and play preferences. In addition, the number and location of available teachers must be sufficient to assist and elaborate on children's play, which affects the success of this approach. Finally, and perhaps most important, the environment must be totally and completely *safe* for children so that they are free to explore and experience the consequences of their actions with minimal restriction. These organizational aspects of infant-toddler care are addressed in Chapter 4.

Focus on Activities of Daily Living

Infants require a great deal of physical care, and toddlers are just beginning to take an active role in their own care. Infants spend a major portion of their awake time either being fed or having their diaper changed. Even most 2-year-olds are not completely feeding themselves and are much better at taking off their clothes than at putting them on. During the toddler period, children also learn independent toileting and other self-care skills, such as washing hands and brushing teeth. All of these daily living activities are important curricular components for infant-toddler programs.

Typically, teachers of older children consider daily living activities to be annoying, although necessary, aspects of child care, taking time from the much more important real curriculum. In infant-toddler care, activities of daily living *are* the real curriculum. With infants, these activities provide the most effective times for teachers to focus one-to-one with a child and have intimate conversations. With toddlers, teachers can use daily living activities to gradually transfer responsibility from the adult to the child, which can be done in a supportive and caring way that builds positive patterns of behavior and a sense of achievement. Thus, teachers must be actively involved in daily living activities and consider these tasks to be as important to their teaching role as reading books, painting pictures, or building with blocks.

Within the approach to infant-toddler care presented in this book, the importance of daily living activities is recognized by the considerable time that is devoted to them each day. By designating time for diapering and toilet training, serving and eating meals and snacks, getting ready for naptime, and putting on shoes and coats to go outside and then taking them off again, teachers have time to interact individually with babies as they provide care and can actively *teach* self-care skills to toddlers without feeling pressure to get on to more important things. Teaching routines for daily living activities are presented in Part III of this book.

Focus on Social Play and Communication

A major advantage of the child care setting as a learning environment is the presence of a group of other children. Infants and toddlers are inherently interested in what other children are doing and spend extensive amounts of time watching one another do what adults consider to be inconsequential things. Therefore, the availability of peers enhances chil-

dren's learning opportunities. In addition, babies and toddlers who have a stable group of peers with whom to play are given the chance to learn about friendships and to develop the skill of being a friend and having friends, important components of healthy social-emotional development.

When very young children play together, their play increases in complexity, with greater amounts of imitation and more verbal exchanges than toddler–preschooler or even toddler–adult play (Rothstein-Fisch & Howes, 1988; Rubenstein & Howes, 1976). Among toddlers, imitation games frequently turn into extended bouts of interaction accompanied by shared laughter (Eckerman, Davis, & Didow, 1989; Eckerman & Stein, 1990), which may be an important precursor to more elaborate language-based play. Particularly when young children are well acquainted with each other, their play incorporates game-like aspects and repetitive "scripts" that appear to be early forms of pretend play (Goldman & Ross, 1978; Howes, Unger, & Seidner, 1989; Mueller & Brenner, 1977).

Child care settings also provide many diverse opportunities for the development of communication skills. By late in their first year, most children are making sounds and gestures that have reliable meaning to their parents and other familiar caregivers. When children have experienced health problems or chronic illness during infancy or when their home environments are not supportive of their development, their early language and communicative development is often delayed. Children with speech and language delays or problems make up the largest proportion of children identified as having delays during the preschool years. Delays in communication development can occur in conjunction with delays or disabilities in other areas, or they may be the primary cause for concern about a child's development (Shewan & Malm, 1990). Communication skills are crucial to later school success and social adjustment, which, if disrupted in the early years, can have lifelong implications (Parker & Asher, 1987). Therefore, a focus on language, communication, and literacy is central to high-quality infant-toddler care.

Taking an ecological approach to quality child care involves using particular environmental arrangements to foster both social play and communication. Certain types of toys, such as large play equipment, dolls, blocks, and games, are known to elicit high rates of peer interaction in preschoolers (Shapiro, 1975; Shure, 1963; Smith & Connolly, 1980, 1986). Play with house toys and pretend vehicles tends to be more complex than other kinds of play (Rubin, 1977), and toys that resemble real-world objects are more commonly used by young children in pretend play than abstract toys (McLoyd, 1983). This knowledge can be incorporated into the environmental design and curriculum for infant-toddler care.

Research has also shown that the nature of the play context influences the behavior of adults as they play with children. When parents play with their toddlers, they talk more and encourage more language from the children when playing with dolls as compared with shape sorters or trucks (O'Brien & Nagle, 1987). Similarly, parents and children play in close proximity with feminine sex-typed toys (e.g., dolls, kitchen toys), whereas they play at a distance with masculine sex-typed toys (e.g., blocks, trucks) (Caldera, Huston, & O'Brien, 1989).

Similar context-specific patterns of language use have been observed among teachers of toddlers (O'Brien & Bi, 1995). When playing in the house and doll area, teachers actively attempted to teach language to the children, labeling objects and asking children a lot of questions. By contrast, when teachers and children were playing with blocks and trucks, teachers described ongoing events more frequently and asked fewer questions. This unintentional strategy on the part of teachers was actually associated with a higher rate of child language and more complex toddler speech than the effortful attempts to get children to talk that occurred in the house and doll context. In large motor play, teachers' predominant style was directive and repetitive; this context elicited the least child speech but offered much opportunity for the development of receptive abilities.

Knowledge of the ways in which classroom ecology influences both teacher and child behavior can be incorporated into practice through the design of activity areas and can suggest teaching goals that flow logically from the typical interactions occurring naturally as infants, toddlers, and teachers play.

Focus on Relationships

Building trust and confidence in parents and other familiar adults is a crucial developmental task throughout infancy and toddlerhood (Bretherton,

1992). A quality child care program fosters this process by working to support the parent–child bond, by strengthening the ability of parents to provide the best possible care for their child, and also by being a secure and consistent place for children to spend their days. Teachers of infants and toddlers must be responsive to children's initiatives, sensitive to their needs, and alert to their attempts to communicate. Furthermore, teachers must be accepting of each child's individual characteristics and of the family's approach to parenting, viewing themselves as playing a supportive role with families (Powell, 1989; Simeonsson & Bailey, 1990).

Teachers of infants and toddlers must not hold back their commitment to loving relationships because they know that their time with the children is short. *All* of the positive and affectionate relationships children have with reliable and sensitive adults contribute to their development of a strong self-concept and a recognition of themselves as competent and valuable people. Separation and loss are difficult and painful for teachers as well as children, but teachers who invest their own emotional energy in developing relationships with children and families also receive the greatest rewards, knowing they have contributed in vital ways to children's long-term mental health.

SUMMARY

An inclusive child care program for infants and toddlers that is based on developmental and ecological principles can provide both quality care and early intervention for all children. The developmental approach requires a recognition of the uniqueness of the infant and toddler periods. This is reflected in a program focus on activities of daily living, an emphasis on understanding and accepting children's needs for emotional support, and an individualized teaching approach built around play materials suited to infants' and toddlers' skill levels.

The ecological approach to program design is based on the principle that infants and toddlers learn constantly; thus, teachers of infants and toddlers are always teaching. An ideal environment arrangement for infants and toddlers promotes children's active exploration, provides a structure for children's experiences with toys and other people that supports learning, and allows individual choice among activities. Children with developmental delays or disabilities can be fully included in such an environment, and typically developing children benefit from the incorporation of early intervention practices into child care.

Chapter 2

Child Care
as a Setting for Early Intervention

Intervention services for children with special needs and child care services for working parents are generally considered to be completely separate types of services. Social change, family advocacy, and altered professional perspectives have all combined to place increased emphasis on the need of *every* family for comprehensive developmental and child care services. As a result, many child care settings include children with special needs, and recommended practices in early intervention services call for services to be delivered in children's natural environments, which include child care settings. This chapter outlines the status of child care and early intervention for children and families in the United States in the late 1990s and describes the many potential benefits inherent in a merger between the two service systems.

HISTORY, REALITY, AND POSSIBILITY

Public interest in both child care and early intervention for children prior to school age has only emerged in the 1980s. Prior to this, daily care for young children was considered to be the primary task of mothers who were generally expected to be at home. When mothers did work outside the home, their children were usually cared for either by a grandmother or an aunt who was not employed or by a female friend or neighbor. A combination of social change and economic demands has led most women, including mothers of young children as well as grandmothers and others who had previously provided care, to seek paid employment outside the home; thus, the urgent need for quality child care has attracted public attention.

Similarly, the recognition that early intervention can help children reach their maximum developmental potential has led to a national trend to provide educational services to children at age 3 or 4, rather than waiting until the traditional age for entry into kindergarten. Head Start, inaugurated in the mid-1960s as part of a national focus on poverty and its effects, is an outstanding example of an early education program that has

captured the hearts of policy makers and the public. Despite reaching fewer than half of those eligible, Head Start has been credited with reducing the need for later special education services for many children (Lazar & Darlington, 1982).

In 1968, the Handicapped Children's Early Education Act (PL 90-538) was passed to encourage the development of educational intervention programs for children with disabilities. This law was followed in 1975 with the Education for All Handicapped Children Act (PL 94-142), which required schools to provide a "free and appropriate public education" for all children, including those with disabilities. In 1986, the Education of the Handicapped Act Amendments (PL 99-457, now encompassed under PL 102-119, the Individuals with Disabilities Education Act Amendments of 1991), provided funds for states to develop comprehensive systems of early intervention for infants and toddlers (Part H, now Part C of the Amendments of 1997) and required states to provide intervention services to all children with disabilities from ages 3 to 5 in order to receive any federal preschool funds (Section 619 of Part B).

Several aspects of PL 99-457, particularly Part C, were highly innovative and have resulted in significant changes in the provision of early intervention services for infants and toddlers. One such aspect is the recognition of the crucial *role of the family* in the development and education of the young child. Under the provisions of Part C, the family sets priorities for intervention and is viewed as the most important context for development. Another feature of Part C is the *requirement that early intervention services be coordinated* across professional disciplines and service agencies. Thus, diverse agencies providing early intervention services were asked to come together and write interagency agreements, a process that has led to much greater communication and collaboration among early intervention professionals in many communities.

To assist families in obtaining services, Part C also requires that a *family services coordinator* be provided for every family of an eligible child; this individual is responsible for assisting the family in obtaining all needed services. Family services coordinators are expected to advocate effectively for families with a variety of service agencies, including both health- and education-focused agencies, to ensure that the needs of the child and family are met. Another important provision of Part C is the development in every U.S. community of a free Child-Find system to foster public awareness, promote developmental screening and evaluation, and compile a directory of available services.

The Importance of Early Intervention

Since the implementation of Part C, an increasing number of children under age 3 are being identified as having disabilities or developmental delays or being at risk for eventual delay. It is estimated that between 8% and 10% of U.S. infants and toddlers—more than 2 million children—are considered to have disabilities or developmental delays that would qualify them to receive early intervention services (Fewell, 1993). These children include those born prematurely or with medical complications, those with chronic health problems or diagnosed physical or mental limitations, and those who show delays or disabilities in social-emotional or adaptive behavior that can be traced to environmental factors. Many developmental delays that are diagnosed in children's first 3 years have no known organic cause. Because developmental disabilities and risk factors have cumulative effects and a deficit or delay in one area of development often "spills over" into other areas, small delays in very young children tend to build into much larger concerns as these children grow. Thus, early detection of potential developmental problems and subsequent intervention to address these problems have the potential for minimizing the accumulation and generalization of disability (Simeonsson, 1991).

Under the provisions of Part C, children are eligible for early intervention services if they have a diagnosed physical or mental condition that is "highly likely" to result in developmental delay or if they show a delay in one or more areas of development (cognitive, communicative, physical, social-emotional, or adaptive). The definition of developmental delay varies from state to state because federal law gives the states authority to determine who should be eligible for early intervention services. Individual states may also choose to provide services to children who are considered to be at risk for later developmental delay.

The Potential of Preventive Intervention

Given our knowledge about the cumulative effects of even small developmental delays, it is clear that early intervention has the potential to be truly preventive. It seems likely that early intervention programs would have the greatest effect in preventing further developmental delays if they fit the definition of *indicated preventive intervention* (Mrazek & Haggerty, 1994). Using this approach, children would be eligible to receive services if they were identified as being at high risk for developmental delays even though they were showing only minimal indicators of delay at the time of intervention. When children are required to demonstrate extensive delay or disability in order to receive special services, as in most school-based special education programs, interventions are no longer preventive; they are *remedial*. A more widespread but expensive approach to preventing developmental delays would be *selective preventive intervention* (Mrazek & Haggerty, 1994), in which all members of groups considered to be at risk, such as children born at low birth weight or children living in poverty, would be targets for intervention. Head Start is an example of a selective preventive intervention program.

Preventive intervention, either indicated or selective, is particularly appropriate for infants and toddlers. During the infant and toddler stages of development, many children who are identified as having a delay or disability in one area of development, such as eye–hand coordination or speech, will be on track in all other areas of development. Eventually, however, even a single area of developmental delay will affect the child's progress in other areas of development. Appropriate and timely intervention at this early stage may effectively boost the child's performance enough to avoid such a spillover of disability. In addition, the incorporation of early intervention practices into child care settings, where *all* children can benefit from such practices, has the potential of offering preventive services to a much broader spectrum of children at relatively low cost.

Child Care for Infants and Toddlers

By the mid-1990s, 57% of the mothers of children under the age of 3 were employed outside the home (Children's Defense Fund, 1996). As a result, most children in the United States are being cared for by someone other than their parents for most of the years before they enter school. Child care is just as important for children with disabilities and children at biological or environmental risk as it is for children who have no known developmental concern; however, a 1990 survey found that relatively few privately operated child care centers accepted children with physical disabilities, mental retardation, or complex medical needs (Crowley, 1990).

Most full-day child care in the United States—both regulated, center-based care and home-based child care—serves only typically developing children. Until the 1980s, care for infants and toddlers was provided almost entirely by parents, relatives, or others in home settings, but the availability of organized infant-toddler care in centers is increasing. Although many home-based child care providers offer high-quality and sensitive child care (NICHD Early Child Care Research Network, 1996), center-based care tends to be more educationally oriented; therefore, therapeutic intervention techniques will usually be more readily incorporated into child care centers than into other types of child care.

Lack of staff training for children with disabilities is cited by center directors as a difficulty and a strong argument against including children with disabilities in their programs (Crowley, 1990). This concern is very understandable because state requirements for child care staff are generally minimal. Even when teachers have training in child development or early education, it is unlikely that they have learned about disability and developmental delay. Most training programs for early childhood educators or child care workers, including Child Development Associate (CDA) programs, offer little information about children with special needs. Lack of information and experience with children who have disabilities and developmental delays undoubtedly leads many teachers and directors of child care programs to be cautious about including such children in their classrooms.

Yet child care centers are considered public facilities under PL 101-336, the Americans with Disabilities Act (ADA) of 1990 (Rab & Wood, 1995). Therefore, according to law, *all* children and families should have equal access to child care settings. Increasingly, as individuals with disabilities become more visible in the community and participate more actively in all aspects of society, more parents of children with disabilities will request enrollment of their children in existing child care programs. In addition, Head Start programs have taken the lead in including children with disabilities and developmental delays in their programs, and the Early Head Start initiative continues this focus.

Furthermore, because developmental delays are often not detectable in very young children, many child care centers that are not considered to be inclusive programs already enroll children whose special needs will be diagnosed in the future. With expanded Child-Find activities in many communities, increasing numbers of these children will be identified during community screenings. Parents of these children are likely to want their children to remain in their familiar child care settings, surrounded by their friends and teachers who know them as individuals.

Given these trends, it would be most beneficial for *all* quality child care programs serving infants and toddlers to begin actively including children with disabilities and developmental delays into their classrooms. Such an effort to support quality child care could be aided by changes in public policy and expanded funding. In addition, child care programs that include children with special needs require the commitment and involvement of special service providers who are trained to provide early intervention services and willing to assist and support child care staff. With such a collaborative approach, however, incorporation of early intervention practices into child care settings serving typically developing children is not only possible, but also likely to be beneficial for all children.

THE POTENTIAL OF INCLUSIVE ENVIRONMENTS

The inclusion of infants and toddlers with special needs into child care programs serving typically developing children has advantages for all children and families. In addition, inclusion offers opportunities for professional development and personal growth to child care program staff.

Including Children with Special Needs in Child Care Programs

In many ways, child care settings can be considered as one of the *best* locations in which to provide early intervention because they represent the natural environment for a large number of children. It is recommended practice within the field of special education for even remedial services to be provided in *inclusive* environments, settings in which typically developing children and children with identified disabilities are educated together (Wolery & Wilbers, 1994).

In an inclusive child care program for infants or toddlers, some of the children will be developing typically and will not be considered to be at risk, some will appear to be developing on schedule but will have a known medical or environmental risk factor, and some will have already been identified as having a delay in at least one developmental domain or will have been diagnosed as having a biologically based disability. Often, visitors to such a program will not be able to determine which children fit into each of these categories; this is one of the goals of inclusion—for *all* children to participate fully without being set apart as *different*—and this goal is perhaps most readily met in infant and toddler care.

Infants and toddlers are not expected to be functionally independent. In infant and toddler classrooms, *all* of the children need help with daily living activities, and few of the children are toilet-trained. Thus, children can participate in the full range of daily activities appropriate for infants and toddlers even when they have clearly recognizable disabilities or developmental delays. Also, any group of typically developing infants or toddlers will include children with a wide range of skill levels and abilities, making individual children's developmental delays in particular areas almost invisible. Furthermore, the physical environment of a child care program serving infants and toddlers needs no modification to accommodate children with special needs. These settings already have space and facilities for diapering children, and toddler-size wheelchairs can fit easily through standard doorways. Finally, the skills that are important for infants and toddlers to learn do not differ substantially from those considered important for young children with disabilities and developmental delays.

For toddlers, one of the primary developmental tasks involves the shift in focus from home, family, and parents to peers and friends. Older infants and toddlers are ready and eager to learn from one another by observation, imitation, and interaction. This is true for children with disabilities and developmental delays as well as for typically developing children. Children with special needs enjoy the same types of activities as other children—they like to touch, bang, and taste toys; be sung to and read to; and wear flowing scarves, baseball hats, and grown-up shoes. A child care setting that is carefully designed to enhance development can, therefore, be an ideal site for early intervention with all children.

How Inclusion Benefits Child Care Programs

Teachers and program directors who have little training and experience in the care of children with special needs tend to be fearful of including *special* children in their classrooms; they often express concern regarding the extra demands for care such children may bring. It is true that integrating early intervention services into infant-toddler child care programs requires a high level of organization of teacher time. One reason that this may not seem feasible to some teachers and program directors is that there have been relatively few guidelines available for organizing infant and toddler care so that it is uniformly of high quality. Instead, many professionals and even parents view infant and toddler care as babysitting and have relatively low expectations for its operation.

Using the guidelines presented in this book, however, it is possible to organize infant and toddler care settings so that they are responsive and supportive teaching and learning environments. In such a program, the focus is on *teaching* as the primary responsibility of classroom staff. Teaching is integral to all care routines as well as planned play activities.

Such a focus adapts well to the inclusion of children with special needs. It is essential that inclusive infant and toddler classrooms be well organized and that child care staff view themselves as *teachers* and *interventionists*, providing responsive care and education to all children. This increased professionalism benefits all of the children in attendance and also benefits the teachers themselves.

Furthermore, involvement in early intervention automatically means involvement in a communitywide network of infant-toddler service providers. Community-based interagency coordinating councils for infant-toddler services were established under Part H of the Education of the Handicapped Act Amendments in 1986 as a necessary step toward increasing collaboration and cooperation among professionals from different disciplines and agencies with diverse missions. The participation of child care programs in the community network of service providers promotes professionalism among teachers and establishes child care as a critical part of the total service picture for children and families. Although the urgent need for child care is a reality for many families, special service providers and school districts have not always acknowledged parents' needs for quality care while they are at work.

When child care programs provide early intervention, they can often receive higher rates of reimbursement from public agencies for these services, thereby increasing the program's resource base. Thus, incorporating an intervention program into an infant-toddler care setting offers promise for improving the quality of care offered to all children, as well as making infant and toddler classrooms more attractive working environments for teachers.

THE ROLES OF TEACHERS IN INCLUSIVE INFANT-TODDLER CARE

Teachers of infants and toddlers, especially those in inclusive care settings, have a different role to play from that of preschool teachers. The role of teachers of infants and toddlers is one that requires the skills of a number of different professionals: teacher, nurse, occupational therapist, speech-language specialist, and even musician, comedian, and performance artist! Infant and toddler teachers are most successful when they are able to think like children and view the world from the perspective of young children.

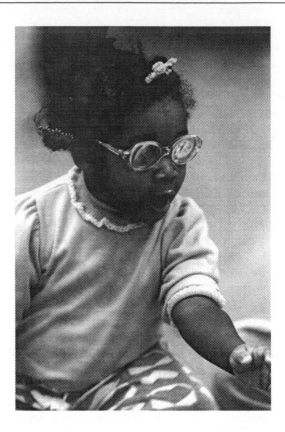

When children have developmental delays or disabilities, they often need more help and support to progress intellectually, socially, and in many other ways than children without special needs, whose learning often appears effortless. Typically developing babies and toddlers are learning constantly from everything that happens and from everything they do. Children with developmental delays or disabilities do not learn as automatically as other children do; they need to have activities and events paced more slowly, see things happen more often, and get more adult help in eliminating distractions and finding ways to succeed (Wolery, 1994). Thus, it is necessary for teachers in inclusive care settings to take on additional roles.

Caregiving

Infants and toddlers require a lot of physical care. Their diapers need to be changed frequently, and toddlers need to be guided through the process of toilet training. Infant feedings are time-consuming and some-times stressful, and many toddlers are messy eaters, requiring adult help to learn to feed themselves. Infants' clothes need to be changed frequent-ly; and toddlers are not able to dress and undress themselves, put on coats, tie their shoes, or even get their shoes on the right feet.

Even more important, infants and toddlers require a lot of emotional care. The daily separations—from parents in the morning, from a favorite toy when it's time to clean up, from consciousness at naptime—are hard for children and often lead to emotional outbursts and loss of control. Even by age 2, children have only a fragile understanding of their own feelings and how to manage them, and all infants and toddlers need the empathetic and caring intervention of sensitive adults to help them regulate their emotions.

Caring for infants and toddlers can sometimes be exhausting. It is necessary for successful teachers of infants and toddlers to be in constant control of their own emotions, setting their personal needs aside so that they can respond sensitively to children's needs. Teachers of infants and toddlers assume a big responsibility because they work with children who are very dependent on adults but who demand independence and individual recognition in challenging ways. Furthermore, teachers in infant-toddler care are in almost constant physical contact with children— lifting and carrying them, holding their hands, wiping their noses, and, of course, hugging and cuddling them.

The physical and emotional dependence of infants and toddlers on adults makes the teacher's job difficult but also rewarding. During their first 3 years, children make what sometimes seems to be a transformation from babyhood to personhood. Not only do teachers watch children make gains in competence and individuality, but they also know they are making an important contribution to these changes by being active participants.

Teaching

Infants and toddlers have a lot to learn, and they are learning all of the time with everything they do. This characteristic can make it appear that the teacher of infants or toddlers has an easy job, but actually it is a very difficult task. Successful teaching of infants and toddlers is open ended and often ambiguous. Teachers of older children often follow a lesson plan with specific goals and generate a finished product as a demonstration that the child has learned or accomplished the objective. This approach is not possible or desirable with infants and toddlers.

Teachers of infants and toddlers may plan creative, play-focused learning activities and conduct these activities with enthusiasm and energy, but children will often appear to be paying no attention, and, in fact, will begin to cry, go to sleep, or get up and leave just at the moment the teacher is getting to the point of the activity. When the play activity is block building, the toddler may be interested in wrapping a block in a baby blanket. When the teacher's goal is to get children to make animal sounds, the children may want to experience rolling on the floor. To the casual observer, what infants or toddlers are learning may not be apparent.

Alert teachers who understand infants and toddlers will begin activities with the expectation and anticipation that their plans will be interrupted and diverted by the children. This does not mean that the teacher does not have to plan. If a teacher has not thought about the play activities he or she will lead and has not viewed the activities and materials from the viewpoint of a child, the teacher will not be successful in attracting children's attention to the activity or involving them with the materials available. Thus, the teacher's planning also involves thinking about what a child can learn from each activity, toy, and material presented, and about how the teacher can make the activity and materials attractive and interesting enough that children will want to become involved with them. It is also important for teachers to think about ways in which specific intervention techniques can be incorporated into play activities.

Having thought through the play activity from the child's perspective, the next step is for the teacher to get involved in the activity. Often, when a teacher begins an activity, he or she is alone in the toy area. The teacher's job is to begin playing with and talking about the toys in a way that attracts the children's attention and interest. The teacher's enthusiasm will bring children to the teacher's side. Because infants and toddlers function best in small groups, it is good to have several different activities underway at once to prevent crowding and to increase opportunities for individualized adult attention.

Once children begin to pay attention to or come near the activity, responsive teachers continue their own involvement while at the same time paying careful attention to what the children find interesting about the activity. While children are playing, the teacher's role is to support, extend, and elaborate on their play by providing a label or description of what children are doing, suggesting a more complex way to use a toy, capitalizing on opportunities to encourage social play, or building a sequence of actions into a repeatable script for play. Teachers cannot assume that babies and toddlers instinctively know how to play. Using toys for play is a learned ability, just as other skills are also learned.

As teachers work to enhance play and integrate therapeutic intervention activities into children's play, it is important for them to avoid restricting children's play in order to meet the teachers' goals. Instead, creative teachers are open to the many varied possibilities that toys present and make use of opportunities to expand the range of children's experiences in play. The most meaningful way for infants and toddlers to explore and experience the world is by following their own intrinsic interests and curiosity. Teachers can guide them toward interesting and challenging opportunities and can prevent dangerous and destructive behavior, but teachers cannot compel children to do things the way adults think is the *right* way.

Infants and toddlers are much more interested in process than in product. They will poke at the Play-Doh but really will not care about making a snake, or they will splash endlessly in the water and never succeed in getting the red paint off their fingers. Often, teachers (and parents) want tangible evidence that children have accomplished a task or learned something new. This desire leads adults to forget the infant's or toddler's viewpoint and ask children to stack blocks on demand, produce artwork that matches a teacher-made model, or demonstrate that they can match the yellow cubes with the yellow square on the piece of paper. These types of tasks are not as meaningful to infants and toddlers as the experiences they seek out for themselves with sensitive teachers at their side to help them interpret, investigate, and invent.

At times, teachers of infants and toddlers will feel they are not truly teaching because they do not see tangible outcomes every day. However, the signs of children's learning are all around them: a child selects the two giraffes out of the animal bin and holds them up together, or a toddler builds a complicated bridge and asks for the *blue* car to go under it, or another toddler goes through all of the steps of making pretend pizza and putting it in the oven. Sensitive teachers of infants and toddlers look for the results of their efforts in the energy, enthusiasm, and curiosity of the children around them, characteristics that are crucial to children's healthy long-term development.

Intervention

In the approach to inclusive infant-toddler care described in this book, teachers play a primary role as interventionists. Because classroom teachers spend a lot of time with the children in their care and know them very well, they are best able to adapt general classroom activities to meet the individual—or special—needs of *every* child, including those with and without developmental delays and disabilities. Teachers need support through consultation with specialists who are knowledgeable about particular aspects of the development of young children and who can share with teachers ways to help all children learn and grow to their maximum potential. These specialists are most effective if they teach teachers early intervention techniques, and these techniques become part of the everyday teaching and caregiving routines in the classroom.

The philosophy behind this approach is that *all* children benefit from the use of early intervention techniques. Furthermore, the children who have developmental delays or disabilities or who are at risk for developmental delays especially benefit from having intervention or therapy available to them for many hours a day rather than the brief sessions that most specialists are able to provide.

When children with special needs are included in an infant-toddler program, teachers need to be aware of the outcomes desired for each child and work toward these goals. Each child with special needs has an individualized family service plan (IFSP; see Chapter 3), in which the outcomes desired by the child's intervention team, including the parents, are described. It is essential for teachers to be aware of the plans for each child so they can help on a day-to-day basis in supporting the child's progress toward those outcomes by incorporating learning goals into all classroom activities.

Facilitating Inclusion

One of the roles of teachers in inclusive child care settings is to serve as *inclusion facilitators*. Facilitating inclusion simply means making sure that children with special needs are incorporated into all of the ongoing activities of the classroom, including daily living activities as well as play activities. An emphasis on facilitating inclusion ensures that children who have disabilities are not set apart from the other children, such as by eating separately because they need individual care, being kept indoors when the other children are on the playground, or being entertained by one teacher while other children are involved in group activities. One-to-one care is not true inclusion. Children with disabilities or developmental delays, even those who are immobile or have complex medical needs, can take part in general classroom activities, eat lunch with the other children, and join the play activity of their choice.

If staffing allows, inclusion facilitation is a responsibility that can be assigned to a specific teacher during specific times of the day. This teacher would then be responsible for helping children with special needs participate more fully in the ongoing activities of the classroom. When, as it often happens, there is not an extra teacher who can be specifically assigned to be an inclusion facilitator, it is still necessary for the job to be done for a program to be truly inclusive. Therefore, all teachers need to make inclusion facilitation part of their regular daily routines.

Although this sounds like an additional task to put on top of an already hectic job, well organized infant-toddler care routines already incorporate many of the techniques that facilitate inclusion. The environmental organization described in Chapter 4 and the responsive teaching approach described in Chapter 6 support inclusion by giving children choices and by encouraging teachers to observe children carefully and then select their teaching goals based on children's exploratory activity with the materials provided. These practices are readily adaptable to the inclusion of children at all ability levels. Similarly, the routines for activities of daily living outlined in Part III allow for a maximum amount of individualization and, therefore, can accommodate a wide range of special needs.

TEACHERS OF INFANTS AND TODDLERS AND THE INTERVENTION TEAM

Classroom teachers are a crucial part of the intervention team for children with special needs. Collaboration among teachers, family members, and special service providers takes work but is the most effective approach to early intervention.

The Team Approach

Providing early intervention to young children and helping their families offer the best possible environment for their children requires collaboration among parents and professionals from several different disciplines. In most child care programs, directors and lead teachers are likely to have training or degrees in child development or early childhood education. Many of the classroom teachers will not have degrees in early childhood education and at times may have minimal formal training in child development.

It is even more likely that child care staff will not have any training or experience in the care of children with special needs. Sometimes this presents a barrier to inclusion because teachers fear that excessive demands for care of children with disabilities may affect the quality of care that other children receive and may increase their own significant workload. When teachers are provided adequate support from administrative staff and are involved in the planning for inclusion, however, good teachers of infants and toddlers can also be successful early interventionists (Rab & Wood, 1995).

One crucial factor in this transition from child care provider to interventionist is an atmosphere of positive collaboration with special service providers. Early intervention services are *cross-disciplinary*. Teachers and administrative staff in child care programs must learn to welcome into the classroom professionals from other fields who work with young children and their families, and these professionals must learn to work alongside teachers in the child care setting. Table 2.1 describes how teachers and specialists can teach one another and contribute equally to providing early intervention within child care settings.

Supportive and positive collaborative relationships are usually not established easily (Bruder, 1994). It is difficult for teachers to have outsiders coming into the classroom, and not all specialists are sensitive to the needs of other children and classroom teachers. It is recommended

Table 2.1.   Collaborative efforts between teachers and specialists

Knowledge to Be Shared	
By teachers	**By specialists**
The roles and responsibilities of teachers in the classroom	Professional role and nature of their training
Classroom organizational strategies that promote quality child care	Types of services they can provide to children, families, and teachers
Characteristics of individual children and each child's overall development in the family and classroom context	Characteristics of developmental delays or problems within particular domains of development
Times and situations in the classroom when intervention techniques can be used successfully	Effective intervention approaches to address specific developmental delays or problems
Effective ways to work with children in groups	Assessment of children's progress
Collaborative Roles in Intervention	
Teachers	**Specialists**
Seek out specialists to get answers to questions about individual children	Serve as consultants and make themselves available to answer questions from teachers
Routinely observe children and bring concerns to the attention of specialists	Follow up on teacher concerns
Use intervention techniques on a daily basis in the classroom	Help teachers gain confidence in using intervention techniques
Suggest adaptations of intervention techniques that fit more easily into classroom routines	Ask teachers' advice on incorporating intervention techniques into everyday routines

that special service providers have a regular schedule of visits so their arrival can be anticipated and included in the day's events. Furthermore, classroom teachers must be assertive with service providers to be certain that they are working in accord with ongoing activities, rather than interfering with them.

Early intervention is a team effort. If it is to be successful, it is crucial that classroom teachers view themselves as equal members of the team, even if they are from different educational backgrounds. It is essential that classroom teachers, like parents, be respected by specialists for their knowledge of individual children and of the classroom setting in which the children spend their days. For both teachers and specialists, the goal is to provide the best possible living and learning environment for the babies and toddlers in their care. This can only be accomplished in an atmosphere of trust and mutual respect.

Many of the specialists who work in intervention with young children have received most of their training and experience from working with preschool-age and older children or even adults. Early intervention with infants and toddlers is a relatively new focus for professional training and is only now becoming a specialization in preprofessional training programs (Bricker & Widerstrom, 1996; Klein & Campbell, 1990). Therefore, it is especially important that classroom teachers, who have extensive experience with the developmental stages of infancy and toddlerhood, be active and contributing members of the intervention team. It is equally important for families to be full participants in all decisions made concerning their children.

Increasing Family Involvement

The traditional approach to early intervention with children under the age of 3 has involved extensive participation by parents. Special services have been provided either in the family's home or in clinic settings that the parent and child attended together. Often interventions have been designed as brief therapy sessions directed by a professional, who then instructed parents in therapeutic techniques for use at home. This approach has some disadvantages, particularly for employed parents and those with little education or an unwillingness to take on the role of therapist as well as parent (Seitz & Provence, 1990; Simeonsson & Bailey, 1990). Nevertheless, one major advantage of this type of intervention is the recognition of the importance of parents in the young child's life.

When child care settings are also the location for early intervention services, it is crucial that special efforts be made to ensure that parents are as actively involved as they wish to be. It is often the responsibility of inclusive child care programs to initiate active parent-involvement efforts.

Child care programs offer unique opportunities for family involvement and service coordination. The transfer of responsibility for the child from the family to the classroom every morning and then back to the family in the evening means that it is necessary for child care staff and parents to have regular daily contact with each other. When these contacts are well-utilized, they represent outstanding opportunities for parents and child care professionals to communicate and collaborate. With a family services coordinator as part of the child care and intervention program staff, an inclusive child care program can become the focus for developmental assessment, service coordination, parent education, and family support for *all* families, rather than just for those families whose children have special needs.

Understanding the Roles of Special Service Providers

Teachers in inclusive infant-toddler child care settings typically come into contact with a large number of professionals whose training and experience is quite different from that of the early childhood educator or child care provider. Most specialists have been trained to provide services in a one-to-one situation, often in a clinic or other setting that is not part of a child's usual daily environment. Because of the increased focus within early intervention on inclusion, many service providers have had to modify the ways in which they work. This is not always an easy transition, even though the service provider may support the change.

Classroom teachers can help ensure that children in their care are receiving the best possible services and support for their development by being active participants in early intervention services (see Table 2.1). It is important for teachers in inclusive programs to have opportunities to observe the evaluation and therapy sessions conducted by special service providers; to ask questions and receive complete, understandable answers; and to learn how to apply specialized techniques in the everyday care of particular children. Special service providers will vary in their willingness to share their expertise, but program directors can help by clarifying the expectation that classroom teachers are the primary interventionists for children enrolled in the child care program.

Teachers will be able to communicate most effectively with specialists and know when to request consultation about a particular child if they have an idea of the background, training, and goals of particular professional fields. This section includes a brief description of the typical roles and areas of training for some of the professionals with whom teachers are likely to work.

Early Childhood Special Educator

The Early Childhood Special Educator usually has a bachelor's or master's degree in special education and experience with assessment, goal setting, and curriculum planning for children with special needs. Special education professionals may be responsible for development and implementation of the IFSP (see Chapter 3), may serve as family services coordinator for some families, or may deliver special instructional services to individual children.

Speech-Language Specialist

The speech-language specialist is knowledgeable about disorders and developmental delays in communicative development and oral-pharyngeal disabilities. Consultation with a speech-language specialist is suggested if children appear to have delays in their communication skills, fall behind their age-mates in the clarity of their spoken language, or have difficulty with eating or swallowing. Speech-language specialists can also help classroom teachers identify particular sounds to practice with children who have speech or language delays, and they can help incorporate communication-focused goals into general classroom activities. In addition, speech-language specialists can help teachers and children learn and use assistive communication devices.

Audiologist

The audiologist focuses on the identification and treatment of hearing loss. Children who have chronic or frequent ear infections and those who do not appear to be developing speech and language as expected for their age can receive a hearing screening or evaluation from an audiologist.

Occupational Therapist

The occupational therapist is concerned primarily with the development of functional everyday skills, play and sensory processing skills, and motor abilities involving positioning and postural control. Occupational therapists can be helpful in suggesting environmental adaptations to promote full inclusion of children with disabilities or developmental delays and are knowledgeable about special adaptive equipment that is often available on loan through state or local agencies.

Physical Therapist

The physical therapist focuses specifically on motor development reflecting neuromotor, muscular, or skeletal deficiencies or disabilities. Physical therapists can teach classroom staff appropriate exercise, movement, and positioning techniques to assist individual children. Consultation with a physical therapist is suggested whenever a child appears to be having difficulty with movement skills.

Clinical Child Psychologist

The clinical child psychologist is knowledgeable about family functioning and psychopathology in childhood. The psychologist may be consulted when a child appears to have consistent difficulties getting along with other children or when a child's family situation appears to be having a disruptive influence on his or her development. A clinical child psychologist may do regular developmental testing for children in the child care program and may be involved in the development and implementation of IFSPs.

Social Worker

The social worker's training usually involves a broad view of children's development within a family and community context. Social workers can be helpful in identifying a family's needs for additional services that will help them provide the best possible environment for their child. Often, social workers will serve as family services coordinators, either for the child care program or for individual families, and will work in this capacity to coordinate community resources in the best interests of the child and family. Whenever a child's family is receiving welfare services or a child is in state custody or in a foster care living arrangement, a social worker will be involved with the child and will be an active member of the intervention team.

Health Professionals

Physicians and nurses are excellent resources for classroom staff when a child has special health care needs, was born prematurely or at risk for developmental delays, or has been diagnosed with a specific medical condition or disability. It is helpful for the child care program to obtain copies of such a child's medical history in order to better understand the situation and support the child's development. When a child needs daily medical care, such as for an ostomy, receives oxygen, or requires the use of any other medical device, it is important for a nurse and parents to visit with classroom staff to explain in detail the necessary procedures for care or use of the equipment. A conference such as this also allows parents to gain confidence in the quality of care provided for their child.

Approaches to Cross-Disciplinary Collaboration

Despite everyone's good intentions, cooperation and communication among individuals from different backgrounds and perspectives does not always go smoothly. Professionals working in early intervention have recognized three different types of team approaches (Bruder, 1994).

The *multidisciplinary team* is not really a team at all. In this approach, often occurring by default or lack of effort, each professional working with a child and family essentially operates independently. Service providers may share information, usually in written form, but they do not collaborate in planning or carrying out recommendations for the child. Often, parents are also relatively uninvolved in this team, receiving reports but not being consulted about decisions before they are made.

The *interdisciplinary team* represents a step forward from the multi-disciplinary team, particularly in the sharing of information among service providers and collaborating on describing the desired outcomes of intervention for the child. Each service provider and the child's family have an opportunity to meet together and talk about the child's level of functioning and what they would like to be accomplished through the provision of special services. Often, however, evaluation and actual implementation of intervention practices are carried out independently, as if each service provider were responsible for one small part of the child's development.

The *transdisciplinary team* is a truly collaborative effort in which the child is seen as a whole person and each area of development is recognized as influencing other areas. On a transdisciplinary team, all service providers and the child's family are in regular communication with one another, make joint decisions, and help carry out the intervention procedures that have been decided upon as they work together.

This transdisciplinary model of cross-disciplinary intervention is the basis for the program design presented in this book. It is important for program directors to recognize, however, that achievement of a true transdisciplinary team effort is very difficult because of such factors as personality clashes, concerns over turf, and lack of time. In addition, reimbursement requirements for early intervention services are often established based on medical models that do not fit well into transdisciplinary team approaches. Nonetheless, the transdisciplinary model is undoubtedly in the best interest of children with developmental difficulties and their families.

Within the transdisciplinary model, responsibility for children's care and education is shared among the family, child care program staff, and special service providers. All participants on the team have equal opportunities to contribute to planning, decision making, and problem solving, and each participant is respected for his or her unique relationship with the child and contribution to the team. Because parents and teachers spend the most time with the child, they are responsible for incorporating intervention practices into everyday interactions and activities, and they are also responsible for making careful observations of the child's responses. Specialists draw on their training and experience to suggest effective teaching and therapeutic approaches and help parents and teachers learn and use these approaches. The focus is on the child as a developing person, who is embedded in the context of a caring family that is supported by the child care program and other community services. This is the goal of inclusive child care.

SUMMARY

Incorporating early intervention practices into child care programs for infants and toddlers is in everyone's best interest, benefiting children, families, and teachers. Because quality child care for infants and toddlers is highly individualized, children with special needs can be readily incorporated into all daily activities. The roles of teachers in inclusive child care programs are expanded to include intervention as well as caregiving and teaching; however, teachers who have the support of administrators and help from special service providers and families are capable of assuming these added responsibilities. Finally, families of *all* children have a right to high-quality child care while they work, and a collaborative parent–teacher relationship can contribute in many ways to children's healthy development.

Chapter 3

Parents as Partners

Working in close collaboration with families is necessary for any program that has the goal of promoting children's healthy development. Children grow and learn in the context of their homes and families. Therefore, effective child care and early intervention programs focus not only on children but also on the needs and concerns of the entire family.

Parents, like all people, come in many different varieties. No one sort of family is typical or ideal, and it is important for teachers to focus on the strengths of each individual family, regardless of its structure. The multi-cultural nature of U.S. society requires teachers to be aware of the variation in child-rearing values and practices of families from many different ethnic backgrounds and to work to support these different approaches to parenthood. Fathers from all ethnic and economic groups are becoming increasingly involved in their children's care, and the range of family involvement activities offered by child care programs needs to expand to include fathers as well as mothers.

Parents also differ in their attitudes toward child care. Some parents view child care programs primarily as a convenience for themselves, whereas others are interested mainly in how a program can assist their child's development. Some parents become actively involved and work alongside child care staff to make a program better, and others like to complain about a program but show no desire to help. There are some parents who resist efforts to involve them. Learning to accept, respect, and work with parents who have all of these different points of view is an important goal for teachers.

In an inclusive child care and early intervention program, there is likely to be an especially wide range of parents' needs and backgrounds. Parents of children with disabilities are usually most interested and concerned about the developmental services their children are receiving and also about the extent to which their children are being accepted and included in the group by teachers and other children. Parents of children who are at risk for developmental delays may be facing overwhelming challenges in all aspects of their lives and may simply be glad that their child is cared for during the day. In addition, some children considered at risk for developmental delays will be in the care of foster parents, grandparents, or other relatives whose needs and concerns are somewhat different from those of most parents. Parents of typically developing children are likely to be extremely busy balancing careers and family demands, and they sometimes may seem to take quality child care for granted.

Furthermore, many parents in all of these described categories may have no experience with organized child care prior to enrolling their child in an infant or toddler classroom. Some parents may feel guilty about placing their child in care, and most parents will know little about what is expected of them or what their role in the program may be. Teachers and other child care program staff have the responsibility to invite parents to become involved with their child *at whatever level is comfortable and desirable to the parent.* At the same time, regardless of the parents' degree of involvement, teachers need to accept the primary role of the parents in the child's life.

THE UNIQUE ROLES OF PARENTS

Parents are truly experts about their own children. Their knowledge of their children's personalities, extensive experience with their children in many different situations, and close emotional relationship with their children give parents insights and understanding that no one else can have. Parents are also the people who assume lifelong responsibility for their children, so their full involvement in all decision making is essential.

Parents as Experts

The parents of a very young child are the people who know the child best and are also the people responsible for making decisions about the care, treatment, and education of the child. Furthermore, parents' reports of concerns about their children have been found to be the best early indicators of developmental delay (Glascoe, 1994). Despite the fact that teachers usually have much more training in child development and early childhood education than parents do, it is essential for teachers to take a secondary role in evaluating a child's needs and deciding how to meet them.

Fortunately, most parents like to talk about their children, so it is usually easy to encourage parents to share their expertise with teachers. Even prior to a child's first day in the classroom, it is helpful for program staff to visit with the family and ask about the child's usual day, routines surrounding eating and sleeping, favorite toys and activities, and what the child does *not* like. Some familiarity with how the classroom environment and routines differ from what the child is accustomed to will help teachers prepare for and understand children's initial acceptance of or resistance to classroom practices.

The parents' knowledge can also be helpful whenever classroom staff have a concern about the child's development or when the child is having difficulty adjusting to a particular situation. Rather than raise the issue as a problem, teachers can involve parents in conversation about the child and simply ask if parents have noticed a child's troublesome behavior or an unusual developmental pattern. A casual question (e.g., "Does Cindy ever seem to ignore you when you talk to her at home?") is less threatening and alarming than a statement suggesting a developmental delay (e.g., "We think Cindy may have some hearing loss"). Furthermore, children's behavior is frequently quite different in a child care classroom from their behavior at home. Thus, any concerns about development or behavior that arise in the classroom need to be verified by parents and others who see the child in different contexts prior to seeking consultation from a specialist.

Teachers' acceptance of the parents as experts is often most difficult when parents appear not to take responsible care of their children. Some families, particularly those with very low incomes, little formal education, and limited problem-solving skills, may not meet the middle-class standards of cleanliness and parenting behavior of most teachers. In these situations, it is, of course, important to try to determine if a parent is truly neglectful (i.e., providing inadequate nutrition, medical care, or supervision so that the child's life or health is seriously endangered). If this is not the case, then teachers are most helpful if they stretch their range of acceptance in recognition that parents can deeply love their children even when their ideas about appropriate child care differ from those of teachers. An approach that emphasizes the importance of infants' and toddlers' emotional *relationships* with their parents can help teachers see that children's underlying needs can be met in many different family situations.

Parents as Members of the Intervention Team

When a child has a disability or developmental delay, parents' involvement, advice, and knowledge are especially important. Parents are the most crucial members of the child's intervention team, not only because they are the experts about their own child but also because they will be with the child throughout all of the child's growing years. The parents are most likely to see the positive results of intervention during infancy and toddlerhood; or, alternatively, to have to cope with the difficulties if the child does not receive appropriate services in the early years. Teachers and special service providers can make an important difference in children's (and families') lives and can build strong and supportive relationships with children, but it is the child's relationship with the parents that is enduring and constant.

First, parents—including fathers, mothers, and extended family members who regularly provide care—need to be involved in all team meetings that concern their child. Because of this requirement, meetings will often need to be held at inconvenient times for program staff and special service providers, and meetings are usually most effective if they are held in parents' homes, rather than in professional conference rooms. This will often require some team members to give up personal time or even to work without pay if they can be reimbursed only for actual therapy services. Agencies serving infants and toddlers and their families and the local interagency coordinating council for infant-toddler services may need to develop policies that emphasize the importance of parental participation and allow time and support for team meetings.

Second, parents need to be consulted and informed about their child's program and progress on a regular basis. The individualized family service plan (IFSP), which outlines the nature of the child's special needs and how classroom staff can help the family meet their goals for their child, requires twice-a-year updates. These updates are not enough to ensure that parents are fully informed and consulted about the services their child is receiving. When classroom teachers and special service providers collaborate in keeping a child log or scrapbook (see Chapter 6), parents need to be aware of its location and be encouraged to read it and add their own notes and observations. When regular developmental checks are made to keep track of children's progress, parents' observations can be helpful and results of the checks should be shared with parents in whatever format works best for each family: in writing or during an informal conversation at arrival or departure, a home visit, or a telephone call.

The involvement of parents as part of the intervention team also entails some responsibilities on their part. Whenever a child has special medical needs that require individualized care or the nature of a child's disability is such that alterations to classroom procedures are needed, parents can be invited to take a lead role in training teachers to provide for their child's individual needs. If parents feel awkward or unsure about their role as trainers, special service providers can also be invited to participate in the training. Such training sessions clearly recognize parents' expert role and encourage increased communication and collaboration between families and classroom staff.

PROVIDING OPPORTUNITIES FOR
PARENT COMMUNICATION AND INVOLVEMENT

There are many opportunities for interaction and communication between parents and teachers of infants and toddlers. Personal relationships are developed between families and teachers as a result of parents' and teachers' daily conversations at arrival and departure, special events held at the child care center, and visits by teachers to children's homes. Effective communication with parents requires teachers to use tact and skill.

Meaningful Daily Communication

Most parents get information about their child's daily care and about the people who provide that care during the seemingly casual conversations they have with teachers as they drop off and pick up their children from a child care center. It is important for teachers to take responsibility for ensuring that parents receive accurate and complete information during these times. Parents have confidence in the quality of care their child is receiving when they feel they know on a personal level the people providing care. Unless teachers make active efforts to get to know parents and to communicate with parents about themselves, this personal connection will never be made.

Some parents may give the impression of wishing to minimize conversation and communication. They may avoid looking directly at teachers, respond to questions or conversational overtures with monosyllables,

or even ignore teachers' initial efforts to engage them in conversation. Teachers cannot assume these parents are unfriendly or uninterested in getting to know them but can instead be subtle yet persistent in their efforts to build a relationship. The parents may simply not know what is expected, be shy or uncertain about their English proficiency, or feel guilty about leaving the child in someone else's care. The most effective point of connection is always the child, and few parents can resist hearing about cute and intelligent things their child has done.

At the other extreme are parents who monopolize the greeting teacher's time in the morning or afternoon or who ask questions about the other children in the classroom that teachers cannot answer without violating confidentiality. In this situation, teachers can politely excuse themselves to greet or talk with another parent or to bring another child to the greeting area. The best response to parents who are curious about other children is to redirect the conversation to focus on the parents' own child. For example, if Kristin's dad says, "Rudy seems to be pretty ornery lately, doesn't he?" a teacher can reply with "Kristen is a very sweet-tempered baby. Today she was giving hugs to everyone!" If a parent is insistent in asking about another child's disability or diagnosis, a teacher may simply need to say something like "I'm not qualified to diagnose the children; I treat every child as a special child." Then the teacher can once again redirect the parent to talking about his or her own child.

When parents raise concerns or issues at arrival or departure that the greeting teacher believes are best discussed privately, he or she will have to use good judgment in either moving with the parents to a private place or arranging to talk with the parents at another time. The immediate care of all of the children is the most important consideration. If the teacher is needed in the classroom to provide supervision for other children, he or she cannot leave, no matter how urgent the parents' concern may be. Usually, however, if teachers communicate meaningfully and completely at each arrival and departure of the parents, major concerns will not arise so suddenly that they need immediate attention. Furthermore, when a family services coordinator is part of the program staff, parents will know they have an advocate with whom they can discuss any concerns privately at any time.

In addition to daily conversations with parents, infant-toddler programs can provide parents with some basic information about their child's day. Knowing when and how long their child slept, when their baby last ate, and whether their toddler is making progress in toilet training helps parents to plan their evening and also gives them confidence that classroom staff are providing high-quality and individualized care. When children have disabilities or complex medical conditions, parents may need to keep daily records of bowel movements and amounts of food eaten. A simple Take-Home Report, such as that shown in Figure 3.1, can be used to provide this information to parents without taking a major amount of teacher time away from interactions with children.

In an infant classroom, the children's Take-Home Reports can be kept in the feeding area, where the most complex records are needed. The lead

What I did today ______________ by ______________
DATE CHILD'S NAME

My arrival time: ______________ News from home? ______________

I ate: ______________

and slept:
from ______ to ______
from ______ to ______

I generally felt:

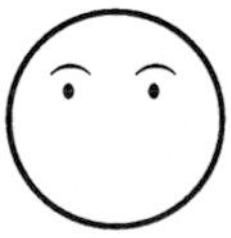

I really enjoyed: ______________

My diapering report: ______________

Figure 3.1. A sample take-home report for use in inclusive infant-toddler care.

teacher can then transfer information about diapering from the Infant Diapering and Sleep Record (see Appendix D) periodically during the day, and the child's naptimes can be recorded every time a child wakes up. In a toddler classroom, it is most efficient to keep the Take-Home Reports in the diapering and toilet area, where the child's toilet-training progress can be recorded at each diapering and toilet time. Unless a child has special feeding needs, information about meals and snacks is usually less important for toddlers than it is for infants, and teachers can simply record a statement about the child's eating. For example, a teacher may record that "Luis loved the peaches at lunch and ate very well." Teachers who are supervising toddlers during naptime can often be responsible for recording meal and nap information on the Take-Home Reports. Toward the end of the day, it is useful for the lead teacher to record an indication of the child's general mood or disposition so that parents can be prepared for a happy or a fussy evening.

It is not necessary to write a lot of descriptive information about children's development or participation in play activities on the Take-Home Reports if parents are given weekly or monthly schedules of planned play activities to take home and if they receive regular updates on their children's developmental progress. It is best to keep the Take-Home Report short and simple, use personal contacts for more detailed information, and devote the teachers' time to direct involvement with the children.

Parent Participation in the Classroom

Although many parents of children in full-day child care programs will have full-time jobs that occupy their time and attention while their child is in the classroom, some parents may be interested and willing to participate in classroom activities on a regular basis. When parents express an interest in this level of involvement, teachers and program staff can, of course, welcome them into the classroom. Although a parent will not usually replace a regular teaching position in the classroom, a parent volunteer can be given a schedule of activities that complements and supports the ongoing classroom activities. Initially, a parent might be paired with one of the teachers and participate in the activities supervised by that teacher. Ultimately, however, as a parent gets to know all of the children and feels comfortable in the classroom, the parent may take over responsibility for certain activities that match his or her talents. A parent who plays a guitar, for example, might offer a music activity on a regular basis or a parent who enjoys sports might organize toddlers into a semblance of a soccer team. It is best for a parent who is a regular visitor to have a specific activity to do with the children. Otherwise, teachers will feel a need to entertain the visitor, taking their own time and attention away from the children in their care.

At times, families may be referred to an early intervention program because of parents' needs for support and education with regard to child care and child rearing. With these families, the family services coordinator can play a major role by involving parents in the classroom and using these experiences to provide the parents with information about and demonstrations of infant or toddler care routines. When these parents are in the classroom, they need to be paired with a teacher who is warm and accepting of diverse family backgrounds and who can devote his or her attention to the requirements of the parents. Usually, the family services coordinator will be trained in and knowledgeable about infant and toddler care routines and play activities used in the classroom and may be the person who provides an educational experience for these parents. In addition to basic care routines such as feeding and diapering, parents who are at risk of providing inadequate parenting can be given information and practice in interacting positively with their child, the types of limits and rules infants and toddlers can be expected to understand, and tools for managing behavior that parents do not like. The suggestions for teachers regarding responsive teaching (see Chapter 6) and responsive guidance (see Chapter 7) can be adapted and simplified for use with parents, even those with relatively little education and experience with children.

Special Events

Infant-toddler programs can help families develop personal relationships with the teachers who care for their children and with other parents of young children by sponsoring social events that bring teachers and parents together in a relaxed and informal context. These events do not need to be elaborate or costly. Often simple social events are the most conducive to making parents feel comfortable and welcome.

Classroom open houses can be held in the late afternoon, extending the classroom hours to permit parents with long work hours to attend. Depending on parents' familiarity with the program, teachers may want to station themselves in daily living and play areas where they can explain the classroom routines and activities as parents move around the classroom. For this kind of open house, it is useful to have a "program" that guides the parents to move from one area to another. Also, open houses can have no agenda, rather simply being opportunities for conversation and communication with the children as the focus.

Teachers may also want to schedule special parent–child events around holidays. It is best to choose low-key holidays, rather than major ones when families are often overcommitted and overstressed. A Valentine's Day dance ("Come and dance with your sweetheart!") is a lot of fun, and a Labor Day picnic on the playground can offer young families a chance to get together in a place that is safe for their children. Halloween is a popular holiday with many adults and older children, but most infants and toddlers are frightened when familiar people no longer look familiar and when their own faces are covered by masks. Infant and toddler classrooms can most calmly and successfully celebrate Halloween by bringing out the classroom's dress-up clothes and having an Autumn Ball in the classroom. Teachers also need to be cautioned against wearing elaborate or frightening costumes.

Many parents want to help celebrate their child's birthday. Because of the difficulties of serving party food in the classroom (see Chapter 8), parents may be encouraged to bring themselves, rather than bringing food. Singing "Happy Birthday" a dozen times and playing games with the children is a rewarding way for parents to participate in the classroom on their child's birthday.

Home Visits and Conferences

Child care program staff can obtain a more complete picture of a child's living situation and family relationships, therefore providing more sensitive and appropriate care for the child, if the staff take time to visit with parents and children in their homes. It is recommended that an initial home visit be made with each family prior to the child's enrollment, so that information can be exchanged and questions asked and answered in a comfortable environment in which the parents feel in control of the situation. The lead teacher, family services coordinator, or program director who visits with the family may take to the home visit a videotape of the classroom that illustrates some of the daily activities. This can serve as a starting point to discuss the philosophy of the program with the parents. The initial home visit should not replace the family's visit to the classroom, where they can meet the teachers and observe caregiving and play activities for themselves; however, it is often difficult to provide a lot of information to parents when they visit the classroom. A home visit is usually more informal and gives parents a chance to get more complete answers to their questions.

Home visits are also useful for developing and updating IFSPs for children with special needs. Rather than being called in for a teacher conference, which many families regard with anxiety, an IFSP meeting in a family's home is usually a relaxed and supportive opportunity for parents and service providers to talk together and for parents to ask questions or share ideas about their children. Regular home visits to all families, not just those whose children have disabilities or developmental delays, build strong relationships with parents and provide parents with support in their difficult job of child rearing.

Some families are uncomfortable with the idea of having classroom staff visit them at home. This preference also needs to be respected. However, a program that conducts home visits regularly for communicating with parents and providing developmental information cannot take a single "No" as a definitive answer. Parents may be contacted individually each time a home visit would be appropriate, and as the parents become more familiar and comfortable with teachers and other program staff, their reluctance may diminish.

Parents who do not want visits at home may be invited to arrange a time to meet with classroom staff in another setting. This does not necessarily have to be a formal conference-type situation. A staff person might suggest a meeting over coffee in a pleasant restaurant or a brown-bag lunch near the parent's workplace. Some parents may prefer or expect a more formal meeting. The important aspect of the meeting is the communication between parent and teacher, rather than the location or formality of the meeting.

Effective Communication with Parents

Conducting home visits or meeting with families in other settings requires some specific skills. It is better for parent–teacher meetings to be held as a regular part of the child care program so that visits are amicable and nonstressful. Holding meetings only when a problem arises or for once-a-year progress reports can remind parents of their own childhood experiences with parent–teacher conferences or receiving grade cards from school. Teachers and other classroom staff who meet with parents need to be aware of techniques that help parents feel comfortable and encourage open and thorough communication among participants.

Listen

The most important communication skill for a professional in any meeting with a parent is *listening*. Teachers show they are listening through their facial expressions and body language as well as through their responses. Just as in working with young children, teachers need to avoid being so intent on their own agenda that they do not focus on the parent's concerns. If the parent brings up an unexpected issue or a concern of which the teacher was previously unaware, the teacher needs to make sure that he or she has heard and understood the parent by restating the parent's question or comment. For example, a teacher might say "It sounds as though you are worried that Kevin is being left out of a lot of activities, and this might be because of his birthmark." This restatement gives a parent an opportunity to correct any misimpression the teacher might have and also communicates to the parent that the teacher accepts and shares his or her concern. In any meeting between a parent and teacher, the parent's important role needs to be acknowledged by making sure the parent talks at least half of the time.

Avoid Labeling the Child or the Child's Behavior

When talking with parents about their children, teachers are most effective when they try to use concrete and specific descriptions of behavior, rather than adjectives that place the child in a category. It is always better to say "Gloria often watches the other children for a while before she is ready to play" than "Gloria is shy." Categories have different meanings to different people. While a teacher might feel that being shy is a positive trait, a parent with a different idea and a different history of experiences might be alarmed or think something is wrong. If the teacher does have a concern about a child's behavior or development, he or she can raise it by asking the parents what they have observed (e.g., "Does David pull up on the furniture at home?"). Typically, if teachers have noticed an unusual developmental pattern, parents will also have noticed and will be happy to share their thoughts. Teachers need to be especially careful never to give a diagnostic label to any child or even to suggest a possible diagnosis.

Accept Parents' Concerns or Observations as True and Important

Parents and teachers sometimes have different priorities and tolerances. A situation that a parent may view as a problem (e.g., "Kari came home the other day with someone else's sweatshirt on!") may seem relatively unimportant to a teacher. Nevertheless, teachers and other child care program staff who view parents as partners need to be open to the concerns expressed by parents, accept these concerns as being significant because they are important to the parents, and be willing to work with the parents to find solutions.

Unless professionals believe that a parent is behaving in a way that is truly detrimental to a child's well-being, it is not their job to change the parent's attitudes or behavior. It is important for teachers to accept that parents vary in their values, their ways of looking at the world, and their conceptions of what should be encouraged and discouraged in children. If parents do not see a particular situation as a problem, they are not likely to want to change anything to solve it. However, if parents do think there is a problem, it is not worthwhile to try to convince them otherwise.

Talk in Everyday Language

Professionals develop ways of talking about children and classroom activities that are not always understandable to all parents. Talking down to parents should be avoided, but teachers can think about what they are saying to be sure they are not using professional jargon or abbreviations that are unfamiliar to parents.

Help Parents Arrive at Alternatives that Fit Their Family

Sometimes teachers may feel that there is only one way to address a particular concern or situation and may want to give advice or instructions to parents on how to solve a problem. Usually, however, when parents bring up concerns, they want support and empathy, rather than solutions. In addition, often one person's solution is not right for another person. When a concern is raised, teachers need to clarify the concern and come to an agreement with the parent on the desired outcomes for the child.

Teachers can certainly make suggestions when they are asked their opinion, but they need to avoid giving advice or proposing solutions for the parent. When professionals do offer suggestions, it is important that they are not presented as expert solutions. Instead, teachers can phrase their ideas as coming from experienced parents (e.g., "Lots of parents find . . ."), or as affirmations of the parents' own experience (e.g., "You probably already know this . . ."). An even better approach is to work through a concern or problem with the parent and encourage the *parent* to think of several possible alternative approaches. The teacher can then ask the parent some gentle questions about how each solution would influence the rest of the family or their daily activities.

For example, if during a parent–teacher conversation a father expresses his fears that his son who has developmental delays will never be coordinated enough to learn to bowl, which is the dad's favorite recreational activity, the teacher needs to avoid jumping in immediately with advice, no matter how good the advice may be. Because it is the father who has the concern, he needs to find a comfortable solution. The teacher can ask questions (e.g., "What makes you think he won't be able to learn to bowl?" or "Has he gone with you when you've been bowling?") to start the father's train of thought, but the teacher's primary objective is to encourage the dad to come up with some positive steps he can take to enjoy being with his son right now. The effective teacher will help the parent leave the meeting with a plan of action and a feeling that the child care program will support his efforts.

Present Concerns without Blame or Accusations

When teachers talk with parents about problems, the teachers' goal is usually to enlist parents' assistance and support. This is best accomplished by presenting the issue objectively and describing how the teacher feels about it without implying that the parent is doing something wrong. For example, if the teacher wants to encourage more regular attendance by a child, he or she might say "When Jamie doesn't come in the morning, I worry that something may be wrong and I want him to be able to spend as much time as possible with the other children." Teachers may also empathize with the complex demands on parents and offer support and assistance, such as "Is there any way we can help you to make mornings less stressful?"

Be Aware of Community Supports for Families

When meeting with parents, teachers may face a situation in which a parent points out a concern or personal problem that is not directly related to the child's care. Teachers need to know where their sphere of responsibility ends and not try to help parents with marital problems, financial difficulties, tenant–landlord conflicts, or disputes with relatives. It is useful to have a directory of community services available, but the teacher should also be familiar with those services so he or she can direct the parent to the appropriate place to call, rather than just hand the parent a folder with a list of names and telephone numbers in it. In the parents' presence or later with their permission, the teacher may even volunteer to make a call for them.

Follow Up After Meeting with Parents

Whenever professionals agree to take any action or obtain information during a meeting with parents, they must be sure to follow through on those commitments immediately and communicate the result to parents. If no action was needed, a brief but personal note to the parents thanking them for their time, their hospitality, or their insights can help to promote positive relationships.

HELPING FAMILIES HELP THEIR CHILDREN

Child care centers support families by providing helpful services and offering information and education to parents. The addition of a family services coordinator to the staff of a child care program clearly establishes the importance of families as partners. The use of IFSPs for all families enhances collaboration between parents and teachers and helps promote shared goals for children.

Child Care as a Family Support Service

Most early childhood educators think of their task as helping children grow, learn, and develop to their maximum potential, and this is an important role. But child care also serves a broader function as a support and extension of the family. Without child care, many working families would not be able to earn enough money to support their family at the level they desire. Furthermore, inclusive child care makes it possible for parents of children with special needs to have employment opportunities equal to those of other parents. Some families may rely on child care to obtain the education or job training they need to move themselves and their families out of dependence on welfare.

In addition to providing this support, a child care and early intervention program can serve as a center for a range of services that help families provide the best possible care for their children. Child care programs can offer parents information and education sessions, provide literature on child health and development, promote children's good health by making sure they receive regular medical care, provide referrals to other specialized services in the community, and even organize toy or clothing exchanges. Through newsletters or fliers, child care programs can promote positive child rearing by providing information on nutrition and recipes for foods that toddlers can eat, information on car seat safety, descriptions of play and learning activities parents and children can enjoy together, and information on toy safety. The opportunities for child care to make a difference in parents' and children's lives are limited only by teachers' ingenuity, imagination, and, of course, time.

The Family Services Coordinator

When an inclusive child care program has a staff position for a family services coordinator, the opportunities for providing family support are enhanced. A family services coordinator, who may be trained in early childhood, social work, special education, or psychology, assists families in whatever ways they identify as helpful to them in providing the best possible care and developmental environment for their child. Sometimes this means seeking out special services required because of a child's special needs. For other families, it means helping them find financial resources to pay for child care or arrange transportation for their child. The family services coordinator may visit a family at home to help them see how to fit toilet training into their busy lives or just to give parents a chance to talk about their hopes and dreams for their child. The range of family-related issues that a family services coordinator may address is unlimited.

The family services coordinator also helps teachers and other members of the intervention team understand parents' points of view. Most parents can help classroom staff provide the best possible care for their child. This is especially true when children have special needs. However, parents are often shy or reluctant to offer advice to teachers whom *they* view as experts in child care and child development. The family services coordinator can promote open two-way communication between child care staff and families and make parents feel they are an integral part of the program.

A family services coordinator may also assume responsibility for enrollment of children and for maintaining a waiting list and handling referrals to the program from other community agencies. When new children are enrolled, the family services coordinator and lead teacher can visit the family at home to explain the program, obtain necessary enroll-ment information, and get acquainted with the child and family. Families may also be invited to visit the classroom with their child prior to the child's first full day.

For children who have special needs, the family services coordinator, the child's family, and the intervention team work together to develop an IFSP. The family services coordinator is then responsible for overseeing implementation of this plan and updating it periodically. When children are approaching age 3, it is also the task of the family services coordinator to assist the child and family with the transition to a new program.

The family services coordinator can also take a major role in devel-oping a range of educational and informational services for all families, rather than just for those families whose children have disabilities or developmental delays. Organizing opportunities for parents to talk with one another about shared child-rearing concerns, putting together newsletters or handouts on topics of interest to parents, or just being available at arrival and departure times to greet and talk to parents are all functions that the family services coordinator can perform.

The Individualized Family Service Plan

Children who are eligible for Part C services under the criteria set by their state are required to have IFSPs. These are official documents, but they are also informal records of families' hopes for their children. Most IFSPs are handwritten in a collaborative effort by families and professionals. IFSPs are meant to be living, growing, changing descriptions of the child, the family, and where they are going together.

The IFSP should never be prepared in advance by classroom staff or special service providers and then presented to the family for their approval. Instead, the IFSP should be jointly written in a meeting that includes as many of the members of the intervention team and family members as possible. Usually, the intervention team is made up of at least one member of the classroom staff, any special service providers who are currently involved or expected to be involved with the child, and the fam-ily services coordinator who is selected by the family to help them obtain any services needed for optimal development of their child. In addition, the intervention team includes all of the family members who are direct-ly involved with the child. *Family* should be broadly defined to mean mother, father, grandparents if they live nearby, a friend or neighbor who is an important source of support to the family, and a regular respite care provider or other involved person. Together, the intervention team will actually *write* the individualized plan for the child and family.

Some parents are intimidated or overwhelmed by meetings that include a large number of professionals who are more articulate and assertive than the parents. When families are unfamiliar with the IFSP process, it is helpful for their family services coordinator to meet individ-ually with them prior to the IFSP meeting. The family services coordina-tor can explain the goals of IFSPs and each family's central role in the process of IFSP development. Parents who are prepared in advance tend to be more active participants in IFSP meetings (Campbell, Strickland, & LaForme, 1992).

Included in an IFSP are results of developmental evaluations of the child, usually carried out by classroom staff, special service providers, or representatives of the interagency coordinating council for infant-toddler services, which is responsible for screening and evaluation. Unlike many educational documents, however, the IFSP presents developmental information in a way that encourages parents' understanding and contribution. Thus, instead of a listing of scores on standardized tests, the IFSP contains a narrative description of the child's current level of performance in each of the major developmental domains, and both family members and professionals can offer descriptions to be included here.

Even the way developmental domains are described on IFSPs is different from the way most educators have been taught to talk about them, because the labels used need to be focused on the types of skills and abilities cared about by families. Rather than cognitive development, an IFSP label might read as *thinking and problem solving*. Similarly, gross motor development could be listed as *muscles and movement;* fine motor development as *reaching and playing;* communication as *talking, listening, and understanding;* social and behavioral development as *getting along with others;* and adaptive or functional skills as *daily living*. When presented in these terms, the discussion about the child's development can be shared equally between parents and professionals.

The IFSP provides an opportunity for a description of the *resources and strengths* the family brings to raising their child. As parents will often be modest about offering ideas about this topic, teachers can often suggest ways they view the parents as supporting the child's development: providing love, affection, attention, a stable and comfortable home, and appropriate early intervention services, for example. Family strengths might also include the presence of an involved extended family, loving siblings, a network of friends and co-workers, support from a religious community, the parents' active involvement in play with the child, the parents' interest in learning about early intervention, or a desire to get more education or become employed. Once professionals begin suggesting and writing down some of these resources and strengths, parents will usually add others to the list. If the child is present during the IFSP meeting, professionals can make specific comments about the positive ways family members interact with him or her and point out how this involvement promotes the child's development. The end result of an IFSP meeting should be a feeling of pride on the part of parents as they see the many contributions they make to their child's development.

Central to the IFSP is the description of *outcomes* desired for the child. The wishes of parents are given first priority here, and the best outcomes are written in the parents' own words. If parents suggest an outcome that is too developmentally advanced for the child to achieve in the next 6 months, professionals can ask questions that help parents identify the first steps toward that outcome and express these in clear terms so that the parents will be able to see their child's progress. If, for example, the parent of an almost 1-year-old expresses a desire for the child to be out of diapers and toilet trained, that outcome can be written on the list, but teachers might ask about the family's approach to diapering and suggest focusing on a skill such as learning the sign for TOILET or cooperating during diaper changes—whatever immediate steps the parent feels would make diaper changing more successful and less burdensome at the present.

Professionals also have an opportunity to suggest outcomes that they would like to be included in the IFSP. In a collaborative planning process, all of the participants are able to express their viewpoints; however, professional opinions should never outweigh the desires of the parents. If the outcomes desired by professionals are not seen as valuable or important by parents, the resulting IFSP will not be useful. Families may also be invited to add to the list any desired outcomes for themselves or for their family that would help them provide better care for their child with special needs. For some families, finding a better job, improving their education, or simply having time for recreation may be important concerns and can be included as goals. If families do not wish to talk about their own needs, it is not necessary for family outcomes to be listed on an IFSP.

Once the outcomes are determined, parents and professionals talk about the ways in which they envision the child reaching the outcomes. Family members are asked for their ideas, and the approaches to intervention need to be evaluated to determine if they fit readily into the family's typical daily schedule. Some outcomes will be more appropriate for parents and others in the home environment to address, whereas others will become a part of the classroom program. Most outcomes can be addressed in all of the environments in which the child spends time. When parents and teachers talk together about ways to reach their goals, there is a greater likelihood of combined efforts and consistency across contexts that benefit the child. The specific settings for intervention are listed in the IFSP, and the service agencies and service providers involved are identified. If the intervention settings are not inclusive or natural settings, the reasons the services cannot be provided in such settings should be identified. All of the services required for the child's best involvement in intervention are listed. If the family needs transportation to get the child to a special service provider or to the classroom every day, that need is identified clearly in the IFSP. If there are adaptive devices or positioning equipment that would increase the child's opportunities for involvement in classroom and family activities, consultation and assistance in obtaining these are included on the list of necessary services. The dates, frequency, and anticipated duration of services are also specified, and a plan for the child's transition to preschool services included.

When developed collaboratively, with parents as full partners, the IFSP provides an opportunity for professionals to assist parents of children with special needs in taking a step back from the stresses and struggles of everyday life and expressing their hopes and dreams for their child. These dreams will usually be very similar to the dreams of all parents, and so the IFSP process also serves as a constant reminder to professionals to put less emphasis on the child's disability or developmental delay and more emphasis on the child as a unique person growing in a family context.

Once the IFSP is complete, classroom staff and special service providers work to translate the outcomes desired by families into a concrete plan of action that can be incorporated into the daily living and play routines of the infant-toddler classroom. Suggestions for incorporating IFSP outcomes into classroom activities appear in Chapter 6.

An IFSP for All Families

High-quality inclusive infant-toddler child care programs encourage all families to think about the outcomes they wish for their children and to communicate these goals to classroom staff. This process gives teachers a better idea of parents' priorities for their children. Some parents will emphasize the learning of preacademic skills, some parents will be most interested in how their child gets along with others, and some parents will simply want their child to be happy and contented during the day. All of these outcomes are important and realistic, and being aware of what parents most want to know about their child can help teachers communicate more effectively with them.

When applied to children who are typically developing, the IFSP process can be simplified to meet families' individual needs. Some families may enjoy talking over their goals and desires for their child in a home visit or other meeting with a teacher or the family services coordinator, but some families may feel this takes too much time from their busy lives. These parents can be asked to fill out a simple questionnaire, such as that shown in Figure 3.2, that gives some basic information about their child and their own priorities. It is helpful to have parents provide this information at the time of enrollment and about every 6 months thereafter, using a schedule similar to that required for the more formal IFSPs of children with special needs. The outcomes desired by parents can also be used in conjunction with a parent feedback form (see Chapter 11) to

Child _____   Age _____   Date _____

How we would like to see our child develop this year:

    in thinking and problem solving

_____

    in play and movement

_____

    in talking, listening, and understanding

_____

    in getting along with others

_____

    in daily living

_____

How our child is growing and changing right now:

_____

_____

We would like the infant-toddler program to help our family with:

    _____   meeting other parents

    _____   learning more about children's development in general

    _____   learning more about *our* child's development

    _____   getting information about nutrition and health in childhood

    _____   toilet training for our child

_____   _____

PARENT SIGNATURE   FOR THE INFANT-TODDLER PROGRAM

Figure 3.2.   A sample short-form IFSP for all children and families.

determine whether the child care program is providing for the individual needs of children and families.

SUMMARY

Families are at the center of infants' and toddlers' lives, and quality child care programs give families a central role as well. Regular communication between teachers and parents is essential for all children, and the full participation of parents in planning for the care and education of children with special needs enhances these children's opportunities. A focus on family collaboration within inclusive child care programs requires a commitment of resources and teacher time but contributes substantially to overall program quality and children's development.

Chapter 4

Organizing Inclusive Infant-Toddler Care

An infant-toddler child care program needs to be highly organized in order for its staff to provide responsive, sensitive, and individualized care to all of the children. When children with special needs are included in a child care program, the tasks remain the same, but there is a greater need for effective organization. This chapter describes a tested and workable plan for operating an inclusive full-day infant-toddler care program that incorporates early intervention practices into daily routines and play activities that are appropriate for all children.

THE ORGANIZATION FOR CHILDREN

First and most important, an infant-toddler care environment must be organized to meet children's individual needs for care, stimulation, and adult attention. The physical environment needs to be comfortable and nonstressful. Furniture and equipment must be of appropriate sizes for very young children, rather than for adults or preschool-age children. Floor surfaces need to be softly carpeted, and colorful plastic-covered foam mats add gentle definition of activity areas. It is most comfortable and homelike if neither children nor teachers wear shoes in the classroom, and this practice also helps keep the carpet clean.

Second, the number of children cared for in a group needs to be small enough to minimize stress and ensure that every child receives a lot of individualized teacher attention. At the same time, group size needs to be large enough to offer diversity and to support the required number of adults to do all of the necessary tasks. The program descriptions in this book are based on inclusive child care and early intervention classrooms operated at the University of Kansas for 9 infants, ranging from 3 to 15 months of age, and 10–12 toddlers, ranging from 15 to 30 months of age for typically developing children and from 15 to 36 months of age for children with disabilities or developmental delays. Children with disabilities or developmental delays should be enrolled in classrooms with their age-mates and should make transitions from the infant to the toddler classroom at approximately the same chronological age as other typically developing children.

Three teachers are needed to staff each of the classrooms described in this book. For a group size of 9 infants and 10–12 toddlers, there is an adult:child ratio of 1:3 for infants and at least 1:4 for toddlers. Although adult:child ratios and group sizes are emphasized in most child care licensing regulations and in descriptions of child care settings, the absolute number of adults present is also very important to quality infant and toddler care. It is extremely difficult to maintain high quality in infant-toddler care with fewer than three teachers in the classroom. Regardless of the number of children, there are often three tasks that must be accomplished at any one time. Thus, with group sizes of fewer than 9 infants or 12 toddlers, it is still recommended that 3 teachers be available in the classroom.

Third, the day's schedule of events for children needs to be varied yet predictable, encouraging children's full participation by allowing them to anticipate events. The daily schedule for an infant classroom is organized around infants' self-determined needs for feeding, sleeping, and diapering and to take advantage of their awake, active periods. Toddlers can be expected to cooperate with a daily schedule that provides a lot of individuality but also arranges meals and naps at the same time each day. A typical schedule for a toddler classroom appears as Figure 4.1.

Fourth, the physical environment for infant-toddler care needs to be consistent and clearly defined, with play areas separated from eating, diaper-changing, and sleeping areas. Infants need a play space that is not only large enough for active movement but also small enough for one teacher to closely supervise all children. A spacious and open room arrangement that includes active play equipment can accommodate toddlers' desire to be constantly "on the go." Children need cozy areas and soft corners as well as open spaces. Also, it is very important for an infant-toddler environment to be completely safe so that children can explore without interference and without endangering themselves or others.

Children with disabilities and developmental delays need the same type of classroom organization as typically developing children. The balance between comfort and challenge that fosters security and exploration in typically developing children is just as beneficial for children with special needs. Responsive, individualized care in a safe and stimulating environment should be available to every child, regardless of disabilities and developmental delays.

In the program model described in this book, infants' and toddlers' time is spent in two general types of activities: exploration and experience—including independent play and teacher-led play activities—and activities of daily living—including diapering, feeding, naps, and transitions between activities. Throughout the day, children are given many opportunities to choose their own activities. Whenever possible, two or three planned play activities that are each supervised by a teacher are offered to children during exploration and experience times. Children may also choose to play independently by using toys that are displayed on shelves within children's reach or by taking a material from an activity area to another place for play. Although children must participate in daily living activities, such as diaper changing and meals, their transitions into and out of these activities are individualized so that children have a

Time	Primary activity	Teaching opportunities: Exploration and experience	Teaching opportunities: Activities of daily living
7:30–8:30	Arrival	Doll play Parallel play	Separation from family Diapering/Toilet Health check
8:30–9:00	Breakfast	Building activity	Washing hands Eating breakfast
9:00–10:30	Exploration and Experience	House, building, and active play activities Music: instruments, rhythm, songs, finger plays, and dancing Small groups: sensory experiences, science, water play, messy play, and art projects	Diapering/Toilet
10:30–10:45	Transition to outside	Small groups continue Parallel play	Dressing for outside
10:45–11:30	Outdoor play	Active play activities, nature activities, sensory experiences, water play, and adventures	
11:30–12:00	Lunch	Parallel play	Washing hands Eating lunch Cleaning up Diapering/Toilet
12:00–12:30	Quiet play	Stories and finger plays	Diapering/Toilet Going to sleep
12:30–2:30	Nap	Listening to stories and music	Going to sleep
2:30–3:00	Quiet play	Puzzles and building activities	Getting up from nap Diapering/Toilet
3:00–3:15	Snack	Parallel play	Washing hands Eating snack Cleaning up
3:15–4:15	Exploration and Experience	House, building, and active play activities Music: instruments, rhythm, songs, finger plays, and dancing	Washing hands
4:00–4:15	Transition to outside	Finger plays and songs	Dressing for outside
4:15–5:00	Outdoor play	Active play activities, nature activities, sensory experiences, water play, and adventures	
5:00–5:30	Departure	Active play activities	Diapering/Toilet Reunion with family

Figure 4.1. A typical toddler classroom schedule.

chance to make some decisions for themselves. The goal of giving children choices among activities is to increase their involvement by building on their naturally occurring curiosity and interests.

Play activities for infants and toddlers need to be focused primarily on having fun, on exploration of materials and the environment, and on gaining experience with a wide variety of objects and other people. In many early intervention approaches, activities are focused on acquisition of specific skills; in such programs, children may be "tested" repeatedly to track their progress or urge them to achieve a new skill. A more effective and relaxed learning environment is one in which teachers are alert to naturally occurring opportunities to teach that arise out of children's own curiosity about the world and involvement in play and other activities. Intervention to assist children who have special needs can best take place within the ongoing activities of the classroom, and intervention can be implemented by teachers with the help and consultation of specialists so that all children receive the benefits of early intervention practices.

When enough teachers are available, their time can be scheduled in a way that allows them to anticipate children's needs for care and be ready to meet those needs quickly. This kind of organization means that a hungry baby or a toddler with an urgent need to "go potty" will not have to wait for care and attention until a teacher finishes another task. Without placing unreasonable demands on any of the children, this approach to infant-toddler care effectively meets the individual needs of children who vary widely in abilities, including children with developmental delays or disabilities.

In high-quality infant-toddler care, the children's needs and concerns have first priority. Expectations for children's behavior are based on realistic and reliable information about children's development. Teachers understand and respect the developmental stages of infancy and toddlerhood, and children are neither pushed to meet expectations that would be appropriate for older children nor disrespected by having everything done for them. In such a caring and supportive climate, infants and toddlers at all levels of ability are accepted as valuable and competent people, are able to explore the world according to their own schedules and interests, and are given opportunities to experience and learn from a wide variety of play and social situations.

THE ORGANIZATION FOR TEACHERS

In order to provide an environment for infants and toddlers that is not only undemanding and comfortable but also rich in social contact and intellectually stimulating, teachers need to be very highly organized and plan their activities in advance. Thus, it is important for teachers to work from a clearly defined schedule that specifies the area or activity for which each teacher is responsible throughout the day.

Experienced teachers of infants and toddlers may feel that following a schedule is unnecessary because they already know what children need. It is true that many infant-toddler child care programs that are considered to be individualized actually do not use a schedule but try, instead, to

meet children's individual requirements simply by responding whenever a need becomes evident. In these situations, however, children are given attention primarily when they are uncomfortable, such as when they need a diaper change, or when a problem arises, such as when one child hits another. Rather than individualized care, this approach leads to crisis orientation, because teachers are constantly reacting to one problem after another. Children who are undemanding and do not cause problems—or children whose disabilities make it difficult for them to signal their discomfort—can easily be overlooked in such programs.

By contrast, when teachers follow a carefully arranged schedule, they can avoid crises through advance planning and organization and also divide their attention more equally among all children. For example, when a teacher has a scheduled time to change diapers and help children use the toilet, he or she can devote full attention to each child who is diapered or uses the toilet during that time. This changes the emphasis placed on diapering and toilet training. Instead of being viewed as interruptions in the day's activities, these daily living activities are given value as important aspects of the program, as they should be for infants and toddlers. Similarly, transitions to outdoor play and toddlers' transitions to naptime are given their own place on a schedule, recognizing that infants and toddlers need time to learn to dress and undress without pressure, teachers need time to help them without stress, and toddlers need to prepare for sleep in a relaxed and supportive environment.

A carefully designed schedule of teacher activities ensures that teachers will be available to anticipate children's needs and to provide care to all children without running from one emergency situation to another. According to the schedules presented here (see Figures 4.2 and 4.3), at any given time, each of the three teachers present in the classroom will usually be doing something different. That is, one teacher may be supervising the children's play while another teacher is feeding infants and the third teacher is changing diapers. At another time, two different teacher-led play activities may be conducted while the third teacher handles diapering. During each day, teachers rotate from activity to activity, following the schedule so that all teachers get variety in their day, but all children's activities are always supervised.

A fourth teacher is a great asset when the classroom includes a number of children whose special needs require a lot of individualized attention or specialized care. Adding a fourth teacher allows a more realistic division of responsibilities among teachers—for example, one person can then greet parents as children arrive, lend a hand during transitions, provide special care as needed for children with disabilities, and help facilitate involvement of children with special needs in all classroom activities. Teacher schedules shown in Figures 4.2 and 4.3 can simply be expanded to include four, rather than three, different teacher responsibilities.

Other than contributing predictability to the day, the daily schedule teachers follow is not noticeable to children. In fact, the schedule has the effect of allowing children maximum flexibility in choosing their own activities and receiving individualized care, and it virtually eliminates downtime for children. For teachers, the schedule specifies not only the tasks they will do but also the division of responsibility. With a well-planned schedule, every teacher always has a clearly defined area of responsibility. When a teacher is not scheduled to be responsible for an area that is not clearly visible to other teachers, that area can be physically closed to children. The clear designation of assigned duties helps avoid situations in which children are not adequately supervised because of vague or shared responsibilities of teachers.

Play activities also need to be planned and scheduled in advance to provide both variety and familiarity for children. By discussing the specific activities planned for the week, teachers can develop new and interesting ways to present materials and integrate intervention approaches into play. The activity plan itself is posted in the classroom where parents and other visitors, as well as teachers themselves, can see it. Advance planning helps teachers successfully involve children and respond effectively to children's interests and initiations during play.

According to the sample schedule for infant classrooms (see Figure 4.2), three teachers take turns with the basic infant care routines of diapering, feeding, and supervising children who are awake and playing. According to this schedule, the teacher who is responsible for diapering can also supervise children's naps, putting to bed those children who are sleepy after their diapers are changed and taking children who are awake out of their cribs to be diapered before going to the feeding or play area. Any teacher assigned to diapering or feeding during a time when no child

Teacher	7:30	7:45	8:00	8:15	8:30	8:45	9:00	9:15	9:30	9:45	10:00	10:15	10:30	10:45	11:00	11:15	11:30	11:45	12:00	12:15
Lead Teacher	arrival			diaper			play 1			diaper		play 2	diaper		play 1			diaper		play 1
Teacher B	play 1	diaper & health check			play 1		diaper		feed				play 1		play 2	feed older babies		feed		
Teacher C	diaper & health check		play 1		feed				play 2		play 1	clean		feed		diaper		play 1		diaper

Teacher	12:30	12:45	1:00	1:15	1:30	1:45	2:00	2:15	2:30	2:45	3:00	3:15	3:30	3:45	4:00	4:15	4:30	4:45	5:00	5:15	5:30
Lead Teacher	play 1	diaper		play 1		play 2	diaper		play 1		diaper		play 2	play 1		departure				set up	
Teacher B	feed clean	play 1		diaper		feed			play 2	clean	play 1			diaper		play 2	play 1		diaper	clean & set up	
Teacher C	diaper	feed			clean	play 1			diaper		feed			clean	play 2		diaper	play 2	play 1		clean & set up

Figure 4.2. A sample teacher schedule for an inclusive infant classroom.

67

Top table (7:30–12:15)

Teacher	7:30	7:45	8:00	8:15	8:30	8:45	9:00	9:15	9:30	9:45	10:00	10:15	10:30	10:45	11:00	11:15	11:30	11:45	12:00	12:15
Lead Teacher	arrival		diaper & health			break-fast	bldg act B	active play act A	house area act C	bldg act D	music	small group #1	tr to out	outdoor play		tr		lunch	quiet play	tr to nap
Teacher B	diaper/toilet & health check				bldg act A	house area act A		bldg act C	active play act B	house area act D	music	small group #3	clean up	outdoor play		tr	diaper/toilet			
Teacher C	doll play		parallel play		breakfast		clean up	house area act B		diaper/toilet	outdoor play	small group #2	tr to out	outdoor play	setup	setup	lunch	lunch	stories & quiet play	

Bottom table (12:30–5:30)

Teacher	12:30	12:45	1:00	1:15	1:30	1:45	2:00	2:15	2:30	2:45	3:00	3:15	3:30	3:45	4:00	4:15	4:30	4:45	5:00	5:15	5:30
Lead Teacher	nap						stories	parallel play		put away cots set up snack	snack	music	active play act C	house area act B	tr	outdoor play		departure			setup for next day
Teacher B	tr to nap	nap					diaper/toilet				parallel play	music	house area act A	bldg act B	tr to out	outdoor play			diaper/toilet		clean
Teacher C	tr to nap	nap					puzzles	bldg act A	doll play		snack	clean up	diaper/toilet			outdoor play			active play act D		clean

Figure 4.3. A sample teacher schedule for an inclusive toddler classroom. (act = activity; bldg = building; out = outside; tr = transition.)

68

needs care in that area joins the children in the play area, carrying out thematic (or Play 2) activities (see Chapter 5). The teacher conducting Play 2 activities is not responsible for supervising the entire play area, so he or she can become involved in more elaborate activities with one or two children.

The lead teacher in an infant classroom is never assigned to feed babies. Instead, the lead teacher is the one person whose schedule allows the flexibility to respond to immediate needs—a parent dropping by the child care center, the telephone ringing, a visit from a special service provider, or a child whose temperature needs to be taken. Feeding is the least flexible of the infant care routines; therefore, it is not well suited to the other responsibilities of the lead teacher.

The sample toddler schedule shown in Figure 4.3 is more complex because the tasks needed in toddler care are more complex. Teachers are assigned to carry out specific play activities keyed to a daily schedule (see Appendix B) that provides variety and also repetition of concepts and experiences to suit the slower paced learning that is typical of toddlers' development. Most play activities are planned to last only 15 minutes so that toddlers' (and teachers') interest stays high, and several activities are conducted simultaneously. Even when all teachers are involved in the same play activity, such as during music and small group times, parallel play and active play toys, as well as dolls and house equipment, are available for those children who do not choose to participate in the planned activity. Time is provided in the schedule for the transition to outdoors (coming inside is much quicker!) and to nap, so children are not rushed and teachers are not stressed.

These sample schedules are presented as examples of the principle of dividing up specific teacher duties into clear time blocks in an approach that emphasizes responsive, individualized care. In practice, of course, each of these schedules would include more than three people each day so that teachers could have needed breaks and work a reasonable number of hours. Actual classroom schedules need to be developed to match the work hours of individual teachers. The ages and ability levels of children in the group also influence the daily schedule, so changes must be made in the tasks to be done and the number of people needed to do the tasks in order to adapt to the particular needs of any program at any particular time.

THE ORGANIZATION OF THE PHYSICAL ENVIRONMENT

Classrooms for infants and toddlers must be flexible and inviting as well as highly organized. Children, parents, and teachers should all feel comfortable in infant-toddler programs. Space needs to be appropriately designed for children who are nonmobile, for those who are just learning to crawl and walk, and for toddlers who are constantly in forward gear. The classroom must also be an efficient and pleasant work environment for teachers.

Space requirements for infant-toddler care vary from state to state, and how rooms are organized usually depends on existing arrangements and available plumbing. As a guideline, nine infants need at least 350 square feet of play space, 30 square feet for diapering, 80 square feet for feeding, and a sleep area that will accommodate nine cribs with a minimum of 3 feet between each of them. Ten to twelve toddlers require somewhat more space: 600 square feet of play space (that can double as a nap area), a diapering/toilet area of at least 50 square feet, and an eating/special activity area of 100 square feet. In addition, a child care program can never have too much storage space.

Space for Exploration and Experience

A large portion of the classroom space in an infant or toddler program is devoted to play. A good basic design for play space is an open floorplan that invites children's movement. Within the overall play space, it is helpful to have separate toy or activity areas where similar types of materials are grouped together or certain types of activities generally take place. For example, a classroom for infants might have an area that is kept free of small toys and clutter, furnished with large blocks or foam shapes around which beginning walkers can cruise safely and without impediment.

The best play space for infants and toddlers is open and carpeted, decorated with interesting items to touch and look at that are displayed at child height, and stocked with toys on open shelves where children can reach them. Toys must be selected carefully, for safety as well as for appeal to all of the senses. At least three similar or identical versions of all toys should be available to minimize squabbles and promote social play. Included within an infant play space is an area designated for nonmobile babies and an open, uncluttered area for crawlers and beginning walkers. For toddlers, play space is divided into several different toy areas that are clearly differentiated by furniture placement, area rugs, or soft, colorful foam mats. Varying floor surfaces afford tactile as well as visual cues about location and also provide challenges to toddlers' developing motor and balance skills. The basic arrangement of the room and placement of furniture should be fixed so that all children—including those with visual impairments—can move about securely.

Play space needs to be open for active movement, wheelchair accessibility, and constant teacher supervision, but at least one soft, cozy corner is also needed where children can separate themselves from the other children or be encouraged to soothe and calm themselves after being upset. It is necessary for the design of the play space to allow children active choice among several different toys and activities and provide a balance between familiarity and novelty.

Once they begin to crawl or walk, infants and toddlers are on the move most of the time. They also like to carry toys with them from place to place. When infants and toddlers become interested in something new, however, the toy they are carrying will be dropped and forgotten. To the casual observer, this constant movement of children and toys gives the appearance of a disorganized classroom. In fact, it is important that infants and toddlers be cared for in a highly organized environment. Teachers must be careful not to confuse neatness with organization and must remember that organization appropriate for infants and toddlers is different from organization suited to older children and adults. The most important aspect of organization in infant and toddler care is teachers' planning and anticipation of children's needs, accompanied by a carefully considered schedule.

A variety of toys needs to be available at all times for play in infant and toddler classrooms. Furthermore, children should not be required to use toys in a specific area, even though that would contribute to a neater classroom appearance. Toys not in use should be put away frequently during the day to keep the play space safe and attractive. Children usually enjoy picking up toys if colorful containers are available and teachers also enthusiastically participate.

Teachers in the play area are responsible for carrying out simple play activities that are fun and that also help children gain new experiences, learn new skills, discover new ways of using toys, make new sounds or say new words, and practice or build on previously acquired skills. (Responsive teaching practices and early intervention techniques appropriate for infants and toddlers are described in Part II of this book.) The play activities for each day can be based on a theme for the week, which helps teachers organize their teaching goals and can be shared with parents to extend learning across settings. Themes for play, like the activities themselves, need to be very simple, matched to the developmental level of infants and toddlers, and allow a lot of individual creativity and expressiveness on the part of teachers. (See Appendix A for sample themes and curriculum plans; see Appendix B for play activities suitable for infants and toddlers.) Planned activities provide a framework within which teachers must do their own planning and use their creativity and ingenuity to make the best use of the materials available for enhancing children's play and development.

On several surfaces in the play area that are out of children's reach, space needs to be provided for tissues and wet wipes, plastic containers for used tissues and wipes (a gallon milk container with the top cut off makes a good play area trash container), and a plastic tub for toys that need to be washed. It is impossible (and unnecessary) to stop infants and toddlers from chewing on toys, so it is important to wash toys frequently. Whenever a teacher notices that a toy is in a child's mouth, he or she should not take the toy but should wait until the child's attention is distracted or the child moves on to something else before picking up the toy. Collected toys are then thoroughly washed and air-dried when teachers have time after feedings or at the end of the day. In addition, all infant toys should be washed after they have been out for children's use, all small toys used by toddlers should be washed at least once every week, and larger toys should be washed about every month or so or at regular intervals.

Teachers must also keep watch with an alert eye for any potentially dangerous materials in the play area. Toys should, of course, be inspected carefully for safety at the time of purchase, but all toys break sooner or later. Any toy can develop sharp edges or break into small pieces that can cause injuries. Whenever teachers are conducting activities, picking up toys to prepare for a new activity, or washing toys, they should look for and remove any toys that could possibly present danger to a child.

Space for Activities of Daily Living

Space for daily living activities is distinct and separate from the play areas of the classroom. Furniture and equipment in these areas should be designed so that they work for teachers—counters and storage units must be placed conveniently and at the right height to minimize bending and reaching. Adequate storage is a necessity, and everything must be easy to clean. At the same time, these areas should also be attractive to children and adults and decorated with the same care as the more public play and greeting areas.

Daily living areas—diapering, feeding, and entry areas—need to be off limits to children unless a teacher is specifically responsible for supervising them. A room can be effectively divided into areas by low (2.5 feet high) walls with latched doors in them (wide enough to be toddler-size wheelchair accessible) for teacher and child movement. Low walls allow teachers to visually supervise children from one area to another and move rapidly (by stepping over the wall) between areas, and low walls also promote communication among teachers.

Greeting Area

The greeting area is where children and parents are welcomed and responsibility for children's care is transferred from parent to classroom staff in the morning and from classroom staff to parent at the end of the day. Parents should be welcomed into the classroom at any time, but on most days, parents and children will say good-bye in the greeting area. If parents do wish to enter the classroom with their child, they should be encouraged to remove their shoes, just as everyone else in the classroom does.

In the greeting area, children's belongings, as well as the children themselves, are transferred from home to classroom and back again. A cubbyhole storage unit, with each cubby labeled with a child's first name, is useful for storage of children's possessions. Plastic bins, also labeled with children's names, help make the transfer of items within the classroom more convenient. As children's belongings are placed in their labeled bin, a diaper bag, backpack, or other container from home can be stored for the day in the child's cubby. In order to save space in the greeting area, children's outdoor coats and shoes can be stored separately on a coat rack with shoe bins or in boxes stored on a shelf. Teachers' personal possessions and outdoor coats should also be stored elsewhere so that the greeting area is uncluttered and pleasant. Also, office supplies (especially scissors and staples) and other materials used in the greeting area must be kept well out of children's reach at all times. Parents will often set a child down on a counter without paying attention to potentially dangerous items left on the counter. A pen or pencil with the attendance record can be attached with a short ribbon or string to a notebook or clipboard so that it cannot be easily picked up by a child.

One important activity that takes place in the greeting area is the exchange of information between parents and classroom staff. Teachers must remember to ask parents about special requests or schedule changes and then effectively communicate this information about children's individual needs with other classroom staff. Similarly, any news from the children's day needs to be communicated to parents in the afternoon.

Because parents will get their primary opinion of a child care program from the greeting area, it is important that this space be well organized and attractive. Like all areas in the classroom, the greeting area must be accessible to everyone, including parents and children in wheelchairs. A small bulletin board for pictures of children involved in classroom activities and a display of children's artwork can help make the greeting area inviting to parents and children. It is also helpful to use a bulletin board near the greeting area to post information for parents, including notices about upcoming community events and specially designed informational posters.

Diapering or Diapering/Toilet Area

In a classroom for infants or toddlers, it is absolutely necessary to have a sturdy diapering table that is at a good working height for adults and is located adjacent to its own sink. The diapering table must have a 3-inch lip to prevent children from rolling off of it; also, teachers should always keep one hand on a child who is on the diapering table. In a classroom for infants, one of the teachers will almost always be working in the diapering area. Therefore, it is best if the diapering area is open to the rest of the room and the person diapering infants is facing the play space. In a classroom for toddlers, the diapering/toilet area must be large enough to accommodate children in wheelchairs, include "potty" seats and, if possible, a child-size toilet and a child-size sink, in addition to the sturdy, safe diapering table and adult-height sink. Sinks used for diapering must be completely separate from sinks used for other purposes.

The diapering or diapering/toilet area should be just as attractive and child-friendly as all other classroom spaces. A mobile, a mirror, and other wall decorations should surround the diapering table, and pictures need to be displayed where children can see them while sitting on the toilet. Some toddlers will enjoy looking at books (either washable cloth books or books with wipe-off plastic-coated pages are best to use), holding a doll, or playing with another small toy while "going potty," so a supply of attractive (and washable) toys should be kept in the area. Sometimes children will be more willing to sit on the toilet with background music; a musical crib toy or other wind-up musical toy can be attached to the wall near the potty seats.

Because cleanliness in the diapering and diapering/toilet area is so important, safe and childproof storage space must be provided for diapers, extra clothes, cleaning supplies, laundry, and used disposable diapers and diaper wipes. Laundry and trash containers need to be lined with plastic bags and tightly covered. Disposable gloves should be used routinely for all diaper changes and cleanup tasks. Teachers will appreciate hand lotion to help protect their skin from the frequent exposure to water and cleaning solutions.

Feeding or Eating Area

An area with an easily washable floor covering that is separated from the main play space is best for infant feedings and toddler meals. In a classroom for toddlers, this area can also be used for individual or small group activities that may involve messy play, as with water, sand, or paint.

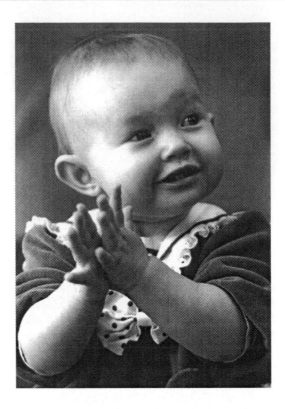

Infant feeding is most convenient if teachers can sit on comfortable adult-size chairs, facing a counter on which are secured sturdy reclining seats for infants. This allows a teacher to hold one child who is being bottle-fed while feeding another child solid foods. Older infants who can sit independently should use feeding chairs or high chairs. Toddlers do not need high chairs; they can sit on low chairs at toddler-size tables. Nearby should be an adult-height counter on which to place food for serving, adult-height and child-height sinks, and, as always, storage facilities. Mealtime materials that need to be stored include cups with lids, paper towels, bibs, special plates and utensils for children with special needs, and cleaning supplies. Art supplies and other materials used in special activities should also be kept in storage near or in the eating area if they are used for play activities. All storage areas must be childproof.

For safety reasons, a feeding or eating area should be closed to children unless there is an adult in the area. When art and science projects or other individual or small group activities are taking place in the area, children should be individually invited to participate, and there must always be an adult supervising children in the area.

A Safe and Healthy Environment

Health and safety are crucial to quality infant and toddler care. Program directors and lead teachers must be knowledgeable about state standards for health and safety, and they should also consult child care licensing officials with regard to environmental design and caregiving procedures that contribute to a healthy child care setting. In 1992, the American Public Health Association (APHA) and the American Academy of Pediatrics (AAP) prepared a set of health and safety standards for child care, *Caring for Our Children,* that is recommended as a guide for child care directors.

Children's safety can best be protected by careful design of the physical environment, close supervision of children by teachers, and careful selection and inspection of all toys and materials that children use. Suggestions for promoting a safe environment are included in the area descriptions above, and a safety check appears at the end of this chapter.

A classroom that is designed for children is much safer than the typical home (Kopjar & Wickizer, 1996; Rivara, DiGuiseppi, Thompson, & Calonge, 1989), where dangerous substances afford a considerable risk. Most of the accidents involving infants and toddlers in child care centers result from falls (Kopjar & Wickizer, 1996); thus, teachers should be particularly alert when children are using indoor or outdoor climbing equipment.

The child care environment, especially including the routines established for child care, can also help protect children's health. All of the child care routines outlined in Part III of this book involve practices that minimize the spread of infections. Frequent hand washing by teachers and children (including infants) is one of the most effective, yet most often overlooked, of all preventive health measures. Furthermore, regular use of disinfectant solution (1 part chlorine bleach to 10 parts water), which can be conveniently stored in labeled spray bottles that are kept out of children's reach, helps keep surfaces free from infectious agents. Frequent, thorough toy washing by using a four-step process—soap and water, clear water rinse, dip into disinfectant solution, and complete air drying—is also a necessity in infant-toddler care.

The most common illnesses experienced by infants and toddlers in the United States are respiratory infections, gastrointestinal infections resulting in vomiting or diarrhea, otitis media or ear infections, and skin rashes (Giebink, 1993). Children who are enrolled in child care centers tend to have more frequent illnesses than those who are cared for in child care homes or in their own homes, especially during their first year of enrollment (Wald, Guerra, & Byers, 1991). A thorough daily health check that includes observation of the child's mood and behavior as well as physical symptoms (see Chapter 9) can help detect early warning signs of illness.

Some child care programs exclude from attendance all children who show symptoms of even minor illness. However, medical experts believe that this is an unnecessary rule, because children with respiratory infections tend to be most contagious before their symptoms are evident (Giebink, 1993). Thus, the criteria for excluding children who have minor respiratory illnesses should be based on whether the children appear to be feeling well enough to participate in classroom activities. Children with severe illnesses, defined by fever, lethargy, persistent crying, difficulty breathing, uncontrolled diarrhea, frequent vomiting, or pain, should be excluded from attending a child care program. It is useful to have a clearly stated policy regarding exclusion for illness so parents can anticipate needs for substitute care for their children.

Teachers in infant and toddler care need to be knowledgeable about the symptoms of common childhood illnesses, but teachers should never try to diagnose a child. Instead, teachers who suspect a child has chickenpox, conjunctivitis, otitis media, a streptococcal infection, or another contagious illness should let the parent know the child is ill and request that a physician be consulted before the child returns to the classroom. Furthermore, if a child becomes seriously ill during the day, has a seizure, or is having unusual difficulty with breathing, teachers should not try to provide treatment themselves nor should they delay in seeking emergency medical help if parents cannot be reached immediately.

Similarly, all teachers of young children should know basic first aid procedures but should defer to health care professionals unless immediate emergency treatment is necessary. Most commonly, children will receive bumps or scratches that can be treated with soap and water, a brightly colored Band-Aid, and a lot of love. All treatment of even minor cuts or abrasions and all child care that brings the teacher into contact with body fluids (e.g., cleaning up after a child who is vomiting or has diarrhea) should be carried out in accordance with recommended public health measures for management of blood and body fluids as determined by local or state health officials. In all cases, teachers should wear disposable plastic gloves and a washable smock that is removed and cleaned as soon as treatment is completed, and teachers should place all used first aid and cleanup materials in a plastic bag that is tightly closed and labeled as containing contaminated material. Local public health officials should be consulted regarding the disposal of such material.

When children have complex medical needs, the procedures for promoting a healthy environment become even more important. If special health care practices are needed for a particular child, parents and public health nurses should be enlisted to demonstrate and teach these practices to all teachers who care for the child. Just as most individuals who become parents of children with special needs do not have prior medical training, learning "on the job" instead, teachers can also learn through experience how to provide the required care for children with special needs. As teachers gain knowledge about caring for children with disabilities and special health care needs, they learn that these children, for the most part, are no more fragile than typically developing children. In addition, supervised practice with special medical procedures can give teachers confidence in their own capabilities and in the abilities of children to communicate their needs to teachers, thus building a stronger relationship between teacher and child.

Because children in child care centers experience more frequent illness than those cared for in smaller groups or at home, parents of children with impaired immune systems or those with children who are particularly susceptible to severe respiratory illness or otitis media should consult their child's physician to determine if an inclusive child care program is the best option for their child (Heagarty, 1993). The risks involved in enrolling these children, even in the case of children who are HIV positive, are to the susceptible children themselves, rather than to other children or teachers (AAP, 1991). Thus, parents in consultation with the child's physician are best able to decide on the appropriate caregiving environment for any individual child, and inclusive child care programs should not establish general policies regarding the exclusion of children based on the nature of their disability or illness.

SUMMARY

An organized environment is the key to high-quality care for infants and toddlers. The organization described in this chapter relies primarily on a well-thought-out schedule of teacher responsibilities that ensures the availability of a teacher to provide for each child's individual needs and to supervise every child at all times. When teachers in an infant classroom prepare and follow such a schedule, babies do not have to be scheduled, but they can eat, sleep, have their diapers changed, and play according to their own internal timetables. Similarly, in a toddler classroom, a teacher schedule offers children the freedom to choose among several activities, allowing the children to select those activities that are most interesting to them and, therefore, provide the most effective learning opportunities.

Space must also be well-organized in an infant or toddler classroom. Teachers are most efficient and children are most comfortable in a consistent environment in which specific areas are designed for specific types of activities. When the physical and social environment is well-organized and safe, infants and toddlers can explore and experience their world with the support of unstressed teachers whose full attention can be devoted to the children.

Quality Check ✔

Safety in Infant-Toddler Care

Teachers, directors, and visitors can use this guide to check the class-room for safety. After watching teachers and children for 10–15 minutes and walking through each area of the classroom, all answers should be YES.

1. Is every child always supervised by a teacher?   YES ☐   NO ☐

2. Are all teachers always aware of their area of responsibility?   YES ☐   NO ☐

3. Do all teachers continuously scan their area of responsibility and act quickly to prevent any potentially dangerous situations?   YES ☐   NO ☐

4. Can all children move freely without getting into potentially dangerous situations?   YES ☐   NO ☐

5. Are all objects within children's reach safe for children to touch and put in their mouths?   YES ☐   NO ☐

6. Are all children lifted and carried with appropriate support for their heads, backs, and limbs?   YES ☐   NO ☐

7. Are all furnishings in daily living areas stable and used appropriately (children buckled into feeding chairs, not left unattended or allowed to stand on diapering table or counters)?   YES ☐   NO ☐

8. Are all furnishings in the play space of appropriate size for infants or toddlers?   YES ☐   NO ☐

9. Is all playground equipment of appropriate size for infants or toddlers?   YES ☐   NO ☐

10. Are all fixtures, walls, and floor coverings in good repair?   YES ☐   NO ☐

Inclusive Child Care for Infants and Toddlers: Meeting Individual and Special Needs by Marion O'Brien © 1997 Paul H. Brookes Publishing Co., Baltimore.

Part II

TEACHING AND LEARNING
IN INCLUSIVE INFANT-TODDLER CARE SETTINGS

In any infant-toddler care environment, the quality of the relationships between adults and children is the most important factor that determines the overall quality of care. Teachers can build strong and positive relationships with children by providing consistent and sensitive care, by recognizing and respecting children's individual differences, and by learning to read and respond to children's emotional states.

When teachers invest fully in their relationships with children, they create a climate of acceptance and love that encourages learning. Children who feel secure in their surroundings and know that they can rely on the adults around them are able to explore and experiment freely, gaining the direct experience with the world that is crucial to infant and toddler learning. In turn, teachers can feel comfortable encouraging children's active exploration when they know that the environment is completely safe and that enough teachers are available to provide supervision for all children.

Children's exploration and experience, which are the keys to infant-toddler education, sometimes appear to the casual observer to be unplanned and disorganized. In fact, careful planning is necessary so that the experiences available are interesting and attractive to children who have a wide range of abilities; these experiences must have teaching and learning potential for every child. Infants and toddlers need opportunities to learn in a variety of situations: in one-to-one activities, such as when assembling puzzles with a teacher; in peer contexts that involve watching and imitating one another's actions, such as when pretending to wash windows; and in exploring objects on their own without adult intervention, such as when closely examining the movement of wheels on an axle or making faces in the mirror. The teacher's role is to set the occasion for involvement and then to watch and listen for the perfect chance to extend children's experience, help them see and solve a problem, or encourage them toward mastery of a recently acquired skill.

Responsive teaching practices require teachers to be careful observers of children and to understand how the world looks to an infant or toddler. Teachers of infants and toddlers cannot decide in advance what and when children will learn. Children are learning constantly, and much of their learning is so basic that adults have forgotten they had to learn these things themselves. The responsive teacher is guided by the child's interest in objects and actions and helpfully provides labels for them, notices when a child is trying to do something difficult and offers just enough help so that the child can succeed, and uses both familiarity and novelty to create situations for learning. Although intuition and timing help teachers be responsive to children, there are also specific techniques that teachers of infants and toddlers must learn and use in order to take advantage of their teaching opportunities. The individualized nature of the responsive teaching approach, which assumes that each child will learn something different from any activity, is especially useful for children with disabilities or developmental delays.

One of the major tasks for infants and toddlers is learning how to get along with other people. Even the youngest infant finds another person more fascinating than any inanimate object, and toddlers are highly gregarious. Despite their fascination with the social world, however, infants and toddlers do not automatically know what is required for harmonious interactions. Teachers who use responsive guidance approaches can help children begin to understand others' perspectives, regulate their own emotions and behavior, and learn the basics of positive social interaction.

This section focuses on teaching and learning in infant-toddler care. Chapter 5 describes ways to organize play and learning activities for infants and toddlers in order to promote children's involvement and, therefore, children's opportunities to learn. Chapter 6 explains in detail responsive teaching techniques for all children, including techniques adapted from early intervention approaches. Chapter 7 discusses children's behavior and offers guidelines for helping children grow socially and gain a positive sense of themselves as valued and valuable people.

Chapter 5

Exploration and Experience

One reason infants and toddlers are so engaging to adults is because they represent unlimited possibilities. Teachers are especially able to see the future potential in the bright eyes and happy faces of young children. The world is just as full of possibility to infants and toddlers themselves. Everything is fair game for touching, tasting, banging, throwing, and learning. This characteristic of infants and toddlers applies equally to those with special needs and to typically developing children. This chapter describes ways of organizing infants' and toddlers' experience and exploratory activity so that children have many opportunities for learning throughout the day.

CURRICULUM FOR INFANTS AND TODDLERS

Dictionary writers usually define *curriculum* as a "course of study." Because babies and toddlers are curious and interested in *everything*, the appropriate curriculum for them includes every activity and event of the day, every toy or other object with which they come into contact, and every experience they have with another child or teacher. Their course of study is life itself.

Within infant and toddler classrooms, teachers must be aware that children are learning constantly and therefore teachers need to be teaching constantly. Young children learn primarily through exploration of the physical and social environment and through direct experience with objects and events. Other important curriculum components for infants and toddlers are activities of daily living, which are described in Part III.

Teachers of infants and toddlers must plan learning activities that give some structure to children's exploration and experience. To meet the needs of babies and toddlers, a curriculum plan must balance novelty with familiarity, be flexible and adaptable to a wide range of developmental levels and abilities, and provide opportunities for children to follow the path of their own interests and curiosity.

Infant Play

Infants' play is primarily exploratory. They touch, taste, bang, reach, push, pull, and generally try to find out about things through their senses.

Infants learn by experiencing the world directly and by having the world react to their actions. The teacher's job is to guide infants' exploration, provide both variety and consistency, and keep them safe.

A curriculum for infants includes variety in materials so children are interested and stimulated by the toys around them; planned and organized social play supported by teachers; and individualized, one-to-one opportunities for building close relationships. In this chapter, two types of play activities for infants are described: materials-based and theme-based. Materials-based activities, labeled *Play 1 activities,* should be scheduled to take place all day long. A preplanned schedule guides the Play 1 teacher in providing new materials every 15 minutes. Theme-based activities, labeled *Play 2 activities,* are one-to-one or small-group playtimes with the primary goal of having fun and extending the range of experiences available to children. These activities are scheduled whenever a second teacher can be in the play area.

Toddler Play

Play activities that are appropriate for toddlers are quite different from those activities that are typically presented to preschool-age children. Toddler play activities must be uncomplicated and open-ended, with an emphasis on presenting materials in a way that sets the occasion for children's exploration and experience. By contrast, many teachers view play-focused curricula as being tied to skill development, with activities selected because they allow children to practice a particular cognitive, language, or motor skill. In a skill-based model, the teacher's role is to direct children so that they use the materials provided to practice the designated skill.

The approach taken in this book is not skill-oriented, but rather experience-oriented. The goal of play activities is for toddlers to have opportunities to explore objects and materials as well as themselves and other people. As an activity progresses, the children are just as responsible for the direction the activity takes as the teacher is responsible for guiding the activity. Thus, when the activity is playing with trucks and blocks and the theme is "Ins and Outs," the teacher begins the activity by getting out the toys, exclaiming over them to attract children's attention, and beginning to build a garage that suits the concept of *in.* As toddlers join the teacher's play, they may be more interested in seeing how fast they can make the trucks go on the floor. This is an opportunity for the responsive teacher to place blocks on an incline so the trucks can roll down them, thereby enhancing the children's play but keeping it *on the topic selected by the children.*

By focusing on the children, teachers make the activity relevant to the children's interest. When teachers try to change the children's focus to match their own teaching goal, children are likely to tune out the teacher or, even worse, walk away. Ideally, then, the teacher's role in play activities is facilitative, rather than directive. In addition, themes for the day and the week provide guidelines that help teachers incorporate concepts into their play, rather than restrictions that limit the range of activities and events available to children.

Themes for Play

Organizing a curriculum plan around weekly themes helps teachers provide a balance between novelty and familiarity. When a classroom's activities are based on a theme, there is an increased opportunity for repetition of activities that allows children to build on previous learning and experience. During a week, sensitive teachers can present variations on activities so that a pretend grocery-shopping activity, for example, can become slightly more complicated with each new day. This encourages children to begin to build a play script around the materials provided. Similarly, teachers can encourage mastery in more task-oriented activities, such as puzzles, by offering the activity every day throughout a week and using the same puzzles each day. In this way, children can gain a sense of accomplishment and the pleasure that comes with mastery of a skill. When the activity's purpose is primarily to experience materials, such as during water play, teachers can plan a range of activities that allow children to learn about water by utilizing all of their senses, or teachers can focus on different uses for water.

Themes based on uncomplicated concepts that can be experienced in a variety of ways also help teachers build content into their play with infants and toddlers. Teachers need to think in advance about the possibilities for learning offered by each of the toys and activities they present to children, or they will not be prepared to capitalize on the many opportunities for teaching during play activities. Unless teachers plan and prepare to make the children's play as rich and stimulating as possible, they can easily lapse into a passive and reactive role of simply watching children's play and preventing problems, rather than the active and responsive role of enhancing and extending play that is appropriate for a teacher to practice.

A theme also encourages teachers to use the same set of words frequently during a week. For example, with a theme of "So Big," in which concepts of size are the primary focus, the words *big, little, large, small, tall,* and *short* are likely to be repeated over and over again. This repetition is helpful to children who are just beginning to sort out which sounds go with which objects, events, or properties. By concentrating the use of a relatively small set of words into a week's time, children are more likely to grasp the concepts behind the words and also to remember and repeat the words themselves.

TYPES OF PLAY ACTIVITIES FOR INFANTS AND TODDLERS

Activities such as playing with dolls and household objects, building with toys, playing outdoors, experimenting with water and paint, reading books, and singing songs allow children to learn new skills while experiencing the world around them. Play presents opportunities for learning when materials are attractive and appropriately challenging, activities are open-ended, and teachers are alert and responsive to children's interests.

House and Doll Play

Activities with house toys and dolls usually focus on everyday types of materials and events that infants and toddlers are likely to experience at home as well as in the classroom. Infants and toddlers do not require elaborate props for their play; in fact, they prefer familiar toys and materials, especially those that resemble real objects or that *are* real objects. Most toddlers also are not able to participate in complex pretend play, but they can take part in simple role-playing activities, especially with the help of an adult who can label the roles and suggest extensions of the role-playing script.

Building Toys

Building toys are those that come in sets with lots of pieces that fit together or can be used together to create a play scene, such as a farm or airport. Many infants and toddlers will have never seen or used building toys anywhere else, and they will not automatically know how the toys can be used or how they go together. The ability to stack blocks or connect Lego blocks is a learned skill. Thus, it is the teacher's job to invite children to get involved with the toys, to help by demonstrating the use of toys and assisting the children's efforts, and to elaborate on children's play through language, demonstration, and encouragement of cooperation. Sometimes, construction toys are more interesting to toddlers if they are used in an unusual place, such as on a table in the house area, a special activity area, or outdoors.

Interesting combinations of building area toys, such as wooden blocks with farm animals or Lego people with nesting cups, are usually more attractive to infants and toddlers than a single type of toy. In addition, these combinations provide teachers with variety and increased opportunities for creativity and imagination. When planning to conduct building area activities, teachers need to think in advance about the properties of the toys to be used, the aspects infants and toddlers are likely to find interesting or new about the toys, and how desired outcomes for individual children can be incorporated into play with the toys. During the activity, teachers must be attuned to children's exploration so that they can take advantage of opportunities to extend play, enhance children's experience, and help build children's fine motor, language, and cognitive skills.

Active Play

Active play activities are primarily intended to be fun for everyone involved and do not necessarily have to focus on specific skill acquisition. As with other types of play activities, the teacher's goal is to encourage involvement with the materials in use, build on children's interests and curiosity in order to elaborate on their skills and toy use, and help children gain confidence in their own abilities.

Parallel Play Toys

Large toys for individual or parallel play often provide useful ways for children to start the day. Many children will discover favorite toys, and these toys provide a good transition from home to school. Favorite toys should be kept out the entire day on low shelves for individual play and rotated (unless a child *really* has a favorite toy that he or she relies on) about every month.

Outdoor Play

In general, several teachers will play outdoors with the infants and toddlers, and it is helpful for each teacher to have a specific responsibility on the playground, just as in the classroom. Thus, one teacher may supervise the sandbox area and lead an activity with sand toys, a second teacher may be responsible for supervising children on a climber, and a third teacher may take a few children at a time on a nature crawl or walk through the bushes. It is important for each teacher to encourage active involvement in outdoor play by all children and to provide variety and stimulation for all children on the playground. As with indoor play, teachers must plan ahead and be actively involved in play on the playground if this time is to be used effectively for learning. Children may appear to be busy outdoors, giving teachers the idea that their role is less important or that this is a time for a break from the demands of teaching. However, the responsive teacher of infants or toddlers will use outdoor play as a time to expand children's experience with the natural world in ways that are not possible indoors.

Art and Sensory Experiences

Usually activities incorporating art and sensory experiences work best when small groups of children work closely with one teacher. The goal of art and sensory activities is to provide children with *experiences*, such as handling and using a variety of different types of materials, using all of their senses, and making things happen. The goal is never to produce a final product that looks like the teacher's example—or any final product at all.

Although all children should be exposed to art and sensory activities and invited to participate, messy play is not for everyone. Some infants and toddlers find touching gooey substances to be unpleasant, while other children are so tactilely sensitive that they do not even enjoy water play; still other children just like to be out in the open play area, rather than closed within a smaller space. These individual preferences need to be accepted and respected. Once children express a dislike for a particular type of activity or situation, however, they should continue to be invited to participate each time that activity is scheduled. Children's preferences do change, and what may seem awful on one day might be quite fun on another day a few weeks or months later. Children should never be forced to participate in any activity or punished in any way for not taking part in an activity. An alternative activity always needs to be available, and children who wish simply to watch the others should be given a chance to do just that.

Teachers often like to have children produce artwork that can be used for display in the classroom and on the bulletin board or that can be sent home with the child, and parents love to receive the projects their children make at school. There is no reason not to save everything children make and every reason to display children's art on the walls, but responsive teachers of infants and toddlers must understand that it is the *experience* of doing the activity, rather than the final product, that is important to a toddler. Infants and toddlers are finished with an art project when they are tired of the activity involved, rather than when their project looks the way they want it to look. In fact, infants and toddlers appear to have no concept of how their project looks. Thus, they will continue to color or paint over what they have already done until the entire paper is brown from the combination of colors in layers. Some of the best art projects for infants and toddlers are, therefore, works in progress: collages on clear Contact paper that can be constantly created and recreated, group murals on large sheets of newsprint on which each child contributes to the overall effect, or paintings made with water on the outside walls.

Books and Stories

Infants and toddlers love books. As with all things, however, they experience books differently than older children and adults. Infants and toddlers use all of their senses, including taste, to explore all of the properties of books. To an infant or toddler, a book is not just something with which one sits quietly. A book can be cargo in a truck, a substitute for a hat, or something that feels slippery between the toes. All of these are useful ways for infants and toddlers to experience books, and children should not be prevented from having these experiences.

At the same time, children need to learn that books are most valuable because of the pictures and words that make up their stories. Therefore, children should be given opportunities on a regular basis to explore some books in infant and toddler fashion; these books can be old paper-covered books that are already somewhat worn out, cloth and heavy cardboard books, or books with plastic-coated pages. The cost of providing books for infants and toddlers to experience is well worth the price because of the strong connection between early opportunities to become familiar with books and subsequent lifelong enjoyment of reading. Eventually, when they have explored books enough, children will shift their attention to the pictures, words, and pages. Some books should be saved for reading only. Favorite stories, books that incorporate touchable textures or smells, and picture books with lots of detail to spark teacher–toddler conversations need to be stored out of children's reach and used during storytimes.

Although children are often attracted to books as if by magnets, there are times when a teacher will get out a book to read and everyone will be off doing a different activity. To encourage children to come listen to the story, the teacher in this situation can simply narrate—loudly—what he or she is doing. For example, a teacher may say, "I'm going to read about *Spot!*" and then sit down with the book and an available lap and begin reading and exclaiming about the pictures. Before the second page is turned, the infants and toddlers will have gathered to listen and participate.

Some of infants' and toddlers' favorite books are homemade. These books may be photo albums of children and teachers going about their daily activities, pictures from home, or picture books created from magazine or catalog pictures that have been laminated or enclosed in plastic sleeves for protection.

Songs, Rhymes, and Finger Plays

Music, songs, and finger plays should be constant companions of infants and toddlers. Even teachers with monotone-like voices can sing beautifully for infants and toddlers who enjoy hearing the rhythm and the rhyme, rather than the quality of the voice. Teachers can use singing and rhyming to make many otherwise tedious tasks pass quickly and pleasantly. In addition, finger plays are magical ways to settle down restless infants or toddlers who are in the midst of a transition or who are otherwise temporarily unoccupied.

Singing, reciting simple rhymes, and performing finger plays also are ways to contribute to children's use and understanding of language. Children often repeat rhyming words before they can be expected to know their meanings and can imitate the motions that go with songs and finger plays before they can participate in singing or chanting. Infants and toddlers with few language skills will use the finger motions of songs to ask teachers to sing, and these sophisticated, nonverbal requests should be noticed and honored if at all possible. Parents are often delighted to learn the words and actions of popular finger plays; they can then understand and respond to children's gestures from the songs. Songs and rhymes contribute to children's long-term enjoyment of spoken language, which also translates into interest in words, reading, and writing.

Many audiotapes and compact discs for children are available on the market. Unfortunately, most of these are recorded at a speed that is beyond the listening power of infants and toddlers. Although teachers may enjoy hearing music at certain times of the day, children will benefit more from homemade tapes that present songs or stories at a slower pace. Infants and toddlers often do enjoy rock and roll music from the 1950s with its clear and steady beat. Music that is also popular includes the sound tracks from children's movies or children's TV shows such as *Sesame Street* or *Barney.*

It is not necessary to use "real" songs or rhymes with infants and toddlers. Creative teachers can make up their own songs and rhymes that incorporate the children's names and familiar events, and these songs and rhymes will often be the children's favorites. Some ideas for using songs and finger plays in infant-toddler classrooms appear in Table 5.1, and a selection of popular finger plays appear in Figure 5.1.

ORGANIZING AND CONDUCTING PLAY ACTIVITIES WITH INFANTS

Successful play activities for infants require energy and enthusiasm on the part of teachers. Young infants are much more interested in people than in objects and are unable to sustain their own involvement with toys for more than a few seconds. Once older infants discover locomotion, they want to *move*, rather than sit and play. All infants exhaust their limited toy manipulation skills very quickly. Thus, infant play activities must be organized in a way that provides variety and stimulation, and teachers must be actively involved with infants in the play area.

Planning Play Activities for Infants

Two types of activities, materials-based and thematic, can be used to provide opportunities for infants' exploration and experience in the play area. For both types of activities, the toys used are often less important to infant learning than the teacher–child interaction that accompanies the toys.

Table 5.1.   Using songs and finger plays with infants and toddlers

Do them *slowly* so that children can process the words, the rhymes, and the actions.
Make your own audiotapes, slowing down the speed of the songs and repeating the same song several times—infants and toddlers need to hear things over and over in order to be able to anticipate and participate.
Look for children to use a finger action to request a song from you a long time before they can ask in words for the song.
Use finger plays and songs during the entire day, whenever a diversion is needed—during transitions, while waiting for the bus, to distract a child intent on getting someone else's toy, or to calm a crying baby.
Repeat songs and finger plays several times before going on to the next one so that the infants and toddlers can remember and be ready to try the actions themselves.
Do not worry if you cannot carry a tune or do not know the tune (or all of the words, for that matter)—the children will enjoy the rhythm and the older ones will correct your mistakes and love it!
You cannot repeat songs or finger plays too often—you may become bored, but the children never will!

My little hands can clap, clap, clap
My little fingers can snap, snap, snap
My little hands reach for the sky
My little hands can wave good-bye

1, 2, 3, 4, 5
Birds up in a tree
Watch them flying all around (make hands fly)
Landing next to me (hands on floor next to body)

Pop, pop, pop (clap hands)
Pour the corn into the pot
Pop, pop, pop (clap hands)
Take and shake until it's hot
Pop, pop, pop (clap hands)
Lift the lid—what have we got?
Pop, pop, popcorn! (clap)

Little Bo Peep has lost her sheep (hold up hands and wiggle fingers)
And can't tell where to find them (hide hands behind back)
Leave them alone and they'll come home (bring hands to front)
Wagging their tails behind them (wiggle fingers)

Two little monkeys jumping on the bed (two fingers jump on palm)
One fell off and bumped his head
Mama called the doctor (dial telephone)
And the doctor said
NO MORE MONKEYS JUMPING ON THE BED!

Itsy, bitsy spider went up the water spout
Down came the rain and washed the spider out
Out came the sun and dried up all the rain
And the itsy, bitsy spider went up the spout again

Here is a nest for the robin (cup hands)
Here is a hive for the bee (put fists together)
Here is a hole for the bunny (finger and thumb form circle)
And here is a house for me (fingertips together make a roof)

I am an icy snowman (stand with arms out)
Standing on his lawn
I melt and melt and melt (start slumping)
And pretty soon I'm gone (to the floor)

Jack Frost is a fairy small (show small with thumb and pointer)
I'm sure he's out today
He nipped my nose (point to nose)
And pinched my toes (point to toes)
When I went out to play

Away up high in the apple tree (point up)
Two red apples smiled at me (form circles with fingers)
I shook that tree as hard as I could (shake tree)
Down came the apples and mmm! they were good (rub tummy)

Figure 5.1.   Some popular finger plays.

Materials-Based Activities (Play 1)

When teachers in an infant classroom move from area to area and share the responsibilities for infant care, as shown in the sample teacher schedule in Chapter 4, there is usually one teacher supervising the play area at a time. This responsibility, labeled *Play 1* on the sample teacher schedule, involves providing a variety of materials for infants to explore and experience, interacting with each baby in the area in ways that extend and enhance his or her play, providing a lot of love and affection, and having fun. It is helpful to have a schedule for rotation of toys throughout the day, as shown in the sample in Figure 5.2. A schedule such as this ensures that infants have experiences with a range of toys without having too many toys out on the floor at one time, which leads to clutter and confusion and is often overwhelming to infants. A regular toy rotation also contributes to infants' health; when it is time for the next Play 1 toy to be introduced to the room, the old toys are washed or set aside for washing before they are used again.

The toys scheduled for use by Play 1 teachers need to be readily available in the classroom. The best Play 1 toys are those that are adaptable to a wide range of ages—from tiny babies to walkers. There should be enough replicates of each toy type available so each child in the play area can have his or her own toys. If building toys are used, they must be easily manipulated and have large pieces that can be used independent of the building activity or combined with containers that allow children to fill, dump, and carry the building toys in case the manipulative activity is too difficult for them.

Teachers should not feel limited to using *only* the toy listed on the rotation, but they should be encouraged to add other materials to those scheduled in order to make the area attractive and fun for children. Usually, teachers are more interested in play if they can choose to play with something they enjoy themselves. Teacher involvement is the key to infant involvement, so teachers need to have a choice of materials they can use. However, having an established toy rotation ensures that all of the materials available are used sometimes, and teachers are not simply selecting the same materials every time they supervise the play area.

The primary job of the Play 1 teacher is to encourage all of the children to remain *busy*. For some children, being busy may mean watching the teacher or other children; for others, it will mean active exploration of the toys; for still others, it will mean practicing movement skills by pulling up on and cruising around the furniture, oblivious to what anyone else is doing. If there are several children in the play area, usually they will not all be involved with the same materials. It is not the teacher's job to get children to do the planned activity, but rather to follow the children's lead and help incorporate what children want to be doing into a useful learning activity. This means that teachers may have to shift their focus of attention from one child to another and from one type of activity to another every few minutes. In addition to helping children explore the properties of toys, teachers can use toys as props for a range of social play activities or become involved in social play that does not involve toys. Some suggestions for fun activities to do with babies appear in Table 5.2.

A.M.	Monday	Tuesday	Wednesday	Thursday	Friday	P.M.
8:00	Small balls	Push-down/pop-up toys	Musical instruments	Stacking rings	Mega Blocks	12:45
8:15	Books	Pull-apart/put-together toys	Animals and sounds	Telephones	Baby songs	1:00
8:30	Mega Blocks	Large balls	Shapes and bowls	Balancing bunnies	Chew and squeak toys	1:15
8:45	Baby songs	Plastic blocks	Photo albums	Large foam blocks	Toys with wheels	1:30
9:00	Chew and squeak toys	Rattles	Push-down/pop-up toys	Musical instruments	Stacking rings	1:45
9:15	Toys with wheels	Small balls	Pull-apart/put-together toys	Animals and sounds	Telephones	2:00
9:30	Stacking rings	Books	Large balls	Shapes and bowls	Balancing bunnies	2:15
9:45	Telephones	Mega Blocks	Plastic blocks	Photo albums	Large foam blocks	2:30
10:00	Balancing bunnies	Baby songs	Rattles	Push-down/pop-up toys	Musical instruments	2:45
10:15	Large foam blocks	Chew and squeak toys	Small balls	Pull-apart/put-together toys	Animals and sounds	3:00
10:30	Musical instruments	Toys with wheels	Books	Large balls	Shapes and bowls	3:15
10:45	Animals and sounds	Stacking rings	Mega Blocks	Plastic blocks	Photo albums	3:30
11:00	Shapes and bowls	Telephones	Baby songs	Rattles	Push-down/pop-up toys	3:45
11:15	Photo albums	Balancing bunnies	Chew and squeak toys	Small balls	Pull-apart/put-together toys	4:00
11:30	Push-down/pop-up toys	Large foam blocks	Toys with wheels	Books	Large balls	4:15
11:45	Pull-apart/put-together toys	Musical instruments	Stacking rings	Mega Blocks	Plastic blocks	4:30
12:00	Large balls	Animals and sounds	Telephones	Baby songs	Rattles	4:45
12:15	Plastic blocks	Shapes and bowls	Balancing bunnies	Chew and squeak toys	Small balls	5:00
12:30	Rattles	Photo albums	Large foam blocks	Toys with wheels	Books	5:15

Figure 5.2. A sample toy rotation for an infant classroom.

Table 5.2. Suggestions for playing with babies

Tiny babies (up to 4 months)	• With baby in an infant seat or bouncer or sitting on your lap, look at him or her face-to-face and talk, sing, make faces, stick out your tongue, smile, blow gently, or coo.
	• Hold small toys in front of baby's face to encourage reaching; be sure to give the baby the toy whenever he or she tries to reach for it.
	• Play peekaboo by hiding your face behind your hands or under a blanket; occasionally put the blanket over the baby's head but remove it quickly.
	• Help the baby practice rolling over from stomach to back, then from back to stomach.
	• With baby on his or her stomach, put your hands behind baby's feet so he or she can push forward; it is even better if there is a toy there to encourage baby.
	• Help baby dance, providing a lot of support at hips and trunk.
	• Play horsie, bouncing baby gently on your knee; stop the bouncing periodically and wait for baby to "ask" for more.
	• Look at pictures in books or photo albums with baby.
	• Look in a mirror together, and make faces, stick out your tongue, open your mouth, or look upside down.
	• Call baby's name; when he or she looks at you, open your eyes wide and smile, smile, smile.
	• Play "This Little Piggy Went to Market."
	• Play pat-a-cake.
	• Carry baby in a front pack while doing housekeeping chores or running errands.
Middle babies (4–7 months)	• Before baby can sit alone, support him or her with pillows or nestle baby inside a plastic crate lined with pillows and blankets so that baby can reach small, easily graspable toys. In front of a mirror, take hats on and off of your head and baby's head.
	• Listen to and imitate baby's sounds; "talk" together.
	• Look at pictures in books together and help baby turn the pages.

(continued)

Table 5.2. (continued)

Middle babies (4–7 months) (cont.)	• Roll a small, soft, graspable ball to where baby can reach it; when baby drops or pushes the ball, roll it back. • Shake toys that make noise or ring a bell in front, to the side, and behind baby; when baby responds, open eyes wide and smile, smile, smile. • Practice greetings by waving *hi* and *bye*, blowing kisses, doing high-fives, and shaking hands. • Play "Where's BABY?" and use all of the babies' names; when you find them, say "There she [or he] is!" and clap and cheer. • Stack small objects and let baby knock them down—many times. • Change your tone of voice from loud to soft; change your pitch from high to low.
Crawlers (8–12 months)	• Sing, recite rhymes, play peekaboo, and play pat-a-cake. • Play "chase" with balls and other toys that roll. • Babble along with baby, using *ba*, *da*, and *ka* sounds; after a string of one sound, change to another sound and watch for baby's reaction and imitation. • Hide small toys in a cup or under a blanket while baby watches; help baby find them. • Hold and pretend to feed dolls and stuffed animals; hug and kiss them and let baby imitate you. • Make hats and capes out of scarves or bandanas; put them on baby and look in the mirror. • Play "sleep": You pretend to go to sleep, then wake up; let baby be in charge of when you go to sleep and wake up. • Have lots of small containers available for filling and dumping, filling and dumping, filling and dumping. • Help baby pull him- or herself up to stand and cruise around furniture; use sturdy push toys so baby can practice walking. • Play name games: use the baby's name in songs, rhymes, "Where's BABY?" and when saying *hi* and *bye* and playing peekaboo and pat-a-cake.

(continued)

Table 5.2.   *(continued)*

Crawlers (8–12 months) (*cont.*)	• Collect family pictures in an album and play "find Mama," "find Dada," "find Sis," "find Nana"; also find baby's pets! • Look at pictures in books and give a label to everything, encouraging baby to point.
Walkers (12–15 months)	• Help baby stack objects, starting with big items and moving to progressively smaller ones. • Practice exchanging objects with baby, using "please," "thank you," "may I?" and alternating "yours" and "mine." • Say single simple words clearly, moving your mouth carefully so baby can watch and imitate. • Roll balls and toys with wheels down inclines. • Do a lot of water play: Watch toys float and sink, stir up soap bubbles, paint with water, dip and pour with containers; in warm weather, sit in water. • Give baby control of real mechanisms by allowing baby to practice turning lights on and off, opening and closing doors and drawers, using real working flashlights, or turning radio or audiotape player on and off. • Crumple paper and let baby handle different types of paper (but put paper away when baby starts to eat it). • Draw and write with crayons together on large sheets of newsprint. • Have containers with handles available, such as baskets, purses, and paint pails, for filling, carrying, and dumping. • Play with sounds and words, especially with rhymes and words with interesting sounds, such as *crash*, *whoosh*, *bubble*, *vroooom*, and *pop*. • Sing, dance, whistle, or play the harmonica; laugh and smile together.

Note: Activities for middle babies, crawlers, and walkers also may include those activities listed for each preceding age group.

The nature of Play 1 activities encourages parallel play, rather than interactive play. Because the teacher conducting these activities is responsible for supervising the entire group of children, he or she cannot become completely absorbed in play with only one or two children. Instead, the Play 1 teacher should try to spread his or her attention evenly among the children, using opportunities for responsive teaching as they arise.

Thematic Activities (Play 2)

When more than one teacher can be in the play area at one time, one of the teachers can have more flexibility in conducting play activities that involve large motor movement and interactive play because he or she does not have to supervise every child. Thematic activities are labeled Play 2 on the teacher schedule in Chapter 4, and these activities also should be conducted whenever a teacher assigned to supervise feeding or diapering does not have any children who need care in that area and, therefore, can join children in the play area. The two teachers in the play area can divide the children between them, perhaps according to the developmental level of the children in the area, or can let the children choose what most interests them. The Play 2 teacher can then devote his or her full attention to only a few children, which results in encouraging more elaborate play and interaction than is possible for the Play 1 teacher who must supervise all of the children in the area.

Play 2 activities can focus on the weekly classroom theme and are organized around the categories of house and doll play, building, active play, and art and sensory experiences. Specific activities that can be used as Play 2 activities for each of the suggested classroom themes are described in Appendix B. Descriptions of scheduled play activities and suggestions for conducting them need to be available in the classroom, but teachers should also be expected to plan ahead and think of interesting and creative ways to adapt the week's theme, use the toys, and present the activities to the infants in ways that will address the learning goals for the week.

Teachers need to be aware of the theme for the week and the Play 2 activities to be conducted. By focusing on the overall teaching goals for the week's theme, teachers can plan ways to adapt each activity for tiny babies, noncrawling babies, older babies, and for infants with special needs. Teachers must plan for flexibility and expect the unexpected.

Because the exact times that teachers will be available to conduct Play 2 activities cannot always be predicted in advance, it is not usually possible to schedule these activities. Instead, teachers can simply select a Play 2 activity that matches the week's theme. Descriptions of the activities can be easily organized in a card file, in a notebook, or on a clipboard located in an accessible place in the classroom. The first teacher conducting a Play 2 activity can use the first activity in the sequence, for example, a building activity, and then transfer that activity description to the bottom of the set of activities for that week. The next teacher to conduct a Play 2 activity can use the next activity in the sequence, for example, a doll play activity, and so forth. When all of the activities have been used, teachers can begin the sequence over again. Repetition of activities during the week and even within the same day is helpful in teaching infants whose learning is enhanced by seeing the same events or having similar experiences over again after only a short period of time.

Included with the activity description should be a list of materials to use and their location if they are not available in the classroom all of the time. It is most efficient to have activity materials gathered together into bins or cartons in advance so Play 2 teachers can simply get the appropriate container from the shelf and conduct the activity. Sometimes, a teacher will be available to conduct a Play 2 activity for only a few minutes before a child needs care in another area, but if the materials are assembled in advance, this easily can be enough time to provide enjoyable and educational experiences for the babies.

Conducting Play Activities with Infants

Teachers conducting Play 1 and Play 2 activities are responsible for introducing the materials, getting children involved in play, and then watching the children's activity, using their cues to what is interesting, difficult, or puzzling as guides to what the learning goals for the activity can be. Teachers must be *actively* involved in children's play, rather than passively watching, simply holding a child, or interacting only enough to keep children "out of trouble." The goal of play is for the infants to have a maximum of opportunities to learn and experience new materials and events with involved adult guidance. Teachers need to be alert for opportunities to extend and enhance infants' play and experience with materials; to use responsive teaching techniques to enhance children's communicative, motor, and social development; and to promote specific outcomes for children with special needs. Teaching techniques to promote learning of all children, including those with special needs, are described in Chapter 6.

The Play 1 teacher is also responsible for the safety of all of the children in the play area as well as for maintaining a healthy environment. Usually there will be nonmobile infants, crawlers, and walkers in the play area at the same time. It is most effective for the Play 1 teacher to stay within arm's reach of the nonmobile children nearly all of the time. Teachers who are actively involved in play, noisy and enthusiastic in response to babies' actions, and funny and silly will entice the crawling and walking children to come to them. As children become more independent, they will often come near the teacher to "check in," then move away to explore and experience toys on their own, looking back at the teacher now and then and coming close to the teacher when they feel the need for adult attention. However, the Play 1 teacher needs to be constantly aware of the location and activity of every child in the area. Therefore, he or she should sit against a wall or partition, facing the play space with as good a view of the entire area as possible.

Even when another teacher is in the play area, the Play 1 teacher is the person responsible for knowing where every child is at all times, keeping track of the children's movement into and out of the area, and ensuring that all of the children have access to interesting and appropriate play materials and to social interactions with teachers and other children.

Teachers conducting play activities need to position children with special needs right next to them, where these children can readily see and hear what is happening. Teachers can help children with limited movement skills to hold and touch the materials used during the activity. It is important that teachers think about the outcomes anticipated for the child with special needs and try to address some of these outcomes in the context of the activity. Furthermore, teachers can encourage interaction between other children and the child with special needs during the activ-

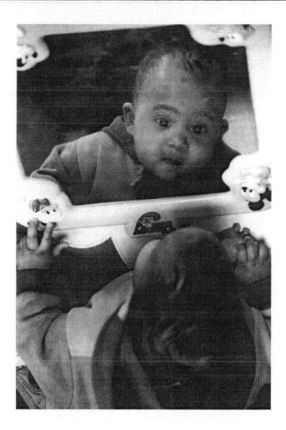

ity. Suggestions for including children with disabilities in group activities appear in Chapter 6.

The goals of planned play activities are to attract and hold the attention of the child by presenting materials in ways that are appropriate to each child's developmental level, to encourage exploration and manipulation of objects, and to promote social interaction between the teacher and child. Teachers need to be flexible about the use of toys—children may show teachers new ways to play with toys if teachers are open to learn.

Teachers who have an idea for making a planned activity more fun should try their idea with the children. If the children do not respond, the teacher should not become discouraged, but rather try the idea again in a few minutes; sometimes babies are slow to catch on to new ways of doing familiar activities. If the idea doesn't attract the children's interest, teachers cannot give up and withdraw from involvement. Instead, they need to be flexible and able to adapt their play and teaching agenda to the children's immediate interests.

Children are not required to demonstrate that they have learned a specific skill in order for an activity to be a success. Teachers may be surprised an hour or a day later to find children repeating some aspects of an activity, especially when the children seemed to have been paying no attention during the time the activity was carried out! Teachers' energy and enthusiasm are attractive to infants and they will respond to *any* activity if the teacher who is leading it is active and involved.

Teachers also need to be alert to health and safety precautions while supervising play. This involves noticing when children place toys in their mouths, picking those toys up when children lose interest in them, and putting the used toys in the washing bin. Teachers must also frequently wipe runny noses (using a clean tissue for each child and wiping their own hands between noses with a wet wipe). In addition, teachers must check and adjust children's clothing as needed. Mobile children can trip over trousers that are too long or socks that are too loose.

Teachers prevent problems in the play area by encouraging children to play, by being actively involved in play themselves, by interacting energetically with children, and by closely supervising the area. If conflicts arise among children, teachers need to use responsive guidance techniques appropriately when necessary (see Chapter 7 for guidelines in handling social behavior).

The Quality Check for play in infant care on page 105 can help program directors and teachers determine whether play activities are being planned and carried out effectively in order to create a comfortable and stimulating learning environment. It is vitally important for teachers to have fun when conducting play activities. The most enjoyable plaything for a baby is a happy, enthusiastic, and interested adult who has nothing more important to do than play! Teachers sometimes need to learn—all over again—to be silly and childlike, and to value play for its own sake.

ORGANIZING AND CONDUCTING PLAY ACTIVITIES WITH TODDLERS

Scheduling play activities for toddlers involves providing a balance between the familiar and the new, between active and quiet play, and between individual and social activities. Toddlers need to have as much choice as possible so that they are intrinsically interested in what they are doing and open to learning from their play. The teacher's role is to supervise toddlers closely and at the same time to take advantage of opportunities to enhance experience, teach a new skill, and promote positive social development.

Planning Play Activities for Toddlers

During exploration and experience times in a toddler classroom, each teacher can be scheduled to carry out a specific activity organized around the major activity areas in the classroom: house and doll play, building, active play, and parallel play. Thus, at any one time, two or three different activities will be available for toddlers to choose from (see Figure 4.3). Even when the primary activity is a daily living activity, such as snack- or mealtime, it is best for one teacher to be available to supervise play so that children can make individual transitions into and out of the daily living activity.

The daily schedule of play activities in a toddler classroom needs to be planned to balance variety with familiarity. Toddlers like to know what to expect, but they are also attracted to novelty. Rotating toys regularly, modifying "old favorite" activities by adding new and different variations, or combining familiar materials in unexpected ways can help maintain a high level of interest in both children and teachers.

Suggestions for play activities to fit the learning goals of particular themes are included in Appendix B. These suggestions are by no means an exhaustive list, however. Many of the best toddler play activities are invented on the spot by teachers who know the toddlers well—and some activities are even invented by toddlers themselves! A schedule of activities should, therefore, be used as a guide, rather than a rigid requirement or restriction on teacher or toddler ingenuity.

Materials needed for play activities should be organized in advance and available inside or adjacent to the classroom, rather than being stored in areas that require teachers to leave the room or scattered so that teachers must spend precious teaching time gathering the items needed for an activity. Teachers should also be encouraged to add materials to the suggested list of toys to use in an activity. Combinations of toys are almost always more interesting and offer more opportunities for creative play than a single type of toy.

Usually play activities will be conducted in the designated toy area, but sometimes it is a good idea to switch areas and conduct activities in different places, thereby adding a new twist to a familiar activity. For example, teachers might want to use the table in the doll and house area for a building toy or an art activity or take dolls and blankets to a soft climber. Teachers need to communicate with one another to be sure responsibilities are clear and all of the children are supervised.

When more than one activity is scheduled at a time, children should be free to choose among them and move from one activity to another as their interest calls them. This is in contrast to many preschool programs where children are divided into groups—often based on age or developmental level—and participate in preacademic activities with their group. Prearranged grouping is useful in a toddler classroom only for activities that require close guidance and supervision of an adult; these activities are labeled as small group activities in the curriculum guide in Appendix B. In all other situations, toddlers are more cooperative and open to learning if they have selected the activity for themselves and are allowed to leave the activity when they are no longer interested in it. In this arrangement, teachers are responsible for making their activities engaging enough that children *want* to participate and stay around long enough to learn a new skill or concept.

Conducting Play Activities with Toddlers

Successful play activities depend on planning; teachers should know the weekly theme, learning goals, and their scheduled activities in advance. Teachers can then think about how each activity can be adjusted for toddlers of different developmental levels and for those toddlers with special needs. Suggestions for the types of play that suit the abilities and interests of toddlers appear in Appendix B.

If there are nonmobile children in the classroom, their active inclusion in play activities is important. The guidelines in Chapter 6 for including all of the children apply to every type of play activity used in a toddler classroom. Usually, it is best to position a nonmobile child right next to the teacher, but the other children should be encouraged to also touch and interact with the nonmobile child. The goal of keeping the child near the teacher is not for protection, but rather to provide as many opportunities for the child's active involvement in the play activity as possible. Play activities need to be adapted to address the specific outcomes anticipated for any child with a disability or developmental delay; in most cases, there will be other children in the group who can also benefit from these teaching activities.

The primary goal of play activities is to involve children and give them experiences with different types of materials and events. Although toddlers sometimes seem to be paying no attention to a teacher during an activity, they are often absorbing what is going on around them; toddlers learn from everything they do. Responsive teachers do not insist that toddlers "look here" or perform a skill on demand. Instead, they are aware that toddlers are learning to make sense of the world and all of their experiences. Toddlers often need time to process what they see and hear before they can demonstrate what they have learned.

When toddlers are choosing what they want to do, not all of them will participate in the planned activities. Therefore, while a teacher is conducting a play activity, he or she is also responsible for supervising the independent play of children who are nearby. To do this successfully, teachers must constantly scan the entire area and be alert to the activities of all of the children. Teachers also need to communicate with one another to be sure that all of the space in the play area is adequately supervised.

Supervising toddlers' play means more than just watching. Teachers in the play area must also encourage toddlers to become involved with the materials available, enhance children's play by teaching language and appropriate toy use, prevent disruptions and aggression, and respond to children's individual needs. To encourage toddlers' involvement in play, teachers must first watch what children are doing and then imagine their way of thinking. Successful teachers of toddlers follow the children's lead, comment on their actions, and encourage more elaborate play or language. Specific suggestions for responsive teaching practices appear in Chapter 6.

Teachers will encourage children to congregate near them and participate in activities if teachers do something that is fun, somewhat loud, and silly—singing and dancing, organizing a "train" of bikes, making funny faces or mouth noises, or imitating animal walks and sounds. Teachers must be involved in their activity, but they must also be aware of the other children who are nearby so that all of the children are closely supervised.

At the same time as they are conducting play activities, teachers need to be alert to children's health and safety. Toys that have been in children's mouths must be separated from the other toys for washing as soon as they are put down by children. Teachers must interrupt their play to wipe children's noses (using a clean tissue for each child and a wet wipe for the teacher's hands in between), adjust children's dangling trouser legs and socks, and pick up scattered toys to remove tripping hazards. At the same time, however, teachers must not waste their activity time on nonessential housekeeping chores; they should take advantage of these valuable teaching and learning opportunities.

An alert and active teacher can also prevent most episodes of aggression or conflict between children. Children who are busy at play are not as likely to interfere with others or endanger themselves as children who are bored, so it is important for teachers to try to encourage all of the children to be involved in play. However, no one can be everywhere and see everything, and there will be times when children will get into fights or endanger themselves or another child. Positive redirection *before* the conflict actually occurs is the most effective technique to prevent conflicts. When redirection is not possible, short, firm corrections (*No* or *Stop*, said once) can be used to interrupt children's dangerous or aggressive behavior as well as to display disapproval by the teacher (see Chapter 7).

One way to encourage positive involvement in play is for teachers to direct most of their conversation and play to children who are occupied with toys or other people. It is not the teacher's job to find an activity for every child to do. Children will choose the activity that they want to do, and then teachers will help children do the activity better or talk with them about what they have chosen. Children who are doing nothing should not be coaxed to "find something to do" or be picked up and held by a teacher. Instead, these children should basically be left alone, unless they appear to be ill or troubled. Some children like to watch what other children or teachers are doing; if they appear to be intent on watching others, teachers can try to get these children to talk about what they are observing. Children will most likely join a group when the activity looks like fun to them, and this will usually be when the teacher is involved, having fun, and frequently complimenting and showing obvious affection to the children who are participating in the activity.

All teacher-led activities need to be continued for the entire scheduled time, which is usually at least 15 minutes. Teachers should be encouraged to vary the activity, add to the materials being used, and completely transform the nature of the activity—but to keep the activity going, even when, at first, children do not seem to be especially interested. The lack of children's participation is a sign that the teacher is not involved or having a good time in play. This is when the teacher needs to find something really fun—and usually really silly—to do with the toys. Activity times are not times for a teacher to chat with another teacher, make personal telephone calls, relax while holding a child on his or her lap, or find something easier to do (like looking at books, cleaning the play area, or joining another teacher's activity). Several different play activities are scheduled at one time because it is beneficial for toddlers to be exposed to a wide range of different materials and events and to be able to choose among them. Sometimes it *is* difficult to keep an activity going for 15 minutes; it takes effort and creativity, but the accomplishment is worth the extra work!

Similarly, teachers need to wait until the last minute to pick up the materials from the activity. Children can help with the cleanup and will often enjoy doing that as much as the activity itself! If another activity is scheduled in the area during the next 15 minutes, teachers should provide children with a transition to that activity. For example, while putting away some of the materials from a pretend grocery-shopping activity, a teacher can explain that "Vicky is going to play Pizza Delivery here now; let's help her get out the pizza pans." It is not necessary for the teacher to set up the next activity, but simply to provide some continuity for children. When teachers pick up all the toys and end an activity abruptly, they interrupt children's ongoing play and involvement and leave them with nothing to do. In such a situation, teachers can expect conflicts among children and loss of control related to children's lack of involvement in play.

The Quality Check for play in toddler care on page 106 lists the key ingredients of a successful play area for toddlers. When program directors, teachers, or other visitors find all of these elements present, they can be assured that a stimulating and responsive learning environment has been created.

Scripts for Toddler Play

Toddlers are particularly able to benefit from play activities that follow regular scripts. When they participate in scripted play, toddlers can learn the basic script so that they can anticipate what is going to happen next and, therefore, participate more actively in the play. In addition, toddlers can begin to understand and take part in pretend play when scenarios are established and repeated frequently. By sharing experiences of scripted play, it is also likely that toddlers will establish a basis for social interaction and communication with one another within the context of such activities.

House and doll play activities are the most obvious situations for use of scripted play. It is helpful for teachers who are assigned to doll play at certain times of the day (at arrival in the morning or after naptime, for example) to develop basic scripts to follow at these times. By repeating a similar play scenario from day to day, teachers can expect to see increasing involvement by children.

Some sample scripts are illustrated in Table 5.3. To use scripted play, teachers should begin with very simple scripts that they repeat several times during one scheduled activity time. The pace of this play needs to be slow, following the children's patterns of attention and activity. If children do things that are not part of the script, they should not be corrected, but rather what they do should be incorporated into the script and used as part of the play activity the next day.

As children begin to follow and participate in scripted play, teachers should elaborate on the script. To do this, teachers can add fine points to the scenario, add additional steps to the routine, and have individual children take different roles in the play. Teachers using scripted play need to find a satisfactory balance between the repetition the children require and the variety that teachers themselves may need to keep the scripted play activity interesting and fun for everyone.

Table 5.3. Scripts for doll play with toddlers

Script for the Morning	1. Have babies in bed and covered. 2. Babies wake up (stretch and call for Mom/Dad to come and help babies get out of bed). 3. Mom/Dad comes and babies get up (getting diaper changed or "going potty"; routine of picking out clothes and getting dressed). 4. Babies go to the table. 5. Babies eat breakfast (choosing foods and preparing breakfast; cleaning up after breakfast; Mom/Dad reading the paper and having conversation during breakfast). 6. Babies go to school (ride in car or bus, look out window, and sing songs). 7. Babies arrive at school (see friends and play with favorite toys).
Script for Feeding Babies	1. Babies are hungry; tell Mom/Dad/teachers they want lunch. 2. Babies go to the table. 3. Babies eat lunch (choosing foods and preparing lunch; talking about lunch and the foods being served). 4. Babies clean up by clearing their places at the table (wash dishes, put things away).
Script for Putting Babies to Bed	1. Babies are sleepy (get fussy, rub eyes, and cry). 2. Babies get diaper changed or "go potty." 3. Babies hear a story or song to get ready for bed. 4. Babies hold a favorite blanket or stuffed toy during this time. 5. Babies go to their beds (are tucked in and have their backs rubbed briefly). 6. Babies are asleep—sssh!

(continued)

Table 5.3. *(continued)*

Script for Dressing Babies	1. Babies want clean clothes (having a party, going shopping, going to school, etc.).
	2. Babies take off clothes.
	3. Babies get a (pretend) bath or have hands and face washed.
	4. Babies put on clean clothes (choosing clothes and matching outfits).
	5. Babies put on shoes and coats to go outside.

SUMMARY

The daily experiences of infants and toddlers provide constant opportunities for learning. High-quality child care programs organize children's experience in ways that capitalize on these opportunities. For example, basing a week's play activities on a theme gives direction to children's play and promotes the repetition of events and vocabulary that helps infants and toddlers learn. A planned schedule of play activities that provides variety but is flexible enough to accommodate children's (and teachers') preferences and interests encourages teachers to think in advance about the play activities they will present and how to use them to teach specific developmental skills. The selection and presentation of toys and activities are important to children's learning, but the involvement, attention, and active participation of teachers with children is what defines quality in infant and toddler care.

Quality Check ✔

Play in Infant Care

Teachers, directors, and visitors can use this guide to quality in play. After watching teachers and babies for 10–15 minutes, all answers should be YES.

1. Does every child receive individual attention and interaction from a teacher?   YES ☐   NO ☐

2. Is every child able to watch or interact with other children?   YES ☐   NO ☐

3. Are children quickly moved or given attention when bored or unhappy?   YES ☐   NO ☐

4. Do all children have space to move freely?   YES ☐   NO ☐

5. Can each child reach some toys?   YES ☐   NO ☐

6. Do teachers smile often and use a positive tone of voice with children?   YES ☐   NO ☐

7. Do teachers touch children frequently with gentleness and affection?   YES ☐   NO ☐

8. Is each child encouraged to learn through exploration and experience?   YES ☐   NO ☐

9. Is each teacher's attention focused primarily on the children?   YES ☐   NO ☐

10. Does the play space appear attractive and inviting?   YES ☐   NO ☐

Inclusive Child Care for Infants and Toddlers: Meeting Individual and Special Needs by Marion O'Brien © 1997 Paul H. Brookes Publishing Co., Baltimore.

Quality Check ✔

Play in Toddler Care

Teachers, directors, and visitors can use this guide to quality in play. After watching teachers and toddlers for 10–15 minutes, all answers should be YES.

1. Does every child receive individual attention and interaction from a teacher?   YES ☐   NO ☐

2. Do children have more than one activity from which to choose?   YES ☐   NO ☐

3. Are teachers actively involved in play and enthusiastic about the activities?   YES ☐   NO ☐

4. Do all children have enough space and the freedom to move around as they wish?   YES ☐   NO ☐

5. Are all children busy and involved with play or people most of the time?   YES ☐   NO ☐

6. Are children's interactions with one another mostly positive?   YES ☐   NO ☐

7. Do teachers smile often and use a positive tone of voice with children?   YES ☐   NO ☐

8. If aggression or upsets occur, do teachers handle them positively and sensitively?   YES ☐   NO ☐

9. Do teachers touch children frequently with gentleness and affection?   YES ☐   NO ☐

10. Do teachers notice and respond to children's efforts to communicate?   YES ☐   NO ☐

11. Is each teacher's attention focused primarily on the children?   YES ☐   NO ☐

12. Does the play space appear attractive and inviting?   YES ☐   NO ☐

Inclusive Child Care for Infants and Toddlers: Meeting Individual and Special Needs by Marion O'Brien © 1997 Paul H. Brookes Publishing Co., Baltimore.

Chapter 6

Responsive Teaching
Techniques for Infants and Toddlers

Effective teaching of infants or toddlers is a difficult job. Young infants seem to pay only fleeting attention to events occurring outside their own bodies, and older babies and toddlers appear to have little organization to their behavior. Infants and toddlers can be joyful one minute and teary-eyed the next minute. Even the oldest toddlers do not understand much language and, therefore, do not follow verbal directions. Thus, teachers cannot simply announce the lesson and expect babies or toddlers to sit quietly and listen.

Primarily, infants and toddlers are learning about themselves and the world around them. Much of what they are learning the rest of us have forgotten we had to learn—such as how it feels to be dizzy, what happens when a container of water is turned upside down, and how small a space will accommodate a curious finger. It is the responsibility of the teacher of infants or toddlers to help children learn these skills, yet these are not the sort of skills that appear on developmental checklists or that are highly valued by most educators.

In order to be successful, teachers of infants and toddlers must strive to see the world through the children's eyes. It is not adequate for teachers to set learning objectives based on the developmental or cognitive skills that adults have defined as important for babies or toddlers. Instead, responsive teachers need to think ahead about aspects of materials or activities that children are likely to find interesting and then be alert to opportunities for teaching that come about through children's exploration.

Teaching infants and toddlers requires energy. The teacher must be constantly alert and aware of the activities of every child in the vicinity, and the teacher needs to be ready to intervene and redirect whenever a potentially dangerous or destructive situation arises. The teacher also needs to participate in play and daily living activities with enthusiasm and pleasure in order to hold the children's attention. If children's attention can be captured for a sufficient length of time, opportunities will arise for teachers to enhance children's play and capitalize on their experiences. Therefore, the teacher's full attention must be focused on the children, rather than on personal plans for later in the day, family troubles, or other events.

Effective teaching of infants and toddlers often appears to be unplanned and casual because it happens as part of children's ongoing activities, rather than during structured teaching and learning times. However, the responsive teacher actually plans carefully in advance to create opportunities for teaching. Some of the aspects of this teaching skill simply require that the teacher remains highly alert and attentive to what is happening with the children in his or her care. Other teaching aspects involve specific techniques for interacting with children so that opportunities for teaching and learning occur frequently.

TEACHING AS ENHANCING LEARNING AND DEVELOPMENT

Using responsive teaching techniques, teachers of infants and toddlers can strengthen children's desire to learn, help children build communication and motor skills, and promote children's social development.

Enhancing Children's Desire to Learn

Successful teachers of infants and toddlers understand that their most important job is to help children discover the pleasure of exploration and enjoy the process of learning. Therefore, the best teachers of infants and toddlers are people who seek out new ideas and experiences themselves and who are able to view the world from the perspective of a baby or toddler. The most enduring learning infants and toddlers are doing involves *attitudes* about themselves, their relationships with other people, and everyday life, rather than facts, concepts, or skills. The following sections describe a number of ways in which teachers of infants and toddlers can contribute to the development of children's positive attitudes toward their own competence and ability to learn.

Emotional Involvement

Teachers of infants and toddlers must come to work with a willingness to become emotionally involved with the children in their care and to show clearly their affection and caring. Babies and toddlers know the difference between a person who truly cares for them and a person who is indifferent. Young children are aware of their dependence on adults, and this dependence makes young children more alert to adults' behavior that is directed toward them than many people realize. Children will more readily respond to the efforts of teachers who are emotionally involved with them than to teachers who are just going through the motions.

Although all babies and toddlers are not equally appealing, teachers cannot have favorites. Some children are less attractive or less cuddly than others, and some children may have less ability to attract adult attention and affection than their age-mates. Teachers need to work at developing strong emotional relationships with all of the children in their care, regardless of children's appearance or social competence. Relationships do not just happen—they require effort and attention. Infants and toddlers are not able to work consciously at developing relationships with teachers; therefore, teachers must be the ones who devote time and energy to becoming attached to the children. Children will reciprocate the relationship, to the enjoyment and benefit of both!

Teachers can build positive relationships with children by being active and animated when they are working with children and by showing clearly that they genuinely enjoy being with the children. When teachers smile a lot, children not only smile back but also interact more frequently with teachers. Through repeated successful interactions, teachers and children learn to depend on the responses of one another; this predictability is the basis for a secure relationship. Furthermore, teachers who are happy, enthusiastic, and energetic during daily living and play activities attract and hold children's attention and, therefore, gain more opportunities to share experiences with children. These shared experiences form the foundation for meaningful interactions about real events in which both parties are interested.

Sometimes teachers allow their knowledge about a child's family background or difficulties to influence their responses to the child. Although teachers must work to be supportive of a child's family, when they are with the child, they should try to develop a relationship that is independent of other aspects of the child's life. Thus, teachers should not develop a relationship with a child based on pity because a child has been abused, neglected, or is living in a foster home; nor a relationship based on protection because a child has complex medical needs; nor a relationship based on vigilance because a child is frequently aggressive. Instead, the teacher–child relationship must be built on honest efforts to get to know the child as an individual and acceptance of the child's positive and less positive characteristics.

The Child's Agenda

Most of our experience with teachers occurs in situations in which teachers are in charge of the activity. Therefore, we tend to expect that the teachers in a classroom determine most of the decisions about lessons that are taught and learned, activities taking place, and how children are involved. For teachers of infants and toddlers, this is true only in the broad sense that the day's schedule is planned and the type of play activities that are provided are organized in advance. The teaching agenda is left almost entirely to the children to decide.

This approach of allowing children to choose activities and set a direction for learning is particularly effective with infants and toddlers, whose primary task is to gain experience with the world. Almost any experience has potential learning value to a baby or toddler. As a child becomes more involved in an experience, it is more likely that he or she will learn a new concept, a new insight into how his or her body works, or a new skill. The teacher who does not try to be in control of a child's experience will be more successful at keeping the child's interest and involvement high and, therefore, will be able to accomplish more effective teaching.

Studies of parents interacting with their babies and young children have shown that the most harmonious interactions and the most successful interactions in terms of enhancing children's later socioemotional and intellectual development are those in which parents follow the children's lead (Isabella, 1993; Tomasello, 1990). For example, when parents allow their children to choose a toy and then focus their attention on the children's selection, the interactions are more successful than when parents try to attract children's attention to a toy in which the parent is interested. Teachers of infants and toddlers can use this same technique of allowing children to make choices during all of their interactions with children.

One way for teachers to practice giving children more control over activities is to match or imitate children's actions with toys. For instance, when Marty selects a doll with which to play, the teacher can select a similar doll. When Marty covers the doll with a bandana, the teacher can also cover his or her doll. This matching of actions must be done with an honest effort to capture and share the child's experience, rather than as mimicry or teasing of the child. As the sensitive teacher becomes involved in matching the child's actions, he or she can talk with the child about their shared experiences and identify opportunities to expand on the child's actions. The teacher's more complex play then flows naturally out of the child's involvement, and the child is more likely to notice and imitate the teacher's actions. This teacher has successfully taught the child a new skill or a new idea without ever having to redirect the child's attention.

When teachers feel that they must be in charge of children's play, they reduce children's initiative to explore and discover ideas and skills for themselves. By being nondirective and allowing children to choose the topic for learning, teachers encourage children's intrinsic motivation to seek out experiences and learn from them.

Nondirectiveness must not be confused with passivity. The nondirective teacher waits to allow the child to show the way, but once the child begins to play with a toy, the teacher is attentive and involved, looking actively for opportunities to introduce concepts or elaborations of the child's selected activity. A passive teacher, however, is content to watch children play and does not take advantage of the teaching opportunities presented by children's involvement with toys or activities. Nondirective teaching also does not mean that the teacher begins an activity by doing nothing; on the contrary, it is often crucial for the teacher to start an activity by being highly visible and animated so that children are attracted to the area where the activity is taking place. The responsive teacher then takes the role of supporting and enhancing children's play, rather than just organizing play or simply observing.

Enhancing Communication Skills

The acquisition of communication skills, particularly language, is a crucial developmental task for infants and toddlers. The beginnings of language lie in nonverbal communication—gestures, facial expressions, and body language that one person uses to let another person know what he or she is feeling or thinking. These movements and expressions are gradually accompanied by sounds, and these sounds eventually become intelligible words. By age 3, most children are talking in full sentences and are able to effectively communicate their thoughts and wishes to others.

Many adults do not begin to respond to children's efforts to communicate until the children produce intelligible words, and for some children, this lack of response is discouraging. Effective teachers of infants and toddlers must try to be responsive to *all* communicative attempts produced by children. Individual children within a group of infants and toddlers will vary widely in their ability to make themselves understood, either verbally or nonverbally. It is important for teachers to pay just as much attention to the gestures and sounds of the youngest or least competent child as to the four- or five-word, beautifully articulated sentences of the most verbally proficient child.

Teachers of infants and toddlers need to spend a lot of time talking about everything that they and the children are doing. Most effective are simple, short sentences spoken with melodic tones that vary in pitch; this manner of talking to children has been studied by researchers who have

termed it *motherese* because it is a nearly universal way that mothers talk to their infants. In addition, babies pay more attention to speech when the pitch changes frequently, the sounds are interesting and varied, and the words or sounds have rhyme or rhythm. Teachers can captivate a baby by singing (either on- or off-key), cooing, babbling, making rude mouth noises, or saying silly rhymes. While teachers are having fun, the children will be learning some of the basics of communication.

An infant or toddler classroom is also an ideal environment for the use of *total communication,* which involves incorporating some sign language into teachers' everyday interactions with children. When children are somewhat slow to start talking or have hearing impairments or other disabilities that affect speech, the use of some sign language can help these children learn that they can communicate effectively with others. Sign language can help all children bridge the time period from being nonverbal to being able to express themselves with words. Signs do not have to be explicitly taught to children because when teachers learn *and use* certain signs all of the time, children easily pick up these signs and use them, too. Teachers do not necessarily have to be fluent in American Sign Language in order to use signs effectively; using a few signs simply takes practice. Especially useful—and easy—signs for teachers to use on a regular basis are those signs for MORE, STOP, POTTY, EAT, DRINK, BABY, BOOK, SHOES, SOCKS, PLEASE, HELP, FINISHED, and WASH.

There are many techniques that teachers can use when interacting with infants and toddlers that help to promote children's active participation in conversations. Some of these techniques have been developed in programs of speech and language therapy for use with children with delays in their language development or impaired functioning of their speech-language-hearing systems. Thus, these intervention techniques are useful for children identified as having communication delays or problems. In addition, these are effective techniques to promote language learning in all children and are particularly useful for infants and toddlers at the beginning stages of language development. Therefore, these are techniques that all teachers of infants and toddlers need to learn and use all of the time during their interactions with children.

The techniques described here do not come naturally to adults, but rather must be learned and practiced, just as with other teaching skills. Adults without training in working with infants and toddlers (including parents) tend to have conversations that consist largely of questions. In one study, some beginning teachers questioned children during almost 85% of their interactions with them (O'Brien & Bi, 1995). When first learning to talk with babies and toddlers, it can be helpful for teachers to wear a small tape recorder and then listen to themselves later (in private), keeping track of the number of questions they ask and directions they use.

Self-Talk

As teachers conduct their regular activities with children, including both play and daily living activities, they need to describe what they are doing, seeing, hearing, smelling, and feeling. These descriptions should be simple and slow-paced so that children can focus on the sounds and the mouth movements associated with the words, and there should be repetitions and pauses between sentences so that children can imitate or participate in the conversation.

Self-talk can be used anytime. A teacher using self-talk during diapering might say, "I'm lifting Jason now. Up we go!" and then later, "Off with the old pants . . . on with the new pants" and "Let's fasten the tape, tape, tape" followed by "Turn on the water and wash our hands." Teachers need to practice the use of self-talk with infants and toddlers because it is a different type of conversation from those adults typically share with young children. Self-talk is an alternative to questions, and self-talk is encouraging to young preverbal and language-learning children. Questions are demands, and the child who is not skillful with using language often retreats from the demands of a teacher to a more comfortable place where no one will insist on a response—which sometimes means a retreat to solitary play. Self-talk does not make any demands of the child, but rather opens opportunities for the child's participation in conversation.

At first, teachers may feel awkward or foolish talking about themselves, especially because children will often seem not to be paying attention. It is true that babies and even toddlers will not always understand the entire substance of what the teacher is saying, but the constant use of words and the opportunity to connect words with objects and actions is not lost on the child who is just beginning to learn language. As teachers become comfortable with self-talk, they will notice the children repeating their sounds and words more frequently and eventually initiating conversations themselves.

Parallel Talk

When a child is actively involved in play, eating, or any other activity, teachers need to describe in concrete terms the child's actions at that moment. These comments should be focused on labeling objects and actions, providing descriptive words for the toys children are using, and generally narrating the ongoing scene like an announcer at a sporting event. As with self-talk, the pace of the teacher's conversation needs to be slow, with a lot of pauses that give the language-learning child a chance to process the teacher's words and say something in response. In contrast to the way older children and adults respond to language, infants and toddlers do not automatically understand words. They must listen and think about the sounds they hear, and this takes time. Adults often do not wait long enough between their sentences for children to participate in the conversation.

Parallel talk requires the teacher to pay close attention to the *child's* actions. When using parallel talk, the teacher does not make suggestions for the child's play or ask the child about what is happening. The teacher simply narrates, describing what happens or what the child is looking at or doing. For example, if a child is involved in a beanbag toss game, the teacher's parallel talk might proceed like this: "Danny has a red beanbag" then later, "The red beanbag hit the blue circle" and a short time later, "Danny is holding two beanbags." When using parallel talk, teachers can also insert sound effects (e.g., "Kabowee!" "Kerplunk!") that help to attract children's attention, but teachers should be sure to focus most of their talk on concrete labels for objects and active, descriptive verbs.

Parallel talk can also be used to help children learn the words for more abstract experiences, such as smells, sounds, and feelings. When a child's attention is distracted by a loud sound in the hallway, the teacher can use parallel talk to let the child know the experience has been shared (e.g., "Big boom, huh, Retta?"). If a child is working hard at a putting a puzzle together but the pieces just will not fit into the right spaces, parallel talk can reflect the child's frustration and be encouraging to the child at the same time (e.g., "You're mad at that doggie's foot. You know where the foot goes, but it's not fitting.").

Parallel talk is effective because it helps create a clear connection between words and the child's experience, and parallel talk also lets the child know that the teacher is interested in the child's activity. Shared interest is the basis for communication. By demonstrating that he or she is involved in the child's activity, the teacher shows respect for the child and arranges a situation in which meaningful communication is most likely to happen.

Expansion

When children begin to talk, teachers can use their early words and even their sounds or signs as the basis for conversation. Whenever a child says a word or makes a sound or sign that is clearly communicative, a teacher can add information to the child's statement. Thus, if a child says, "Tuck" while holding a bright red fire truck, the teacher responds with, "You have a red truck." As children begin to connect words into short sentences, expansion can be used to provide more elaborate sentence structure. If Mindy says, "Do book," the teacher can respond, "Mindy wants to read a book."

Expansion is not used to *correct* a child's errors in speech, but rather to model correct speech and sentence structure. Thus, the child is not asked to repeat the teacher's words, and the teacher does not make a point of the fact that the child incorrectly says a word. Expansion is more than just simple repetition along with better articulation of the child's speech. When teachers use expansion, they try to frame their responses into short and clear but complete sentences.

Continuation

As a child's language progresses, a teacher can encourage more complex and descriptive speech by responding to the child's brief statements with new information that may be of interest to the child or may help the child's understanding of the world. As an example, if Vincent is on the playground and says, "Big bug," the teacher can respond, "That big bug is a June bug." Similarly, in the building activity area, as the block tower falls and Luisa exclaims, "Fall down!" the teacher continues with, "They fell down when that big long block went on top."

The teacher using continuation should try to incorporate the words the child used as part of the response so that the child can easily grasp the connection between his or her language and the teacher's language.

Toddlers who appear to be quite verbal actually process speech more slowly than adults, and teachers need to give toddlers as many hints and cues as possible so that they can participate more fully in conversations.

Enhancing Motor Skills

Anyone who visits an infant or toddler classroom can plainly see that babies and toddlers are constantly practicing their large motor skills. At times, toddlers especially will seem to be in constant motion, and their practice with motion is not limited to the types of movements that are typical of adults and older children in classrooms. Babies are as likely to roll across the floor as they are to crawl, and toddlers can be seen repeating a movement, such as climbing in and out of a large carton, until even an observer tires of watching.

The successful teacher of infants and toddlers realizes that young children need to learn how their bodies move and also how to gain control over these movements. Checklists of large motor skill development milestones tend to focus on the child's progression from crawling to walking to running and the associated body movement skills accompanying this progression, such as jumping, standing on one foot, and climbing stairs. Some of the bases for large motor competence are missing from this developmental sequence—specifically, the ability to balance, the ability to anticipate shifts in weight that accompany body movements, and the ability to keep the body aligned as the child changes positions.

Teachers of infants and toddlers need to learn to observe children's balance and posture and to provide opportunities to practice balance as well as offer support and assistance, as needed, to help children maintain postural control. These aspects of children's motor development are particularly of concern when children have disabilities that affect their muscular or bone structure or their muscle tone, such as cerebral palsy, spina bifida, or skeletal deformities, or when children are delayed in learning to walk. Like most techniques originally developed to assist children with disabilities, postural and balance control interventions are helpful to all children, including typically developing infants and toddlers.

Balance

Children who have difficulty with balance are at risk for continued difficulties with movement and eventual limitations in their ability to participate in recreational activities. Difficulties with balance may be responsible for the clumsiness that characterizes the movements of some toddlers and may result in some children being reluctant to attempt some activities, such as playing on the rocking boat or slide.

A *balance reaction* is the tendency of the body to keep itself in alignment with gravity. For example, when people walk up a slope, they lean forward; on a ship or airplane, people will attempt to keep their body and head from tilting with the movement of their seat.

Teachers can promote the development of children's balance reactions by providing them with supported opportunities to experience tilting and returning to center. Whenever a child is sitting in a teacher's lap, the teacher can bend one leg so that the child slides to one side or, holding the child by the hips, the teacher can repeatedly roll the leg on which the child is supported to one side, then to the other side. The child will enjoy the game and the physical contact and at the same time will be gaining experience with the sensation of being off-balance and keeping control over the alignment of head and body.

Children can also be challenged to develop their balance reactions by having a variety of surfaces available on which to sit, crawl, stand, and walk. Surfaces that are flexible, moveable, or uneven require postural adjustments to maintain balance. Defining play areas with plastic-covered foam mats of different heights so that children must crawl or step up and down in order to move around the classroom is one way to incorporate regular practice in balance and movement into the children's daily activities. Outdoors, a sandbox in which to play, real grass and uneven earth to walk on, or a hill to climb are all useful ways of developing balance.

Postural Control

Children need to be able to bend and reach while maintaining control over the rest of their body. Sometimes teachers will observe children who are quite competent at walking and running but who fall to the side when they are sitting on the floor and trying to reach around an obstruction or up high to obtain a toy. Children are not hurt by these falls, but they need practice in order to gain the stability to maintain their position and to move their arms and upper trunk freely and flexibly at the same time.

Teachers can help children practice maintaining their balance by offering children toys that are just out of their reach so that they must stretch and bend to obtain the toy that they want. This technique should not be done in a teasing manner, but rather as a way of encouraging children's control over their own movement. Younger children may need a teacher behind them to support their hips as they reach for a toy above or out in front of them. Children can practice postural control when they are sitting or kneeling on the floor, sitting on large square or round foam blocks, riding foot-powered bikes, sitting on chairs at the lunch table, or standing on the floor. In addition, climbing into and out of cardboard boxes or plastic crates, walking up and down stairs, and crawling up and down a ramp all help children develop postural control.

Enhancing Children's Social Development

During the toddler years, children's social focus shifts to a large degree from adults to peers. The development of communication skills contributes to this shift of attention. When babies or young toddlers play together, their social exchanges are generally very brief and end abruptly because neither partner is competent in assisting the other with communicating. By the end of the toddler period, however, children are typically able to carry on extended conversations and also to play cooperatively together.

The difficulty that babies and young toddlers have with interacting and playing jointly with their peers is not an indication of their lack of interest in the activities of other children. In fact, some infants and toddlers spend a great deal of time intently observing the behavior and play of other children, and it is clear that even very young children learn from watching and imitating other children's behavior. This early imitation, which is often accompanied by smiling and laughter as children become aware of it, has been suggested as a bridge between solitary and social play (Eckerman & Stein, 1990).

Children's growing involvement with peers also does not mean that the influence of adults in their lives is diminished. On the contrary, children who have strong and positive relationships with adults, including teachers as well as parents, apply skills learned from their social experiences with these adults to play with their peers. Teachers are often babies' and toddlers' first friends—people who are not members of the children's own family with whom children have loving and caring relationships. Children who spend their days together in an infant or toddler group are also likely to become friends. Thus, teachers have a unique opportunity to make children's initial experience of friendship a positive and supportive one.

As with all of the important developmental tasks of infancy and toddlerhood, becoming a competent play partner and a good friend are not the types of abilities that are easily taught by presenting a set of defined tasks that allow children to acquire skills sequentially. Instead, teachers need to work to provide an overall environment that encourages and supports positive, affectionate, and rewarding social interactions between adults and children and among children themselves. Also, the social climate must be one in which each child is accepted and cared for as an individual so that children can develop the confidence to give up some of their hard-won autonomy in order to gain friendship with other children.

All of the play activities described in Appendix B potentially provide this type of welcoming social environment. The use of the techniques described previously for enhancing communication skills plays an important role in promoting social development, and the efforts teachers make to understand infants' and toddlers' behavior and respond to problem behavior in effective and thoughtful ways (see Chapter 7) help children learn positive ways of getting along with others. In addition, there are some specific ways for teachers to encourage the development of more complex social interactions and cooperative play with infants and toddlers.

Investing in Relationships with Children

One of the most important ways teachers can promote children's social development is by building their own emotional relationships with children. Adult–child relationships form the basis for children's later peer relationships. Infants and toddlers need the security and predictability that comes from consistent and sensitive interactions with caring adults. Teachers do not replace parents when they develop relationships with children. Instead, they extend children's experience in close relationships so that children's ideas about how people get along together are enhanced and given depth.

Teachers of infants and toddlers must be willing to become emotionally involved with the children in their care. There is a risk to this involvement because babies and toddlers grow up quickly and move to new classrooms, and sometimes their families move to new cities. However, even if the loving and secure relationship between a teacher and child lasts only a year, it will contribute to the child's sense of his or her own worth and will eventually contribute to the child's ability to develop relationships with other adults and children.

Creating Opportunities for Shared Experience

Social interaction is based on shared experience. Because babies and toddlers have had relatively little life experience and lack knowledge about other people's perspectives on experience, their opportunities for social interaction are limited.

Teachers can use familiar play activities to build a foundation of shared experience that can serve as a framework for interaction and joint play. For example, teachers can use parallel talk to describe the similar actions of Julie and Gus with the sand toys, making the children aware of their parallel play. Furthermore, teachers can help children create play scripts by conducting the same or similar activities several days in a row, each time following the same series of steps in sequence but then adding a new dimension that extends the play. Such scripts are perhaps most readily developed with dolls and house toys, where rudimentary pretend play is most common among even young toddlers, but the same approach can be used in play activities with building toys and in active play as well.

When teachers notice that certain children appear to have common interests, they can also plan opportunities for the children to repeatedly play together for brief periods of time. These same two children can be invited to "potty" at the same time or to eat lunch together in order to add to their shared experiences. Teachers should not always decide which children sit together, however, because children should be allowed to select their own companions. Teachers can make it possible for certain children to do activities together and then let the children take over to determine whether a friendship develops.

Whenever two or more children are involved in an activity with a teacher, the teacher can be alert to opportunities to encourage friendly interactions between children. For most infants and toddlers, these interactions will need considerable support from the teacher. For example, in a pretend grocery shopping activity, the teacher may suggest that Jay push his cart to the table, where Robbie has a monopoly on the plastic vegetables, and ask for a tomato. Yet, if Jay follows this suggestion, the teacher's task is not finished. The teacher will need to follow along with Jay so that when Jay makes his request, Robbie understands the question. If Robbie is particularly attached to the tomatoes, some negotiation for another vegetable might be needed, and again, the teacher will need to be involved. It is quite likely, however, that when a vegetable is placed in Jay's cart, he will smile at Robbie and offer a cheery and unsolicited "Thank you!" This is the teacher's reward and marks the first step toward cooperative social play.

Activities that involve turn taking, although sometimes frustrating for infants and toddlers, can be used as opportunities to talk about shared experience. For example, a teacher may instruct children on how to take a

turn with a game, "First Megan pushes the button, then Sam pushes the button." Waiting for a turn is difficult but can be eased by teachers who exaggerate the alternation of activity, make a song out of the situation, or point out that it is funny to be taking turns. The shared laughter that becomes part of the game will make the experience more memorable to the children, who will then want to repeat the experience again and again. The next day, the teacher may find Megan and Sam playing the same game together without a teacher involved to guide them.

Showing Affection

When teachers are affectionate with the infants and toddlers in their care, they create an environment in which caring and concern for others are clearly valued. When children spontaneously display affection toward one another, teachers can describe what they are doing and get in line for their own hugs. It is easy for a child who is on the receiving end of such affection from another child to misinterpret the intent, however, turning a gesture of love into an instant conflict. To encourage children to put their caring for others into practice, teachers can play affectionate games with dolls and stuffed animals, making it easier for children to imitate hugging and kissing without invading another child's personal space.

Teachers can also help children practice turn taking and joint use of toys by encouraging children to "share" toys with dolls, rather than with other children. The concept of sharing requires that infants or toddlers recognize other people's perspectives, which is an inappropriate expectation for children at this age. Thus, practice with actual sharing can generally be successful only by asking children to "give away" toys in which they are not interested. This technique is best accomplished when there are several similar toys or replicates of toys available so everyone can find a satisfactory toy.

Older infants and toddlers can also be taught to make requests for toys by using words or signs and also to be somewhat assertive in resisting other children's efforts to take toys in their possession. Sometimes a timid child can learn to say or sign "No!" or "Stop!" in a forceful enough manner to discourage other children from taking toys. Teachers can play giving and receiving games with children by asking politely for a toy and saying an elaborate "Thank you" at even the slightest movement of the toy toward the teacher. It is fruitless and frustrating to expect infants and toddlers to share or to insist that they give up favorite toys. Giving should be practiced in the context of enjoyable play, rather than when possession really matters to a child.

One of the most enjoyable and successful ways to encourage smiling and affectionate behavior—in both teachers and children—is to sing songs about hugging, smiling, and loving that use the children's names. Almost any familiar song can be adapted for this purpose (e.g., "David's happy and he knows it . . . smile wide"), or teachers can simply make up their own rhymes (e.g., "I see Lisa; happy, happy Lisa"). Smiling is truly contagious. It is almost impossible to avoid smiling back at someone who beams a big, honest smile in your direction—just the act of smiling makes most people feel happy. Teachers of infants and toddlers can make frequent use of this delightful human characteristic.

TEACHING AS INTERVENTION

All of the teaching approaches described in this chapter are equally useful for children with disabilities or developmental delays as well as for typically developing children. Many of the techniques included here were initially developed in early intervention or in special education programs. Used routinely with all children, these techniques can be expected to minimize secondary delays, to reduce the decline in developmental progress that is often noticed by teachers in children's third year of life, and also to enhance the developmental progress of children without disabilities or developmental delays.

In addition to these general approaches to teaching and learning, however, it is often important for children who have been diagnosed as having disabilities or developmental delays to receive individual help and support from teachers. Teachers can best promote the development of children with special needs by making sure all of the children receive equal opportunities to participate in classroom activities, by encouraging social interactions between children, and by focusing some of their teaching interactions on the specific outcomes desired for individual children.

Facilitating Inclusion of Children with Special Needs

The caregiving routines and responsive teaching practices described throughout this book are appropriate for children with disabilities and developmental delays as well as for typically developing children. The primary challenge for teachers is to ensure that children who have disabilities participate fully in classroom activities so that they can benefit from all of the play and daily living activities. The following suggestions can help teachers facilitate the inclusion of all children in classroom activities.

1. *Teachers should provide opportunities for nonmobile and nonverbal children to indicate an activity preference.* High-quality infant-toddler care is based on children's self-selection of activities. When children cannot "vote with their feet" by physically entering and leaving activities, teachers must offer and follow through with choices. For example, if the activity choices at a particular time are pretending to have a tea party or playing with waffle blocks, a teacher can present toys used in each of these activities to any child who cannot move independently between the activities. The teacher then can ask, "What would you like to do next? You can go to a tea party (holding up a teacup) or play with waffle blocks (holding up a block)." Depending on the child, a preference may be indicated by a smile, a nod, or simply by the focus of visual attention on one of the two choices. Similarly, teachers can notice when an activity captures the attention of a nonmobile child. If the child appears to be watching an activity in progress at the other end of the room, the teacher can reposition the child so he or she can be a part of that activity. Clearly, this is a practice that applies to young infants who are not yet mobile as well as to children who have disabilities that affect their movement.

2. *Teachers must frequently reposition children who are nonmobile.* Any child who cannot move to a new location or change positions on his or her own should be repositioned at least every 15 minutes. This applies to nonmobile infants who may be seated in infant seats, resting in bouncers, or lying under a cradle gym as well as to older children with disabilities who are unable to crawl or walk. No child—at any ability level—should be left in a container that restrains movement (including a swing) for more than 15 minutes at a time, even if he or she is not complaining. Every child needs opportunities to view the world from different perspectives, to exercise all of his or her muscles, and to experience a variety of social situations.

3. *Teachers need to position children in an activity area for best participation.* The best position for a child will depend on the nature of the activity and how the other children are positioned. If all of the children are gathered around a small table, the child who is nonmobile or has special needs should be placed in a positioning chair, in a standing apparatus, or on a teacher's lap so he or she can also play at the table. If children are lying on the floor listening to a story, the nonmobile child should be positioned on the floor as well. If a group of toddlers is moving about in an active play activity, the teacher can either "be" the child's legs (by carrying the child and playing the game like a toddler), or the teacher can position the child in his or her wheelchair and push the wheelchair in order to help the nonmobile child keep up with the other children.

4. *Teachers can encourage participation at whatever level is appropriate for or desired by the child.* All children in an infant or toddler classroom must be taught as individuals. Within a group, no two children will

participate in planned activities in the same way or with the same level of enthusiasm. Often, just touching or holding the materials and watching and listening to the other children is enough stimulation for a child, and this is especially true for children who have severe disabilities. Other children with special needs may be able to participate more actively if they are given the right amount of support and assistance. Each child learns a different concept, skill, or ability from each activity. Teachers need to be alert for small signals from children with disabilities and should encourage all levels of involvement from these children.

5. *Teachers must avoid the tendency to do everything for the child with special needs.* The teacher's job is to promote and support every child's involvement in classroom activities and in interaction with other children. Teachers need to avoid separating a child with special needs from the other children and entertaining the child with individual activities, such as reading books. Even if a child has a severe disability or has complex health care needs, the child should be involved in regular daily activities—including meals and outdoor play—along with typically developing children.

Furthermore, teachers should not encourage other children to do activities *for* the child, but rather to do activities *with* the child who has special needs. Very young children quite readily accept differences in other children. Toddlers will behave in a caring and compassionate way toward a child with a severe disability who cannot walk or talk, but toddlers will also expect that child to be a part of everyday activities. Teachers can take their cues from the children and consider the child with special needs, first of all, to be a child.

Encouraging Peer Play

Teachers can also help children interact with one another. All infants and toddlers need help if their social interchanges are to be successful. Most young children's communication attempts are even difficult for familiar adults to recognize and understand. When the receiver is also a child who is equally new at communicating, there is a very high possibility for missed signals. If they have a little help, however, children with special needs can participate as equals because social interaction among infants and toddlers is fairly basic. Interaction among children can be encouraged in a variety of ways:

1. *Encouraging children to share information:* Teachers can notice and remember certain aspects about individual children and use these as conversation starters (e.g., "Susie likes to drink hot chocolate. Tell Susie what you like to drink for snack").

2. *Encouraging children to give or receive toys:* Infants and toddlers do not share happily but can be enticed to exchange objects as part of a play activity (e.g., "Gary has a cool necktie. Would you like to see how it looks on you? Let's see how your fancy hat looks on Gary").

3. *Providing information about one child to another child, thus pointing out areas of shared knowledge and experience:* Recog-

nizing that you have a common interest with another person is the basis of communication and social interaction. Teachers who know children well can help them find a common ground (e.g., "Elaine has a big black dog at home. I know you have a dog too. What's your dog's name?").

4. *Encouraging children to help each other:* Older infants and toddlers enjoy the feeling of competence they gain from helping another child, and they especially enjoy teaming up with a teacher to do something nice for someone else (e.g., "David and I will hold the paper while you color. Then you can hold our paper for us").

5. *Making statements that point out the activities the child with special needs is capable of doing:* Interactions involving children with disabilities need to focus more frequently on abilities (e.g., "Craig can hold on tight to the parachute" or "Wow! Look at Maxine crawl!") than on disabilities.

6. *Answering children's questions about the child with special needs:* Teachers can help typically developing children make sense of their experiences with children who have special needs by describing disabilities in simple language (e.g., "Tracey's legs don't work like yours. The wheelchair lets Tracey go fast!").

Incorporating IFSP Outcomes into Play and Daily Living Activities

Each child who qualifies for services under Part C of the Individuals with Disabilities Education Act Amendments of 1997 (PL 105-17) will have an individualized family service plan (IFSP; see Chapter 3), and a major part of that plan will be the outcomes desired for the child by the intervention team, which includes the child's family, the classroom staff, and special service providers. These desired outcomes must be incorporated into the teaching approaches and goals used in the classroom. Teachers will find that they are already addressing many of the outcomes for children with special needs if they are using responsive teaching techniques to enhance the learning of infants and toddlers.

Although they are common in special education programs, elaborate skill-based charts and extensive daily record keeping are not necessarily the only effective way to serve children with special needs. Teachers can discuss the outcomes for individual children during their regularly scheduled staff meetings and share ways to incorporate these outcomes into daily classroom activities. Some desired outcomes for children, such as the acquisition of specific speech sounds, may be best addressed during the one-to-one context of diapering, whereas other outcomes, such as the ability to bear more weight on the legs, can easily be incorporated into all play activities. Furthermore, the play activity schedule can be adapted to include activities that are focused toward a specific outcome for a particular child. For example, if special switch-operated toys are available for a child who has significant motor impairment, these toys can be the focus of a play activity that is available to all children. Another example could be blowing bubbles, which is an excellent context in which to practice the "b" sound. Experienced teachers can complete simple self-checks on a weekly basis to monitor their own involvement in promoting children's outcomes, or the lead teacher or program director can observe each teacher on a regular basis and provide feedback regarding the teacher's effectiveness in adapting activities to meet children's individual needs (see Chapter 12).

One easy system for providing reminders to teachers regarding the outcomes for particular children is to print sheets of adhesive labels bearing each child's name and a brief description of one of the outcomes desired for that child. The lead teacher or family services coordinator can attach these labels to existing record sheets and schedules for activities in which the outcomes can be practiced—on play activity schedules or descriptions, the diapering record used in the classroom, or the child's menu for the day. Long-term progress can be tracked through regular skill checks or developmental assessments conducted by the family services coordinator or a special service provider (see Chapter 12).

Another means of encouraging teachers to be aware of outcomes for particular children is for the family services coordinator to develop an attractive poster for each activity area of the classroom that lists at least one outcome that can be addressed in that area for each child with an IFSP. These posters need to be placed where teachers can easily see them and must be frequently revised or they will become part of the background, rather than active, useful documents.

It is useful to encourage parents of typically developing children and parents of children who are considered to be at risk for developmental delays but who are not eligible under Part H criteria to provide a list of the outcomes they desire for their children similar to those outcomes included on IFSPs (see Chapter 3). Teachers who know the goals parents have for their children can communicate more effectively with families. Furthermore, the expectations parents have for their children may, at times, indicate that teachers need to shift their teaching emphasis in particular areas, and in some cases may identify a family's need for information about child development.

Communication between special service providers and teachers can be facilitated by using a child logbook or scrapbook, an inexpensive notebook or record book in which each special service provider who works with a specific child records a brief description of each therapy or educational session. As specialists teach teachers intervention techniques to address particular outcomes, they may wish teachers to record their experiences and the child's responses in this same record book. If parents also want to receive frequent reports about the services provided for their child, a family-friendly report form can be developed (see an example in Figure 6.1). Keeping photocopies of these reports in a loose-leaf notebook, which also serves as the child's logbook, avoids the need for teachers to record descriptions twice.

The most important goal in working with children who have special needs is for teachers to incorporate the intervention practices appropriate for each child and each child's desired outcomes into the everyday care and play routines of the classroom. As teachers learn and practice new intervention approaches that are intended to meet individual children's

---

HOME REPORT for _____

What we did today

Progress noted   How child liked it

_____   _____
Service provider signature   Date

Figure 6.1.   A sample home report to keep parents informed about special services.

needs, they should also, whenever possible, use these same approaches with *all* of the children, including typically developing children. In this way, every aspect of every child care and teaching routine will contribute toward intervention for all children in the classroom.

SUMMARY

Responsive teaching involves paying attention to each child as an individual and adapting activities and routines to create a learning environment that is appropriate for every child. Teaching techniques developed as intervention approaches for preschool-age children with special needs are particularly useful for all infants and toddlers, including those children who are developing typically as well as those children who have disabilities or developmental delays. Promoting the development of language and communication, enhancing motor skills, and encouraging positive social relationships with others are important aspects of teaching infants and toddlers.

Inclusion of children with disabilities or complex medical needs into a group of typically developing infants or toddlers does not require a major classroom reorganization because all infants and toddlers require a great deal of physical care and a lot of individual attention, regardless of disabilities. When teachers are aware of the developmental level of each child in their care, they are able to incorporate specific learning goals into regularly scheduled play activities and daily living routines. Similarly, responsive teaching means recognizing the needs of infants and toddlers for guidance in learning to develop positive relationships with other people.

Chapter 7

Responsive Guidance
for Infants and Toddlers

From the moment of birth, it is clear that human infants belong to a socially oriented species. Throughout infancy and toddlerhood, children are very interested in and responsive to other people, and their social behavior becomes increasingly complex and differentiated as they grow older. When gathered together in a group of age-mates, however, the immaturity of infants' and toddlers' social behavior is often more obvious than its growing sophistication. This chapter presents suggestions to help teachers understand infant and toddler behavior and cope with some of the troublesome and frustrating situations that can arise in group infant and toddler care.

UNDERSTANDING INFANT AND TODDLER BEHAVIOR

Many teachers of infants and toddlers express considerable frustration about the behavior of the children in their care. When an infant cries and teachers can find nothing wrong with the child, they feel helpless and may lose confidence in themselves as caregivers. Babies' schedules vary considerably from day to day, and older babies will appear to have settled into a regular routine during one week, only to behave completely differently during the next week. This unpredictability of infants can be unsettling to teachers who like to know what to expect each day.

Teachers frequently describe toddlers in terms that evoke the image of the "terrible 2s," with their tantrums, defiance, unprovoked aggression, and noncompliance with adults. Toddlers also do the unexpected, such as standing on tables, rather than sitting on chairs, wearing grocery baskets on their heads, and objecting loudly when asked to play with fingerpaints. Teachers can easily become exasperated with their efforts to correct toddlers or to teach them to conform to standard rules.

Teachers who become frustrated with infants' and toddlers' behavior usually have inappropriate expectations for very young children. Infants have immature nervous and digestive systems, and their varying internal states influence how they feel and behave on any given day. For many babies, crying is a necessary release of tension and does not reflect on the quality of care they are receiving.

The teacher who sees only the negative aspects of a toddler's behavior is looking for competencies appropriate to preschoolers. The toddler's understanding of the world and knowledge of other people is quite different from that of an adult or an older child. Furthermore, most toddlers have limited comprehension of language, so they cannot be expected to respond to spoken requests or verbal explanations.

By looking at the world through the eyes of an infant or toddler, the teacher can come to understand the *reasons* that children behave as they do. This allows the teacher to work *with* rather than against the child, set appropriate expectations, and enjoy the delightful aspects of caring for infants and toddlers.

Examining Reasons for Behavior

When infants and toddlers act in ways that teachers do not like, the teachers often label the children's behavior as *misbehavior*. Actually, however, most behavior of very young children, including behavior teachers like as well as behavior they dislike, occurs in reaction to the immediate situation surrounding the children. Teachers (and other adults) tend to attribute too much intentionality to infants and toddlers. If infants' and toddlers' behavior is considered to be intentional, teachers feel that they must *react*, usually negatively, in order to teach the children right from wrong or to preserve their own authority. Sensitive caregiving of infants and toddlers demands that teachers inhibit their initial reactions, think about the situation from the child's point of view, and then *respond* in a positive manner that helps the child gain social and self-understanding.

Some of the exasperating behavior of infants and toddlers and possible reasons for their behavior are listed in Table 7.1, along with guidelines for positive responses by teachers.

Setting Limits for Behavior

Although infants and toddlers should not be expected to follow a large number of rules or very complicated rules, they do need to have some limits established for them. A good basic set of rules for behavior is as follows:

1.   A child cannot intentionally hurt another person.
2.   A child cannot intentionally hurt or endanger him- or herself.
3.   A child cannot intentionally damage classroom equipment or toys.

In all other situations, children's behavior should not be corrected and they should not be told "No" or "Don't." Infants will almost never be corrected because very little of their behavior can be considered *intentional*. With toddlers, teachers must learn to separate annoying behavior from destructive behavior or behavior that intentionally hurts someone. For example, toddlers should be allowed to run in the classroom . . . as long as they are not endangering themselves by running into an area in which there are a lot of toys on the floor or hurting other children by repeatedly running into them and knocking them down. It is also acceptable for infants and toddlers to use loud voices inside the classroom.

Table 7.1.   Why infants and toddlers behave the way they do

When a child:	He or she may be:	And the teacher's best response is:
Pulls another baby's hair Rolls over on top of another baby Pushes a truck over another child's body Throws a toy	Experimenting—trying to find out how the world works	Use a sense of humor Use redirection to keep children involved in play Use responsive teaching to reinforce learning from the experience
Pulls on a toy another baby is holding Stands on another toddler's foot Knocks down a tower built by another child	Unaware his or her behavior is troublesome to someone else Trying to help	Use patience Give a brief explanation of the problem from the other child's point of view Use redirection to keep children involved in play
Uses bad language	Repeating behavior observed in others	Ignore it
Persistently uses toys in dangerous or destructive ways (e.g., throwing toys, standing on breakable toys, pounding one toy with another)	Seeking adult attention	At the moment, remove the toys and work harder to make other activities more attractive (e.g., sing, blow bubbles, dance) Overall, increase attention when children are behaving positively
Takes toy away from another child	Wanting to play with the toy	Closely supervise and redirect before the toy changes hands Involve both children in play with interesting toys Buy more toys so there are several replicates of those toys that children like

(continued)

Table 7.1.   *(continued)*

When a child:	He or she may be:	And the teacher's best response is:
Refuses to do what the teacher asks	Unable to understand the directions Testing his or her power	Make sure directions are clear and specific Limit directions to situations in which the child *must* follow them Follow through whenever a direction is given Withdraw from conflict and avoid viewing the child's behavior as a challenge to authority Use more creative approaches to gain the child's cooperation
Occasionally hits, kicks, pushes, pinches, pulls hair, or bites other children in anger	Feeling hurt and upset	Stop the aggression and separate the children Mildly correct the child by saying "No" or "That hurts" or "Touch gently" Work harder to make activities fun and interesting
Frequently hits, kicks, pushes, pinches, pulls hair, or bites in anger, especially toward one particular child	Developing a hostile and antisocial approach to others	Stop the aggression and separate the children Increase supervision and keep the children apart as much as possible Intervene to prevent aggression whenever possible Keep track of the child's behavior Increase efforts to involve the aggressive child in play and teach appropriate social behavior through positive attention and affection

(continued)

Table 7.1. (continued)

When a child:	He or she may be:	And the teacher's best response is:
Has an occasional temper tantrum	Frustrated or not feeling well	Make sure the child is safe and stay nearby Comfort and support the child when he or she is calm
Has frequent tantrums or episodes of head banging or breath holding	Seeking adult attention Developing a dangerous pattern of self-injurious behavior	Make sure the child is safe Monitor the child carefully but from a distance Ignore the behavior until the child is calm Keep other children busy elsewhere Keep track of the child's behavior and inform parents, especially if the child has other special needs

However, if the noise level becomes too high, teachers need to encourage quiet activities by changing the available toys, starting to read a story, or playing quiet music.

These rules are simple and basic enough to apply to children with disabilities and developmental delays as well as to typically developing children. Furthermore, by reducing the classroom rules to absolute basics, teachers can avoid the correction, nagging, and lecturing of children that is as frustrating as it is ineffective. Instead, teachers can spend their time and energy encouraging appropriate behavior by providing an environment that meets the interests and abilities of infants and toddlers, by offering children choices among interesting activities, and by working to promote each child's active involvement with toys, people, and play activities. An active, interested child is much less likely to display problem behavior than a bored, frustrated child.

A TOOLBOX FOR TEACHERS OF INFANTS AND TODDLERS

Understanding the reasons that infants and toddlers sometimes behave in troublesome ways helps teachers avoid overreacting when they do not like children's behavior. The next step is for teachers to learn to overreact to behavior they *do* like! Teachers need to recognize that their responses to infants and toddlers have a major influence on children's learning.

Therefore, teachers must learn to respond enthusiastically to behavior they want to encourage and respond minimally to behavior they want to discourage. Guiding infants and particularly toddlers toward appropriate social behavior requires considerable self-control on the part of teachers. A "top 10" list of responses to children's undesirable behavior that teachers should avoid and suggestions for responses to use instead appears as Table 7.2.

In the following sections, techniques that help teachers guide their responses to children's behavior and the situations in which these techniques can most effectively be used are described. All of these techniques require teachers to have considerable control over their own behavior so they can analyze a situation and respond appropriately, rather than simply react to children's behavior.

Time-In: A Background of Positive Acceptance and Love

What it is: Positive and affectionate interactions between teachers and
   children
When to use it: Every day, all of the time
What children learn: That they are valued and accepted and that teachers
   like them

Time-in is the necessary background to all other teaching techniques and, in fact, to all quality child care. Teachers need to be active participants at all times with children in ways that encourage the children in their care to be actively involved with the toys, play activities, and daily living routines in the classroom. A child who is not actively involved or not interested in continuing involvement is not motivated to do what adults ask. It is the desire to gain the approval of people who are important and obviously care about the child that is behind a child's efforts to learn appropriate social behavior.

A visitor to an infant-toddler classroom will notice time-in primarily through the feeling of warmth and acceptance communicated to children by teachers and a sense that teachers and children are enjoying what they are doing. This does not mean that there are never any upset children or conflicts, but when disturbances occur, teachers respond to the children with calmness and caring.

Time-in is also evident in frequent interactions between teachers and children, including gentle, affectionate touching and talking. In a classroom in which time-in is the basic approach to teaching, there will be many more positive than negative interactions between adults and children and among children. In addition, both children and teachers will be actively involved in play or a daily living routine and will appear to be calm and content.

The positive interactions teachers have with children must be genuine reflections of their feelings. If teachers praise children frequently but their praise is intended as manipulation, children will know this. Time-in is effective only when teachers truly care about and enjoy the children in their care.

Table 7.2.   Top 10 responses to avoid using when working with young children

Do not . . .	Instead . . .
Focus attention on children who are doing things you do *not* want them to do	Get involved and excited with children who are doing things you like
Interpret children's behavior as if they are specifically trying to ruin your day	Recognize that children behave in ways that meet their own immediate needs
Tell children how *you* feel about their behavior	Encourage children to feel good about themselves
Shout, scold, nag, or use a negative tone of voice with children	Sing, laugh, smile, play, and have fun with children
Label children with negative-sounding nicknames, even just for fun or even if parents use such nicknames	Build on children's strengths and talk to them about their positive characteristics
Correct children unless their actions are dangerous or destructive	Brainstorm and use creative ways to redirect children toward positive activities
Be afraid to touch and hug children	Show affection in a lot of little ways
Say negative things about children "over their heads"	Treat every child with respect
Threaten children	Give *real* choices when they exist
Allow children's behavior to make you feel angry or frustrated	Get lots of sleep and enjoy relaxing and recreational activities in the evenings

Redirection: Preventing Problems

What it is: Refocusing a child's attention in a positive way

When to use it: When a child appears to be getting bored, an activity is getting too messy or loud, or a child's behavior is escalating toward a destructive or dangerous action

What children learn: Exploration and involvement are more interesting and enjoyable than aggression or other dangerous or destructive behavior

Infants and toddlers are easily distracted by a new and interesting toy or activity, especially if an adult appears to find the toy entertaining. Teachers can use this appealing characteristic as a preventive approach to almost all situations in which aggression or other dangerous or destructive behavior is likely to occur. It is crucial that redirection be used *before* any problem behavior occurs. Redirection should never be used *after* a child has broken a rule.

Teachers must try to intervene and redirect in order to prevent aggression and to interrupt situations in which a child's actions appear to be esca-

lating toward dangerous or destructive behavior. Teachers must not watch and wait until a rule is broken so that they can provide a consequence to the behavior. With an infant or toddler, it is always better to interrupt the child before a rule is broken. Infants and toddlers, including those children with disabilities or developmental delays, learn most effectively in a positive environment. Redirection helps keep children actively and positively involved in play and learning activities in which they are practicing appropriate social behavior and receiving positive teacher attention.

Redirection requires teachers to be extremely vigilant and alert to all of the activities around them and to *prevent* conflicts whenever possible. For example, teachers should always try to intervene *before* one child hits another child, takes a toy that another child is using, or climbs onto the rocking boat in front of another toddler. Redirection is also helpful to separate children when they have congregated in a large group and are so close together that their personal space is being violated. Redirection requires the presentation of a positive alternative, rather than nagging and correction (e.g., "Let's make a tent" rather than "Don't cover Julie with that cloth" or "I'm going to read a book over here. Angela and Chris, come see!" rather than "Let's break it up here!"). Thus, in addition to being very alert, teachers must see the possibilities in children's activities and redirect them creatively. Interrupting children's activity by putting toys away where children cannot reach them is not redirection. Instead, if a group's activity seems to be heading in a negative direction, the teacher must think like an infant or toddler to find a variation on the activity that is fun and interesting but less problematic.

Infants and toddlers are not limited by knowledge of how toys are supposed to be used; therefore, they tend to use toys in ways teachers may consider inappropriate. Unusual ways of using toys are not troublesome unless children's play is becoming dangerous, destructive, or aggressive. Teachers must be careful not to redirect just because children are playing unconventionally. Redirection should be saved for situations in which a teacher believes a child could be hurt or something could be broken.

When using redirection, teachers need to focus on the new toy or activity, rather than the activity or behavior that teachers want to stop. Teachers also need to be sure that they have the child's attention before redirecting. Thus, a teacher wishing to redirect a child from jumping up and down on a doll could say, "Josie, my pizza is ready to go in the oven. Come help me" in order to encourage the child to leave the potentially destructive activity that he or she is doing and begin a new, constructive activity. Teachers should not refer to the behavior they want to interrupt (e.g., "Stop that jumping" or "That poor doll" would be inappropriate comments). If the child does not move to the suggested activity or another activity within about 5 seconds, the teacher should follow through, gently and positively, to move the child to a new activity. Once the child has shifted to a new activity, the teacher should try to stay involved with the child for a few minutes to demonstrate that he or she really wants and values the child's participation in the activity.

Mild Correction for Mild Problems

What it is: Interruption of aggressive, dangerous, or destructive behavior, accompanied by a firm but brief explanation

When to use it: When the teacher has missed the opportunity to use redirection

What children learn: Teachers disapprove of certain types of behavior

Despite the use of careful, creative redirection by teachers, some conflicts and potentially dangerous situations will arise in the classroom. When these situations occur, teachers need to be prepared to respond calmly, quickly, and consistently to the conflicts. It is most important for teachers to separate children who are entangled in physical conflict or ensure the safety of a child who has become involved in a dangerous situation. Thus, physical intervention is needed. Teachers must gently but firmly move a child out of the situation. At the same time, teachers need to provide a friendly but firm verbal correction. With very young children, a simple but firmly spoken "No" said just once is adequate. As children gain more of an understanding of language and social situations, correction should be positively phrased, telling the child the appropriate behavior (e.g., "Touch your friends gently" or "Toys are for playing, not throwing"). Teachers cannot correct children effectively from across the room. Thus, teachers should never shout "No" or "Stop" to a child from a distance, but rather should move quickly to the child and call for his or her attention before correcting the inappropriate behavior.

The message in mild correction is conveyed largely through tone of voice and body language. When correcting children, teachers need to avoid making direct eye contact and should speak abruptly and firmly but not harshly. Any physical contact between teachers and children during corrections should be minimal, rather than the usual cuddly and warm contact teachers share with children. The entire interaction surrounding a correction should last only a few seconds.

Usually, a child being corrected will be moved to a different area away from the conflict or troublesome situation. He or she should always be located near a teacher and within easy reach of toys. In other words, a child should not simply be moved to the middle of a room in which there is nothing to do and no play activity available. Teachers must think in terms of moving a child *to* another activity, rather than just away from trouble. No further mention of the situation should be made, and the child should be greeted by other teachers as if nothing has happened. Also, the teacher who corrected the child should make a special effort to notice and play with that child within a few minutes of the episode, without making any reference to that event. This will demonstrate to the child that it was the particular behavior or situation that made the teacher unhappy, rather than the child him- or herself.

Planned Ignoring: The Unexpected *Lack* of Response

What it is: Brief withdrawal of teachers' attention from a child

When to use it: When a child is behaving in a negative way that is generally guaranteed to attract teacher attention—having a temper tantrum, for example—but is not endangering him- or herself or others

What children learn: That the most reliable way to get teachers' attention is by being involved in classroom activities

Infants and toddlers need—and deserve—a lot of adult attention. For the most part, they are not able to play on their own, and their social interactions with other children are brief and infrequent. Furthermore, infants and toddlers are very responsive to affectionate physical contact with adults, which delivers a lot of messages that they are not yet able to comprehend in language. Therefore, teachers should pay a lot of individual attention and show a lot of affection to all of the children in their care.

Nevertheless, there are some times when children should *not* receive adult attention. Sometimes children are doing something that teachers do not like, but the action is not hurting anyone or anything and is not likely to become dangerous or destructive. In such a situation, teachers should avoid nagging children to stop the action and should not actively redirect them. Instead, teachers need to ignore children's behavior, giving their conspicuous attention to other children who are involved in more appropriate play. For example, a child who is kicking the wall or climbing on toddler-size furniture can be ignored until he or she discovers that no one is paying attention. Then, when the child begins doing something more constructive, teachers can show their interest and affection.

Similarly, when children have frequent temper tantrums or exhibit other forms of angry behavior that are not directed at another child, but rather appear to be efforts to gain the teachers' attention, the best response is no response—until the child has calmed down and returned to involvement in an activity. At that time, no mention needs to be made of the child's tantrum or anger; instead, the child should be welcomed to the group and given a big dose of teacher attention. Discussion of angry as well as happy feelings is a necessary and important part of teaching infants and toddlers, but such conversations are best saved for less emotionally intense situations or when the child's anger is in response to a social situation, rather than an attention-getting effort. When a child appears to feel angry because another child has taken away a toy or has interfered with his or her play, this is a good time to label the child's feelings.

It is most appropriate to use planned ignoring with children who frequently use tantrums or other angry outbursts to manipulate others. If a child who is normally calm and in control of his or her behavior has a tantrum, teachers should stay nearby and provide support and comfort to the child as needed. Such an episode may be a sign of illness or stress in the usually cheerful and active child and can be startling and even frightening to the child. Therefore, an expression of respect and care toward the child is needed from the sensitive teacher. It is when a child's tantrums become frequent and purposeful, with the intent to attract attention or get one's own way, that planned ignoring should be used.

Planned ignoring is not as easy as it sounds. To use planned ignoring, teachers must avoid looking directly at the child and must show no facial expression that indicates their feelings about the child's behavior or actions. Also, all teachers must work together when ignoring the child, so there must be quick and quiet communication among the teachers in the classroom. Teachers must also try as much as possible to redirect other children away from the child being ignored, because the attention of peers can be just as valuable to a child as the attention of teachers. All teachers need to stay very busy and actively involved in play with other children, saying nothing either *to* or *about* the child who is being ignored.

Within a few seconds of the time during which the child stops his or her action, one teacher should go to the child and touch or talk to him or her in a positive way. This teacher should say nothing about the child's previous inappropriate behavior or about the fact that the child has stopped behaving in an annoying or inappropriate way. Instead, the teacher needs to comment on the child's current activity or, if necessary, positively redirect the child's attention and activity. If the result of the child's negative behavior is a mess that needs to be cleaned up (e.g., the child was spreading glue on the table instead of on paper), the teacher needs to direct the child, in a friendly fashion, to clean up the mess, following through to be sure the child helps with cleanup. The purpose of planned ignoring is lost if teachers refer to the undesirable behavior after it has stopped. Therefore, using planned ignoring requires a lot of self-control on the part of teachers.

Planned ignoring can only be effective in classrooms in which time-in is used all of the time. If children are accustomed to being ignored, then planned ignoring will not be any different from their usual experience. Ignoring children's behavior needs to be an uncommon event, used only for specific instances of undesirable behavior that are not dangerous but appear to be intentional on the part of the child and aimed at gaining attention.

Following Through: Teaching Children to Follow Directions

What it is: Working together with children to achieve a common goal
When to use it: Any time a teacher gives a direction that *must* be followed
What children learn: The pleasure of cooperating with a teacher in a task

Infants are not usually expected to follow adults' directions, but as soon as children become toddlers, people often think of them as noncompliant, doing only what they please, rather than doing what teachers or other adults ask of them. However, when teachers give directions that toddlers understand, toddlers actually are very willing to go along with their requests.

It is important for teachers to monitor their own requests to children. Many teachers use far too many instructions, give vague and general directions, and use language that is too complex for young children to understand. Teachers must also put themselves in the children's place and give directions in ways that emphasize goals the children share with teachers. To give children practice in following directions, teachers can ask for a "high five"; they are guaranteed to get cooperation!

There are times when teachers are leading play activities—as in active play games, for example—when giving directions is important and necessary. In these cases, teachers need to accompany their directions with actions so that children can imitate the teachers and are not required to understand all of the words. However, many play activities are better conducted by using descriptive language (e.g., the techniques of self-talk and parallel talk, described in Chapter 6), rather than directions. Describing actions of other children and teachers is a responsive teaching technique that focuses children's attention on the connection between ongoing events and language, and this technique provides many natural opportunities for children to imitate sounds and words and participate in conversations at a level comfortable for them.

When teachers want to enhance children's play, they need to give instructions in a way that makes it clear to children that they are not required to comply. Gently phrased suggestions (e.g., "What about . . ." or "Let's try . . ." or "What would happen if . . .") are better than directives (e.g., "Put it here" or "Do it this way"). The technique of following through is not generally needed when teachers are leading play activities. In fact, teachers' efforts to encourage children to do *everything* they want is likely to make children defiant and oppositional.

At certain times, however, teachers give children directions that *must* be followed. For example, children do need to have their diapers changed and leave the playground when the other children do. If children get into dangerous situations, they need to respond to teachers' instructions in order to get out of those situations. Also, there are many daily living situations in which teachers should expect children to comply with their requests. Children should help pick up toys to get ready for new activities; toddlers should practice dressing themselves in socks, shoes, and coats to go outside; and children should cooperate during mealtime. When regular, predictable daily routines are established and followed, infants and toddlers generally meet these expectations quite happily. Children are less compliant when the requirements change from day to day or moment to moment, based on how teachers are feeling or which teacher is present.

Even in a well-organized and relaxed environment, however, there will be times when children do not follow a direction that a teacher thinks is important, and situations will arise in which the child's refusal interferes with the activities of other children. During these times, teachers should use following through. First, the teacher must make sure the child is aware that the instruction is intended for him or her and understands what to do. Thus, the teacher needs to address the child by name to get the child's attention and should rephrase the request, using simpler words and gestures. Unless the child is in a dangerous situation, the teacher should give the child about 5 seconds to begin to comply with the request.

If a child shows no signs of following the teacher's direction or runs in the opposite direction, the teacher needs to move closer to the child and repeat the direction, using the same simple expressions and gestures as before. At the same time as the direction is repeated, the teacher can begin to move the child gently but insistently through the task. Often, a child will begin to cooperate with only a gentle nudge from a teacher. If the child does begin to cooperate, the teacher should step away and allow the child to complete the job him- or herself.

If the child continues to resist direction or becomes more active in his or her resistance, the teacher should ignore any behavior that is not related to accomplishing the task. Thus, if the child says "No," squirms and wrestles with the teacher, collapses in a heap on the floor, or cries, the teacher should continue to move the child gently and calmly through the task until it is completed. The child's participation is not required. Once the task is finished, the teacher should say "Thank you" in a friendly and cheerful tone of voice, even if the teacher did all of the work by him- or herself. The teacher needs to maintain involvement with the child once the task is done by doing a fun activity with the child or by redirecting the child to an alternative activity. If the child's resistance turns into a temper tantrum, the teacher can use planned ignoring until the child recovers control.

To follow through effectively, teachers must listen to themselves talk and be aware of when they are giving instructions and when those instructions need to be followed. Teachers also need to be aware of children's responses to their directions so that they can say an honest and meaningful "Thank you" and offer a hug and a kiss when children do what teachers want the first time they ask. If teachers issue a lot of meaningless and unimportant directions, children will get the (accurate) impression that it is up to them whether to comply. Then, teachers will have to work hard when they really want compliance. When teachers are responsive, respectful, and encouraging, they will not have to use the technique of following through very often.

HANDLING COMMON SITUATIONS

Teachers of infants and toddlers need to be prepared to handle a number of difficult situations involving the behavior of children in their care, including fights over toys, persistent crying, biting, and hostile aggression. In addition, socially withdrawn children who avoid interacting with other teachers and children also require patience and support from teachers.

Fights over Toys

The most common problem teachers of infants and toddlers identify is when one child grabs a toy away from another child. Unless accompanied by a hit, push, kick, or other physical attack, toy grabbing does not endanger the child who is left without a toy. Infants and toddlers do not understand the concept of sharing; therefore, children who take toys or try to take toys from others should not be told to "share." However, even young toddlers can begin to grasp the idea of taking turns. If a teacher is close by when one child takes a toy from another, he or she can gently remove the toy and say, "Angela's. Your turn next" and return the toy to the first child. It is also helpful to find a similar toy for the child who did the grabbing and who probably just wants to play.

Teachers should not assume an aggressive intent whenever one child takes a toy from another child. Most infants and toddlers have not yet learned how the world looks through another person's eyes; thus, they do not know that the child who has lost the toy feels hurt and upset. Teachers whose primary experience is with older children sometimes approach conflicts among children with the attitude that children need to learn to work out their own conflicts. These teachers may react to fights over toys with attempts to discuss social behavior with children. Although this approach can be helpful for older children, infants and toddlers simply do not have the cognitive or communication skills required to understand concepts of right and wrong.

Teachers should not make a big fuss over toy taking. Teachers should never follow a child across a room to retrieve a toy that the child grabbed out of another child's hands. Instead, teachers should be alert to children's activities at all times and work to *prevent* fights over toys. Teachers can successfully prevent fights by being constantly alert to children's focus of attention. When they see a child reach for a toy that someone else is holding, teachers can physically block the child's attempt to take the toy and quickly redirect this child to an alternative toy. Teachers who try to hasten the process of a developing child's skill in seeing the perspective of other children by nagging or scolding about sharing will only succeed in setting up an unpleasant situation for everyone in the classroom. Teaching about sharing and other children's perspectives is best accomplished at times when there is no conflict and as a positive aspect of play with others. The concepts of giving, receiving, and turn taking can be incorporated into many different play activities.

Often, fights over toys occur when there are not enough attractive toys available for the children or when teachers are not fully involved as active participants in the children's play. If fights over toys begin to occur frequently, teachers need to introduce some new, different toys, begin a new activity, and increase their own enthusiasm and energy to encourage involvement of all of the children.

Persistent Crying

Crying is an important means of communication for infants and toddlers, who have few truly reliable ways to signal their needs. Usually, crying communicates an unmet need, and so a crying infant should be responded to quickly, calmly, and sensitively. Teachers who know infants well can usually identify the reason for a baby's crying very quickly and fix the problem by shifting the baby's position, providing a new focus for the baby's attention, giving the baby a bottle, changing the baby's diaper, or settling the baby down for a nap. Although feeding is a reliable way to stop babies' crying, it should not be the first choice unless it is clear to teachers that the baby is actually hungry. If the baby who is crying has eaten less than 2 hours ago, teachers should work to find other ways of soothing the baby because it is easy to overfeed a fussy baby.

Babies differ in their amount of crying. Some babies almost never cry, and teachers know instantly that something is definitely wrong when these babies do cry. Other babies seem to have a need to cry for a period of time each day. This tendency may reflect immaturity of the infant's central nervous system, a need to release tension, or simply a greater sensitivity to internal discomforts. Severe, persistent crying is termed *colic* and usually diminishes after 3 or 4 months of age.

When a baby cries persistently, teachers need to be sure that there is nothing really wrong. Then, if the crying continues, teachers should not feel guilty or responsible for the crying, nor should teachers work frantically to try to stop the baby's crying. Crying *is* stressful and unpleasant, but teachers need to remain calm and patient, or they will contribute further to the high stress level in the classroom.

Persistent crying tends to be less common after the child's first birthday, as children learn other ways to communicate their needs and gain a wider range of possibilities for play. However, some toddlers cry a great deal when they first attend a classroom program. It is easy for teachers to feel sorry for these children, give them a lot of special attention, or even hold and carry them for long periods of the day. A better strategy to cope with children's distress is to empathize with the child but focus on the adjustment period as a time of learning and growth for the child. When viewed this way, teachers can see children's efforts to overcome distress as a sign of strength, rather than concentrating on the crying as a weakness.

At times, children who have seemed perfectly well adjusted to child care may enter a period of crying and distress. This may be associated with changes occurring in the classroom, such as the departure of a friend or favorite teacher, or with events occurring at home. It is not always necessary, or even helpful, for teachers to know the precise reason for a child's crying. Instead, as with the adjustment process, teachers can emphasize the child's efforts to overcome distress, rather than fretting over the cause of the crying.

In situations of persistent crying, teachers must themselves exercise great self-control, finding a way to provide comfort without rewarding the child's crying. Because toddlers are not skilled at describing or understanding the reasons for their feelings, teachers should not try to prompt them to talk about their distress, as would often be appropriate with older children. Instead, teachers can most successfully minimize persistent crying while still showing concern and caring if they continue to give positive attention to the *child*, rather than to the child's crying.

For example, the distressed child can be positioned next to the teacher, who can then use the technique of self-talk (see Chapter 6), describing his or her own actions with toys. The teacher can include the distressed child in this talk (e.g., "Now I'm putting a hat on Sarah") but should not demand the child's participation by asking questions, making requests, or insisting that the child play. As other children come near, the teacher can talk and play with them as well, providing many positive comments and a lot of affectionate touching. If children ask, "What's wrong with Sarah?" the teacher can reply in a matter-of-fact way, "She's feeling sad" and then continue play without looking at the child or otherwise devoting special attention to the fact that Sarah is crying. If the child shows signs of involvement or interest in the play activity, the teacher can gently respond to these overtures. It is important to allow the child to determine his or her own level of involvement and not interpret any small sign of decreased crying as a cue for elaborate praise and attention. Above all, teachers should avoid making reference to the child's crying (e.g., by making comments such as, "Thank you for not crying" or "Sarah's finally ready to play").

Using this approach, the crying child is not segregated or singled out, but rather is treated respectfully and allowed to choose between crying and involvement in play. In this way, teachers provide support and encouragement for children to learn to regulate their own emotions, rather than making children dependent on teachers whenever they are upset.

Biting

Biting, a primitive response to anger or frustration, is the most troublesome aspect of infant and toddler behavior. For babies and toddlers, much of life is centered in the mouth; they are just learning about food and its pleasures and are also experiencing a good deal of discomfort in their mouths as they begin teething. In fact, some children bite only at times when their mouths are tender and sore as a result of teething. If a child who bites is teething, teachers should keep a good supply of chew toys available to ease the pain of teething.

Children may also be susceptible to anger and frustration if they are hungry or overly tired. It is important for teachers to keep track of the moods and behavior of all of the children in their classroom. A child who refuses breakfast and later appears to be especially irritable might need to be offered a mid-morning snack. A child who has been ill or has not been sleeping well at night also may be particularly prone to aggression, including biting. Because infants and toddlers are unable to express their feelings and moods verbally, their teachers must become particularly good at "reading" children's behavioral cues and responding to each child's individual needs.

The best way to handle child bites is, of course, to prevent them from happening by being alert to children's activities and removing children from difficult situations before they become so angry or frustrated that they lash out at others. Another important preventive measure is to avoid letting children crowd together in a single activity area.

No matter how hard teachers try, however, child bites will occasionally occur in any group of infants or toddlers. It is important for all teachers to know exactly how to handle the situation when one child bites another child. It is also extremely important to avoid exaggerating the situation, calling everyone's attention to the incident, and focusing all of the classroom activities on the child who has bitten another child. These reactions will only reinforce the action of the child who has done the biting and demonstrate to the rest of the children that biting is a sure way to become the center of attention.

Many teachers who observe child bites consider it their duty to lecture the child who bites in order to make him or her understand that biting is wrong and that it really hurts the other child. Unfortunately, infants and toddlers do not learn about behavior from lectures. It is also not useful—or even legal—to bite a child back or to place an unpleasant-tasting substance on the child's tongue.

Because biting is a typical response to frustration in infants and toddlers, the most appropriate way to deal with biting is the same response used for other occasionally occurring forms of aggression. Teachers should, therefore, respond to biting with a mild correction, including a brief but firm, "No biting!"—a sure sign of disapproval that even the youngest child can understand. After correcting the child, teachers' attention needs to be obviously directed toward other children for a minute or two without any mention of biting or misbehavior. Unless a child bites frequently, it is not necessary to take any other action in response to biting. However, if a child appears to be making a habit of biting whenever he or she is frustrated or as an effort to attract teachers' or children's attention, teachers should begin to keep a record of the frequency and pattern of biting. Often, biting only occurs in response to particular situations or during certain times of the day. The only truly effective measure to reduce biting is to teach the child more positive ways of interacting with others. Teachers need to increase their vigilance and also focus on actively teaching social interaction and communication skills to the child who bites. If a child develops a pattern of frequent biting, it may be necessary for one teacher to shadow that child for a week or two, interrupting any attempts at biting. If a frequent biter is prevented from biting for 2 weeks, usually he or she will develop new ways of coping with frustration.

It is most important for teachers to remain calm any time one child bites another child. When teachers get upset, the situation becomes more upsetting to the child who has been bitten and more rewarding to the child who is biting. The child who was bitten should be taken to another area in which there is running water to have the bite washed with disinfectant soap and water and to receive cuddling and comfort. Teachers should wear gloves to tend to bites, as they would for any first aid treatment. Usually children's bites will not break the skin, and the bites are, therefore, not dangerous. However, bites do hurt, and they look painful. It is important, though, not to give too much sympathy and attention to the child who has been bitten. Some children become willing victims of biting because they enjoy the attention they receive when hurt; these children may even place their fingers or hands in the mouths of children who are known to bite occasionally.

Teachers sometimes find it difficult to build a positive and affectionate relationship with a child who bites others. Because biting is unpleasant and causes a lot of trouble, teachers may allow their dislike of the behavior of biting to cloud their feelings for the child who bites. It is important for teachers to demonstrate to the child that his or her *behavior* is the problem. At all other times, teachers need to be just as loving and affectionate with children who bite as with all other children.

When one child bites another child, other children may imitate the biting behavior or pretend to be biting. These attempted or mock bites should be answered with redirection or mild correction and increased efforts by teachers to actively involve all of the children in interesting play activities. The best solution to an outbreak of biting is to keep children busy at activities they like to do, avoid frustrating situations, and increase the rate of positive teacher attention for positive child behavior.

Another difficult situation arises when no one sees a bite occur. In this case, unless a teacher is absolutely certain who is responsible for the biting, teachers have no choice but to simply treat the bite and the bitten child and do nothing about the one who did the biting. Above all, teachers should avoid going on a fact-finding mission, such as asking other children or the child with the bite mark who was responsible for the bite; infants and toddlers are not always reliable witnesses.

Teachers need to keep track of children's bites, just as any injury or other event that involves a child's health or well-being is also recorded. It is particularly important that the teacher who will be greeting parents at departure time knows exactly how the incident happened and the type of treatment given so he or she can explain the bite and the situation to parents. It is not necessary, and it is, in fact, a violation of classroom confidentiality to tell parents who did the biting. While empathizing with parents' concern, teachers should explain to parents that biting is a typical behavior in infants and toddlers and therefore is not as serious a problem as it is in older children. Usually parents will want to know how teachers plan to prevent future bites. This is not a good time to explain responsive teaching and its emphasis on children's positive behavior. Instead, teachers should actively listen to parents' concerns and anxieties, be supportive and understanding, and agree that everything possible will be done to prevent biting from occurring in the future.

Frequent or Hostile Aggression

Occasionally a toddler will be persistently—and hostilely—aggressive to the point that other children's enjoyment of the classroom is being affected. An equally difficult situation arises when a child frequently acts in ways that are so dangerous or destructive that they interfere with other classroom activities. When this starts to happen, teachers should immediately begin recording these instances of aggression or dangerous situations. This record should include time of day, type of activity, and other children involved in the incidents. Using a week's record of the child's behavior, all of the classroom staff can then discuss the problem and determine if the aggressive or dangerous behavior is occurring in response to particular situations (e.g., always immediately before lunch or during small group time), seems to be directed toward a particular child or children, or is occurring in a more general pattern.

Often, the most effective way to help an aggressive child involves changing teachers' behavior, the classroom environment, or the daily schedule in order to give the child more opportunities to receive rewards for behaving positively. If the record of aggressive episodes indicates a pattern that is tied to time of day, crowding, or some other factor, teachers can find a way to prevent the child from being present in that situation. For example, if aggression occurs late in the afternoon after other children's parents start arriving to take their children home, one teacher might arrange for a small group of the later-departing children to play outside on the playground during that time.

In most cases, heightened teacher supervision is the best solution to persistent aggression. It is important to prevent aggression by interrupting the child's negative behavior, moving the child out of crowds, and keeping the aggressive child and any frequent targets of aggression separated from each other. For a while, one teacher may need to closely monitor the aggressive child at all times, redirecting him or her frequently *before* trouble begins in order to provide opportunities for involvement in other activities that result in the child receiving positive attention from the teacher.

If teachers believe that a child needs extra help to replace aggression with more positive social behavior, they need to work to find an approach that suits the individual child. It is not effective to use one response to aggression for all children. Although the common solution in many classrooms is to use time-out, a brief separation from ongoing activities, this technique is usually not helpful. Most children who are involved in a lot of aggressive or destructive activity do not experience very much time-in, so time-out is not an obvious difference to them. Furthermore, maneuvering a child into time-out often involves so much teacher attention that it serves as a reward for aggressive behavior, rather than serving as a deterrent.

A more positive way of intervening to change a child's behavior is to think about the outcome desired, which is usually friendly, or at least neutral, social behavior. Teachers need to identify ways of encouraging, noticing, and actively rewarding the child's nonaggressive behavior, even if the desired behavior is brief and infrequent. Some children may respond to an obvious reward, such as stickers given with a hug or frequent applause during the day. Toddlers have no sense of time and short memories, so delivering stickers according to a schedule (e.g., a sticker for 30 minutes without an aggressive episode) is not particularly helpful. Instead, each teacher might be assigned to give the child four stickers each day during times that they choose. The point of giving an obvious reward is simply to draw the child's attention to the fact that teachers like positive social behavior. It should not be necessary for the child to exhibit wonderful behavior, such as giving up three consecutive turns on the rocking boat, to be rewarded. Simply showing up at a teacher's side without pushing anyone out of the way would be enough for the child to deserve a reward.

Whatever approach is selected, it is important that *all* teachers adopt the approach and use it consistently. One teacher should never make a unilateral decision to try to change a child's behavior, nor should the child receive inconsistent responses from different teachers. It is also important to continue recording instances of aggression or dangerous behavior in order to determine whether the actions teachers are taking are actually working. However, any approach should be used consistently for at least a week before evaluating its effectiveness, because young children often push against new limits before happily accepting them.

The Socially Withdrawn Child

Some infants and toddlers, like some older children and adults, appear to be almost painfully shy. They tend to avoid close contact with other children and sometimes even resist attention from adults. Although they do not cause problems for teachers, these children are as much at risk for long-term social problems as children who are highly aggressive; therefore, they also deserve special care and concern from teachers.

It is important to differentiate the truly withdrawn child from the one who simply likes to "case out" a situation before getting involved. The child who is slow to warm up to others may spend the first half hour of the day alone, on the edges of activities, or intensely watching others play. However, this child eventually will become actively involved and interested in play, begin communicating with teachers, and move freely around the room.

A socially withdrawn child is also different from one who likes to observe what others are doing. Infants and toddlers can learn a lot from watching others, and some children like to watch first and try activities for themselves later. Children who are observers usually watch intently and show interest in the ongoing activity, whereas socially withdrawn children avoid any area in which other children are congregated. Often, withdrawn children also have difficulty involving themselves in play and may spend much of their time in transition or staring vacantly into space.

Truly withdrawn children can easily be overlooked in a group. They may never cause any problems that draw attention to themselves, and they may not initiate interactions with teachers, even if they need care or attention. Therefore, teachers need to be very alert to the patterns of behavior of all of the children in their care so that they notice and discuss the child who has difficulty becoming involved in the social activities of the classroom as well as give attention to the more assertive and aggressive children.

This concern is especially important in an inclusive child care program. If a child is socially withdrawn in addition to having a disability or developmental delay, this combination may create problems at later ages when other children are more selective about their social partners. Children who are socially withdrawn may also have difficulty communicating and acquiring spoken language at the typical rate. A communication delay may then become a secondary disabling condition for a child who already experiences other developmental challenges.

Observing a socially withdrawn child's behavior closely over several days is the first step in helping the child. These observations will often reveal a pattern of preference for certain types of toys or activities or a tendency to play near a certain teacher or near one or more of the children. Detecting these preferences gives sensitive teachers a place to start helping the child become more comfortable in social situations.

Working with the socially withdrawn child requires patience and love. Such children generally do not respond well to the types of positive attention-giving strategies that other children enjoy because socially withdrawn children do not want to be the center of attention. Teachers must focus on building a strong and caring relationship with children as well as enhancing their ability to communicate. These serve as the foundation that allows children to form other relationships on their own. Often, teachers' efforts with socially withdrawn children will not have obvious effects on a short-term basis, which can be discouraging to teachers. Nevertheless, the establishment of positive relationships with adults and the ability to communicate needs and thoughts are crucial to children's later social competence. Teachers can help children move toward greater confidence in themselves and trust in other people.

ENCOURAGING PROSOCIAL BEHAVIOR

The term *prosocial behavior* is used to describe all of the types of positive social behavior adults enjoy seeing in children: sharing toys, showing concern when another person is hurt or sad, allowing another person to go first, and showing affection. Although most infants and toddlers are not *antisocial,* in that they generally react to situations, rather than intentionally hurting another person or another person's feelings, infants and toddlers also are not obviously *prosocial.* In order to be actively prosocial, a child must be aware of the other person's point of view. For example, in order for Maggie to hold the picturebook she is looking at in a position where Jason can also see the pictures, she must have some idea of how the world looks through Jason's eyes. Similarly, when Terri falls on the playground, Damien must be aware that she feels pain or there is no reason for him to be concerned or to show caring.

Teachers can help children learn about their own and others' feelings by responding appropriately to children's displays of emotions and by labeling and describing feelings, including feelings that are negative as well as positive. When teachers respond dismissively to children's crying, such as saying, "That didn't hurt" when a child cries after a fall, or "Let's see a smile" when a child is sad or upset, they miss out on opportunities to teach children about feelings. A more empathetic and descriptive response (e.g., "You're sad that we're putting the trucks away") helps children connect their internal feelings with the words to express those feelings. Then, when teachers describe those same feelings in connection with another event and another child, there is an opportunity for children to understand that other people sometimes feel the same way they do. Therefore, teachers should be alert to children's displays of emotions and label them clearly.

Teachers should also demonstrate empathetic responses, rather than pitying ones, to children who have disabilities or special medical needs and during situations when any child is sad, angry, or hurt. Some children will imitate teachers' prosocial responses even before they gain a thorough knowledge of emotions, and the positive response children receive when they display concern or affection for other children will encourage them to remember and repeat that behavior. Play with dolls and stuffed animals provides opportunities for teachers to demonstrate prosocial behavior and encourage children to participate. In addition, teachers can use situations in which children are, perhaps unknowingly, showing prosocial-like behavior as opportunities for teaching. For example, if Tammy and Jacob are alternating turns of placing blocks on a tower, the teacher can comment on the fact that they are taking turns and make the alternation itself a game, thereby focusing the children's attention on the shared activity, rather than only on the blocks or the tower. Similarly, when Gloria gently pats or hugs Roberto, teachers can respond with more than comments such as "Ahhh . . ." and "Isn't that cute?" Instead, teachers can use parallel talk to describe for the children what is happening (e.g., "Gloria is showing Roberto that she likes him. Roberto feels happy now").

Prosocial behavior is most likely to develop when children are in a supportive and encouraging social environment, when adequate amounts of attractive materials are available, and when adults share their attention evenly and notice positive behavior on the part of children. The overall emotional climate of the classroom is the most important factor in encouraging the development of positive social behavior.

SUMMARY

The behavior of infants and toddlers is often challenging and can be frustrating to teachers. It is important that teachers' expectations for children's behavior match the reality of infants' and toddlers' cognitive and language abilities. Classroom rules must be few and simple, focusing on guiding children away from truly dangerous and destructive behavior. Teaching approaches for managing children's behavior are most effective when they emphasize the many positive acts of children, rather than the few negative ones.

Responsive teachers who are able to look at the world through the young child's perspective will also find much humor and creativity in the unconventional behavior of infants and toddlers. Furthermore, effective teachers are able to turn potentially troublesome situations into opportunities to teach children positive social interaction skills. Labeling children's feelings, helping them follow adult directions, and emphasizing turn taking and shared experience are all ways that teachers of infants and toddlers help children develop their ability to get along with others.

Part III

ACTIVITIES OF DAILY LIVING

Acquiring functional skills is one of the key developmental tasks for infants and toddlers. Fortunately, it is a great pleasure to a young child to be an active participant in all of the activities of daily life, especially if an adult also takes part in these activities. An environment focused specifically toward infants and toddlers must use daily living activities as important curriculum components and provide adequate time for infants and toddlers to participate fully in these activities and, thereby, grow in independence.

Daily living activities are repetitive by nature. Every day people get dressed, go to school or work, have meals, clean up after themselves, and sleep. Similarly, in an infant or toddler classroom, some events occur each day, including arrival and separation from children's families, feedings or meals, diapering or going to the toilet, dressing for outdoor play, taking naps, and reunion with the children's families at departure. This section considers these activities of daily living and describes ways in which they can be used as teaching and learning opportunities.

The repetitiveness of daily living activities makes them seem routine. A *routine* is any predictable, regularly occurring event. In infant and toddler classrooms, a substantial part, perhaps even the majority, of the children's time is spent in daily living routines. Daily living activities are used successfully for teaching and learning when the active involvement of teachers and children is encouraged and valued and when teachers consider child care routines to be an important part of their teaching responsibilities.

Specifying the steps of caregiving routines and ensuring that all teachers follow these basic steps guarantees that the *minimum* level of child care provided is of high quality. Because so much of infant and toddler care involves relationships between teachers and children, every routine is conducted differently by every teacher with every child. Thus, having carefully planned routines is not a substitute for teachers' personal involvement with children, nor do routines limit the opportunities teachers have to be creative and to express their own personalities. Instead, routines for daily living simply provide a clear and unambiguous description of the *basic* elements of quality care for infants and toddlers.

Although each activity of daily living is unique, all of the activities still share much in common. Every daily living routine involves five basic steps: 1) getting ready; 2) inviting or bringing children to the activity; 3) responding individually to each child; 4) involving the child; and 5) cleaning once the child has left the activity. All of the child care procedures included in this section apply these five steps.

Chapter 8 describes routines for infant feeding and for serving meals and snacks to toddlers; this chapter also includes recommendations for introducing solid foods and some hints for encouraging healthy eating habits. Chapter 9 describes diapering and toilet-training routines. Chapter 10 focuses on the transitions of the day: arrival and departure, naps, and transitions to outdoors. Together, these routine activities comprise the majority of most children's time in child care and, therefore, deserve careful attention and a lot of teacher energy.

Chapter 8

Food and Nutrition

Routines and rituals surrounding food and meals are important aspects of social life for people in many nations of the world, including the United States. Most family gatherings seem incomplete without a meal, and for many busy families, mealtimes are the major points of contact between parents and children. Many social conventions are associated with foods and mealtimes. Some ethnic groups have rigid requirements for specific foods that can and cannot be eaten; these customs often date back many centuries. Many cultures have distinct cuisines, and people from different parts of the world vary widely in the types of food they consider good to eat.

Food and feeding also have considerable psychological significance, especially for mothers of young children. Historically, psychoanalysts have emphasized the mother–infant bond and considered it to be strengthened by sensitive interactions between the mother and her child during feeding in the child's early infancy. Parents tend to feel competent if their child eats well and gains weight; by contrast, when a child seems uninterested in food or frequently refuses to eat, parents often feel guilty and responsible for their child's loss of interest in food.

Considering all of the history and folklore surrounding food, nutrition, and children's growth, it is not surprising that feeding their children is of great importance to many parents and a potential source of concern when their infants or toddlers are enrolled in a child care program. Furthermore, many children who have diagnosed disabilities also have difficulties with eating. Thus, teachers in inclusive child care programs must pay careful attention to children's nutrition and to the routines for feeding infants and toddlers.

Feeding guidelines from the U.S. Department of Agriculture Child Care Food Program (U.S. Department of Agriculture, 1988), which assists nonprofit and regulated child care programs to provide nutritious food for children, appear as Tables 8.1 and 8.2. It is helpful to plan a set of menus for each of the age categories defined by the Child Care Food Program and rotate serving these menus so that children receive a variety of foods. It is also helpful for parents to know the foods that will be served to their children on a given day.

Table 8.1.   Feeding guidelines for infants from the Child Care Food Program

Child's age	Morning	Mid-day	Afternoon
Younger than 4 months	Breast milk or iron-fortified formula—4–6 ounces	Breast milk or iron-fortified formula—4–6 ounces	Breast milk or iron-fortified formula—4–6 ounces
4–7 months	Breast milk or iron-fortified formula—4–8 ounces If desired, iron-fortified infant cereal—up to 3 tablespoons	Breast milk or iron-fortified formula—4–8 ounces If desired, iron-fortified infant cereal—up to 3 tablespoons If desired, puréed fruit or vegetable or both—up to 3 tablespoons of each	Breast milk or iron-fortified formula—4–6 ounces
8–11 months	Breast milk, iron-fortified formula, or whole milk—6–8 ounces Iron-fortified infant cereal—2–4 tablespoons Puréed fruit or vegetable or both—1–4 table-spoons of each	Breast milk, iron-fortified formula, or whole milk—6–8 ounces Protein source: meat, fish, poultry, egg yolk, or cooked dry beans or peas—1–4 tablespoons; or cheese—$1/2$–2 ounces; or cottage cheese, cheese food, or cheese spread—1–4 ounces Fruit or vegetable or both—1–4 tablespoons of each If desired, iron-fortified infant cereal—2–4 tablespoons	Breast milk, iron-fortified formula, whole milk, or fruit juice—2–4 ounces If desired, bread or crackers made from whole grain or enriched flour

Source: U.S. Department of Agriculture (1988).

Table 8.2.   Feeding guidelines for toddlers from the Child Care Food Program

Child's age	Breakfast	Lunch or supper	Morning and afternoon snacks
1–2 years	Whole milk— 4 ounces Fruit—¼ cup Enriched or whole-grain bread— ½ slice—or dry or hot cooked cereal—¼ cup	Whole milk— 4 ounces Protein source: Meat, fish, poultry, or cheese— 1 ounce—or 1 egg—or cooked dry beans or peas— ¼ cup or peanut butter— 2 tablespoons Two or more vegetables or fruits—⅛ cup of each Enriched or whole-grain bread—½ slice	Two of the following: 1) whole milk— 4 ounces 2) protein source— ½ ounce 3) juice, fruit, or vegetable— 4 ounces 4) enriched or whole-grain bread— ½ slice—or either hot or cold cereal— ¼ cup

Source: U.S. Department of Agriculture (1988).

Children with special health care needs frequently have special feeding needs, too. In addition, families of different ethnic or cultural backgrounds or families who are vegetarian may wish their children to eat different foods from those on the regularly planned menus. Parents are truly the experts on their children's feeding schedules and the types and amounts of food their children should be given. Parents whose children have special feeding needs or allergies to certain foods can indicate on the menus any changes they would like to make for their children. Depending on the resources available at the child care center, parents may or may not be asked to provide substitute foods.

FEEDING INFANTS

Babies require proper nutrition in order to support their rapid growth, and babies also need individual attention during feedings for healthy social-emotional development. These goals are best met when the feeding area is well organized and teachers follow a feeding routine designed to help them respond effectively to individual infants' feeding needs.

Feeding, Nutrition, and Growth in the First Year

The typical newborn infant weighs about 7½ pounds (3,400 grams); the infant's weight will double by 5 months of age and triple by the end of the first year. Also during the first year, the average baby grows 10–12 inches (25–30 centimeters) in length. This period of extremely rapid growth requires a diet that provides the infant with plenty of energy. Because fats have high caloric density (i.e., provide a lot of energy per amount consumed), an infant's diet must be higher in fat content than the diet of an older child or adult.

Breast milk is generally recognized as the "perfect" source of nutrition for young infants (Garza, Butte, & Goldman, 1993). Cow's milk formulas have been developed to be similar to breast milk in their concentrations of total fat and carbohydrate. Standard infant formulas contain reconstituted skim milk and a mixture of corn, soy, and other oils, with lactose as the sugar. When children are lactose intolerant, they can be fed a soy-based formula that uses sucrose as the carbohydrate. Because standard cow's milk formulas are very low in iron content, the Child Care Food Program requires the use of iron-fortified formula (see Table 8.1).

Infants younger than 4 months of age can be expected to consume about 30 ounces of formula a day (between 3 and 6 ounces at each feeding). Most pediatricians recommend beginning to add solid foods to infants' diets between 4 and 6 months of age. Earlier introduction of solids may contribute to infants' developing allergic reactions to certain foods (Sorenson, Porch, & Tu, 1993). It is not until infants are about 5 months old that they lose their extrusion reflex—the in-and-out tongue action that is very efficient for sucking but results in solid food being pushed out of the front of the mouth, rather than to the back of the mouth where it can be swallowed. When solid food is introduced before this reflex is lost, parents and teachers must not interpret infants' tongue thrusting as refusal or dislike of solid foods. When the sucking reflex becomes voluntary, infants can begin to move their jaws up and down in chewing motions, making spoon feeding more successful and satisfying. At about this same age, infants can reliably bring their hands to their mouths and begin to take small sips from a cup; thus, by 6 months of age, these infants are starting to assemble the range of skills they will eventually need to feed themselves.

For most infants, the first solid food to which they are introduced is enriched rice cereal. Although some children appear to enjoy being spoon-fed, other infants seem to dislike the experience. Teachers should experiment with a variety of thicknesses of cereal in order to find a texture that a child will most readily accept. At first, infants can be expected to eat only a few tiny spoonfuls of solid food, eventually working up to about 3 tablespoons of cereal during breakfast and lunch. Recommendations from the American Academy of Pediatrics regarding the order of introduction of puréed foods after rice cereal are potatoes and carrots; apples, pears, and bananas; beets and artichokes; wheat or oat cereals; and cabbage and broccoli (Agostoni, Riva, & Giovannini, 1995). When introducing solids, it is best to add only one new food at a time to a baby's diet. In this way, if the child has a reaction (e.g., diarrhea, skin rash), the specific food that is responsible can be identified.

By 8 months of age, infants can begin to eat whole-grain breakfast cereals and can also be introduced to citrus fruits, tomatoes, and legumes, such as beans and peas (Agostoni et al., 1995), as well as to meats, cheese, and egg yolks. Depending on the pediatrician's recommendation and the parents' wishes, infants can also switch from formula to whole milk at about this age. By 8 or 9 months of age, many infants show considerable interest (but less skill) in feeding themselves. They should be given opportunities to eat pieces of dry cereal, crackers, toast, and cheese; to hold a spoon themselves, even as they are being fed; and to put their fingers in their food.

Typically developing children who are fed when they are hungry and have opportunities for some autonomy in feeding will learn to enjoy mealtimes and will eat well. Difficulties arise when adults try to control feeding situations and the amounts of food that children eat. It is important that teachers avoid power struggles over meals. A child who refuses food and fusses during one mealtime is showing that he or she is not hungry; rather than fuss back, teachers should pleasantly remove the child from the feeding area. It is most likely that this same child will be hungry at the next mealtime.

It is very common for children with special needs to have skeletal, motor, or nervous system disabilities that interfere with feeding, and their dietary needs may differ from those of the typically developing child. These issues are discussed in the section, Feeding and Nutrition When Children Have Special Needs, in this chapter.

Organizing Feeding in Infant Care

Organization is the key to a calm and pleasant feeding time for babies. If teachers are hectic and rushed, they cannot be responsive to infants' individual needs. Although it is usually necessary for more than one baby to be fed at the same time, each infant can receive individual attention and responsive care as long as the feeding area and the teacher are both well organized. The Quality Check on page 173 can help program directors and teachers determine whether infant feeding times are running smoothly.

One effective way to organize teachers' feeding responsibilities is to schedule each teacher to feed babies during 1-hour blocks of time and to have a teacher assigned to the feeding area during the entire day (see Figure 4.2). This organization gives each teacher enough time to plan feedings and feed babies in a relaxed way and also ensures that a teacher will be available to feed babies whenever they are hungry.

The first step for a teacher who is taking responsibility in the feeding area is to *think* about how the hour will be spent. The teacher's plans will never work out exactly as he or she anticipates because some babies will need to eat sooner or later than usual, but these unexpected feedings can easily fit into the feeding routine if the rest of the preparation and feeding is planned in advance.

With rare exceptions, children should always be fed in the feeding area. Sometimes bottle-fed babies who are getting ready to go to sleep may be given their bottles by a teacher in a rocking chair in the nap area. However, babies should never be given bottles when they go to bed because this can contribute to tooth decay. Unless absolutely necessary, infants should not be fed in the play area. A teacher who is supervising infant play cannot feed a baby and still provide individual attention to the other children in the play area. Bottle-fed babies should always be held while being fed, although some older infants may prefer to be in charge of their feeding and hold their own bottle. Babies being fed solid foods can be in an infant seat or a feeding chair, depending on their age.

Often, more than one baby will be hungry at the same time. Teachers can hold and bottle-feed one baby while also helping one or two other babies who are eating solid foods. Feeding two or three infants at the same time takes skill and a high level of organization.

In order to keep the feeding area calm and minimize babies' frantic crying, teachers should prepare all food and have it ready to eat *before* babies are brought to the feeding area. Infants will quickly learn to associate the feeding area with feeding; they will become excited and agitated when taken into the feeding area. If the teacher brings a baby to the area before his or her food is ready, the baby will not understand the need to wait until the food is prepared. Once an infant becomes very upset, feedings do not go well and spitting up of food is common.

Older infants (children 12 months and older) can begin eating regular table food, such as that served to toddlers, provided that their parents approve. Often, foods for these older infants will need to be chopped into finer pieces or broken into the right size for the children to pick up with their fingers. All food preparation and serving by teachers must be done with utensils, rather than with fingers. It is helpful to feed the older infants in a group together, thereby making lunch a social occasion, and then plan for the children to take a nap right after lunch. This helps accustom these older infants to the lunch-to-nap routine that they will follow when they "graduate" into the toddler classroom.

Feeding Routine for Infants

An effective infant feeding routine includes preparation of foods before infants are brought into the feeding area, provision of individual attention to each of the children, involvement of the children in their own feeding, and attention to healthful practices, such as keeping the feeding area clean and well organized.

Step 1: Get Ready

First, the teacher taking responsibility for an hour in the feeding area needs to plan how that hour will be spent. The times children are expected to eat, based on parents' instructions and experience with the child, should be posted in the feeding area, and the teacher can use these times as guidelines for planning. Babies' schedules change frequently, however, and a feeding plan that works one week may be all wrong the next week. Therefore, it is important for each teacher to check the schedule and plan for each baby who is expected to eat during that hour. A second step before preparing the food is for the teacher who is responsible for feeding to get him- or herself ready to handle food. This involves fastening long hair back away from the face and *thoroughly* scrubbing hands. Hands must be washed again between feedings and also any time the teacher who is feeding the infants goes out of the feeding area and handles toys or other objects.

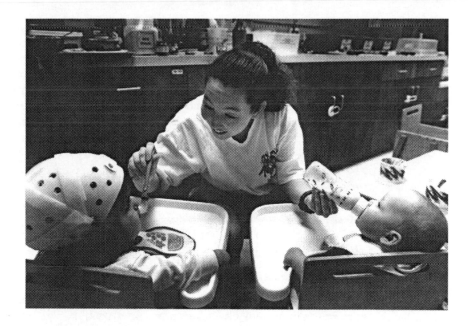

The final step in getting ready for feeding is preparing the food. A menu for the day listing specific foods to be served, based on the Child Care Food Program guidelines, needs to be posted for each age group of children and used to determine the foods that they will eat. To warm formula, the prepared bottle is placed in warm water. To prepare baby food, a small amount of each food to be served is placed in a separate small cup. Infant formula or food cannot be warmed in a microwave oven because of the uneven heating that results in "hot spots" that may burn babies' tender mouths.

After preparing the amount of food a baby is expected to eat, leftover food in the jar can be covered, marked with the date, and stored in the refrigerator. It takes only about 5 minutes to prepare food for an infant, and food should not be left sitting on the counter for more than 10 minutes. Therefore, food should not be prepared while a baby is still asleep or when a young baby is showing no signs of hunger. Instead, it is better to wait until the baby is definitely ready to eat before preparing his or her food.

Step 2: Invite or Bring Children to the Feeding Area

When a teacher picks up a child to take him or her to the feeding area, the teacher should let the child know what is happening. This is also an opportunity to check the child's diaper because every child should have a clean diaper at the beginning of a meal. Each child, except those being held and bottle-fed, should be safely secured into a high chair or infant seat.

Step 3: Respond Individually to Each Child

It is not unusual for teachers to be feeding more than one child at a time. Nevertheless, each child must be given individual attention and sensitive care during feedings. This means letting a child know when more food is coming and waiting for his or her cues (e.g., open mouth, obvious excitement) to show that the child is ready for the next bite of food. Different babies eat at different speeds, and their individual preferences for eating should be respected. Sensitive care also means that the teacher needs to be relaxed and comfortable during feedings, even when he or she feels somewhat harried or rushed. Talking pleasantly with the babies makes mealtime an enjoyable, social occasion. A teacher should take advantage of this time to sit down, slow down, and focus on one or two babies.

Children who drink from bottles also need to be burped gently two or three times during a feeding to be sure they release any air that they may have swallowed. To burp a baby, a teacher can hold him or her upright at the teacher's shoulder (protecting clothes with a cloth diaper) and *gently* pat or rub the child's back. Teachers may also hold a child in a seated position on their lap, leaning the infant slightly forward and supporting his or her tummy and chest with one hand while gently patting or rubbing the child's back with the other hand.

Step 4: Involve Children

As soon as children begin eating solid foods, they enjoy doing some of the work of feeding themselves. Teachers can give all babies a chance to feed themselves some foods, to touch their food, and to hold their cup or bottle. A child should never be left to feed him- or herself completely without help, however. Children should be offered all of the foods on the menu plan, but they should never be forced or nagged to eat or even taste everything. At first, most solid food will be on the outside of children, rather than on the inside, but eventually all babies learn to eat real food. Teachers must be alert to the babies' signals that they are finished eating and not push babies to finish their bottles or "eat just a little more." Instead, teachers should describe aloud what they think babies are telling them (e.g., "You feel full, don't you? All happy and satisfied!").

Step 5: Clean Up After Children Have Left the Eating Area

When children finish eating, their faces and hands must be wiped with a wet cloth or a baby wipe. Unless the children need a diaper change or are ready to nap, they can return to the play area. If one child finishes eating and there are other children in the feeding area, the feeding teacher *cannot leave the area.* Another teacher will need to come and take the child who has finished to the play area. As long as there are children in the area, the teacher who is responsible for feeding must focus his or her attention on these children. Cleanup should not begin until after all of the children have finished eating and have been moved to another area.

It is important to record the types and amounts of food that each child eats for classroom records (see a sample recording form in Appendix D) and for families (see Figure 3.1). Then all of the utensils and dishes used for feeding can be collected and washed. Unused portions of breast milk should be placed in the refrigerator, with nipples of the bottles covered by caps, to return to parents at the end of the day. Unused formula should be discarded and the bottles rinsed or washed. If formula is stored in bottles in the refrigerator, the nipples of the bottles must be covered, and the bottles must be labeled with the child's name and the date.

During each feeding time, certain general housekeeping tasks will also be the responsibility of the teacher who is in charge of feeding, including washing toys, cleaning the feeding counters, and sorting or folding laundry. These tasks should be done during times when no babies need to be fed and when no children are in the kitchen area. By keeping the kitchen area clean all of the time, the need for major, heavy cleaning at the end of the day or week is avoided. Teachers must remember to wash their hands after completing housekeeping tasks and before preparing food.

When a teacher who is responsible for feeding does not have any babies who need to eat and has completed all of the assigned housekeeping tasks, he or she should join the teacher and children in the play area and conduct a thematic, or Play 2, activity (see Chapter 5).

FEEDING TODDLERS

Organizing meals and snacks for toddlers involves presenting foods that toddlers can eat easily with their fingers and encouraging toddlers to become more involved in feeding themselves, drinking from a cup, and using spoons. When mealtime and snacktime routines are well organized, toddlers can participate actively throughout the meal, asking politely for second helpings and clearing their own dishes.

Feeding, Nutrition, and Growth in Toddlers

The extremely rapid growth of infants comes to an end at about their first birthday. During the second year, children's total weight gain is approximately 5½ pounds (2,500 grams), and in later years of childhood, children's yearly weight gain is about 5 pounds (averaging about 2,000 grams per year). The toddler's rate of growth is about half that of the typically developing infant—1-year-olds add about 5 inches (12 centimeters) and 2-year-olds add less than 3 inches (6–8 centimeters) in height.

Along with this slowing of growth, toddlers' interest in food often declines. Many parents who have become accustomed to the amounts of food that their babies consume are distressed and concerned about the often sudden drop in appetite of their toddlers. As long as children are served a healthy, balanced diet and continue to grow and gain weight, parents can be reassured that their children's disinterest in food is not harmful. Typically developing children should be trusted to judge when they are hungry and when they have eaten enough to be full and should not be urged, nagged, or promised rewards to eat more food. In addition, toddlers who do not eat well during one meal should not be given special snacks or preferred foods (e.g., cookies, crackers, sweets, a bottle) before the next regular mealtime or snacktime. Instead, these toddlers should be allowed to get hungry so that they can learn to enjoy eating regular meals.

By the time children enter a toddler classroom, usually at about 15 months of age, they can eat soft table food and drink milk, water, and juice from a cup. The physiological need for sucking lasts only until about 9 or 10 months; after that age, children can be gradually shifted from a bottle to a cup so that by the time they are ready for toddler activities, they will also be able to get through the day without a bottle. Families from some cultural backgrounds are accustomed to breast feeding or bottle feeding their children longer than the first year of age. These parental preferences must be acknowledged and respected, but children can be introduced to drinking liquids from a cup during meals at the child care center. Children can adapt readily to drinking from a cup in the classroom and having bottles when they are at home.

When first drinking from a cup, most children tip the cup but do not tilt their heads to let the liquid run into their mouths. Thus, it is helpful to put lids with spouts on cups for younger toddlers. As children become more familiar with using a cup, they can be given opportunities to drink from cups without lids. To give all children practice drinking from a cup without having to worry about cleanup, cups of water can be taken outdoors while children are on the playground.

Teachers should not spoon-feed toddlers, unless a motor disability makes such help necessary. Toddlers do not become proficient with spoons until the third year of age, so they need to be served foods that can be eaten with their fingers. Foods that must be eaten with spoons should be of a consistency that makes them stick to a spoon without much help from toddlers. Thus, oatmeal, applesauce, and pudding are manageable foods, but thin or creamed soups and cold cereal with milk are difficult for toddlers to eat. Some nutritious foods that most toddlers like and that are easy to serve and eat are listed in Table 8.3, along with a list of foods to avoid because of common sensitivities, allergic reactions, or the possibili-

Table 8.3.   Nutritious foods for toddlers

Good sources of protein	Good sources of energy
Pasteurized cheeses Ham and cheese sandwiches Scrambled eggs Cheese pizza Macaroni and cheese Fish sticks Hamburger and meatloaf Whole milk	Vanilla ice cream Chocolate milkshakes Peanut butter sandwiches Potato chips French fries Mashed potatoes and gravy Chocolate chip cookies Pudding
Popular vegetables and fruits	**Foods to avoid**
Broccoli with cheese Steamed and cooled carrot sticks Steamed and cooled (or canned) green beans Peeled and sliced apples and pears Watermelon without seeds Canned peaches	Berries, grapes, and cherries Nuts Hot dogs Raw vegetables Raisins or other dried fruits Apple skins Shellfish Pineapple—fresh or canned Popcorn

ty of choking. Suggestions to help guide menu planning and food serving in a toddler classroom appear in Table 8.4.

Organizing Meals and Snacks in Toddler Care

Toddler feeding times are running smoothly when toddlers come happily to the table and appear to enjoy most of the food served, and there is pleasant conversation between teachers and toddlers at the table. Meal- and snacktimes are unpleasant when toddlers are frequently being nagged by teachers, children are fussy or there are frequent squabbles or upsets, and toddlers intentionally spill food just to make a mess. Use of an organized routine for meals and snacks that allows individual transitions into and out of the eating area contributes to enjoyable mealtimes for everyone. Teachers and program directors can use the Quality Check on page 174 to look at mealtimes from the toddlers' point of view.

Many young toddlers are given few opportunities to feed themselves at home. Nevertheless, with the exception of children whose special needs make it difficult for them to feed themselves, toddlers, in general, are quite capable of eating independently if the physical setting and foods provided are appropriate. Children can sit on toddler-size chairs at a low table, rather than in high chairs or other seats that restrict their indepen- dent movement, and can be served foods they can eat with their fingers. Toddlers can be given spoons (regular teaspoons are fine) so that they can practice using them, but they do not need knives or forks.

When mealtimes are organized the same way every day and when teachers encourage children's active participation in serving, eating, and cleanup, toddlers rapidly learn and follow the eating routines. They quickly learn to ask politely (using signs as well as words) for second helpings of food, contribute to conversations around the table, and sam- ple a wide variety of foods with gusto. In addition, older toddlers can pour water, juice, or milk for themselves from a small pitcher, and all chil- dren can clear their own dishes from the table at the end of the meal.

Children whose special health care needs or disabilities require them to have help from a teacher at mealtimes can still sit at the breakfast or lunch table with the other children and enjoy the social aspects of eating. Ways of incorporating individual care for children with special needs into mealtime routines are described in the section, Feeding and Nutrition When Children Have Special Needs, in this chapter.

Mealtime and Snacktime Routines for Toddlers

The best mealtime and snacktime routines for toddlers involve the chil- dren as active participants as much as possible. Meals are social times, so teachers should encourage conversation around the table. Toddlers should be given opportunities to eat independently, decide how much to eat, and help with cleanup.

Step 1: Get Ready

First, the teacher who is serving food must get ready by fastening long hair back and *thoroughly* washing his or her hands. Next, the teacher pre- pares the eating area by setting up chairs, wiping tables, and getting out

Table 8.4. Encouraging healthy eating habits in toddlers

Serve toddlers all of the different courses at once; don't save dessert as a reward for those children who clean their plates or for any other reason, or dessert will become an especially desirable type of food.

Plan menus around nutritious foods toddlers enjoy—fruits, cereals, cheese, meatloaf, muffins, peanut butter, fish sticks and so forth, rather than the foods adults think children should learn to like (e.g., brussels sprouts, zucchini, lima beans).

Use food combinations that toddlers like, rather than those that appeal to adults; for example, an all-orange menu of spaghetti, peaches, and steamed carrots may look unappetizing to adults but may be the children's favorite.

Choose foods that are easy for toddlers to eat because they are soft, require little chewing, and can be picked up with toddler fingers.

Do not add salt, sugar, spices, or food additives—infants and toddlers will never miss them.

Serve food at room temperature, rather than either hot or cold.

Bake flaked cereals and oatmeal into nutritious bars, cookies, and muffins that are much easier for toddlers to manage than bowls of cereal with milk.

Most toddlers prefer simple, straightforward food; for example, steamed carrots with dip is a better bet for toddlers than a rice-carrot-cheese casserole.

Steam raw vegetables quickly over high heat to retain nutrients and color and also to make vegetables easier to chew and digest.

Let toddlers sit in small groups at low tables, rather than in high chairs, so mealtime is a social occasion for toddlers, and they have some control over how long they stay at the table.

To prevent choking, avoid hard and chunky foods or foods that require a lot of chewing—nuts, popcorn, raisins (except in baked goods), hot dogs cut in chunks, pineapple chunks, or raw vegetables.

Be aware of children's individual styles of eating and cut food in small pieces for children who tend not to chew their food.

Never nag children about eating. Toddlers will eat when they are hungry and stop when they are full—unless the adults around them turn mealtimes into a power struggle.

Toddlers can feed themselves using fingers and (sometimes) spoons, so they should not be spoon-fed by teachers unless a special medical condition requires it.

Spills and messes are a necessary part of learning to eat. Toddlers can be asked in a matter-of-fact way to help clean up what they spill, but they should never be punished or criticized for making a mess at the table.

Except for children with special health care needs, all toddlers can drink from a cup with or without a spout and do not require a bottle.

Share recipes and information about toddlers' favorite foods with parents, and encourage them to do the same.

supplies and thoroughly washing hands again before handling food. Unless children are helping to serve food, the teacher also places small portions of food on plates or napkins and pours milk, juice, or water into cups, placing lids on the cups as needed. Serving bowls for second helpings should be kept within arm's reach of the teachers but out of reach of children at the table. All foods, including finger foods, must be served using utensils (e.g., spoons, spatulas, tongs). Teachers should never handle children's food with their hands.

Step 2: Invite or Bring Children to the Eating Area

Children rarely need to be coaxed to come to breakfast, lunch, or snack! A general announcement that it is time to eat usually attracts a group of hungry toddlers to the eating area. If a general announcement results in a crowd, teachers can guide children individually to the eating area.

Step 3: Respond Individually to Each Child

As children enter the eating area, the teachers who are serving food should greet each toddler by name and guide those who need help washing their hands. During mealtime, the teachers who are serving food should sit at the tables and talk with the children. Conversations can be about foods and how they taste but may also range far beyond the immediate situation, just as mealtime conversations at home may cover almost any topic. When children finish a helping of food, teachers should give the children attention (e.g., "Theresa *loves* that broccoli!") to encourage requests for more.

Toddlers cannot be required to make verbal requests for second helpings but should indicate in some way (e.g., by nodding, signs, or gestures) that they want more food. Children should also not be required or nagged to taste all of the foods served, clean their plates, or eat more food than they indicate they want to eat. Generally, however, it is a good idea to limit children to three reasonable servings of fruit or sweet foods so that they do not eat only one type of food.

As each child finishes eating, he or she should be encouraged to leave the table to go to another area, rather than waiting for all of the children to finish eating. Children should, however, complete their meals and have empty mouths before they leave the table.

Step 4: Involve Children

It is important to give children opportunities to do as much as they can for themselves, even though it is often quicker for teachers to do things for them. Toddlers can find their own places at the table and seat themselves, but they may need help "scooting" up to the table. If a child accidentally spills food or makes a mess, the teacher should respond calmly and ask the child to help with cleanup (remembering to wash his or her own and the child's hands again afterward). When children are intentionally messy, they are indicating they are not hungry and are ready to leave the table. When they finish eating, toddlers can clear their own places at the table, placing dishes, cups, and utensils in a plastic dishpan and trash in the wastebasket and then washing their hands with help from teachers as needed.

Step 5: Clean Up After Children Have Left the Eating Area

Mealtimes involve fairly extensive cleanup, which should be done without any children present. (Children can help wipe tables, but they should not use disinfectant solution or participate in heavy-duty cleanup.) Tables, chairs, and serving counters need to be wiped with disinfectant solution, the sink used for washing hands needs to be cleaned, the floor swept, and dirty dishes washed.

FEEDING AND NUTRITION WHEN CHILDREN HAVE SPECIAL NEEDS

Children with disabilities or children who are at risk for developmental delays often have feeding difficulties that complicate their care. Infants who were born prematurely and exposed to unpleasant medical procedures, such as suctioning and tube feeding, may develop a resistance to being fed by mouth. When first bottle-fed, premature infants also usually have a very weak sucking reflex and less control over their tongue and lips than full-term infants, adding to the stress of their initial feeding experiences. It is common for children with disabilities to experience frequent gastroesophageal reflux, resulting in discomfort and vomiting. Some toddlers with diagnosed disabilities cannot chew and swallow regular table food, and other children may have dental malformations that affect their ability to eat. For many of these children, eating does not provide enjoyment as it does to most people, but instead is aversive and unpleasant, is associated with discomfort and stress, and, in short, is hard work.

Children at environmental risk may not be accustomed to regular feedings, may not have been exposed to a range of healthy foods, or may be diagnosed with "failure to thrive," a condition in which children do not eat enough food to sustain growth. Occasionally, children who have no disabilities or developmental delays may develop extreme food preferences, such that they will eat only one food or one texture of foods, which can seriously affect the nutritional content of their diets.

Some young children, particularly those who have chronic illnesses or disabilities that have required frequent hospitalization, may have been tube-fed or fed intravenously for much of their lives, as medical personnel and parents were coping with more immediate or life-threatening concerns for these children. It is important for teachers to realize that many of these children need to gain the slow and gradual experience with eating that they have missed. Typically developing children's first experiences eating from a spoon occur at about 4 or 5 months of age, but it is not until 10–12 months later that these children are really comfortable with feeding themselves. Teachers cannot expect children who have had minimal experiences with "regular" mealtimes to accept foods of varying tastes, colors, and textures without a lot of experimentation.

For any child who has difficulty with feeding, lack of adequate nutrition is a potentially serious problem. A child who does not eat enough of the right types of food may not have enough energy to participate in activities in the way typically developing infants and toddlers do. Furthermore, inadequate nutrition may contribute to poor dental and oral health, and children with feeding difficulties often get sick more often than other children. Poor nutrition can also lead to anemia, inadequate skeletal growth and strength, and eventual learning problems.

Many children with disabilities or chronic illnesses will not grow as fast or reach the adult height expected for typically developing children. In addition, toddlers and older children who are nonmobile because of their disabilities usually need fewer calories as a result of their reduced motor activity. It is not uncommon for children with Down syndrome, muscular dystrophy, spina bifida, or cerebral palsy to gain excessive weight in early childhood. Over time, obesity contributes to such illnesses as heart disease, high blood pressure, and diabetes. Thus, an optimal diet and targeted amount of caloric intake for children with special needs should be determined by the children's pediatricians.

In an inclusive infant-toddler child care program, it is important to understand and meet each child's individual feeding needs. A child with severe disabilities may need extensive one-to-one care at feeding time; this usually requires the presence of an additional teacher or special service provider. In general, however, most children who are considered to have problems with feeding can be given individualized care within the context of regular feedings or mealtimes. Many of the difficulties children have with feeding can be successfully resolved with patience, understanding, affection, and a regular routine for feeding.

Mealtimes in child care should always be pleasant and relaxing. When children with feeding difficulties are present, a calm and supportive atmosphere is especially important. The key to helping a child overcome feeding difficulties is to work *with*, rather than *against*, the child. Eating is inherently rewarding when a person is hungry and when other factors do not predominate. Thus, children who have difficulties with feeding should eat when they are hungry, and teachers should not allow themselves to be drawn into power struggles with children, regardless of children's behavior. Some experimentation with the day's schedule may be needed in order to find out when a particular child is likely to be most hungry. A toddler who is typically not very hungry at lunchtime could receive a small snack then and eat a full meal after a nap, when the others are eating only crackers and juice. A shift in schedule or location of eating may also help some children who find the activity of others around them to be highly distracting during mealtimes.

When children accept relatively few types or textures of foods, it is often most successful to introduce new foods or serve a wider variety of foods at snacktimes rather than during meals. Usually, snacktime portions are smaller than portions served during regular meals, which places less demand on the child to eat unfamiliar or unpreferred foods. At mealtimes, when children receive most of their caloric and nutrient intake, children should be offered foods they are known to eat. Also, if feeding is a problem, meals should be stress-free and positive experiences for children, rather than challenges to their autonomy.

Teachers must realize that a feeding problem cannot be solved during one meal or even during one week. The goal for teachers is to reverse the negative associations a child has with food and feeding by making mealtimes positive experiences. This requires time, patience, and love from teachers; it also requires involvement and expertise of special service providers who can help teachers understand and meet the specific feeding needs of individual children with disabilities.

Tube Feeding

When children with disabilities are unable to take in enough food by mouth or if they frequently aspirate, or breathe food into their lungs, they must be tube-fed. The two most common types of tube feeding for infants and toddlers are nasogastric and gastrostomy tubes. The nasogastric tube is inserted through the child's nose and into his or her stomach. Usually, nasogastric tubes are short-term solutions to specific problems, such as building up a child's caloric intake just prior to surgery or providing adequate liquids or nutrition during an illness. Gastrostomy tubes are more long-term adaptations for children who cannot suck or swallow food; who aspirate frequently; or whose mouth, throat, or esophagus is malformed. The gastrostomy tube is inserted surgically through the abdominal wall and directly into the stomach. Because tubes can be pulled out by children, many young children receive gastrostomy "buttons," which are less cumbersome and do not inhibit children's activities.

Teachers in inclusive infant or toddler child care classrooms should receive training from parents and a nurse or other special service provider to learn to tube-feed a child. However, the procedure is not complicated or difficult. The child can sit on a teacher's lap or in an infant seat or can rest on his or her right side during the feeding, which usually takes 15 or 20 minutes. For most children, a large syringe containing formula is attached to the end of the tube and held so that the formula flows through the tube into the child's stomach. Some children need to have the formula flow very slowly by using special tubing that regulates the rate of flow. Formula should be at room temperature or warmed slightly to avoid cramping. After a feeding, a child's gastrostomy tube must be vented for up to 15 or 20 minutes to allow air to escape. Throughout a feeding, a teacher should cuddle and talk to the child to make the feeding a social time. Infants can also be encouraged to suck on a pacifier during tube feedings in order to associate oral stimulation with the satisfaction of a full stomach and also to meet infants' physiological sucking needs. Pacifiers are not recommended for children older than 10–12 months who no longer have a physiological need to suck.

When a child has a gastrostomy tube or button, the skin around the incision must be checked and cared for regularly. The skin around the gastrostomy should be washed daily with soap and water. If there is any drainage, the site should be covered with a gauze dressing. Parents should be informed any time the gastrostomy site looks red or inflamed or if there is a greenish-yellow discharge.

Food Allergies

It is common for young children to have reactions, such as diarrhea, skin rashes, or respiratory congestion, after eating certain foods. Many of these sensitivities to foods never develop into full-fledged allergies and, instead, seem to disappear with age. Nevertheless, these reactions create discomfort for children and concern for parents and should be noticed and cared for. Children whose parents have allergic reactions to a variety of substances are more likely than other children to have long-term difficulties with allergies.

The most likely foods to cause sensitivities or allergies are milk, wheat, and eggs. When teachers or parents identify what they think is a food sensitivity or allergy, the child should see a pediatrician for specific instructions on altering the child's diet. Often the offending food does not have to be completely eliminated from the child's diet, but the quantities consumed should be reduced. Unless a child has had an extreme allergic reaction, foods that are eliminated should be reintroduced to the child's diet every few months to determine if symptoms of sensitivity have disappeared.

Food allergies should not be confused with reactions to inappropriate foods. Many children experience diarrhea when given high-fiber foods such as pineapple or beans. These are not allergic reactions but simply reflect the inefficiency of the young child's chewing and the immaturity of the toddler's digestive system.

Medical Conditions Affecting Feeding

Several medical conditions require children to be restricted to specific diets or affect their physical abilities to eat and drink.

Phenylketonuria (PKU)

Although always associated with severe mental retardation when untreated, PKU is now the focus of a universal screening program in U.S. newborns that allows immediate preventive treatment. Children identified with PKU must eat a highly restrictive diet that controls phenylalanine, an amino acid found in such high-protein foods as meats and dairy products. The child's pediatrician, in consultation with a nutritionist, must prescribe the specific diet required for the child.

Cystic Fibrosis

Individuals with cystic fibrosis are unable to digest fat, protein, and fat-soluble vitamins without receiving enzyme-replacement supplements. Even with such supplements, children with cystic fibrosis must increase their caloric intake substantially above that of a typically developing child in order to obtain adequate energy. However, children with cystic fibrosis are still likely to be small for their age and underweight for their height. Chronic respiratory disease accompanies cystic fibrosis and often causes death in early adulthood.

Sickle-Cell Disease

Children with sickle-cell disease have unusually shaped, fragile red blood cells that tend to clog blood vessels and interfere with the delivery of oxygen throughout the body. The lack of oxygen causes episodes of severe pain, restricts the child's activity, increases susceptibility to infections, and affects growth. By age 2, children with sickle-cell disease are usually showing signs of growth retardation, and these signs tend to increase with age. Increased caloric intake, in order to provide good nutrition and increased energy, may help reduce the frequency of infection that often precipitates acute phases of the disease.

Cerebral Palsy (CP)

Cerebral palsy is marked by abnormal muscle tone, which affects posture and movement. Less obvious but equally disabling is the impact on feeding as CP also influences lip movements, tongue retraction, jaw closure, and swallowing. Some infants with CP tend to arch their backs when held, making feeding difficult and stressful. Each child with cerebral palsy will have a different pattern of dysfunction. It is important that classroom staff consult with parents and special service providers regarding a child's individual needs and receive training in the best feeding practices for each child with CP.

Cleft Lip and Palate

When children are born with a cleft in their lip, they are unable to close their mouths tightly around a nipple in order to suck. This can make feeding time-consuming and frustrating for children and teachers alike. Furthermore, children with cleft palates have difficulty swallowing, and liquids and food can enter the nasal cavity. Also, these children typically undergo an extended series of surgeries and attendant hospitalizations that may interfere with their development. Parents and occupational and speech-language therapists can help teachers in an inclusive infant-toddler classroom learn effective feeding techniques for children with cleft lip and palate.

FAMILIES AND FEEDING

Most U.S. parents look with pride on a chubby baby and with alarm at a skinny baby. The conscientious parent's desire to satisfy a child's needs often seems to be focused on feeding, in which success can be easily defined by an empty bottle or a clean plate. Child care staff and directors often find issues regarding feeding, foods, and menus to be at the top of parents' concerns about quality care for their children.

Inclusive child care programs that follow the guidelines of the Child Care Food Program (see Tables 8.1 and 8.2) can inform parents of their participation in this U.S. nutrition program and also can refer to it in setting policies about feeding. If parents wish their children to eat a diet that does not match the food program guidelines and this diet is not determined by a physician in response to the children's special needs, classroom staff can discuss with parents, in a nonthreatening manner, their understanding of children's nutritional needs in infancy and toddlerhood. A compromise for classroom staff might be to offer the types of foods the parents prefer in conjunction with the regular menu, giving the children an opportunity to sample a wider variety of foods. This approach has the advantage of accepting parents' ideas while not jeopardizing the teachers' standards or the food program requirements with regard to nutritional adequacy of menus.

Parents who are vegetarians may wish their children to eat a vegetarian diet. As long as milk, eggs, and cheese are included, this represents no threat to children's health. Vegetarian diets that exclude all animal products are not recommended for young children (Dwyer, 1993). Child care programs should not agree to place children on strict vegetarian diets without clear directions from a pediatrician.

Diets vary widely from culture to culture. It is helpful for an inclusive child care program to use menus that incorporate dishes representing a range of cuisines, especially those from ethnic groups common in the geographic region of the child care center. Some families from non-Western cultural backgrounds may still find the food strange. Typically, children adapt readily to eating foods that other children are eating, but some parents may have more difficulty accepting new foods as being adequate for their children. In this situation, teachers and parents should talk through their ideas about food and work together to ensure that these children are eating adequate amounts of healthy food.

Because many parents feel strongly about their children's diets, it is often helpful to share information about children's food preferences and dislikes with their parents and also to exchange recipes when a toddler has indicated a favorite food. Sometimes parents continue feeding commercially available baby food to children long after their need for the puréed texture has passed. Some suggestions of simple-to-make substitutes may encourage these parents to be more adventuresome in preparing foods for their children at home.

If classroom staff believe a child is not being adequately fed at home, they should raise their concerns with the family services coordinator and the program director, who can consult with other service providers working with the family or make a home visit themselves. Resources are available in most communities to help families meet their children's nutritional needs, and the family services coordinator can connect the family to these services.

Families often want to celebrate their children's birthdays in the classroom where their children's friends can be present. Although 1- and 2-year-old children do not really understand the concept of birthdays, they love a party! Because of the varying nutritional needs and potential dietary restrictions of children, families should be discouraged from bringing cake or other treats to serve in the classroom. If there are children with special feeding needs present, they may not be able to participate in a party that centers on cake and ice cream, and other children may be allergic to some of the ingredients in the party food. Instead, parents can bring themselves, their talents, and their love to share with the children and teachers. Parents might bring a favorite book or some special music they enjoy at home. Some parents may have a wonderful skill they can share: juggling, playing the guitar, or even patting their head while rubbing their stomach! The idea is to focus the celebration on *people*, rather than on food. Teachers can also plan special birthday activities that include parents and siblings so that they will also be a part of the child's experience.

SUMMARY

Providing nutritious foods in a comfortable and nurturant environment is a key element of high-quality care for infants and toddlers. By establishing and following regular routines for feeding infants and serving meals and snacks to toddlers, teachers contribute to children's healthy enjoyment of mealtimes and thus to their growth and overall well-being. Although children with special needs often require individual attention while eating, they can also participate with other children in the social aspect of mealtimes, eating alongside other children and joining in the conversation. In feeding, as in all basic care routines, teachers should strive for low stress and a lot of individual attention to children.

Quality Check ✔

Feedings in Infant Care

Teachers, directors, and visitors can use this guide to quality care in feeding infants. After watching teachers and infants for 10 minutes, all answers should be YES.

1. Does every child receive individual attention and interaction from a teacher?   YES ☐   NO ☐

2. Is food always ready to serve before children are brought to the feeding area?   YES ☐   NO ☐

3. Do all children appear comfortable and happy while eating?   YES ☐   NO ☐

4. Do all children have a chance to touch their food and help feed themselves?   YES ☐   NO ☐

5. Does the teacher who is feeding infants smile often and use a positive tone of voice with children?   YES ☐   NO ☐

6. Does the teacher who is feeding infants touch children frequently with gentleness and affection?   YES ☐   NO ☐

7. Is the teacher's attention focused primarily on the children?   YES ☐   NO ☐

8. Does the feeding area appear clean, attractive, and inviting?   YES ☐   NO ☐

Inclusive Child Care for Infants and Toddlers: Meeting Individual and Special Needs by Marion O'Brien © 1997 Paul H. Brookes Publishing Co., Baltimore.

Quality Check ✔

Mealtimes in Toddler Care

Teachers, directors, and visitors can use this guide to quality care at mealtimes and snacktimes for toddlers. After watching teachers and toddlers for 10 minutes, all answers should be YES.

1. Does every child receive individual attention and interaction from teachers?　YES ☐　NO ☐

2. Is food always ready to serve before children come to the table?　YES ☐　NO ☐

3. Do all children appear comfortable and happy while eating?　YES ☐　NO ☐

4. Do all children have a chance to touch their food and feed themselves?　YES ☐　NO ☐

5. Are teachers involved in the meal, sitting at the table, talking with children, and responding to children's efforts to communicate?　YES ☐　NO ☐

6. Do teachers smile often and use a positive tone of voice with children?　YES ☐　NO ☐

7. Do all children appear to be enjoying the food and have enough food?　YES ☐　NO ☐

8. If spills or other upsets occur, do teachers handle them positively and sensitively?　YES ☐　NO ☐

9. Is each teacher's attention focused primarily on the children?　YES ☐　NO ☐

10. Does the eating space appear clean, attractive, and inviting?　YES ☐　NO ☐

Inclusive Child Care for Infants and Toddlers: Meeting Individual and Special Needs by Marion O'Brien © 1997 Paul H. Brookes Publishing Co., Baltimore.

Chapter 9

Diapering and Toilet Training

Diapering and toilet-training times should be relaxed and comfortable for children; these should be times when children can expect and receive a teacher's undivided attention. In the diapering and toilet area, a teacher's basic responsibilities are to see that all children's diapers are checked and changed if needed and that the older children have an opportunity to "go potty." Once children are toilet trained, going to the bathroom becomes something of a nuisance that takes them away from more interesting activities. This perspective of children needs to be acknowledged and respected, as older toddlers may make very quick trips to the toilet, not wanting to waste their time being cuddled or read to in the toilet area.

Cleanliness during diapering is of utmost importance in a child care center. Teachers cannot wash their hands too often when working with infants and toddlers, even when using plastic gloves, and teachers *must* wash their hands after handling any child's diaper or after assisting any child who is going to the toilet. The diapering table and toddler toilet-training chairs must be cleaned thoroughly with disinfectant solution after each child uses them, and each child's hands must also be washed thoroughly before he or she leaves the diapering or toilet area. Diarrheal infections can spread rapidly from child to child—and to teachers, too. Only consistent, conscientious attention to cleanliness can prevent such infections from spreading among children.

ORGANIZING DIAPERING AND TOILET TRAINING IN INFANT-TODDLER CARE

Diapering and toilet training are important activities in infant and toddler care, and teachers need to give as much thought to the organization of these areas and care routines as to more traditional teaching and learning activities. In an infant classroom, diapering provides babies and teachers with opportunities for one-to-one interaction. With toddlers, teachers need to be patient and encouraging as they help children gain independence. Following well-defined routines in the diapering and toilet area promotes individualized care and ensures high standards of cleanliness.

Diapering Infants

In the sample infant classroom teacher schedule shown in Figure 4.2, teachers are assigned diapering responsibilities for half-hour periods. During the half hour of diapering, the teacher should think about what children are doing and think ahead about what children will soon be doing, then check and change diapers in a way that makes sense. For example, if it is late in the day, it is helpful first to check and change diapers for children whose parents tend to arrive early. Also, the teacher who is diapering should be aware of which children have been napping for a long time and are likely to awaken soon and which children are getting ready to eat or to lie down for naps. Children will need to have their diapers changed before they go to the feeding area or before they go to sleep. After anticipating the immediate needs of these children, the teacher responsible for diapering can finish checking the diapers of the other children who are awake and in the play area.

Once all of the children who are awake have had their diapers checked and changed (if necessary), the teacher in charge of diapering should complete any housekeeping tasks needed in the area. When these tasks are finished, teachers who are diapering children should ask the lead teacher where they are needed or conduct a thematic, or Play 2, activity in the play area (see Chapter 5).

Although diapering is not a glamorous job, it is a crucial part of quality infant care. The Quality Check on page 190 can help child care directors and teachers determine whether diapering is contributing positively toward a quality infant care program.

Diapering and Toilet Training Toddlers

At the time that they first join a toddler group, most children will not be toilet trained. Learning how to use the toilet independently is one of the basic skills toddlers must master; therefore, it is a crucial skill for teachers to help toddlers learn. Children do not suddenly become *ready* to be toilet trained, although there are some helpful precursors. Rather, toddlers learn to "go potty" through observation, practice, and trial and error, just as they learn everything else. Assisting children with this task is an important component of a toddler care program. Every child in a toddler group, regardless of whether he or she is in the active toilet-learning stages, needs frequent trips to the toilet area for diaper checks and changes, one-to-one attention, cuddling, hand washing, and changes of clothes.

Because toddler group sizes are usually larger than those for infants and because most toddlers will need time to sit on the toilet or potty seat, each teacher should be assigned to the diapering and toilet area for 45 minutes or an hour at a time (see Figure 4.3). During this time, the teacher responsible for the toilet area should bring the children who are in the process of learning to "go potty" into the area first. If these children do not use the toilet but have dry pants, the teacher can try to bring them back to the toilet area at the end of the diapering time for a second chance. Success in toilet training depends on providing toddlers with many opportunities.

During a typical day, some toddlers may spend as much time in the diapering and toilet area as they spend playing outdoors. Therefore, it is important for teachers to be involved with children and interact responsively and sensitively during diapering and toilet training. To keep track of the toddlers' experiences in diapering and toilet training, teachers and child care directors can use the Quality Check on page 191.

Diapering and Toilet-Training Routine for Infants and Toddlers

The routine for the diapering and toilet-training area is basically the same for all children (infants as well as toddlers), regardless of their degree of independence.

Step 1: Get Ready

First, the teacher gets ready by checking that all supplies are available and within easy reach beside the diapering table, including diapers, extra clothing, ointment, baby wipes, disinfectant solution in a spray bottle, and plastic gloves. Before any child comes to the diapering area, the teacher must thoroughly wash his or her hands and put on clean, disposable gloves. Also, the changing table must be wiped with disinfectant, and a clean paper towel must be placed on top of the changing table pad. Children must always be changed on a thoroughly washable surface topped with a disposable cover.

Step 2: Invite or Bring Children to the Diapering and Toilet Area

Once the area is ready, the teacher responsible for diapering should let other teachers and children know that the diapering and toilet area is "open for business." Other teachers should be aware of which children need a diaper change or are showing signs of being ready to "go potty" and can then send or take these children to the diapering and toilet area. Also, the more independent children may use this announcement as a reminder to come to use the toilet or potty seat on their own. The teacher responsible for diapering can never leave the diapering or toilet area if there is a child there. Thus, other teachers must take or guide children to the area as the teacher who is diapering is ready for them. This requires active communication and cooperation among all teachers.

Some toddlers will come readily when the teacher who is diapering calls them; others take the call as a challenge and run in the other direction. The teacher responsible for diapering must avoid turning this situation into a power struggle; the teacher should call a child only once or twice, then either ask another teacher to bring the child to the area or use the technique of following through and retrieve the child him- or herself. Children should not be expected to interrupt their involvement in an activity at the instant the teacher who is diapering wants them to come to the diapering area. Instead, the teacher responsible for diapering should be flexible, caring first for children who are in transition from one activity to another and then giving 2-minute warnings to children who are busily occupied so that they can prepare themselves for the interruption. For example, with younger infants, the teacher who is diapering could announce, "Glenn is next" while picking up Chelsea. Then the teacher could tell Glenn once again the reason he is being picked up (e.g., "Glenn, come with me and get a nice, clean diaper!"). Children should never be picked up and taken somewhere without being told in advance what is happening to them.

Step 3: Respond Individually to Each Child

The teacher responsible for diapering should greet each child warmly and take the time for some individual attention and cuddling. This one-to-one time is often one of the most pleasant and relaxing times in an infant classroom.

Teachers should know the stage of toilet training each toddler has reached and his or her individual likes and dislikes with regard to undressing, being changed, or sitting on the toilet or potty seat. The ability to accommodate children's idiosyncrasies so that they feel completely comfortable and trusting is what distinguishes an excellent teacher from a mediocre one. It is best to have two toddlers in the diapering and toilet area at one time, making use of toddlers' natural learning processes of observation and imitation. At the same time as a more independent child sits on the toilet or potty seat (and perhaps looks at a book), a younger child can practice sitting on the toilet or potty seat and then have his or her diaper changed. The teacher must give both children individual attention and care.

Step 4: Involve Children

With older children (and adults), bathroom time is generally considered an interruption in the day's more interesting activities. For infants and most toddlers, however, diapering and "going potty" are just as interesting and fun as most other things they do, and there are just as many opportunities for teaching and learning during diaper-changing times as during planned curricular activities. Therefore, diapering and toilet training should not be rushed. Diapering babies gives teachers a chance to talk and sing and to cuddle and tickle. During toilet-training times, toddlers should be given opportunities to work on undressing and dressing skills, toilet flushing, and hand washing. The teacher responsible for diapering must pay careful attention to children in the area because of potential health or safety hazards, but he or she should also allow children a chance to explore safely. It is also important for the teacher to keep track of how long a child sits on the toilet or potty seat. Usually, a child who is going to use the toilet will do so within about 2 minutes. Sitting longer than 2 minutes can become unpleasant, and some children may view this as punishment. (Of course, some children go through phases when they *want* to sit on the toilet or potty seat for a long time; they should be given some extra time but encouraged to finish and return to play or other activities within 5–10 minutes.) All children's hands must be washed—in running water, if possible—before they leave the diapering area. Teachers should allow toddlers to do as much of the washing and drying as possible for themselves.

Step 5: Clean Up

Although the teacher responsible for diapering must pay close attention to children in the area at all times, cleanliness is so important in the diapering area that it is not possible to save all cleanup chores until there are no children in the area. Diapers, tissues, baby wipes, and plastic gloves must be disposed of as soon as a soiled diaper is removed from a child and the child's bottom is clean. Teachers must keep one hand on the child while clearing away these items and while wiping their own hands with a baby wipe.

Once the child has left the area, the paper towels used as a changing surface must be thrown away, and the diapering table must be cleaned with disinfectant solution before it is used by another child. Potty seats must be emptied and disinfected after each use. If a child uses a toddler-size toilet, the seat and rim also need to be cleaned with disinfectant before another child uses it. Record keeping for the classroom (see the Infant Diapering and Sleep Record and the Toddler Diapering/Toilet Record in Appendix D) and for families (see Figure 3.1) should also be done in between diapering children, during times when there are no children in the diapering and toilet area.

The Health Check

The easiest time for a teacher to conduct a health check is during the child's first visit to the diapering or toilet area each day. The daily health check helps to protect the health of all children and teachers by identifying early signs of communicable illness. A health check involves a teacher's inspection of each child from head to toe, looking for any changes in the child's condition or any signs of illness or injury. An alert teacher will also notice the child's general disposition because illness is often evident in a child's behavior before any other signs appear. When a child has special medical needs, health checks may involve keeping records requested by parents or health professionals; these may include noticing particular aspects of the child's behavior or changes in his or her physical condition. Any changes or symptoms noted in any child should be shown to the lead teacher and recorded on a daily Health Check Record after the child has left the area (see Appendix D).

To conduct a health check, teachers must look carefully at the child from head to toe, following this procedure:

1. **Examine the child's scalp.** Look for cuts, scratches, rash, flaking dry skin, hair loss, itching, lumps, or sores.
2. **Look carefully at the child's face.** Note the child's general expression (e.g., happy, enthusiastic, anxious, fearful, tired) as well as any cuts, scratches, rashes, sores, bruises, swelling, or unusual color (e.g., pale, flushed).
3. **Notice the child's eyes.** Are they watery, puffy, red or inflamed? Is there crustiness or discharge? Does the child look glassy-eyed? Are the eye movements uncoordinated? Does the child squint or seem unusually sensitive to light? Is the child rubbing his or her eyes frequently?
4. **Look at the child's ears.** Check for drainage or redness.
5. **Examine the child's nose.** Look for discharge or skin irritations; notice frequent sneezing or congestion.
6. **Open the child's mouth.** Look for new teeth coming in; red or swollen gums; mucus or sores on the lips, tongue, or throat; red or white patches or spots on the roof of the mouth; or cracked lips.

7. **Feel the child's neck.** Touch the neck gently, feeling for enlarged glands.

8. **Examine the child's trunk and back.** Lift or remove clothing, looking for signs of injury, rash, or unusual perspiring.

9. **Watch the child's breathing.** Note wheezing, rattles, breathing through the mouth, shortness of breath, or frequent coughing.

10. **Look on the child's arms and legs.** Look for cuts, scratches, sores, bruises, and rashes. Examine hands and feet, too. When a child stands and walks, check posture, coordination, and leg positions.

11. **Examine the genital area and bottom.** Removing the child's diaper or pants, look for redness, rashes, swelling, or bruises.

12. **Be aware of the child's behavior and disposition.** Changes in activity level, alertness, compliance, appetite, sleep, irritability, and coordination may all indicate illness.

TOILET TRAINING TODDLERS

It is useful to consider the process of learning to use the toilet independently as a sequence of stages, in which certain components of the overall skill of "going potty" are emphasized in each stage. As children demonstrate their acquisition of skills at each level, they move to a new stage that is identified by a change in the type of clothing they wear and by small changes in the diapering and toilet-training routine.

At each stage of toilet training, the skill considered most important to be learned can be rewarded (e.g., giving children a sticker or a small cracker), if desired. Giving children an obvious reward for demonstration of a particular skill at each level appears to help children move through the toilet-training process somewhat more quickly than if tangible rewards are not given. It may be that giving stickers has the effect of focusing teachers' attention on the specific skill each child needs to learn, making teachers more effective in teaching that skill. Of more importance than rewards are the encouragement and attention teachers give to children during toilet-training times. All children's visits to the diapering and toilet area should be pleasant and positive experiences.

Teachers should keep records of each child's diaper changes and progress in toilet training and share these records with parents. Records can help teachers and parents identify early signs of illness as well as provide the information teachers need to determine when to move children to a new stage of toilet training. When children have disabilities or developmental delays, teachers should consult parents about possible modifications in the stages of toilet training to meet the children's individual needs. Issues surrounding diapering and toilet training for children with complex medical needs or identified disabilities are discussed in "Diapering and Toilet Training When Children Have Special Needs," a later section of this chapter.

Stage 1: Pretraining

In the pretraining stage, children wear diapers and teachers check and change the children's diapers as necessary. Children in Stage 1 are not

expected to be able to control their bladder or bowels or to have dry pants. During this stage, it is helpful for teachers to talk with children about the difference between wet pants and dry pants and to encourage children to think of clean, dry pants as more comfortable and pleasant than wet, dirty pants. Some children just do not seem to mind wearing wet diapers, however, and no amount of talk is going to change their opinion. Teachers should never display disgust or make unpleasant faces when changing children's diapers.

In Stage 1, children should receive a lot of enthusiasm and possibly a sticker any time that they answer correctly in response to the question, "Are your pants dry?" Knowing the difference between *wet* and *dry* is not a necessary skill for toddlers to begin the process of toilet training, however, so teachers should not wait until children can answer correctly before they are moved into the next stage.

When pretraining children come to the diapering area, teachers should give them a chance to sit on the toilet or potty seat if they ask to sit, and teachers should encourage them to sit for a brief period at least once each day, at an unhurried time, so that the children get accustomed to how the toilet or potty seat feels. Initially, reluctant children may be encouraged to sit on the toilet or potty seat while they are fully dressed. Once children have become accustomed to this experience, they can sit on the toilet or potty seat in just their diapers and then without their diapers. It is often helpful to bring two children to the diapering and toilet area at one time—an older child who is close to being toilet trained and a younger child who is just beginning. Younger children learn a great deal by observation of other toddlers.

In practice, when a pretraining child comes to the diapering and toilet area, teachers do the following:

1. Ask if child's pants are dry, check diaper, and give a hug (and possibly a sticker) if child answers correctly.
2. Change diaper if necessary.
3. Wash child's hands.
4. Return child to play.
5. Record the diapering.

The criterion for beginning a new stage of toilet training is that the child frequently asks to sit on the toilet *or* the child is 23 months old.

Stage 2: Familiarization

As children approach their second birthday, they need to become familiar with the routine of sitting on the toilet or potty seat long enough to experience success. This is the easiest and quickest way for children to learn what toilet training is all about. The resulting applause and excitement from teachers makes the event memorable and allows children to begin to understand what is expected of them. Thus, children should frequently sit on the toilet or potty seat at times when success is likely.

Because children sometimes resist sitting on a toilet or potty seat unless they have become accustomed to doing so early, familiarization should begin when children are 23 months old, at the latest. It is not necessary for children to recognize *wet* and *dry* or have other prerequisite skills to begin familiarization. The goal of familiarization is not for children to become toilet trained quickly, but rather to accept the routine of sitting for a brief period of time in order to have an opportunity to use the toilet. This is also a good time to be sure that children know the sign for POTTY or can say "potty" so that eventually they will be able to signal their needs.

While in the familiarization stage, children continue to be dressed in diapers because they are expected to be wet more often than they are dry. The major task for children in this stage is to be cooperative in sitting on the toilet or potty seat calmly and without protest. Therefore, teachers should encourage children and reward them with a lot of attention (and possibly a sticker) any time that they sit on the toilet or potty seat for at least 2 minutes. Of course, if a child should happen to have success during those 2 minutes, great enthusiasm and more rewards should follow.

In practice, when a child in the familiarization stage comes to the diapering and toilet area, teachers should do the following:

1. Ask if child's pants are dry, check pants, and praise child if he or she answers correctly.
2. If change is needed, remove diaper completely, or just pull diaper down for child to sit on toilet or potty seat if diaper is clean and dry.
3. Have child sit on toilet or potty seat and give child a hug (and possibly a sticker) if he or she sits for at least 2 minutes.

4. If child has success on toilet, respond with enthusiasm, hugs, and another sticker.
5. Wash child's hands.
6. Return child to play.
7. Record child's progress.

The criterion for beginning a new stage of toilet training occurs when the child sits for 2 minutes at least twice each day for 10 consecutive days and is successful at least once.

Stage 3: In Training

During the in-training stage, children are gaining more of the skills they need to learn how to use the toilet independently. Children in training wear heavy training pants—if these are cloth training pants, they should be covered by plastic pants. This new underwear is a sign to the child that a change has taken place, and it allows the child independence in pulling pants up and down. During this stage, some form of tangible reward—a sticker, small toy, or cracker—for success helps to focus the child's attention on the task at hand. The reward clearly marks the child's progress in a way that he or she can remember and thus repeat.

Frequently during the day, teachers should remind in-training toddlers to "go potty," and teachers should take toddlers to sit on the toilet or potty seat whenever the children show signs of needing to use the toilet (possibly more than once during a scheduled toilet time and between these regularly scheduled times as well). Teachers can never use too much enthusiasm for in-training children who are successful at using the toilet or at dressing or undressing themselves. It is impossible for teachers to give too many hugs or to express too much pleasure in children's accomplishments at this stage.

Teachers should not, however, expect in-training children to have clean and dry pants when they come to the toilet area. At this stage, children have generally not yet learned to inhibit urination, even though they may be able to use the toilet successfully. Teachers should change children's wet or dirty training pants in this stage, expressing just as much acceptance as they do when changing the younger children's diapers. Teachers should never complain about dirty pants to children (or to other teachers), make faces that indicate disgust, or show displeasure in any other way that would make a child feel shame for needing a change of pants.

In practice, when a child who is in training comes to the toilet area, teachers should do the following:

1. Ask if child's pants are dry, check child's pants, and praise child if he or she answers correctly.
2. If wet or dirty, remove pants either while child stands in bathroom or while child is lying on diapering table; clean child's bottom if needed.
3. If dry, praise with enthusiasm.
4. Have child sit on toilet or potty seat for at least 2 minutes.
5. If child is successful, respond with enthusiasm, applause, and a sticker.

6. Encourage child to participate in dressing him- or herself.
7. Have child wash hands.
8. Return child to play.
9. Record child's progress.

The criterion for beginning a new stage occurs when the child is successful at least twice each day for 10 consecutive days.

Stage 4: Transition to Independence

A child in the transition stage of toilet training has learned the basics of using the toilet, demonstrating regular success. However, some children can use the toilet regularly when asked and yet have wet pants frequently during the day. Children in the transition stage still need many reminders to "go potty." Their primary remaining task is to recognize, before it is too late, when they need to use the toilet. Therefore, children in the transition stage should receive teachers' attention (and possibly a reward) not just for using the toilet but for staying dry *and* "going potty." Children at this stage can still be expected to have frequent accidents in which they wet their pants, however, and teachers must greet these accidents with equanimity—and a quick cleanup.

Children in the transition stage of toilet training will vary in their ability to dress and undress themselves, and teachers should encourage them to do as much as they can independently. Teachers must demonstrate considerable patience in working with children in the transition stage. It is much quicker and easier to dress a child than to stand by while he or she works clumsily at the task. At times, other demands may interfere, but whenever time permits, teachers should give children opportunities to try dressing themselves and provide help without doing the entire task for the child.

Children in the transition stage are helped in learning how to undress and dress themselves if they wear easily removable outer clothes—elastic-waist trousers or shorts are best—over training pants. Teachers should ask parents to send children to the child care center in simple, user-friendly clothes and save the cute overalls, fancy tights, and jumpsuits with a million buttons for other occasions. If children do not arrive in clothes that they can remove on their own, teachers should dress them in sweat pants or shorts for the time that these children are in the classroom.

In practice, when a child in the transition stage of toilet training comes into the diapering and toilet area, teachers should do the following:

1. Ask if child's pants are dry and praise child if he or she answers correctly.
2. If pants are wet or soiled, remove pants and clean child's bottom as needed.
3. If pants are dry, praise and celebrate.
4. Have child sit on toilet or potty seat, encouraging child's independence in undressing.
5. If child was dry *and* is successful, respond with enthusiasm and a sticker.
6. If child was wet and is successful, respond with just as much enthusiasm but no sticker.

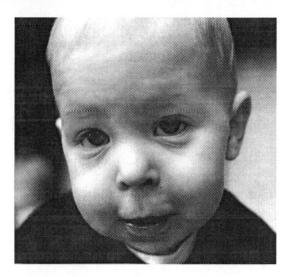

7.   Encourage the child to dress independently, helping only as needed.
8.   Have child wash hands.
9.   Return child to play.
10. Record child's progress.

The criterion for beginning a new stage occurs when the child is dry all day at least 8 of 10 consecutive days.

Stage 5: Independence

The independent child has mastered the toileting routine. He or she is aware when a trip to the bathroom is needed and can manage on his or her own in the toilet area with a minimum amount of help from an adult.

Independent children can wear regular underpants or cloth training pants without plastic pants. Sometimes, the event of graduating to real, grown-up underpants is very exciting to toddlers, especially for girls who are now able to wear frilly underwear with lace and bows; often these girls will insist on proudly showing everyone their frilly underwear. This is an opportunity for teachers to celebrate children's achievements with them, and the significance will not be missed by other toddlers who are close to independence in toilet training. There is no need for teachers to point out to other toddlers why one child is allowed to wear fancy underpants and others are not; they can figure this out for themselves.

Teachers still need to remind children who have reached independence to use the bathroom, but teachers should trust independent children when the children say they do not need to use the toilet. When these children come to the toilet area, it should be on their own, and they will need little help. Although independent children will not need as much time or care as other children who are involved in toilet training, the teacher in the toilet area should notice and pay attention to them. Children at the independent stage should only receive a sticker if they come to the toilet area independently (without being reminded or physically guided). They should not receive a tangible reward for "going potty," but teachers should continue to praise children enthusiastically when they use the toilet. In this way, teachers gradually phase out the use of rewards as children become more competent in using the toilet.

In practice, when an independent child comes to the toilet area, teachers should do the following:

1. Greet and give a sticker to the child if he or she came into the area on his or her own without a teacher calling or reminding the child.
2. Ask if the child needs help.
3. If pants are wet or soiled, give help as needed without scolding or becoming upset.
4. If pants are dry and child uses the toilet, show pleasure enthusiastically.
5. Have child wash hands.
6. Return child to play.
7. Record child's progress.

It is not uncommon for children who reach the transition and independent stages to have periods of regression when they have wet pants several times a day or even refuse to sit on the toilet or potty seat. If a child shows such a pattern for several days in a row, teachers can shift the child back to the procedures of an earlier stage of training until this phase has passed.

Such regression is quite normal in a typically developing child and does not necessarily signify psychological disturbance, although it may occur in conjunction with stress in the child's life. Even if there is an indication of stress, teachers can continue the usual toilet training procedures and avoid making a radical change in their approach to the child in toilet training. Any child who is experiencing stress or a troubling time at home will need teachers' increased support, attention, and affection throughout the day. It is best, however, if the child is expected to continue participating in the regular classroom routines, which provide predictability and stability for children.

If a child shows a persistent change in patterns of toileting over several weeks, this may be a symptom of illness or a complication from a disability. Teachers should bring this change to the attention of the child's family and encourage the family to consult with their pediatrician in order to determine whether there is a medical cause.

DIAPERING AND TOILET TRAINING WHEN CHILDREN HAVE SPECIAL NEEDS

Many children who have complex medical needs or identified disabilities need special care in the diapering and toilet area. Because the diapering and toilet-training routines described in this section are very individualized and include procedures that maximize cleanliness, they are readily adaptable to a wide range of special needs.

Parents may be reluctant to try to toilet train toddlers who have mental retardation, cerebral palsy, and general developmental delays, but the gentle procedures described are valuable for children who learn slowly.

Children can stay in the familiarization stage for as long as they need to in order to begin to understand the expectations of toilet training. This way, children with developmental delays or disabilities do not stand out as different and are not given special treatment that limits their opportunities to learn and experience the world along with typically developing children. Instead, all children receive special care in the diapering and toilet area—care that is suited to their individual needs and levels of development.

Often, children who have medical conditions affecting their motor functions also have difficulty with control of the muscles involved in urination and defecation. Classroom staff, including the family services coordinator, must rely on parents' experience and the consultation of health professionals to provide appropriate care for such children. In addition, some children with disabilities commonly have recurring problems with constipation, particularly if their disabilities cause them to be largely inactive or limit their diets. If children have very hard stools, passing them can be painful and difficult. Teachers should notify parents if such conditions occur so that parents can seek medical advice.

Ostomies

Although relatively rare, some children are born with conditions that make it impossible for their bodies to remove wastes on their own. These children will have an *ostomy*, or a surgical opening in the abdomen that allows wastes to be removed without passing through the entire digestive tract or directly from the bladder. When in the large intestine, this opening is called a *colostomy* or *iliostomy*; when in the bladder, it is called a *vesicostomy*.

Children with intestinal ostomies will not recognize the need to have a bowel movement because waste material is passed through the surgical opening into a pouch before reaching the muscles that typically developing children are learning to control as a part of toilet training. The *stoma*, a part of the intestine that is visible at the ostomy site, is covered by the pouch used to collect the stool. Intestinal ostomies are not painful for children, who can be held and physically handled without any problems.

Ostomies do require special care by teachers, and teachers will need to become accustomed to ostomies. Cleanliness while diapering children with ostomies is very important. In addition, children with ostomies often need to follow a special diet and drink a lot of liquids. Diarrhea is of special concern, as it can very quickly become life-threatening for children with ostomies. Most ostomies are temporary and are surgically corrected while children are still toddlers. After surgery, children can be toilet trained the same way as other typically developing children.

Children with vesicostomies also require special attention to be sure that the skin around the surgical opening is kept very clean in order to prevent urinary tract infections, which are critical illnesses for children with bladder and kidney diseases. Unless there are other complications, these children have normal bowel functioning and can be encouraged to follow usual toilet-training procedures, with the exception that they continue to wear diapers to protect the vesicostomy area.

When a child with an ostomy is enrolled in an infant or toddler classroom, the family services coordinator should work along with the family and teachers to ensure clear communication about the child's needs and consultation with medical advisers if necessary.

Catheters

In children with spinal cord injuries or other disabilities that interfere with their ability to control bladder function, catheterization is usually begun at some point during the late toddler or preschool years. For example, most children who are born with spina bifida are not able to control urination and, therefore, cannot be toilet trained. Catheterization involves the placement of a thin tube, or catheter, into the bladder through the urethra. Urine then flows through the catheter, rather than emptying through the urethra whenever the bladder is full. Catheterization is usually done frequently during the day to keep the bladder from being constantly full, which can cause kidney damage.

As with ostomies, careful medical management is crucial when children are catheterized. Families are usually experts in the care of their children when they have complex medical needs, and teachers can learn a great deal from families. In addition, it is helpful for teachers to learn more about these children's conditions from health professionals so that they understand the purpose and importance of all of the procedures that they are asked to conduct as well as gain confidence in their own abilities to provide appropriate care.

FAMILIES AND TOILET TRAINING

Unless a child is very easily toilet trained at a young age, there comes a time in almost every parent's life when toilet training becomes a matter of the utmost importance. The gradual approach described in this chapter makes some aspect of toilet training a part of the daily experience of every toddler. When this gradual approach is clearly communicated to parents, it can help them adopt the same type of realistic, gradual, and nonstressful attitude about toilet training.

Most toddlers respond positively to gentle, matter-of-fact efforts to introduce them to using the toilet but rebel against intense, emotional campaigns about toilet training. If parents are aware of the many small steps involved in learning to "go potty," and follow a routine at home similar to that used in the classroom, toilet training generally proceeds smoothly, and the child is toilet trained before parents become exasperated and desperate.

Toilet-training approaches vary substantially across different cultures and family backgrounds. Teachers must be aware of the individual preferences and customs of the parents with whom they are working and respect these differences. A gentle and gradual approach to toilet training is adaptable to a wide variation in cultural practices. A clear description of toilet-training procedures should be provided to parents at the time of enrollment so that they understand that all children are familiarized with the toilet or potty seat and its use as soon as they enter the toddler classroom.

Teachers should communicate regularly with parents about toilet training and describe the procedures used at each stage of training. Most teachers want parents to follow the same procedures at home as those that are used in the classroom, and it is desirable to have consistency in any type of learning. Nevertheless, teachers must respect parents' rights to follow whatever procedures they wish—even if their choice is not to do *any* toilet training at home. When gentle and positive toilet-training procedures are used in the classroom, children acquire some of the needed skills for using the toilet independently, even if parents are not interested or actively participating in toilet training at home.

At the opposite end of the continuum are the parents who want their child completely toilet trained at a very early age, perhaps earlier than teachers believe is appropriate for the child. Open communication with these parents about the toilet-training approach taken in the classroom can be helpful but will not always be successful in convincing parents to adopt a more gradual approach to toilet training when their cultural or family background emphasizes early training. Teachers should not become adamant about their approach to toilet training and should avoid starting a power struggle with parents over the best way to toilet train their child. Within the classroom situation, the gradual introduction of toilet-training skills can continue, and the child will learn at his or her own pace.

SUMMARY

Diapering and toilet training provide opportunities for teachers and children to have quiet, affectionate interactions away from the hustle and bustle of other classroom activities. Use of a regular routine for diapering prevents this area from becoming hectic and promotes the cleanliness that is so necessary for children's and teachers' health. A gradual and individual approach to toilet training encourages toddlers to learn this important skill without stress or discomfort. Children's special needs can be easily accommodated within regular classroom diapering and toilet-training routines that focus on individualized care.

Quality Check ✔

Diapering in Infant Care

Teachers, directors, and visitors can use this guide to quality care in diapering for infants. After watching each teacher diaper at least one baby, all answers should be YES.

1. Does every child receive individual attention and interaction from the teacher? YES ☐ NO ☐

2. Does the teacher always keep at least one hand on the child being diapered? YES ☐ NO ☐

3. If a child cries or fusses, does the teacher respond positively and sensitively? YES ☐ NO ☐

4. Is every child given a chance to move his or her arms and legs freely while being diapered? YES ☐ NO ☐

5. Is every child talked with, sung to, and cuddled during diapering? YES ☐ NO ☐

6. Does the teacher smile often and use a positive tone of voice with every child? YES ☐ NO ☐

7. Does the teacher touch and lift each child with gentleness and affection? YES ☐ NO ☐

8. Is each teacher's attention focused primarily on the children? YES ☐ NO ☐

9. Does the diapering space appear clean, attractive, and inviting? YES ☐ NO ☐

Inclusive Child Care for Infants and Toddlers: Meeting Individual and Special Needs by Marion O'Brien © 1997 Paul H. Brookes Publishing Co., Baltimore.

Quality Check ✔

Diapering and Toilet Training in Toddler Care

Teachers, directors, and visitors can use this guide to quality care for toddlers in the diapering and toilet area. After watching teachers and toddlers in the area for 10–15 minutes, all answers should be YES.

1. Does every child receive individual attention and interaction from a teacher? YES ☐ NO ☐

2. Is each child in the diapering and toilet area always carefully supervised? YES ☐ NO ☐

3. Is the teacher responsible for the diapering and toilet area actively involved with children and enthusiastic about what they are doing? YES ☐ NO ☐

4. Is each child given opportunities to help undress and dress him- or herself? YES ☐ NO ☐

5. If any child cries or fusses, does the teacher respond positively and sensitively? YES ☐ NO ☐

6. Does the teacher smile often and use a positive tone of voice with children? YES ☐ NO ☐

7. Does the teacher touch and lift each child with gentleness and affection? YES ☐ NO ☐

8. Does the teacher notice and respond to each child's efforts to communicate? YES ☐ NO ☐

9. Does the teacher focus his or her attention primarily on the children? YES ☐ NO ☐

10. Does the diapering and toilet space appear clean, attractive, and inviting? YES ☐ NO ☐

Inclusive Child Care for Infants and Toddlers: Meeting Individual and Special Needs by Marion O'Brien © 1997 Paul H. Brookes Publishing Co., Baltimore.

Chapter 10

Transitions

Infants and toddlers are more sensitive than older children to change and disruption of their activities. Furthermore, very young children cannot be verbally prepared for transitions because they do not understand language, and they have little sense of time. To toddlers, 5 minutes can seem like an instant or an hour, depending on what they are doing and how much they are enjoying their activities.

In this chapter, the transitions of arrival and departure, going to sleep, and moving from indoor to outdoor play are discussed. Each of these transitions can be difficult for infants and toddlers. Some children may resist separation from parents in the morning and also may be so involved in play in the afternoon that they do not want to go home. Difficulties getting infants and toddlers to settle down to go to sleep are common for families at home as well as for teachers in child care settings. Even the pleasures of playing outdoors are not always enough of an inducement for young children to interrupt what they are doing in favor of getting dressed in shoes and coats to go outside. Despite these potential difficulties, with appropriate teacher support and responsive care, infants and toddlers can learn to cope with—and even look forward to—change in their activities.

ARRIVAL AND DEPARTURE

When teachers are organized and ready to greet parents and children in the morning, children's entry into the classroom can be calm and pleasant. An arrival routine for the infant or toddler classroom helps ensure a smooth separation of children from their parents. It is equally important for teachers to be well organized at the end of the day when children are tired and parents often feel in a hurry. Every arrival and departure time is an opportunity to build positive and personal relationships between classroom staff and family members.

Arrival

An orderly and calm arrival in the morning helps children feel comfortable with the classroom situation and with separation from their parents.

If arrivals are hectic and chaotic, children will have difficulty understanding what is happening and are likely to become upset because of the
stress and confusion.

An arrival routine for children includes removing their outdoor
clothing and shoes, saying good-bye to parents, receiving a health check
(and diaper change if needed), and moving into the first activity of the
day, which may be breakfast or play. This routine generally involves all of
the teachers in the classroom; each one should welcome every child
warmly and have something special to say or to do with each child.

For parents, the arrival routine involves transferring full responsibility for their children to the teachers in the child care center, which
may be difficult for some parents. Communicating with the teachers
about any special needs for their children that day is also a part of the
arrival routine for parents. The teacher who is responsible for greeting
parents and children as they arrive must be sure to obtain all necessary
information from parents while making arrival pleasant and comfortable
for the children, and this requires the teacher to use a lot of organization,
planning, and poise.

One teacher (usually the lead teacher) should be available to greet
parents and children as they arrive (see Figure 4.2). When arrival is the
primary responsibility for a teacher, parents will never feel that they are
interrupting a teacher's other activities, but instead feel valued and welcome. It is helpful for the same teacher to greet parents and children each

day because this teacher can then build a personal relationship with parents that encourages effective two-way communication. Also, the greeting teacher can become familiar with the ways that individual children separate from their parents and can be supportive during what is often a difficult transition for older infants and toddlers. Suggestions for making separations easier for both children and parents appear in Table 10.1. A

Table 10.1. Ideas for making separation easier

Set up the classroom to look appealing, using popular and attractive toys, and be sure that teachers are actively involved in playing with those toys and are visible from the doorway of the classroom.

Arrange a second activity area that is visually screened from the doorway of the classroom so that children who have difficulty with separation can be involved in an activity but cannot see their parents.

When parents are having trouble with separation, arrange an informal meeting to give parents a chance to talk openly, without criticism, about their anxieties.

Although parents typically should be welcomed to visit the classroom at any time, during children's first week or two of attendance, it is best to arrange a routine of arrival that involves making the transition from parents to a teacher at the doorway of the classroom.

If parents have difficulty separating from their children at the door of the classroom, encourage them to think about their own responses to separation; for example, would they rather leave to go somewhere exciting or be the ones left behind? When parents come into the classroom with their children and then leave, their children are in the position of being the ones left behind, and this is more difficult than separating from parents at the door of the classroom.

Encourage parents to view their children from an observation area where the children cannot see them or to call frequently during the day, rather than staying in or outside the classroom.

Respond to children's distress at separation with empathy, which involves acceptance and understanding and shows respect for children, rather than responding with sympathy, which involves feeling sorry for children and shows a lack of confidence in their ability to cope with the situation.

Develop an arrival routine for each child, and use it every day, such as a special greeting song, a toy brought out "just for you," a trip around the classroom to look at the pictures on the wall, or any activity that involves the child.

Encourage the use of transition objects from home, such as the children's own blankets or stuffed toys, special cloth diapers, or whatever the children use as comforters in times of stress. Once the children adjust to the new situation, the transition objects will not be needed.

Be aware of cultural differences in families' levels of comfort with the idea of child care. Parents from some cultural backgrounds may experience a lot of guilt and have little support from their extended family for the idea of allowing strangers to care for their children.

Quality Check for arrivals and departures, which appears on page 212, can be used by child care program directors and teachers to examine the experiences of parents and children as they are greeted each morning.

Arrival Routine for Infant and Toddler Classrooms

Teachers need to be prepared for children to arrive each morning and ready to welcome parents. Providing individual attention to each child on arrival helps make the transition into the classroom go smoothly.

Step 1: Get Ready

Before opening the child care center each morning, everything needed should be assembled in the greeting area or near the door, including a place to store each child's outdoor clothes and shoes, a storage bin for diapers and extra clothes for the day, Daily Attendance Records and Medication Request Forms (see Appendix D), Take-Home Reports (see Figure 3.1), and pencils and pens.

Step 2: Welcome Parents and Children

The greeting teacher should welcome each child and parent warmly as soon as they are in sight. Parents can remove their children's coats and shoes and place them in the children's cubbies or lockers. As soon as this is done, the greeting teacher should focus attention on the children first, which can often encourage children to initiate separation from their parents. Entry into the day's activities is also easier for children when other teachers and children also join in greeting new arrivals. For most children, a hug and a loving, yet matter-of-fact, "See you this afternoon!" from their parents is enough reassurance to allow the children to separate from their parents. However, individual children and parents may use or need different ways to say good-bye. Parents can also be encouraged to transfer diapers and extra clothing into the children's bins, giving the children a chance to move into the classroom on their own.

Step 3: Respond Individually to Each Child and Parent

Good personal relationships between parents and teachers are essential to the provision of high-quality child care. The daily conversations between the greeting teacher and parents provide opportunities for establishing trust and encourage open communication that supports the efforts of both parties to provide the best possible care for the children. (See "Suggestions for Talking with Parents" on pp. 200–202 for a discussion of parent–teacher relationships.)

The greeting teacher must be sure to obtain any information needed about changes in the families' or children's schedules or any unusual behavior that parents have noticed. Often a simple question such as, "How is Doug today?", "Did you all have an exciting weekend?", or even "How's everything going?" will jog parents' memories or encourage them to talk about something that is on their minds. The parents or greeting teacher also needs to sign the child into the classroom on the check-in sheet and record any special instructions for the day, telephone number changes, or other information about the child's care on the FYI form (see

Appendix D). This process is easier if the parents are asked to fill out the top portion of a Take-Home Report (see Figure 3.1). Parents provide information needed for their children's care during the day, and, in turn, the classroom staff provide information that helps parents plan and provide care at home in the evening. When a child has special medical needs, the day's routine may need to be discussed. If a child must be given medicine during the day, parents must fill out and sign a Medication Request Form (see Appendix D). If a child has food allergies, the greeting teacher should check with the parents about substitute foods for mealtimes. These conversations with parents are easier and more relaxed if the child has been separated from the parents and is involved in the rest of the arrival routine. However, the greeting teacher must be attuned to and respect individual differences in children's and parents' tolerance for quick separations.

Step 4: Involve Children

Older children who are comfortable with separation from parents should be encouraged to walk into the classroom on their own, thereby demonstrating their independence and also allowing them to enter activities at their own pace. Often, however, infants and younger toddlers do best when they are held by a teacher for a short time after arrival so that they can receive some one-to-one attention. Within a few minutes of arrival, each child also needs to have a health check (described in Chapter 9). This provides an opportunity for the teacher in the diapering and toilet area to have some individual time with each child and give the focused attention that helps each child with the transition into the day's activities.

Step 5: Organize the Area After
Children and Parents Have Left the Greeting Area

There can be a lot of information for a greeting teacher to remember each morning, so it is best to have a place to write down special instructions or reminders from parents. However, as long as parents or children are arriving, the greeting teacher needs to pay attention to them, assisting children's transitions into the classroom and talking individually with parents. If a parent indicates a need for a more extensive conversation, it is best to schedule a meeting at a later time. Once all of the children have arrived, the greeting teacher can organize the special requests or schedule changes from parents and communicate them to other teachers. Then the teacher can straighten the greeting area in preparation for the afternoon.

Departure

Children's reunion with parents is often an easier transition than the morning's separation, but it is complicated by the fact that everyone— children, parents, and teachers—is tired by the end of the day. Sometimes the first parent's arrival triggers a chain reaction of distress in babies or toddlers who appear to have suddenly remembered their parents are not with them. Teachers who are ready to relax with their own families may have difficulty keeping their enthusiasm high, and because teacher enthusiasm is a key ingredient in successful infant and toddler activities, children's involvement is often at its lowest point late in the day. Parents are also tired from their workday and are looking wearily ahead to what is often a hectic dinner and bedtime with their active babies or toddlers.

Despite these potential difficulties, the teacher responsible for departure should do his or her best to help make each child's good-bye a cheerful time. The teacher who is in charge of departure must also communicate with parents regarding anything special that may have happened that day, particularly if it could influence how the child behaves at home in the evening. Departures go more smoothly if parents assume responsibility for dressing their children to go outdoors and if the dressing area is outside the classroom. This way, each baby or toddler can say good-bye to teachers and friends, and then the transfer of responsibility to the parents is made clearly and cleanly. Teachers and child care program directors can use the Quality Check for arrivals and departures on page 212 to determine whether parents and children are leaving each day with a positive impression of the child care program.

Departure Routine for Infant and Toddler Classrooms

Preparing for children's departure from the child care center and welcoming parents when they arrive to pick up their children are important steps for teachers during the departure routine at the end of the day. Teachers need to respond individually to each child and parent and talk to parents about any concerns or special requests parents made that day. Teachers can help parents keep in touch with their child's experiences by remembering and mentioning specific events involving the child each day.

Step 1: Get Ready

Pack children's diaper bags and place shoes and coats on top before parents arrive. If there is artwork, a newsletter, or announcements of upcoming events to be sent home, attach these items to children's take-home reports, and tape the reports to the outside of the diaper bags where they are easily visible to parents.

Step 2: Welcome Parents and Bring Children to the Departure Area

Parents should be warmly welcomed as they arrive to pick up their children, and the teacher responsible for departure should ask parents about their day. There is usually little opportunity for long conversations at departure time, but the teacher in charge of departure can use this time for personal contact with parents that will make parents feel supported and valued (see "Suggestions for Talking with Parents" on pp. 200–202). The teacher responsible for departure must also be aware of how each child typically reacts to his or her parents' arrival. Some children respond as parents expect, with big smiles and arms held out to be picked up by their parents. Other children cope differently with reunion, sometimes becoming shy or even running in the opposite direction from their parents. The teacher responsible for departure should anticipate these responses and immediately bring these children to the door as soon as their parents arrive, rather than calling their names and potentially beginning a power struggle over departure. Because young children show many different ways of responding to others, teachers should avoid making judgments about parent–child relationships based on individual patterns of behavior at reunion.

If at any time a person that the teacher in charge of departure does not recognize comes to the child care center to pick up a child, the teacher should ask for identification and check the identity of the person against the list of people authorized to pick up the child. A child should never be released to an individual whose identity is not known or who is not legally authorized to receive that child.

Step 3: Respond Individually to Each Child and Parent

Many parents who are in a hurry to get home want to rush their children through departure. The teacher responsible for departure can help prevent the inevitable conflict that arises in this situation by assisting with dressing the child to go outside. However, it is common for several parents to arrive at exactly the same time, making it difficult for the teacher responsible for departure to help dress children or even to have a personal conversation with each parent about their child's day. The Take-Home Report (see Figure 3.1), with its record of the basics of each child's activities during the day, can help keep parents informed without making it necessary for them to wait every day to talk with the teacher in charge of departure about their child.

The teacher responsible for departure should make a special effort to talk with certain parents. Any concerns that were raised or special requests that were made in the morning should be followed up with the parents during departure. Also, if the teacher in charge of departure has important information for parents, he or she must find a way to talk briefly with them before they leave the child care center. Because departure time is usually very hectic, the teacher responsible for departure must be sure to write down anything parents say about future schedule changes, concerns, or any other important information, or it is likely to be forgotten.

Step 4: Involve Children

During the transfer of a child from classroom to parents, the teacher responsible for departure should mention specific activities that the child enjoyed doing that day. Older toddlers can be encouraged to talk to their parents about something fun or exciting that happened. These personal comments about a child's favorite toy, a special food that the child ate for lunch or snack, or a new achievement of the child help keep parents in touch with their child's experiences and also give them confidence that teachers are aware of their child as a special person. The teacher responsible for departure should keep track of children's activities during the day so that he or she will have something personal to say to each parent.

Step 5: Clean After Children and Parents Have Left the Departure Area

The teacher in charge of departure should wait for times when no children and parents are present to record departure times, make notes about the next day's schedule, and prepare materials for the next morning. Because everyone wants to get home quickly at the end of the day, there is a tendency for teachers to pick up toys and clean up play areas while children are still in the classroom. This leaves the remaining children with nothing interesting to do, inevitably resulting in disruptions and distress. As some children leave the classroom, one teacher may begin cleanup, but most teachers should continue their involvement in planned activities with children, even if only one child remains.

Suggestions for Talking with Parents

Being an effective teacher means not only working with children, but also working with parents and other family members who come to the class-room on a regular basis. These people are very important to young children, so they are very important to teachers, too.

Often, the lead teacher will have the most contact with parents, but other teachers should also try to build relationships with children's families. Parents like to know the people who care for their children. The following hints can help teachers develop good relationships with parents.

1.   **Teachers should learn parents' names and greet parents by name.** A list of the parents' first and last names can be given to each teacher so that he or she can learn parents' names and greet them in a personal way. Usually, it is best to start a relationship with parents on a formal note by using the parents' last name (e.g., Mr. Johnson, Ms. Adams), and allowing parents to decide if they prefer to be called by their first names.

2.   **Teachers should always initiate conversation with parents in the classroom.** Teachers are sometimes reluctant to start conversations with parents, waiting for parents to take the lead. However, it is important for teachers to remember that they are the hosts or hostesses of the child care program, and it is their responsibility to put the guests, or the parents, at ease. Parents will often feel awkward and uncertain of what teachers expect of them when they first enroll their children in a child care program. Teachers can help parents feel more comfortable by initiating conversation with parents. If teachers see parents or children outside of the classroom (e.g., at the grocery store, downtown), it is best for teachers to be cordial but avoid being too friendly. In these situations, teachers need to allow parents to initiate conversation.

3.   **Teachers do not have to focus all of their conversations with parents on the child.** Parents are people, too, and they have interests and concerns other than those that center on their children. If teachers limit their conversations with parents to concerns regarding the parents' children, the relationship between parents and teachers will always be on a business level, rather than a personal level. Although it is not a good idea for teachers to become close friends with the parents of children in their care, building a personal relationship with parents means learning about parents' lives, including their work, their hobbies, their travel plans, what they think about the day's hot (or cold) weather, or what they are doing during the weekend. In short, teachers should talk with parents just as they would with any other acquaintances.

4.   **Teachers must listen attentively to what parents say.** Arrival and departure times are sometimes very hectic, and it is easy for teachers to find themselves struggling to pay attention to several matters at once.

However, if parents are talking, it is important for teachers to be listening. If parents want to talk and it is not possible for a teacher to listen at that time because of responsibilities for other children, teachers should politely explain this to parents (e.g., "Mr. Sanchez, I think this is really important. Let me find another teacher to take over here so we can talk for a minute"). If a parent gives a teacher instructions or information that affects a child's care, either for that particular day or in general, the teacher must write down what the parent says. This information must then be communicated to all of the teachers in the classroom (if it involves care for that day) and to administrative staff (if the information affects long-term care).

5.   **If parents raise a concern or question that a teacher is unsure of answering, he or she should try to find another staff member who can help the parents.** The lead teacher or the child care program director may be needed to help parents when a teacher is unable to answer specific concerns or questions. If the lead teacher doesn't know the answer and administrative staff are not available, teachers can ask parents when and where they can be reached by phone that day, and then teachers can notify the child care program director of the parents' question and that the parents are expecting a call. Parents' concerns should be addressed as quickly and as thoroughly as possible.

6.   **Teachers should always have a positive experience to share with parents about a child.** When talking with a parent, teachers should think of the child's experiences that day and tell the parent at least one *specific* detail of what happened (e.g., "Josie tried and tried to stand up by herself today. She's so persistent"; "Damien was playing with trucks this afternoon and learned the names of all the big equipment—bulldozer, grader, dump truck—he's really talking a lot!"). No matter how small the incident may seem to teachers, any recollection of a specific event with a child allows the parent to see that teachers truly know their child as an individual.

7.   **When reporting an accident or injury involving a child, teachers must be direct and straightforward with parents about what happened.** The teacher should give the parents specific information about what was happening at the time of the accident and how the child was hurt. The parents should also be told exactly what was done to treat the child's injury, even if the injury was very minor. If there are changes in staff from morning to afternoon, it is crucial that all of the accidents and injuries are described *completely* in writing. Parents will lose confidence in child care staff if they feel that no one knows what happened to their child.

The one exception to informing parents fully is that it is *not* a good idea to tell the parents the names of other children who were involved in an accident or who may be responsible for the child's injury. Even if a child has received a bite from another child, it is not appropriate to tell the parents the name of the child who did the biting. (Older children will probably tell the parents themselves, but teachers should not be the ones who talk about other children with parents.) Furthermore, teachers should not imply to the parents that their own child was responsible for the accident because of his or her bad behavior or lack of control. It is also not required for teachers to assume personal responsibility for the accident. If parents ask about the level of supervision, teachers can explain the situation in a neutral manner, such as by saying, "We have four teachers here all the time and children are always supervised, but sometimes things happen really quickly."

8.   **Teachers must think of themselves as supporting parents' care, rather than substituting for the parents.** Parents are the most important people in young children's lives. Teachers provide an important supplement and support for parents, but they must avoid any feelings of competition with parents. When teachers view themselves as supports to parents, they express themselves as being friendly and helpful, rather than critical or superior.

TRANSITION TO SLEEP

All infants and toddlers need naps during the day, but many resist the transition from wakefulness into sleep. A regular nap routine for infants helps teachers prepare babies for sleep. Toddlers also need a predictable nap routine that allows some individuality and encourages a calm and relaxing transition to naptime.

Naps for Infants

Infants' nap schedules should be determined by their own needs for sleep. Teachers must be aware of and alert to individual children's signals that they are tired. Some children will be very obvious about becoming sleepy and will rub their eyes and yawn, whereas other children will just become cranky or highly active. Parents can be asked to suggest approximate naptimes for their babies. These times can provide a guide to babies' naps, but infants' wake and sleep schedules often vary widely from day to day. A sleepy baby should not be kept in the play area because the schedule suggests that his or her nap is not due for another hour.

Babies also vary in the speed with which they go to sleep once teachers lay them in their cribs and in the techniques they use to go to sleep. It seems that some babies need to cry in order to release tension and relax and may need to be left in their cribs to cry until they go to sleep. Children with special medical needs may have special sleep needs as well, and it is important for teachers to discuss these needs in advance with families. It is helpful for teachers to know all of the children's usual nap routines and how their parents handle naptimes at home. The environment in an infant classroom is clearly different from most homes, however, because in the classroom there are usually several babies sleeping at the same time as well as other children who are awake and playing. Once infants adjust to the classroom situation and the nap routines, babies' sleep is not disturbed by having the lights on or by the sounds of other activities in the room.

It is most important for teachers of infants to have a regular nap routine in order to prepare each baby for sleep. Babies need to do the same activities in the same sequence every day before naptime, and they need to sleep in the same place every day, surrounded with the same familiar objects. Teachers are not responsible for getting children to sleep or keeping them asleep. Instead, teachers are responsible for creating an environment that helps children learn to go to sleep on their own.

The teacher responsible for naps is usually the same teacher who is responsible for diapering (see Figure 4.2), or if a fourth teacher is available, the lead teacher may be responsible for naps. Balancing supervision of naps and diapering is not an easy job, but it is possible because the duties of the teacher who is responsible for diapering are more flexible than those of the teacher in charge of feeding or the teacher supervising play. In some cases, it may be possible to quickly check and change the diapers of all of the children who are awake at once and then concentrate on naps; during other times, the teacher will have to alternate between diapering and naps. Good judgment, knowledge of individual children, and active communication among all teachers are needed to make naps run smoothly.

It is sometimes tempting in infant care to organize the entire day around naps, especially if there is a child who initially has difficulty going to sleep and is fussy and irritable a lot of the time. It is understandable for teachers to want a break from a crying child who simply refuses to sleep for hours at a time. However, the solution to this situation is not to turn out all of the lights and keep all of the other babies quiet. Instead, teachers must stick to a regular nap routine that communicates to the child that it is time to relax and go to sleep.

At around the time of their first birthday, most children can be gradually eased into a routine of taking one nap each day. This nap should be scheduled directly after lunch. In order to ease a child into this schedule, lunch may have to be given very early in the day if the child has been accustomed to napping in the late morning. However, a gradual approach that gently moves the child to lunch at 11:30 A.M. and a nap at noon will help prepare the child for the transition into the toddler classroom. These older infants can also begin to nap on a toddler cot instead of in a crib, which gives them more independence and is safer for an active baby who may attempt to climb out of a crib.

The Quality Check on page 213 can be used by teachers and child care program directors to determine whether naptimes are running smoothly in an infant classroom.

Nap Routine for Infants

A predictable nap routine that incorporates the use of familiar objects, such as a favorite stuffed animal, blanket, or toy, is comforting to an infant and signals to the child that it is time for sleep. Teachers need to be responsive to each infant's naptime preferences but encourage every infant to learn to go to sleep on his or her own.

Step 1: Get Ready

When a child is ready to nap, the teacher prepares the crib or cot by checking the bedding and getting out the child's favorite sleep toy or special blanket. The child's diaper also needs to be checked and changed, if necessary, before the child naps.

Step 2: Invite or Bring Children to the Nap Area

The teacher who will be settling a child down to nap can bring the child his or her favorite sleep toy or blanket. This toy or blanket, which should be used only during naptime, serves as a visual reminder to the child that it is time to sleep and also provides comfort. If a child uses a pacifier at naptime, this is also the time to give the pacifier to the child. Depending on the child's individual routine in getting ready for nap, the teacher should spend a few minutes with the child in quiet talking, singing, rocking, or storybook reading. This quiet time is useful even for the youngest babies because it sets up a routine that will be helpful later when children are more easily distracted and more resistant to naps.

Step 3: Respond Individually to Each Child

Each child should have an individual routine that is followed every naptime. Parents may suggest a routine, or teachers can find one that is comfortable and helpful for the baby. It is important that this routine incorporates the same familiar elements as much as possible from naptime to naptime—the same song, the same storybook, and the same stuffed animal. This routine should last only a few minutes, and then the teacher can say, "Time to sleep," while placing the child gently in the crib. Unless a child has a medical condition that requires laying the child on his or her stomach, a young infant should be placed in the crib on his or her back or side, supported with a tightly rolled blanket or towel. For an older infant, parents will suggest the child's favorite sleeping position.

The teacher may gently rub the child's back if the child likes this and say something soft and comforting, such as, "Sleep tight!" However, the teacher's time at the child's bedside should be very brief, lasting only a few seconds, even if the child begins to cry. A child will go to sleep if teachers have been reading his or her signals correctly and the child is truly tired. Until children adjust to the nap routine, some may cry enough to interfere with others' sleep for a few days. Although this is frustrating for teachers, it is a necessary step in teaching children that sleep is good when one is tired.

The length of time a child should remain in a crib after being laid down to nap when he or she does not go to sleep should be individually determined in consultation with parents. A child who is very tired is as likely to be cranky and crying in the play area as in the nap area and is not in a good frame of mind to play and learn. When a child is in his or her crib and is crying, fussing, or refusing to lie down, teachers should avoid making eye contact with the child. If a child is clearly sleepy, a teacher may go and lay the child down again after 5 or 10 minutes, covering the child with a blanket and briefly rubbing his or her back. The specific approach that works in encouraging a child to sleep is different for each child. Sometimes nothing works, and teachers should not feel that they are responsible for a child's sleeping difficulties. Instead, they must continue to use a regular and comforting routine with each child, who will eventually learn to sleep on his or her own.

Step 4: Involve Children

Once a child awakens, he or she should be removed from the nap area, have a diaper check and change, if necessary, and return to play as quickly as appropriate for that child. Some children wake up ready to go, whereas other children need a few minutes to become fully alert. Also, some children may appear to wake up but go back to sleep after a few minutes if they are not disturbed. It is important for teachers to know the sleeping habits of each baby. Even if a child appears to be content, he or she should not be left in a crib for more than 5 or 10 minutes after awakening from a nap.

Step 5: Clean Up After Children Have Left the Nap Area

Once a child has been taken to another area, the teacher supervising naps should check the child's bedding and change the sheets and blankets if they are wet. Pacifiers and naptime toys or special blankets should be washed if necessary and put away. The times of each child's nap should be recorded on the classroom sleep chart and also on the Take-Home Report (see Figure 3.1) so that parents have a record of when their baby slept during the day.

Naps for Toddlers

Settling in to sleep in a bed that is not one's own is difficult for many people, and toddlers are no exception. Some children sleep well anywhere, whereas other children have difficulty relaxing and resting in any environment other than their own home. These individual differences must be respected and accommodated, and teachers must try not to become impatient with children who do not sleep easily.

Successful toddler naptimes depend on a predictable routine that is followed every day, a relaxed and comfortable atmosphere, a lot of individual attention to children during the transition to nap, and the availability of quiet activities when children awaken. Problems arise when naptimes are hectic and stressful for teachers and children and when routines are not followed. All children should not be expected to sleep or even stay on their cots for the same length of time. Children have different needs for sleep and are on different schedules at home, and these differences must be respected during naptime as well as during other times of day. Children with disabilities or special medical needs may have unusual sleep patterns or require special sleeping arrangements, and these concerns should be worked out with families in order to provide for the individual needs of each child. Child care program directors and teachers can use the Quality Check on page 213 to determine how well naptimes are conducted in their classroom.

Some toddler and preschool programs turn naptime over to substitute caregivers while regular teachers take their lunch breaks, but this practice does not recognize toddlers' need for the reliable presence of familiar, caring people during times of stress. Naptime is a part of daily living for toddlers that requires a maximum amount of sensitivity and responsiveness from teachers.

Young children accept bedtime and go to sleep more readily at home when the time for going to bed comes at the end of a comfortable routine that includes progressively more relaxing activities with parents' involvement. The same principle can be used successfully in child care. When the same routine is followed every day, toddlers can predict what is going to happen next, and this helps them feel in control of the situation. In addition, each child should have a soft blanket, stuffed toy, or other "transition object" that belongs only to that child and that is used only at naptime. These transition objects can be brought from home (if they can be spared), or they can be replicates of the bedtime comforters children use at home. If a child does not use such an object at home, one can be provided in the classroom. For most children, the association of such a soft, comfortable object with sleep provides a useful bridge from active play to rest.

Infant classrooms are usually required to have a separate sleeping area since babies' naptimes are unpredictable. In most toddler classrooms, a separate sleeping area will not be available for children's naps. Space for transition activities before and after nap is very limited when cots are set up in the play area. It is helpful to designate a space for each of the steps in the routine before nap and to move toddlers through the routine individually, rather than an entire group, in order to keep the transition relaxed and calm. At the same time, teachers must recognize and meet children's individual needs for extra comfort or attention during naptime. Toddlers cannot be rushed to their cots and expected to settle down to sleep on their own. Teachers must be aware that the transition into nap is an activity that requires as much of their involvement and attention as the more traditional teaching activities that they do.

Nap Routine for Toddlers

Toddlers need a familiar nap routine that provides signals to them that it is time for sleep. Dimmed lighting, soft music, and quiet activities can help toddlers gradually become ready for naps. It is important for teachers to respond to toddlers individually and recognize that children need varying amounts of rest.

Step 1: Get Ready

In toddler classrooms, naptime usually comes right after lunch. As lunch begins, one teacher can set up cots for children's naps. If at all possible, the light level should be lowered once lunch is over. Also, by playing soft music and talking quietly, teachers can begin to set a relaxed and restful mood. Each child should have a cot of his or her own, set up in the same place every day. Each child's cot should be covered with the same sheet (or at least a sheet of the same color or pattern) and blanket every day.

Step 2: Invite or Bring Children to the Nap Area

As children leave the lunch table, they may cycle through a quiet activity before "going potty" or having a diaper change, then return to the quiet activity, which serves as the staging area for naptime. During this quiet activity, which is recommended to involve reading books or storytelling by a teacher, children should have access to their transition objects, the soft blankets, stuffed animals, dolls, or whatever they prefer to keep with them during naptime. When children have had a few minutes of quiet listening, another teacher can invite or take them to their cots, one at a time, always spending a minute or two—but not more—to help each child settle down to sleep. Affectionate pats or a brief backrub as the child lies down can be reassuring; however, teachers should not assume responsibility for getting children to sleep by rocking them, holding them, or rubbing their backs for long periods of time. Children need to learn to get themselves to sleep, and teachers should demonstrate confidence in their ability to do so.

Step 3: Respond Individually to Each Child

Teachers must become familiar with the individual differences among children in their care so that they can support them in the transition to sleep. Parents can help by describing their children's typical nap patterns at home, but observation of children in the classroom is also necessary. The order in which children are taken to their cots should allow the children who are most tired to get to sleep first. Children who are easily distracted by others' activities should be situated on cots that are on the edges of the sleep area or visually shielded from other children. The goal is to provide an environment that encourages quiet relaxation and sleep without the constant involvement of teachers, whose nagging and other attempts to enforce children's rest can only result in frustration for themselves and the children. Those children who have a particularly difficult time getting to sleep should be the last to leave the lunch table and the last to leave the quiet play activity so that they can have a longer quiet time with a teacher before going to their cots. In this way, most of the other children will already be asleep, the lights can be dimmed even further, and teachers can say, "Have a good sleep" and then withdraw their attention from the child. Sometimes children who have difficulty sleeping can be encouraged to relax by listening through headphones to an audiotape of quiet music or a story, preferably a somewhat boring one.

Step 4: Involve Children

Children have varying needs for sleep; for example, some children may take 2- or even 3-hour naps while others may awaken after only 1 hour or less. Some children wake up energized, whereas other children awaken only gradually. Teachers, in consultation with parents, must become aware of and accommodate children's individual differences. When children do awaken and are finished with sleep, they should not be required to remain on their cots, waiting for other children to wake up or for a specified amount of time to pass. Toddlers can be encouraged to leave the sleep area quietly so as not to disturb other children, and they will enjoy the alliance with teachers as they tiptoe among the cots. A trip to the toilet or a diaper change is first on the agenda after naptime, and a drink of juice or water should be offered. Most children enjoy a quiet activity after nap—doll play, puzzles, or looking at picture books are good alternatives. If there is no space in the classroom for children to play, a teacher can take the first two or three children to awaken from their naps on a walk around the building or, if the weather is warm, to the playground.

Step 5: Clean Up After Children Have Left the Nap Area

In order to avoid awakening children, teachers should wait to fold blankets and put away cots until the majority of the children are awake. Toddlers who are awake can then help to put their beds away. Those children who sleep the longest amount of time are usually not easily disrupted by others' activities. If these children's cots are placed at the edge of the sleep area, regular classroom activities can be resumed while they continue sleeping.

TRANSITIONS TO OUTDOOR PLAY AND BACK INSIDE THE CLASSROOM

Although infants and toddlers generally enjoy outdoor play, they do not like interruptions. Therefore, the process of getting ready to go outside often presents difficulties for teachers. Similarly, once outside and involved in play, infants and toddlers may not be happy when told that it is time to go back inside the classroom. Although the focus of this section is on transitions to the playground, similar situations also arise whenever an entire group of infants or toddlers must be moved to a new location, such as an eating area that is separate from the classroom or during fire or storm drills. Cooperation among teachers, advance planning, and accommodation to the individual styles of children help reduce transition time troubles.

Transitions for Teaching

Transitions are most effectively used as teaching and learning times when teachers involve the children in game-like interactions that keep them actively involved. As in most activities, difficulties arise when infants and toddlers are passive recipients of care or must wait with nothing to do. Therefore, if at all possible, it is best for a few children at a time to go with one teacher to the playground, followed by another small group in a few minutes, until all of the children have completed the transition, rather than having the entire group of children wait until everyone is ready and then move as a group from inside to outside the classroom. If the environment makes gradual transitions impractical, teachers must work to keep all of the children involved in the transition. Toddlers who are more independent can be enlisted as helpers for the younger, less independent children, bringing shoes and coats for younger children and even helping with socks or mittens. Teachers can also use transition songs that are repeated every day so that older infants and toddlers can participate and in this way maintain involvement in the ongoing activity.

Planned transitions to outdoors also provide excellent opportunities for teachers to encourage toddlers to work at learning how to put on their own socks, shoes, and coats. Each child can have at least one task to try, and teachers can provide assistance to ensure success. Watching other children do things for themselves provides incentive to the less skilled children to gain independence. In addition, some children who do not want to dress themselves are eager and willing to help another child, especially a child who has a disability. Teachers can encourage children to help one another and gradually work to transfer the skills learned in this way to children's efforts to dress themselves.

Although transitions in preschool are not considered to be activities, infants and toddlers cannot be rushed from one area to another. Furthermore, all infant programs and most inclusive toddler programs will have children who are not independently mobile and for whom transitions are even more disruptive and difficult. Therefore, transitions in infant-toddler care are accomplished most smoothly when a block of time is planned to be devoted to the process of getting shoes and coats on and going outside and for returning to the classroom and removing clothes worn outside. Transition routines are basically the same for infants as they are for toddlers, and transition routines are among the few daily activities that frequently involve all of the teachers and children at the same time. The Quality Check for transitions on page 214 can serve as a guide to whether transitions are running smoothly in an infant or toddler classroom.

Transition Routine for Infants and Toddlers

A transition routine is needed for infants and toddlers who are in the process of moving from one area to another area, such as from inside the classroom to the playground outdoors. Teachers can use songs or finger plays to make the transition fun and interesting for children. Allowing adequate time for transitions gives teachers opportunities to help all children, including children with disabilities, move toward increased independence in dressing and undressing themselves.

Step 1: Get Ready

About 5 minutes before transition time, the lead teacher should make a general announcement that it is "almost time to go out" or "time to get ready to go in to play." This reminder is effective primarily with teachers because infants and toddlers are not able to understand how long 5 minutes takes. Once they hear the announcement, however, teachers can begin talking with the children in their vicinity about the next activity, and can further signal the coming transition by involving older infants and toddlers in helping to pick up the toys they have been using. Often, children will not seem to pay attention to these announcements or conversations. Nevertheless, the warnings are heard and they help children prepare for an interruption in their activities.

Step 2: Invite Children to Begin the Transition

One teacher should be designated to begin helping children who are walking to put on their shoes. It is best to put only a few children's shoes on at a time so that the majority of children can continue their play. The teacher can begin talking about shoes, such as discussing the colors of the shoes, how they feel, or whether they close with laces, straps, or Velcro. Children who show an interest (and some children will if the teacher is enthusiastic) can be asked to identify the owners of the shoes—young

children are very observant of their peers' belongings. Teachers can help
make the shoe activity more fun and interesting by getting involved
themselves—for example, claiming that a tiny pair of sneakers is theirs
and pretending to put the pair of shoes on.

Coats, coveralls, or snowsuits should be put on children just before
they go outside. No child should be dressed for outdoor play and then
have to wait for other children for more than 5 minutes at most. Toddlers
who use wheelchairs should be dressed, settled in their wheelchairs, and
taken immediately outdoors, rather than being left to wait with nothing
to do while teachers help other children get ready. Similarly, if strollers or
other carriers are being used for infants, babies should not be placed in
them until the trip is ready to begin.

Step 3: Respond Individually to Each Child

Some toddlers will be mostly independent dressers, able to put on and
take off their own socks, shoes, and coats, whereas most children will
need a great deal of help dressing and undressing. Teachers need to be
aware of the degree of assistance each child needs and use daily transitions as times to help move each child toward increased independence.
Even infants and children with motor disabilities can participate in dressing and undressing by holding out an arm or lifting a foot. Sometimes
children who know how to dress or undress themselves have days when
they want to be waited on by teachers. Teachers should accept toddlers'
wavering between being a baby and being a "big kid" and offer help

without criticizing children. At the same time, children who do any part of the dressing or undressing routine on their own or who help other children should be given plenty of attention and encouragement for their achievements. Teachers need to be careful not to take for granted those children who are capable of these tasks, but rather to provide affection and attention to all children.

Step 4: Involve Children

In addition to encouraging the development of dressing and undressing skills, teachers must work to make the transitions to and from the playground times of active involvement for the children. Even the youngest children who are mobile can help push, pull, or carry toys from the classroom to the playground. Toddlers can help a teacher push a child's wheelchair, help pull a wagon with younger children in it, or carry toys. On the way outside or back inside the classroom, teachers should sing to the children (developing a repertoire of "traveling music" is worthwhile). Another good transition activity for teachers and children is "Follow the Leader." Toddlers can be encouraged to "hop like a bunny" or "fly like a bird to the sandbox." One teacher might encourage the older children to talk about what awaits them on the playground or describe what they did while outside, in order to help develop children's narrative skills. Transition times can also be good times for teaching simple songs or rhymes. If any waiting is involved during transitions, teachers should be prepared with a set of finger plays and songs to keep children's minds and fingers occupied.

Step 5: Clean Up After Children Have Left the Area

After the transition is completed, one teacher can be responsible for any cleanup that is needed. This may involve sorting the children's shoes and coats and returning these items to children's cubbies or lockers, putting outdoor toys in their storage containers, and completing any general playground cleanup. A toddler helper can sometimes be involved with a teacher in these activities.

SUMMARY

Transitions typically come as surprises to infants and toddlers because the children do not understand enough language or have a concept of time to be prepared for them. Therefore, transitions in infant and toddler classrooms are most successful when teachers consider them to be activities, rather than interruptions in activities. By allowing time on the daily schedule for children's arrivals and departures, for preparation for naps, and for moving to the playground, teachers can eliminate the frustration that comes with trying to hurry infants or toddlers through a change of activity.

If transitions are to be positive learning experiences for children, rather than wasted time, teachers must be just as involved with children during transitions as during other teaching and learning activities. Music, storytelling, and active games are useful approaches to making transitions pleasant for children and teachers alike. In addition, carefully planned transitions offer opportunities for children to learn and practice functional skills that they can use every day.

Quality Check ✔

Arrival-Departure in Infant-Toddler Care

Teachers, child care program directors, and visitors can use this guide to determine whether arrivals and departures are going well. After watching a few parents and children arrive or depart, all answers should be YES.

1. Does every child receive individual attention and interaction from all teachers?   YES ☐   NO ☐

2. Does every parent receive individual attention and interaction from the greeting teacher?   YES ☐   NO ☐

3. Is separation or reunion handled sensitively for every child and parent?   YES ☐   NO ☐

4. Does the greeting teacher communicate personally with every parent and have something positive to say about every child?   YES ☐   NO ☐

5. Does the greeting teacher smile often and use a positive tone of voice with children and parents? YES ☐   NO ☐

6. Does the greeting teacher touch and lift children with gentleness and affection?   YES ☐   NO ☐

7. Is the greeting teacher's attention focused on parents and children?   YES ☐   NO ☐

8. Does the greeting area appear attractive and inviting?   YES ☐   NO ☐

Inclusive Child Care for Infants and Toddlers: Meeting Individual and Special Needs by Marion O'Brien © 1997 Paul H. Brookes Publishing Co., Baltimore.

Quality Check ✔

Naps in Infant-Toddler Care

Teachers, child care program directors, and visitors can use this guide to determine high-quality care during naptime. After watching teachers and children during naptime, all answers should be YES.

1. Does every child receive individual attention and interaction from a teacher? YES ☐ NO ☐

2. Does every child (unless too sleepy) have a quiet time with a teacher before being put down to nap? YES ☐ NO ☐

3. Is every child encouraged to go to sleep on his or her own? YES ☐ NO ☐

4. When each child awakens, is he or she noticed and invited to get up? YES ☐ NO ☐

5. Do teachers smile often and use a positive tone of voice with children? YES ☐ NO ☐

6. If any child cries or fusses, do teachers respond positively and sensitively? YES ☐ NO ☐

7. Do teachers touch children with gentleness and affection while putting them down to sleep? YES ☐ NO ☐

8. Do teachers notice and respond to every child's efforts to communicate? YES ☐ NO ☐

9. Is each teacher's attention focused primarily on the children? YES ☐ NO ☐

10. Does the sleep space appear uncrowded, attractive, and inviting? YES ☐ NO ☐

Inclusive Child Care for Infants and Toddlers: Meeting Individual and Special Needs by Marion O'Brien © 1997 Paul H. Brookes Publishing Co., Baltimore.

Quality Check ✔

Transitions in Infant-Toddler Care

Teachers, child care program directors, and visitors can use this guide to determine high-quality care during transitions outside. After watching teachers and children throughout a transition, all answers should be YES.

1. Does every child receive individual attention and interaction from a teacher?   YES ☐   NO ☐

2. Is downtime—waiting with nothing to do—kept to no more than 1–2 minutes for any child?   YES ☐   NO ☐

3. Are all children encouraged to help dress themselves and more capable children encouraged to help others?   YES ☐   NO ☐

4. Is every child involved in a transition activity of some type—song, finger play, movement activity, or conversation with a teacher?   YES ☐   NO ☐

5. Do teachers smile often and use a positive tone of voice with children?   YES ☐   NO ☐

6. If any child cries or fusses, or aggression or upsets occur, do teachers respond positively and sensitively?   YES ☐   NO ☐

7. Do teachers touch children frequently with gentleness and affection?   YES ☐   NO ☐

8. Do teachers notice and respond to children's efforts to communicate?   YES ☐   NO ☐

9. Is each teacher's attention focused primarily on the children?   YES ☐   NO ☐

10. Is every child always supervised?   YES ☐   NO ☐

Inclusive Child Care for Infants and Toddlers: Meeting Individual and Special Needs by Marion O'Brien © 1997 Paul H. Brookes Publishing Co., Baltimore.

Part IV

MANAGEMENT AND ADMINISTRATION OF INCLUSIVE INFANT-TODDLER CARE

High-quality programs for children depend on people. All of the teaching techniques and care procedures described throughout this book require a commitment to quality by families, teachers, special service providers, and child care program directors. It is more difficult, more tiring, and more costly to provide high-quality care for young children than to provide poor or merely adequate care.

Inclusive child care and early intervention services have great potential to improve the lives of children and families. They provide employed families support in the difficult job of raising children while working outside of the home. Child care services also promote children's health, growth, and development in ways that contribute to their lifelong well-being. Furthermore, inclusive child care and early intervention services can effectively remediate early signs of developmental delays, prevent secondary disabilities, and maximize the opportunities of individuals with disabilities to lead satisfying and productive lives. Although these contributions are most significant to individuals, provision of quality services to young children and their families offers considerable gain to the society as well. When developmental delays are ameliorated in children's early years, costs of special education services in schools are reduced. Even more important, giving all young children opportunities to learn and grow in supportive and responsive environments can reduce the incidence of behavior problems, serious mental illness, and antisocial acts among adolescents and young adults in the future.

Maintaining high quality in child care programs is not an easy task. The demands placed on teachers are complex and continuous, and the salaries they earn do not compensate for the investment of physical and emotional energy that teachers must make in caring for children. Families want the best for their children, but many families have limited financial resources to contribute toward the real cost of high-quality child care programs. Administrators often find themselves caught in the struggle to keep programs financially afloat, which leaves little time to provide the supervision and support that teachers need to do the best possible job.

The many difficulties in operating high-quality child care and early intervention programs must not deter families, teachers, child care program directors, and other professionals from maintaining their efforts to do so. The personal rewards of high-quality care are constantly apparent in the everyday progress and enthusiasm of children. As the evidence of the effectiveness of preventive approaches to educational and social problems continues to accumulate, it is likely that increased support for early childhood programs will be forthcoming. Until then, individuals with a commitment to quality must continue to advocate in the best interests of all children and families.

This section discusses the management of inclusive infant-toddler care, which is a crucial aspect of high-quality care for young children. Chapter 11 describes the administrative structure that supports the day-to-day work of teachers in inclusive infant-toddler care and also describes techniques for training and supervising teachers on a regular basis in order to ensure high-quality program operation. Chapter 12 describes ways in which the quality of infant-toddler care can be evaluated.

Chapter 11

Administering
Inclusive Infant-Toddler Care

Administrators of early childhood services have several responsibilities that are crucial to the provision of quality care and early intervention for infants and toddlers. A major responsibility of administrators is the selection and training of teachers. The teacher–child relationship is at the heart of all child care situations; therefore, the selection and training of teachers are crucial aspects of quality child care. Administrators are also responsible for supporting and encouraging teachers in their day-to-day work with children.

AN EFFECTIVE ADMINISTRATIVE STRUCTURE

In order to maintain a high-quality, inclusive infant-toddler care program, it is essential to have an effective administrative structure. A lead teacher is needed to make sure that all teachers are providing high-quality care every day. The family services coordinator ensures involvement of families in infant-toddler care, and an intervention team helps meet the needs of each child at risk for or with disabilities or developmental delays. A child care program director's responsibilities involve personnel management and financial aspects of the child care center; the advisory board supports the child care program with fund-raising and publicity.

The Lead Teacher

In most child care programs, one of the classroom teachers is usually designated as a lead teacher, whose primary responsibility is day-to-day management of the classroom. This job may involve daily communication with parents, including making sure that classroom teachers keep accurate records and send home information about the children's activities each day. During the day, the lead teacher usually keeps track of the activities of all children and teachers in the classroom and helps prevent and solve problems that arise. In addition, the lead teacher will usually be responsible for making sure that all of the classroom teachers are providing high-quality and responsive care, all of the children are receiving the individual care that they need, and the classroom is operating smoothly.

If several children with special needs are enrolled in an infant or toddler program, it is most effective if a lead teacher *and* three teachers comprise the classroom staff. In this situation, the lead teacher can assume supervisory responsibilities while handling record keeping and other important administrative tasks that are time-consuming and take teachers' attention away from the children. Furthermore, the lead teacher can promote inclusion by helping children with special needs participate fully in classroom activities, taking charge of providing specialized health care for individual children as needed, and serving as a liaison between special service providers and teachers. At times, the lead teacher in this situation will be directly involved with children by helping the three classroom teachers; for example, the lead teacher may assist with transitions between areas and during outdoor play. When one of the regular teachers is not available, the lead teacher can also assume his or her role, ensuring that the number of teachers present in the classroom never falls below 3.

Frequently, lead teachers will also be involved in training new teachers and will serve as resources for teachers and parents when they have questions or concerns about anything happening in the classroom. The lead teacher shares responsibility with the child care program director for the quality of care and intervention provided to children. The lead teacher is present in the classroom most of the time; therefore, he or she is the best person to be responsible for observing teachers' performance of daily routines, presentation of play activities, and effective use of teaching and intervention techniques. The lead teacher can also provide regular feedback to teachers in a way that helps them become better teachers. Constructive feedback is best provided by the lead teacher in personal conversations with teachers on a daily basis; therefore, the lead teacher should set aside some time every day to observe each teacher and make notes of the positive aspects of teachers' performance and any suggestions for improvement. (See the section on "Feedback from Teachers" in Chapter 12 and Figure 11.1 for procedures for supervision and evaluation of teachers.) In addition, the lead teacher provides help and support to teachers as they conduct their everyday tasks and does not wait until a specified "feedback time" to comment on a successful play activity or make suggestions to help improve teachers' effectiveness.

The Family Services Coordinator

The involvement of families in infant-toddler care and early intervention is one of the hallmarks of a quality child care program. Continuity and communication between children's homes and the classroom are particularly important with very young children. Child care program staff are responsible for providing support to families and extending the care that parents provide to their children, rather than replacing or improving parents' care. More information about family involvement and the role of the family services coordinator is presented in Chapter 3.

The Intervention Team

The most effective services for young children and families use a transdisciplinary model of early intervention, described in Chapter 2, in which

Teacher _____   Date _____

Observer _____

Does the teacher		Comments
1. Conduct child care routines with energy and accuracy?	Always Usually Sometimes Rarely	
2. Interact with children affectionately, sensitively, and enthusiastically?	Always Usually Sometimes Rarely	
3. Cooperate effectively with other child care staff, supervisors, and families?	Always Usually Sometimes Rarely	
4. Successfully involve all children in play and participate actively with children?	Always Usually Sometimes Rarely	
5. Use responsive teaching techniques, modifying teaching goals as needed?	Always Usually Sometimes Rarely	
6. Successfully include children with disabilities in all classroom activities?	Always Usually Sometimes Rarely	
7. Use language facilitation techniques, including signs, to promote communication?	Always Usually Sometimes Rarely	
8. Use motor development facilitation techniques to promote balance and coordination?	Always Usually Sometimes Rarely	
9. Use positive comments and encouragement, rather than correction and criticism?	Always Usually Sometimes Rarely	
10. Supervise children at all times, use responsive guidance as needed, and ensure children's safety?	Always Usually Sometimes Rarely	
11. Focus full attention on the children?	Always Usually Sometimes Rarely	
12. Behave reliably and dependably?	Always Usually Sometimes Rarely	

Figure 11.1.   A sample form for evaluating teacher effectiveness.

parents, teachers, and special service providers work together to provide the best possible learning environment for children. In the approach taken in this book, specialists serve as consultants to the child care program; they teach children's teachers how to use intervention techniques that will help meet the outcomes specified on children's individualized family service plans (IFSPs). Teaching techniques that are recommended by specialists are incorporated into the teachers' repertoire and used with *all* of the children all of the time.

When a child is referred to an infant or toddler program because of a concern with his or her development, the intervention team should conduct a developmental assessment to determine whether the child is showing developmental delays in any area or appears to be at risk for eventual developmental delay. Assessment includes talking with the child's parents about their child's health history and discussing with parents the times that certain developmental milestones were reached by the child. Members of the intervention team will also observe the child in the classroom as he or she participates in everyday activities as well as during standardized testing situations. Team members consult with one another frequently to consider the best ways to meet the child's needs, even if the child does not have any identified delays or disabilities.

As described in Chapter 2, a transdisciplinary team that is supporting the intervention efforts in an inclusive infant-toddler child care and early intervention program will usually include the following professionals who work together to meet the needs of each child: the child's family services coordinator, who may or may not be directly employed by the child care program and may have training in early childhood special education, social work, clinical child psychology, or another discipline; a speech-language specialist, who concentrates primarily on the development of communication abilities; both physical and occupational therapists, who are concerned with the child's motor development and his or her acquisition of functional skills; an early childhood special educator, who may provide special instruction for a particular child; and health professionals, both nurses and physicians, with whom a program may consult regarding a child with special health care needs. Parents and other family members are also crucial members of the intervention team.

The other important but often overlooked members of the intervention team are the classroom teachers, who are usually early childhood educators. The best classroom teachers have the type of broad training in child development that allows them to see the child as a whole person, rather than merely focusing on a set of developmental skills that each child must learn. Good teachers, regardless of their training, are also knowledgeable about how the classroom environment works and can identify times and situations in which intervention approaches can be most successful.

A transdisciplinary team works together to provide intervention that meets individual children's needs. In the model described in this book, the teachers are the primary interventionists outside of the family; the teachers, rather than the specialists, are the people who are expected to implement intervention techniques with children as part of every activity that occurs in the classroom during the day. Although at times a particular child may spend some time with a specialized therapist, teachers provide intervention every day and within every classroom context.

This type of collaboration requires the sharing of roles among all of the people on the intervention team. In other words, therapists must be willing to give away to teachers some of the specialized knowledge about intervening with children that they have learned over years in school and by experience. In turn, teachers must be willing to accept the responsibility of intervening in order to minimize developmental delays in children and be willing to add specialized intervention techniques to their repertoire of teaching skills. Also, therapists must be willing to learn from teachers who understand early childhood environments and classroom routines so that therapists can plan intervention approaches that work in the context of the child care setting. For their part, teachers must be willing to consider changes in classroom organization and routines that may better meet children's individual needs. All of this shifting of responsibility and information does not happen easily or without planning. Instead, it requires time and effort from each member of the intervention team.

Thus, the intervention team must make time to meet so that they can plan the necessary intervention program for each child and also so that they can communicate about *how* to intervene and *when* intervention can best take place within the daily schedule. In addition, specialists must visit the classroom on a regular basis to provide teachers with demonstrations and information about intervention techniques, to help with problem solving, and to give teachers feedback on their use of the techniques that they have learned. Teachers must also communicate honestly and openly with specialists (who must listen) regarding techniques that work and techniques that do not work in the classroom.

The Child Care Program Director

The role of the child care program director is to set policy and ensure financial stability of the program, which includes hiring, training, and supervising lead teachers and family services coordinators; working with the lead teachers to select and train teachers; supporting the collaborative efforts of the intervention team; and maintaining a high-quality early intervention and inclusive child care program. An effective child care program director will be involved in the community's early intervention network, and he or she also will be aware of local, state, and national policies and trends in child care and early intervention services.

Typically, a child care program director will not spend a lot of time in the classroom and will not be involved in direct care of children. Nevertheless, a child care program director must be familiar with all of the classroom routines and activities; be well-acquainted with staff, children, and parents; and be available for consultation and problem solving as needed. The child care program director is an important part of the intervention team; he or she provides access to specialized consultants and information as well as support for the intervention team's ongoing efforts to supply quality services to children and families.

Although a child care program director is responsible for hiring child care program staff and evaluating their work, these duties should be viewed as *supportive* efforts. A child care program director can achieve this by giving lead teachers and other child care program staff frequent, positive feedback, rather than waiting until problems arise and the feedback will most likely be negative. Thus, a child care program director should visit the classroom frequently and conduct structured observations of the program's operation on a regular schedule.

The Advisory Board

Most community-based programs have advisory boards composed of community leaders, representatives of educational organizations, and parents. Advisory boards serve valuable functions in child care program management and community relations. Frequently, the advisory board can be consulted regarding policy changes or fee increases, the members may serve on personnel selection committees, or the members may help to develop or review written materials for families.

Advisory boards often assist child care programs with fund-raising and publicity, which can be extremely helpful. A well-selected and active advisory board can also serve as a professional liaison with the public schools, local institutions of higher education that train prospective child care program teachers and special service providers, and with other child care and early intervention agencies in the community.

In order for an advisory board to be an active and effective participant in the administrative organization of a child care program, the child care program director must be able and willing to delegate meaningful tasks and real responsibilities to advisory board members. Advisory boards generally do not take action without encouragement and direction. Furthermore, the child care program director and other child care program staff must be willing to listen to the suggestions and ideas of the advisory board, or the board will become an administrative burden, rather than a vital and supportive organization.

TRAINING AND SUPERVISION OF CLASSROOM TEACHERS

Responsive teaching of infants and toddlers is a difficult and demanding job, and the individuals hired as teachers must be carefully selected. New teachers of infants and toddlers need thorough training in order to learn the care and teaching routines used in the classroom. Regular positive feedback from supervisors helps support teachers as well as giving them opportunities to discuss performance standards and job responsibilities. Teachers in inclusive child care programs also need to learn about children's special needs in order to care for children with disabilities and developmental delays.

Identifying Characteristics of Successful Teachers of Infants and Toddlers

Although infant and toddler care is difficult and demanding, people who care for very young children are often poorly paid and are not required to have child-related training or certification in early childhood education (Blau, 1991). Partially as a result of such hiring policies, much of the infant care and especially toddler care available in the United States is of low quality (*Cost, Quality, and Child Outcomes in Child Care Centers*, Executive Summary, 1995). If early intervention is to be incorporated into infant and toddler care, child care providers must be trained as teachers and supported in their work.

Many early childhood education programs in community colleges and 4-year colleges and universities include training in infant-toddler care, and the Child Development Associate training program offers a specific certification for infant-toddler care. Teachers whose training programs did not include infants and toddlers in their curricula can receive effective in-service training within the context of a quality child care program, provided that these teachers are observed regularly in the classroom and given frequent and specific feedback on their teaching performance.

Knowledge of child development, particularly regarding the developmental tasks that must be mastered by infants and toddlers and the appropriate developmental expectations adults should have, is an important factor in successful teaching of infants and toddlers. Flexible thinking and a willingness to tolerate change and ambiguity are also necessary because infants and toddlers cannot be expected to behave according to adult standards or even to follow the same schedule from day to day. Teachers must also have an overwhelmingly positive attitude about everything that children do and focus on the strengths and successes of children and their families, rather than on the problems and stresses children and their families may sometimes create.

Successful teachers of infants and toddlers are usually outgoing, energetic, expressive, and openly affectionate; however, the addition of a teacher with a quieter personality, whose lap is readily available and whose manner is always calm, competent, and comfortable, often provides a needed balance in the classroom. Regardless of their personalities, teachers of infants and toddlers must be willing to become actively involved in children's care and play, to be silly and enjoy themselves, and to leave their own cares and troubles behind when they are with the children. Teachers must be alert and intelligent so that they can learn and follow caregiving routines accurately and completely, modify those routines as needed for individual children, and be able to supervise children's experiences closely without interfering with their exploration.

Caring for infants and toddlers requires a team effort; therefore, effective teachers must work well as part of a team. Teachers of infants and toddlers must communicate effectively, value collaboration and cooperation, and be willing to accept suggestions from other teachers and supervisors. Teachers must also be healthy and highly reliable so that they do not miss a lot of work or frequently arrive late.

Teachers with all of these characteristics are ideal candidates for involvement in inclusive infant-toddler child care programs in which they will have opportunities to use all of their many skills every day and to gain increased professional confidence and competence.

Training New Teachers

Within an organized inclusive child care program for infants and toddlers, every new teacher will need a period of training, regardless of his or her previous experience or certification. All of the teachers must learn to use responsive teaching (see Chapter 6) and responsive guidance (see Chapter 7) techniques in all of their interactions with children and follow daily living routines for child care (see Chapters 8, 9, and 10).

Effective on-the-job training can be done relatively quickly and thoroughly. The first step of training is directing a new teacher to read a description of each of the care and teaching routines to be learned and then spend at least a day or two "shadowing" an experienced teacher who can provide demonstrations and guidance. The second important step of training is giving the new teacher regular descriptive feedback about his or her performance of all assigned daily living and teaching responsibilities. This observation and feedback can be provided with the use of the observation checklists included in the appendix at the end of this chapter. For the first few days, the trainer (usually the lead teacher or child care program director) should carefully observe the new teacher and make notes of excellent performance in addition to areas in which improvement is needed. Once the new teacher has demonstrated his or her acquisition of the basic aspects of classroom routines, these checklists may be used as self-training guides, and the new teacher may judge his or her own performance with a checklist as a reminder of what is expected in each routine.

Supporting Teachers Through Regular Feedback

When new teachers thoroughly learn and practice routines for several weeks, it is usually not necessary to continue checking performance at the same level of detail. Instead, teachers can be given regular feedback on their general teaching skills and overall contribution to the child care program; a teacher effectiveness evaluation form similar to that shown in Figure 11.1 is useful for this purpose. No matter how much experience or seniority a teacher may have, this evaluation form serves as a reminder of the qualities valued by a high-quality child care program. When evaluations are carried out frequently (e.g., every month), teachers receive positive feedback that is encouraging and supportive.

It is helpful in training teachers and maintaining quality for child care programs to have regular staff meetings that focus on one item from the teacher effectiveness form during each meeting. Together, teachers and administrative staff can review the standards for high quality associated with that item in a general discussion. This format allows experienced teachers to share their knowledge with new teachers, and it also reminds all of the teachers to strive for the child care program's expectations for quality care. During the interval between meetings, lead teachers or child care program directors can closely observe that particular item from the evaluation form, giving written and verbal feedback to teachers on a regular basis.

When teachers are given frequent feedback and have opportunities to discuss performance standards and job responsibilities with their supervisors, the feedback they receive from supervisors is almost always highly positive. Thus, a system of providing regular, written feedback combined with personal discussions about the classroom and teachers' efforts becomes a means of providing support for hardworking teachers, rather than being a stressful and anxiety-provoking experience. It is recommended that all teachers, regardless of the length of time that they have been employed, receive written feedback (primarily positive) about some important aspect of teacher effectiveness at least once each month.

Helping Teachers Learn About Children's Special Needs

Although a child care program may have experienced and well-educated teachers, the child care staff may be unfamiliar with working with children who have disabilities and developmental delays. In fact, the uncertainty that many teachers have about dealing with the unknown often serves as a barrier to inclusion of children with disabilities in child care programs (Fewell, 1993). Teachers can overcome their fear and anxiety through training that is specifically tailored to the individual needs of particular children who are enrolled in the child care program. It is also helpful for teachers to be reminded that parents of children with special needs are usually not specialists themselves in disabilities or medicine, yet parents are expected and able to provide the care their children need.

Whenever a new child who has special medical needs or a disability that is not already familiar to classroom teachers is enrolled, it is worthwhile to devote a child care staff meeting (or to call a special meeting) to providing teachers with as much information as possible about the new child. Involving the child's family in this meeting is extremely helpful. Family members are the best people to provide perspectives on a child as a person, rather than a patient, and this is how teachers will get to know the child. Parents can also provide some of the direct training that teachers require to meet a child's individual needs. Special service providers who are familiar with the child or the nature of the child's disability can also provide a useful perspective and some hands-on training in positioning, feeding, and other care routines.

As teachers work on a day-to-day basis with any child, they will think of questions about the child's medical history, prognosis, and current treatment and intervention plan that they did not think about when they first met the child. If parents are willing, a follow-up meeting to talk about these questions in more depth may be useful. Often, questions also can be collected by the lead teacher or family services coordinator, who can contact the family and special service providers to obtain the needed information. It is most important that teachers feel free to ask whatever questions they have and receive prompt and complete answers. As they gain more experience with children who have special needs, teachers will learn that not all questions can be answered. Often, the precise cause for a child's disability or delay is not known, the prognosis is uncertain, and the treatment plan is based on the best available knowledge but is not guaranteed to achieve immediate results. These are difficulties that families also face, and these issues can help teachers learn to cope with the uncertainties that are part of caring for children with special needs. Teachers can provide support and encouragement to parents by sharing their experiences and enjoyment of the child with families.

An inclusive child care program should also maintain a small library of books, articles, and videotapes regarding disabilities and developmental delays. Copies of relevant material can be given to teachers to take home, where they can read or view them as they realize their need for further information.

SUMMARY

An effective organizational structure for an inclusive child care program serving infants and toddlers and their families has the goal of supporting the work of teachers and ensuring that the program has adequate financial and community resources to operate successfully. Because the quality of care provided to children to a great extent depends on the personal characteristics, training, and morale of teachers, a primary goal of child care program administrators must be to hire excellent teachers and train them in responsive teaching and caregiving practices that are appropriate for all children, including those with disabilities and developmental delays. Furthermore, the hard work that teachers do must be supported by administrators through provision of a lot of positive feedback and opportunities for professional development.

Appendix
Teacher Training and Performance Checks

Teacher Performance Check: Infant Play 1

Teacher: _____ Week of: _____

++ = excellent   OK = OK   ✔ = improvement needed   N = not observed

Did the teacher:	M	T	W	TH	F
1. Keep the majority of children actively involved most of the time? (Observer should check and calculate percentage during beginning, middle, and end of observation time.)	1 2 3	1 2 3	1 2 3	1 2 3	1 2 3
2. Check schedule board and set out materials scheduled for this time?					
3. Position him- or herself in a location where he or she could see most of the area?					
4. Keep noncrawling infants and those children in positioning chairs or other containers within arm's reach?					
5. Scan the area frequently in order to keep track of every child?					
6. Have verbal and/or pleasant physical contact with every child at least every couple of minutes?					
7. Use language- and motor-development facilitation techniques frequently in interactions with children?					
8. Act quickly to prevent problems and redirect children as needed and handle appropriately any problems that arose?					
9. Have at least 10 positive verbal interactions for every correction or interference? (Observer should tally interactions.)	Pos. Neg.	Pos. Neg.	Pos. Neg.	Pos. Neg.	Pos. Neg.
10. Use the available materials in creative, interesting, and developmentally appropriate ways?					
11. Show consistent energy and enthusiasm throughout the 15 minutes?					
12. Make special efforts to interact with and involve children with special needs in play?					
13. Communicate with the supervisor and other teachers regarding children's transitions into and out of the play area?					
Observer's initials					

Comments:

Inclusive Child Care for Infants and Toddlers: Meeting Individual and Special Needs by Marion O'Brien © 1997 Paul H. Brookes Publishing Co., Baltimore.

Teacher Performance Check: Infant Play 2

Teacher: _____ Week of: _____

++ = excellent   OK = OK   ✔ = improvement needed   N = not observed

Did the teacher:	M	T	W	TH	F
1. Keep most children actively involved in the activity most of the time? (Observer should check and calculate percentage at beginning, middle, and end of observation time.)	1 2 3	1 2 3	1 2 3	1 2 3	1 2 3
2. Check schedule board and have materials needed for the activity ready and available?					
3. Choose a good place to conduct the activity?					
4. Make an active effort to include children with special needs and children from all age groups in the activity?					
5. Have an idea of what to do and introduce the activity in a way that is likely to capture children's attention and interest?					
6. Have constant verbal and/or pleasant physical contact with every participating child?					
7. Act quickly to prevent problems and redirect children as needed and handle appropriately any problems that arose?					
8. Have at least 10 positive verbal interactions for every correction or interference? (Observer should tally interactions.)	Pos. Neg.	Pos. Neg.	Pos. Neg.	Pos. Neg.	Pos. Neg.
9. Present the activity in creative, interesting, and developmentally appropriate ways?					
10. Show consistent energy and enthusiasm throughout the activity time?					
11. Show flexibility in modifying the activity to follow the children's changing interests?					
12. Use language- and motor-development facilitation techniques throughout the activity?					
13. Communicate with the supervisor and other teachers regarding children's individual needs?					
14. Clean and involve children in cleaning during the final 30–60 seconds of the activity time?					
Observer's initials					

Comments:

Inclusive Child Care for Infants and Toddlers: Meeting Individual and Special Needs by Marion O'Brien © 1997 Paul H. Brookes Publishing Co., Baltimore.

Teacher Performance Check: Toddler Play Activities

Teacher: _____ Week of: _____

++ = excellent   OK = OK   ✔ = improvement needed   N = not observed

Did the teacher:	M	T	W	TH	F
1. Check the schedule board and have materials needed for the activity ready and available?					
2. Begin the activity in a way that was likely to capture children's interest and attention?					
3. Make an active effort to include children with special needs in the activity?					
4. Conduct the activity with energy and enthusiasm?					
5. Keep the activity going and have some children involved in the activity for the entire scheduled time?					
6. Handle appropriately any problems that arose?					
7. Have at least 10 positive verbal interactions for every correction or interference?	Pos. Neg.	Pos. Neg.	Pos. Neg.	Pos. Neg.	Pos. Neg.
8. Respond to children's interests and focus of attention, finding ways to teach without redirecting?					
9. Use language facilitation techniques and signs along with words?					
10. Use motor development techniques?					
11. Show flexibility in making the activity fit the full range of development levels of children?					
12. Position him- or herself to be able to see other children in the area who are not actively participating?					
13. Communicate with the supervisor and other teachers regarding children's individual needs?					
14. Clean and involve children in cleaning during the final 30–60 seconds of the activity time?					
Observer's initials					

Comments:

Inclusive Child Care for Infants and Toddlers: Meeting Individual and Special Needs by Marion O'Brien © 1997 Paul H. Brookes Publishing Co., Baltimore.

Teacher Performance Check: Infant Feeding

Teacher: _____ Week of: _____

++ = excellent   OK = OK   ✔ = improvement needed   N = not observed

Did the teacher:	M	T	W	TH	F
1. Wash hands before preparing food?					
2. Consult the food chart to determine which food or formula to prepare?					
3. Prepare food correctly and place partially used food jars in the refrigerator?					
4. Prepare a place for the child and have all utensils ready before bringing the child to the area?					
5. Determine whether the child needed a diaper change before placing the child in a feeding chair?					
6. Fasten the seat belt on the feeding chair?					
7. Talk pleasantly with the child throughout the feeding, describing food and telling the child when the next bite was coming?					
8. Feed the child at the appropriate rate for that child?					
9. Hold each bottle-fed baby and burp the child often enough and correctly?					
10. Wipe the child's hands and face after feeding?					
11. Record accurately the types and amounts of food eaten?					
12. Rinse utensils and place them in the appropriate bin for washing?					
13. Cover partially finished bottles and put them in the refrigerator?					
Observer's initials					

Comments:

Teacher Performance Check: Toddler Meals and Snacks

Teacher: _____ Week of: _____

++ = excellent   OK = OK   ✓ = improvement needed   N = not observed

Did the teacher:	M	T	W	TH	F
1. Wash hands before handling food?					
2. Have him- or herself and area ready and food served before opening area to children?					
3. Communicate with other teachers about hand washing and make sure every child had clean hands?					
4. Greet children individually and encourage them to seat themselves as much as possible?					
5. Sit at the table with children, talking and encouraging pleasant mealtime conversation?					
6. Give children a chance to ask for more food and encourage polite requests?					
7. Use signs along with words?					
8. Make sure children were finished chewing and had clean hands and faces before leaving the area?					
9. Follow all food serving procedures—serve with utensils, wash own hands whenever needed, clean up spills on table and floor?					
10. Record amounts of food eaten accurately?					
11. Put all dishes and utensils back on the food cart and return it to the kitchen at the appropriate time?					
Observer's initials					

Comments:

Inclusive Child Care for Infants and Toddlers: Meeting Individual and Special Needs by Marion O'Brien © 1997 Paul H. Brookes Publishing Co., Baltimore.

Teacher Performance Check: Infant Diapering

Teacher: _____ Week of: _____

++ = excellent   OK = OK   ✔ = improvement needed   N = not observed

Did the teacher:	M	T	W	TH	F
1. Prepare needed supplies before bringing the infant to the area?					
2. Wash hands and put on gloves before handling the infant?					
3. Have at least one hand on the child at all times while the child was on the diapering table?					
4. Clean the infant's diaper area thoroughly?					
5. Talk pleasantly with the child throughout diapering?					
6. Put a clean diaper on the infant correctly?					
7. Change the infant's clothing if necessary?					
8. Record the diaper change accurately?					
9. Dispose of wet or soiled diaper correctly?					
10. Store previously worn clothing in a plastic bag in the child's diaper bin?					
11. Clean the diapering table thoroughly before bringing another child to the area?					
12. Wash hands before bringing another child to the area?					
Observer's initials					

Comments:

Inclusive Child Care for Infants and Toddlers: Meeting Individual and Special Needs by Marion O'Brien © 1997 Paul H. Brookes Publishing Co., Baltimore.

Teacher Performance Check: Toddler Diapering/Toilet

Teacher: _____ Week of: _____

++ = excellent   OK = OK   ✔ = improvement needed   N = not observed

Did the teacher:	M	T	W	TH	F
1. Prepare needed supplies before bringing any child to the area?					
2. Wash hands and put on gloves before handling each child?					
3. Bring children from the play area effectively and communicate with other teachers as needed?					
4. Use signs along with words?					
5. Follow the routine for each child according to his or her stage of toilet training?					
6. Have at least one hand on a child at all times while the child was on the diapering table?					
7. Have each child sit on the toilet for no more than 2 minutes?					
8. Talk pleasantly with children throughout diapering and interact warmly and sensitively with them?					
9. Give children opportunities for independence in dressing?					
10. Wipe or wash children's hands before they left the area?					
11. Record diapering and toilet times accurately?					
12. Dispose of wet or soiled diaper or underwear correctly?					
13. Store previously worn clothing in a plastic bag in each child's diaper bin?					
14. Clean the diapering table thoroughly before bringing another child to the area?					
15. Wash hands before bringing another child to the area?					
Observer's initials					

Comments:

Inclusive Child Care for Infants and Toddlers: Meeting Individual and Special Needs by Marion O'Brien © 1997 Paul H. Brookes Publishing Co., Baltimore.

Teacher Performance Check: Arrival

Teacher: _____ Week of: _____

++ = excellent   OK = OK   ✔ = improvement needed   N = not observed

Did the teacher:	M	T	W	TH	F
1. Have needed supplies in the greeting area?					
2. Greet each parent and child warmly and individually?					
3. Encourage each parent to remove child's coat and shoes and unpack diaper bag?					
4. Notice obvious signs of illness and ask the child's parent to wait for a full health check?					
5. Ask pleasantly for any special instructions, schedule changes, and so forth, from each parent?					
6. Record arrival times of each child accurately?					
7. Have parent sign medicine request form and accept only prescription or other authorized medicine?					
8. Write down any special instructions or schedule changes and communicate them to other teachers?					
Observer's initials					

Comments:

Inclusive Child Care for Infants and Toddlers: Meeting Individual and Special Needs by Marion O'Brien © 1997 Paul H. Brookes Publishing Co., Baltimore.

Teacher Performance Check: Departure

Teacher: _____ **Week of:** _____

++ = excellent   **OK = OK**   **✓ = improvement needed**   **N = not observed**

Did the teacher:	M	T	W	TH	F
1. Have needed supplies in the greeting area?					
2. Have diaper bags packed and ready before parents arrived?					
3. Have Take-Home Report ready before parents arrived?					
4. Greet each parent warmly and individually?					
5. Bring each child immediately to his or her parent?					
6. Ask for identification and check emergency cards for authorized list if necessary?					
7. Follow up with each parent on any special instructions or concerns that were raised in the morning?					
8. Record departure times accurately?					
9. Return all medicine?					
10. Give parent some information about the child's day or classroom activities or encourage the child to talk about the day?					
Observer's initials					

Comments:

Inclusive Child Care for Infants and Toddlers: Meeting Individual and Special Needs by Marion O'Brien © 1997 Paul H. Brookes Publishing Co., Baltimore.

Teacher Performance Check: Infant Naps

Teacher: _____ Week of: _____

++ = excellent   OK = OK   ✓ = improvement needed   N = not observed

Did the teacher:	M	T	W	TH	F
1. Stay alert to the schedule and aware when children were likely to be ready to sleep?					
2. Have crib ready before bringing each infant to the area?					
3. Follow an individual nap routine that provided a quiet time for each child before being placed in his or her crib?					
4. Lay the child down to nap with a loving but firm statement and let the child get to sleep on his or her own?					
5. Show awareness of children as they awakened and get them up appropriately?					
6. Record naptimes accurately?					
Observer's initials					

Comments:

Inclusive Child Care for Infants and Toddlers: Meeting Individual and Special Needs by Marion O'Brien © 1997 Paul H. Brookes Publishing Co., Baltimore.

Teacher Performance Check: Toddler Naps

Teacher: _____   Week of: _____

++ = excellent   OK = OK   ✔ = improvement needed   N = not observed

Did the teacher:	M	T	W	TH	F
1. Have cots ready before bringing any children to the area?					
2. Move children individually to cots, taking those who were showing signs of sleepiness first?					
3. Put each child down to nap with a loving but firm statement and let the child get to sleep on his or her own?					
4. Show awareness of children as they awakened and get them up appropriately?					
5. Record naptimes accurately?					
Observer's initials					

Comments:

Inclusive Child Care for Infants and Toddlers: Meeting Individual and Special Needs by Marion O'Brien © 1997 Paul H. Brookes Publishing Co., Baltimore.

Teacher Performance Check: Infant Transitions to Outside

Teacher: _____ Week of: _____

++ = excellent   OK = OK   ✔ = improvement needed   N = not observed

Did the teacher:	M	T	W	TH	F
1. Prepare children a few minutes ahead of time by announcing the upcoming transition?					
2. Dress only two children at a time for outside?					
3. Have children in coats for no more than 1–2 minutes before going outside?					
4. Move children individually, in groups of no more than two?					
5. Communicate effectively with other teachers so that a child was never left unsupervised and a teacher was never responsible for more than three children at a time?					
6. Involve the children in the transition by talking about what they were doing or using the time to teach a song or finger play?					
7. Stop and talk with the children for at least 1 minute out of every 3 minutes during a walk?					
Observer's initials					

Comments:

Inclusive Child Care for Infants and Toddlers: Meeting Individual and Special Needs by Marion O'Brien © 1997 Paul H. Brookes Publishing Co., Baltimore.

Teacher Performance Check: Transitions to Outside

Teacher: _____ Week of: _____

++ = excellent   OK = OK   ✔ = improvement needed   N = not observed

Did the teacher:	M	T	W	TH	F
1. Prepare children a few minutes ahead of time by announcing the upcoming transition?					
2. Bring only a few children's shoes at a time into the play area or take only a few children to the dressing area?					
3. Dress children individually in shoes and coats, encouraging independent dressing?					
4. Have children in coats for no more than 1–2 minutes before going outside?					
5. Move children individually, in groups of no more than two?					
6. Communicate effectively with other teachers so that a child was never left unsupervised and a teacher was never responsible for more than four children at a time outside the classroom?					
7. Involve the children in the transition by talking about what they were doing, playing a game, or using the time to teach a song or finger play?					
8. Stop and talk with the children for at least 1 minute out of every 3 minutes during a walk?					
Observer's initials					

Comments:

Inclusive Child Care for Infants and Toddlers: Meeting Individual and Special Needs by Marion O'Brien © 1997 Paul H. Brookes Publishing Co., Baltimore.

Teacher Overall Performance Check

Teacher: _____ Week of: _____

++ = excellent   OK = OK   ✔ = improvement needed   N = not observed

Did the teacher:	M	T	W	TH	F
1. Conduct care routines with energy and accuracy?					
2. Interact with children affectionately, sensitively, and enthusiastically?					
3. Cooperate effectively with other child care staff, supervisors, and families?					
4. Involve children successfully in play activities and participate actively with children?					
5. Use incidental teaching techniques, modifying teaching goals to match children's interests and developmental levels?					
6. Include children with disabilities successfully in play activities?					
7. Use language facilitation techniques?					
8. Use motor development techniques?					
9. Supervise children at all times, monitor their behavior, and ensure their safety?					
10. Talk to children frequently and use sign language to promote children's communication?					
Observer's initials					

Comments:

Inclusive Child Care for Infants and Toddlers: Meeting Individual and Special Needs by Marion O'Brien © 1997 Paul H. Brookes Publishing Co., Baltimore.

Infant-Toddler Program

Questionnaire for Supervisor Review

Because you work with your supervisor every day, your evaluation of his or her job performance and suggestions for improvement can be very helpful. Please circle the response to each item that you feel best describes the performance of the supervisor whose name is listed below. Your specific comments on any of these items or other issues not listed here are welcome. Please be assured that your responses are anonymous and confidential, and only summaries of all teachers' comments will be shared with supervisors.

Supervisor's name: _____   **Classroom:** _____

1. Fairness:

     very unfair   unfair   OK   fair   very fair

2. Relationship with children:

     very poor   poor   OK   good   very good

3. Ability to give both positive and negative feedback:

     very poor   poor   OK   good   very good

4. Willingness to respond to suggestions:

     very unwilling   unwilling   OK   willing   very willing

5. Ability to solve problems and deal with everyday situations:

     very poor   poor   OK   good   very good

6. Ability to maintain parent and child confidentiality:

     very poor   poor   OK   good   very good

7. Judgment and decision making:

     very poor   poor   OK   good   very good

Please make any comments about the supervisor's job performance.

Inclusive Child Care for Infants and Toddlers: Meeting Individual and Special Needs by Marion O'Brien © 1997 Paul H. Brookes Publishing Co., Baltimore.

Chapter 12

Evaluating Quality
in Inclusive Infant-Toddler Care

Evaluating quality in child care requires recruiting information from a variety of sources. Families and teachers can best provide feedback about day-to-day program operation. Administrators must also evaluate the curriculum by observing children's involvement in classroom activities, the developmental progress of children, and the number of desired individualized family service plan (IFSP) outcomes addressed and reached by children with special needs. A child care program must also meet the expectations of external evaluators, including licensing officials and accreditation organizations. In this chapter, procedures for evaluating child care program quality are described.

FEEDBACK FROM FAMILIES

One of the most important sources of information about child care program quality is parent opinion. Some parents are vocal in expressing their satisfaction or dissatisfaction with the quality of a child care program and will make their feelings known. Other parents, however, may be less assertive or concerned that complaints or special requests will lead child care program staff to feel negatively about their child. Some parents may even feel that their child's enrollment may be jeopardized if they do not appear to be positive about the child care program. Therefore, it is important to give every parent a chance to express his or her opinion about the child care program anonymously and to actively ask for parents' comments at least twice each year. It is also valuable to ask parents' opinions about the child care program immediately after their child graduates into a preschool program or leaves the program for some other reason because these parents will be less concerned about the effect of any negative comments they might have about the child care program.

A parent satisfaction survey can be very general, composed of just a few open-ended questions, or it may be more detailed, asking specific questions about particular aspects of the child care program. A sample parent survey form is shown in Figure 12.1. It is recommended that administrators mail parent surveys to families at home with an enclosed

Having my child attend the infant-toddler program made it possible for me to

- Continue my education   YES ☐   NO ☐
- Get or keep a job outside of the home   YES ☐   NO ☐
- Get more work done at home   YES ☐   NO ☐
- Have more time for myself   YES ☐   NO ☐

Please describe any other opportunities:

During the past 6 months, my child's development has been helped by the infant-toddler program in the following areas

- Thinking and problem solving   YES ☐   NO ☐
- Play and movement   YES ☐   NO ☐
- Talking, listening, and understanding   YES ☐   NO ☐
- Getting along with others   YES ☐   NO ☐
- Daily living activities (eating, toileting, dressing, etc.)   YES ☐   NO ☐
- Reaching, grasping, and handling toys   YES ☐   NO ☐

Please describe any other changes in your child's development:

The infant-toddler program has helped our family to

- Meet other parents   YES ☐   NO ☐
- Learn more about child development in general   YES ☐   NO ☐
- Learn more about *our* child's development   YES ☐   NO ☐
- Get information about nutrition and health during childhood   YES ☐   NO ☐

Please describe any other ways the program has helped your family:

Since your child has been attending the infant-toddler program, what changes have you noticed in his or her behavior?

What would you change or wish were different about the infant-toddler program?

Figure 12.1.   A sample parent survey form.

stamped return envelope addressed to the child care program director or family services coordinator. This procedure ensures parental confidentiality if they wish it.

A more detailed parent opinion form can be developed that is based on the outcomes families list for their children at their IFSP meeting. Parents can be asked for their subjective opinions about whether each outcome has been met, partially met, or not at all met. Although this type of evaluation cannot be anonymous, it does provide more specific information regarding the child care program's success at addressing parents' priorities. This evaluation might be conducted as part of the IFSP update conference, during which useful discussion of the possible reasons that some outcomes may not be met can take place.

FEEDBACK FROM TEACHERS

In high-quality infant-toddler care, teachers should receive regular feedback from supervisors about their teaching effectiveness, and they should also have the opportunity to *give* feedback to their supervisors about the quality of the child care program and the supervisors' own effectiveness. Competent, caring teachers are the heart of any child care program, and their ideas, concerns, and criticisms should be highly valued. Teachers should also be encouraged to raise questions and help solve problems of all types during staff meetings and to bring concerns or questions to their supervisor at any time. Some teachers, like some parents, are always

going to be more assertive or more confident than other teachers, and they will be the only voices heard unless the child care program director makes an active effort to obtain evaluative information from all teachers.

A sample supervisor evaluation form, intended for providing feedback to lead teachers regarding their day-to-day management of the classroom and the teaching staff, appears as Figure 12.2. This takes very little of teachers' limited time but provides valuable information on teachers' relationships with their lead teacher.

To obtain information about the overall quality of the child care program from the teachers' perspective, the Quality Checks appearing throughout this book are useful. Teachers can be asked to respond to one or more of these checks on a regular basis (monthly or quarterly) and to indicate areas in which they think improvement might be needed, a schedule change might be implemented, or the room arrangement might be changed to promote quality care and children's learning. Each staff meeting might focus on one aspect of quality, and all teachers might contribute their ideas. Alternatively, teachers might prefer to make their suggestions anonymously; these suggestions can then be summarized by the child care program director and discussed by administrative staff.

CURRICULUM EVALUATIONS

In addition to the lead teacher's or child care program director's observation of individual teacher effectiveness, administrators must also look at child care program quality from a broad perspective. A combination of three approaches to evaluating infant and toddler programs plus the parent and teacher evaluations described previously provides a comprehensive picture of the overall contribution the classroom program is making to children's and families' lives. These three approaches include measuring the level of children's involvement in program activities, keeping track of children's general developmental progress, and examining the extent to which outcomes desired for children with IFSPs are being regularly addressed within the context of classroom activities.

Children's Involvement

Children who are actively and positively involved with toys, other materials, and people are most likely to be learning. Thus, one measure of quality that is important to obtain is the frequency with which children in an infant or toddler classroom are actively and positively involved with the activities and materials provided. As the proportion of involved children decreases, the number of upsets and aggressive episodes increases, and the teaching and learning environment will be lower in quality.

Lead teachers should be encouraged to conduct regular involvement checks of the children in the classroom at frequent intervals (see p. 236 for a sample Quality Check for involvement). These checks can be used immediately to guide the lead teacher in organizing staff duties, changing play activities, or providing feedback to teachers about their effectiveness and also can be used in long-term planning of activities and the day's schedule.

Lead teacher's name _____ Classroom _____

Because you work with your lead teacher every day, your evaluation of his or her effectiveness and suggestions for improvement can be very helpful. Please circle the response to each item that you feel best describes the lead teacher whose name is listed above. Your specific comments are also welcome. Please be assured that your responses are anonymous and confidential, and only summaries of all teachers' comments will be shared with lead teachers.

1. Fairness in working with teachers:

> very unfair   unfair   OK   fair   very fair

2. Relationship with children:

> very poor   poor   OK   good   very good

3. Ability to give both positive and negative feedback to teachers:

> very poor   poor   OK   good   very good

4. Willingness to respond to teacher suggestions:

> very unwilling   unwilling   OK   willing   very willing

5. Ability to solve problems and deal with everyday situations:

> very poor   poor   OK   good   very good

6. Ability to work effectively with families:

> very poor   poor   OK   good   very good

7. Ability to maintain parent, child, and teacher confidentiality:

> very poor   poor   OK   good   very good

8. Judgment and decision making:

> very poor   poor   OK   good   very good

Please make any specific comments you have about the lead teacher's effectiveness.

Figure 12.2.   A sample form for evaluating the effectiveness of lead teachers.

In order to conduct an involvement check, the lead teacher or other observer first records all of the activities that are scheduled to be occurring in the classroom at the time of the observation and the names of teachers who are scheduled to supervise those activities. Part of the involvement check involves noting the extent to which the schedule is being followed, such as whether each planned activity is being conducted or not and whether teachers are present and actively involved in their areas. To check on the number of involved children, the observer starts at one end of the classroom and spends a few minutes watching each child who is awake, making a tally for the child's presence and then a tally for involvement if the child is busy. A busy child is one who is actively participating in an ongoing activity (daily living or play activity), being talked to or played with by an adult, clearly focusing on a toy or other material that he or she is holding or a teacher is holding for the child, practicing active movement in a nondangerous or nondestructive way, or intently watching other children or a teacher who is doing an activity. Children are *not* involved if they are holding and chewing on a toy with a vacant expression on their face, wandering around the classroom somewhat aimlessly, sucking their thumb and resting on a pillow, crying, or involved in a dangerous or destructive activity or negative interaction.

An involvement check indicates high quality if all children or all but one child are involved in an activity. More than one uninvolved child indicates that problems may exist in the nature of the activities provided or in the enthusiasm of the teachers in conducting those activities.

It is useful for lead teachers and child care program directors to conduct these involvement checks throughout the day, rather than just during prime teaching times. Often, it is during transitions to outdoors, late in the afternoon, or when lunch is being prepared that children's involvement drops and problems arise. When such low-involvement times are identified, teachers and supervisors can work together to identify interesting activities to increase children's involvement or rearrange the schedule to eliminate downtime.

Developmental Progress

A standard skill checklist is a useful tool for keeping track of the developmental advances of each child enrolled in the child care program. The initial developmental status of a child should be determined shortly after enrollment, allowing for a period of adjustment to the new situation. The skill checklists should then be updated approximately every 4–6 weeks for infants and every 2–3 months for toddlers.

The information obtained from the developmental checklist should be shared with parents in a personal and useful way, which will vary with the needs and schedules of individual families. Parents who have no concerns about their children's development may be happy with a brief, written report and a short discussion with the lead teacher or family services coordinator during arrival or departure times. Other parents may want to be involved in the evaluation, know what developmental milestones are coming up for their child, and have more complete information about their child's performance. Sometimes families like to have the developmental checklist completed in their homes, where they can watch and actively participate and then discuss the results right away.

Any of the standard developmental checklists available on the market are appropriate for this use. Child care program directors or lead teachers should select the measure with which they are most familiar or the measure in which they have the most confidence. The goal of this developmental tracking is not to set objectives for curriculum planning or to determine eligibility for services, but rather simply to determine whether children are moving ahead developmentally in all domains.

When children's special needs make it unlikely that they will show rapid progress in one or more developmental domains, a more specific skill checklist that breaks developmental progress into smaller steps may be useful. Parents often find it encouraging to be able to see change and growth on whatever scale is appropriate for an individual child.

Young children reach developmental milestones at very different ages, for reasons that have to do with their biological heritage and personalities as well as the quality of the learning experiences in which they are involved. However, all of the children enrolled in an infant or toddler program should be making some progress in some areas on a regular basis. Sometimes children's cognitive and fine motor manipulation skills will stand still for several months while children learn to crawl, then stand, then walk. Children's concentration is focused on movement, rather than on eye–hand coordination or toy play. Thus, teachers should not expect uniform progress across all developmental domains and should not be alarmed if one child appears to be moving forward more slowly than another child of the same age. Serious concerns about a child's development require more careful evaluation by a cross-disciplinary team that can examine the child's development within the context of his or her past medical history and current living and learning situations. The developmental checklists used as an in-classroom index of children's progress cannot substitute for such a full-scale evaluation.

If the developmental checklists indicate that several children are making only minimal progress across several domains, then the lead teachers and child care program director should take a careful look at the nature of the play and learning activities provided and the quality of teacher–child interactions in the classroom. Children who spend long hours in unstimulating and unresponsive care environments would not be expected to progress developmentally. If this is the case, then appropriate and interesting play activities must be developed and implemented, and teacher training and supervision must be improved.

IFSP Outcomes

For children with special needs, it is important that the outcomes desired by families and other members of the intervention team be addressed as part of the classroom activities on a regular basis. It is not always the case that the proportion of outcomes met is a reliable key to quality. Sometimes desired outcomes are so globally phrased that it is difficult to decide if the outcomes have been met, or IFSP outcomes may be long-term objectives, such as "getting along with other children," which are difficult to measure. At other times, clearly phrased outcomes may be inappropriate for a particular child. Thus, it is useful for child care program directors, family services coordinators, and special service providers to measure the frequency with which outcomes are being addressed within the classroom context. Appropriate outcomes that are frequently addressed will eventually be met.

Teachers themselves can help in this evaluation effort if forms used in daily living activities have an area for suggesting ways to address specific outcomes within routines. For example, if one of Mindy's desired outcomes is for her to signal when she wants second helpings of food, the posted menus for the week can include a note to remind teachers to encourage Mindy to use the sign for MORE or to say "please" before receiving a second helping. Teachers who address specific outcomes can also make a note of their efforts in the child's logbook or scrapbook of services (e.g., "Today during our 'wheels' activity, we encouraged Gina to reach and grasp toy cars with both her left and right hands").

A more objective but time-consuming way of determining the usual frequency of incorporating outcomes into classroom routines is for an outside observer to spotcheck each child on a regular, perhaps monthly basis, watching the child for eight to ten 5-minute periods throughout a day and recording the number of instances each IFSP outcome was addressed. If teachers are given regular reminders about children's outcomes and are knowledgeable about ways to incorporate outcomes into everyday activities, an observer will see teachers capitalizing on opportunities to address the outcomes frequently throughout the day. When such observation does not result in viewing these occasions, it is likely that the outcomes are not being addressed. In this case, more specific suggestions to teachers or incorporation of new techniques into regular routines will be necessary.

EXTERNAL EVALUATIONS

In the United States, every licensed child care program will be visited by licensing authorities on a yearly or more frequent basis and will be expected to meet state standards of environmental organization, health and safety, and quality of care. Each state's standards are different, but none are more demanding than the caregiving and teaching routines outlined in this book. Thus, child care programs that use the approach described in this book should be readily accepted by licensing agencies.

Some child care programs are accredited by the National Association for the Education of Young Children (NAEYC). The accreditation process followed by NAEYC is based on the highest standards in early childhood education, and the procedures for becoming accredited are time-consuming and extensive. Such accreditation assures parents of a very high-quality child care environment.

When children with special needs are enrolled in infant-toddler care, the state agency responsible for administering the provisions of Part H of the Individuals with Disabilities Education Act (PL 101-476) may also carry out an external evaluation of the child care program in order to determine its eligibility to receive funding from Part H or be listed as a Part H service provider. State standards and requirements vary, but the program described here is designed to meet the individual needs of children and their families through a transdisciplinary approach and should meet or be readily modified to meet agency standards.

Although all of these external evaluations are useful and provide opportunities to gain professional and community input into the child care program, these evaluations cannot substitute for the more specific child- and family-oriented evaluations described in this chapter.

SUMMARY

Child care program directors are responsible for identifying areas of strength within their programs and areas in which improvement is needed or problems exist. These responsibilities involve direct observation of children and teachers in the classroom in addition to requesting information from all of the people involved in the program, including children, families, teachers, and special service providers. Child care programs also are required to meet appropriate licensing and accreditation standards. Administrators must continuously monitor the classroom environment and pay close attention to everyday events and interactions between teachers and children in order to ensure that a program is maintained at the highest quality.

Quality Check ✓

Children's Involvement in Classroom Activities

Observation time Start time: _____ Stop time: _____	What activity is scheduled?	Is it occurring?	Are teachers present?	Are teachers involved?	Tally of children present in area	Tally of "busy" children
Eating area						
Diapering/toilet						
Play: doll/house						
Play: building						
Play: active						
Play:						
Other:						

Inclusive Child Care for Infants and Toddlers: Meeting Individual and Special Needs by Marion O'Brien © 1997 Paul H. Brookes Publishing Co., Baltimore.

References

Agostoni, C., Riva, E., & Giovannini, M. (1995). Dietary fiber in weaning foods of young children. *Pediatrics, 96,* 1002–1005.

American Academy of Pediatrics. (1991). *Report of the committee on infectious diseases.* Elk Grove Village, IL: Author.

American Public Health Association & American Academy of Pediatrics. (1992). *Caring for our children: National health and safety performance standards for out-of-home child care programs.* Washington, DC: Authors.

Americans with Disabilities Act (ADA) of 1990, PL 101-336, 42 U.S.C. §§ 12101 *et seq.*

Barrett, K.C., & Campos, J.J. (1987). Perspectives on emotional development: II. A functionalist approach to development. In J.D. Osofsky (Ed.), *Handbook of infant development* (2nd ed., pp. 555–578). New York: John Wiley & Sons.

Bauer, P., & Mandler, J. (1992). Putting the horse before the cart: The use of temporal order in recall of events by one-year-old children. *Developmental Psychology, 28,* 441–452.

Blau, D. (1991). The child care labor market. *Journal of Human Resources, 27,* 9–39.

Bredekamp, S. (1987). *Developmentally appropriate practice in early childhood programs serving children from birth through age 8* (Rev. ed.). Washington, DC: National Association for the Education of Young Children.

Bretherton, I. (1992). Attachment and bonding. In V. Van Hasselt & M. Hersen (Eds.), *Handbook of social development* (pp. 133–149). New York: Plenum.

Bricker, D., & Cripe, J. (1992). *An activity-based approach to early intervention.* Baltimore: Paul H. Brookes Publishing Co.

Bricker, D., & Widerstrom, A. (Eds.). (1996). *Preparing personnel to work with infants and young children and their families: A team approach.* Baltimore: Paul H. Brookes Publishing Co.

Bruder, M.B. (1994). Working with members of other disciplines: Collaboration for success. In M. Wolery & J. Wilbers (Eds.), *Including children with special needs in early childhood programs* (pp. 45–70). Washington, DC: National Association for the Education of Young Children.

Caldera, Y.M., Huston, A.C., & O'Brien, M. (1989). Social interactions and play patterns of parents and toddlers with feminine, masculine, and neutral toys. *Child Development, 60,* 70–76.

Campbell, P., Strickland, B., & LaForme, C. (1992). Enhancing parent participation in the individualized family service plan. *Topics in Early Childhood Special Education, 11,* 112–124.

Children's Defense Fund. (1996). *The state of America's children yearbook 1996.* Washington, DC: Author.

Cost, quality, and child outcomes in child care centers. (1995, January). (Executive Summary). Denver: University of Colorado at Denver.

Crowley, A. (1990). Integrating handicapped and chronically ill children into day care centers. *Pediatric Nursing, 16,* 39–44.

Dwyer, J. (1993). Nutritional implications of vegetarianism for children. In R. Suskind & L. Lewinter-Suskind (Eds.), *Textbook of pediatric nutrition* (pp. 181–190). New York: Raven Press.

253

Eckerman, C.O., Davis, C.C., & Didow, S.M. (1989). Toddlers' emerging ways of achieving social coordinations with a peer. *Child Development, 60,* 440–453.

Eckerman, C.O., & Stein, M.R. (1990). How imitation begets imitation and toddlers' generation of games. *Developmental Psychology, 26,* 370–378.

Education for All Handicapped Children Act of 1975, PL 94-142, 20 U.S.C. §§ 1400 *et seq.*

Education of the Handicapped Act Amendments of 1986, PL 99-457, 20 U.S.C. §§ 1400 *et seq.*

Fewell, R. (1993). Child care for children with special needs. *Pediatrics, 91,* 193–198.

Field, T. (1994). The effects of mother's physical and emotional unavailability on emotion regulation. In N.A. Fox (Ed.), The development of emotion regulation: Biological and behavioral considerations (pp. 208–227). *Monographs of the Society for Research in Child Development, 59*(2–3, Serial No. 240).

Garza, C., Butte, N., & Goldman, A. (1993). Human milk and infant formula. In R. Suskind & L. Lewinter-Suskind (Eds.), *Textbook of pediatric nutrition* (pp. 33–42). New York: Raven Press.

Gibson, J. (1979). *The ecological approach to visual perception.* Boston: Houghton Mifflin.

Giebink, G.S. (1993). Care of the ill child in day care settings. *Pediatrics, 91,* 229–233.

Glascoe, F. (1994). It's not what it seems: The relationship between parents' concerns and children with global delays. *Clinical Pediatrics, 33,* 292–296.

Goldman, B., & Ross, H. (1978). Social skills in action: Analysis of early peer games. In J. Glick & K.A. Clarke-Stewart (Eds.), *The development of social understanding* (pp. 177–212). New York: Gardner Press.

Handicapped Children's Early Education Act of 1968, PL 90-538, 20 U.S.C. §§ 621 *et seq.*

Hart, B., & Risley, T. (1995). *Meaningful differences in the everyday experience of young American children.* Baltimore: Paul H. Brookes Publishing Co.

Heagarty, M. (1993). Day care for the child with acquired immunodeficiency syndrome and the child of the drug-abusing mother. *Pediatrics, 91,* 199–201.

Howes, C., Unger, O., & Seidner, L.B. (1989). Social pretend play in toddlers: Parallels with social play and with solitary pretend. *Child Development, 60,* 77–84.

Individuals with Disabilities Education Act (IDEA) of 1990, PL 101-476, 20 U.S.C. §§ 1400 *et seq.*

Isabella, R. (1993). Origins of attachment: Maternal interactive behavior across the first year. *Child Development, 64,* 605–621.

Klein, N., & Campbell, P. (1990). Preparing personnel to serve at-risk and disabled infants, toddlers, and preschoolers. In S. Meisels & J. Shonkoff (Eds.), *Handbook of early childhood intervention* (pp. 679–699). Cambridge, MA: Cambridge University Press.

Kopjar, B., & Wickizer, T. (1996). How safe are day care centers? Day care versus home injuries among children in Norway. *Pediatrics, 97,* 43–47.

Kopp, C.B. (1989). Regulation of distress and negative emotions: A developmental view. *Developmental Psychology, 25,* 343–354.

Lazar, I., & Darlington, R. (1982). Lasting effects of early education: A report from the Consortium for Longitudinal Studies. *Monographs of the Society for Research in Child Development, 47*(2–3, Serial No. 195).

McLoyd, V.C. (1983). The effects of the structure of play objects on the pretend play of low-income preschool children. *Child Development, 54,* 626–635.

McWilliam, R., & Bailey, D. (1992). Promoting engagement and mastery. In D. Bailey & M. Wolery (Eds.), *Teaching infants and preschoolers with disabilities* (2nd ed., pp. 229–255). Columbus, OH: Charles E. Merrill.

Mrazek, P.J., & Haggerty, R.J. (Eds.). (1994). *Reducing risks for mental disorders: Frontiers for preventive intervention research.* Washington, DC: National Academy Press.

Mueller, E., & Brenner, J. (1977). The origins of social skill and interaction among play group toddlers. *Child Development, 48,* 854–861.

Nelson, C. (1987). The recognition of facial expressions in the first year of life: Mechanisms of development. *Child Development, 58,* 889–909.

NICHD Early Child Care Research Network. (1996). Characteristics of infant child care: Factors contributing to positive caregiving. *Early Childhood Research Quarterly, 11,* 269–306.

O'Brien, M., & Bi, X. (1995). Teacher and toddler speech in three classroom play contexts. *Topics in Early Childhood Special Education, 15*, 148–163.

O'Brien, M., & Nagle, K.J. (1987). Parents' speech to toddlers: The effect of play context. *Journal of Child Language, 14*, 269–279.

Parker, J.G., & Asher, S.R. (1987). Peer relations and later personal adjustment: Are low-accepted children at risk? *Psychological Bulletin, 102*, 357–389.

Powell, D. (1989). *Families and early childhood programs.* Washington, DC: National Association for the Education of Young Children.

Rab, V., & Wood, K. (1995). *Child care and the ADA: A handbook for inclusive programs.* Baltimore: Paul H. Brookes Publishing Co.

Rivara, F., DiGuiseppi, C., Thompson, R., & Calonge, N. (1989). Risk of injury to children less than 5 years of age in day care versus home care settings. *Pediatrics, 84*, 1011–1016.

Rothstein-Fisch, C., & Howes, C. (1988). Toddler–peer interaction in mixed-age groups. *Journal of Applied Developmental Psychology, 9*, 211–218.

Rubenstein, J.L., & Howes, C. (1976). The effects of peers on toddler interaction with mother and toys. *Child Development, 47*, 597–605.

Rubin, K.H. (1977). The social and cognitive value of preschool toys and activities. *Canadian Journal of Behavioral Sciences, 9*, 382–385.

Seitz, V., & Provence, S. (1990). Caregiver-focused models of early intervention. In S. Meisels & J. Shonkoff (Eds.), *Handbook of early childhood intervention* (pp. 400–427). Cambridge, England: Cambridge University Press.

Shapiro, S. (1975). Preschool ecology: A study of three environmental variables. *Reading Improvement, 12*, 236–241.

Shewan, C., & Malm, K. (1990). The prevalence of speech and language impairments. *Asha, 32*, 108.

Shure, M.B. (1963). Psychological ecology of a nursery school. *Child Development, 34*, 979–992.

Simeonsson, R. (1991). Primary, secondary, and tertiary prevention in early intervention. *Journal of Early Intervention, 15*, 124–134.

Simeonsson, R., & Bailey, D. (1990). Family dimensions in early intervention. In S. Meisels & J. Shonkoff (Eds.), *Handbook of early childhood intervention* (pp. 428–444). Cambridge, England: Cambridge University Press.

Smith, R.K., & Connolly, K.J. (1980). *The ecology of preschool behavior.* Cambridge, England: Cambridge University Press.

Smith, R.K., & Connolly, K.J. (1986). Experimental studies of the preschool environment: The Sheffield Project. In S. Kilmer (Ed.), *Advances in early education and day care* (Vol. 4, pp. 27–66). Greenwich, CT: JAI Press.

Soken, H., & Pick, A. (1992). Intermodal perception of happy and angry expressive behaviors by seven-month-old infants. *Child Development, 63*, 787–795.

Sorenson, R., Porch, M., & Tu, L. (1993). Food allergy in children. In R. Suskind & L. Lewinter-Suskind (Eds.), *Textbook of pediatric nutrition* (pp. 457–469). New York: Raven Press.

Thompson, R. (1991). Emotional regulation and emotional development. *Educational Psychology Review, 3*, 269–307.

Tomasello, M. (1990). The role of joint attentional processes in early language development. *Language Sciences, 10*, 68–88.

U.S. Department of Agriculture. (1988). *Feeding infants—A guide for use in the Child Care Food Program* (Food and Nutrition Service publication FNS–258). Washington, DC: Author.

Wald, E., Guerra, N., & Byers, C. (1991). Frequency and severity of infections in day care: Three-year follow-up. *Journal of Pediatrics, 118*, 590–514.

Warren, S. (1992). Facilitating basic vocabulary acquisition with milieu teaching procedures. *Journal of Early Intervention, 16*, 235–251.

Wolery, M. (1994). Instructional strategies for teaching young children with special needs. In M. Wolery & J. Wilbers (Eds.), *Including children with special needs in early childhood programs* (pp. 119–150). Washington, DC: National Association for the Education of Young Children.

Wolery, M., & Bredekamp, S. (1994). Developmentally appropriate practices and young children with disabilities: Contextual issues in the discussion. *Journal of Early Intervention, 18,* 331–341.

Wolery, M., Strain, P., & Bailey, D.B., Jr. (1992). Reaching potentials of children with special needs. In S. Bredekamp & T. Rosegrant (Eds.), *Reaching potentials: Appropriate curriculum and assessment for young children* (Vol. 1, pp. 92–111). Washington, DC: National Association for the Education of Young Children.

Wolery, M., & Wilbers, J. (1994). Introduction to the inclusion of young children with special needs in early childhood programs. In M. Wolery & J. Wilbers (Eds.), *Including children with special needs in early childhood programs* (pp. 1–22). Washington, DC: National Association for the Education of Young Children.

Appendix A

Themes for Infant and Toddler Play

Organizing infant and toddler play around weekly themes offers teachers fresh opportunities to think about their teaching and learning goals each week. The sample themes included here are uncomplicated and flexible; thus, they are well suited to infants and toddlers. For each theme, suggestions are listed to help teachers look at the world from an infant's or toddler's viewpoint and consider what aspects of that theme the children are likely to explore and experience. Using these anticipated experiences as the foundation, teachers can also work on particular learning goals that can be introduced or practiced in conjunction with the theme and vocabulary during the week. Some of the types of special issues that must be taken into consideration when working with children who have special needs are listed for each theme.

Also accompanying each theme description is a list of some play activities that are particularly well suited to teaching the goals associated with that theme. Specific plans for conducting play activities need to be developed in advance by teachers who know their classroom and their children well. The lists provided here are only suggestions to help creative teachers develop their own repertoire of play activities. Samples of the activities included in these lists are described in more detail in Appendix B.

When a theme is used to organize play and activities are selected to fit a theme, children are exposed to repeated opportunities to learn similar concepts from different teachers in different play situations with different materials. This repetition is especially useful for infants and toddlers, whose processing speed is slower than that of older children and adults. Repetition of the same activities each day during the week, even from morning to afternoon, is not boring to infants and toddlers. Instead, this repetition gives them increased opportunities to practice skills and gain mastery, to display their growing memory capacity in deferred imitation, and to learn scripts or routines for play with certain materials.

It is not necessary—or desirable—for *all* of the week's play activities to be associated with a theme. In every group of infants or toddlers (and teachers), there will be certain activities that are everyone's favorites. These activities should be repeated frequently and included in the week's activity plan, even if these activities do not have a clear relationship to the week's theme. Play should be fun for everyone! In addition, an activity plan needs to provide opportunities for children to practice a variety of different skills and to experience a range of events and materials. Thus, a play activity plan is most effective if it balances novelty with familiarity, active play with quiet play, and easy tasks with challenging tasks.

Classroom themes can also serve as a way of organizing communication with families. Each weekly theme may be the focus for a family newsletter, including suggestions for parent–child play as well as notices of upcoming events in the classroom or community. Classroom staff can also prepare theme-based play packets for families—inexpensive or homemade materials that promote parent–child play and help to transfer learning from classroom to home.

The themes suggested here represent only a small selection of what is possible. Creative teachers will want to develop themes that fit their classroom, their climate, and their children's interests. Teachers and children often enjoy seasonal or holiday themes—although teachers must remember that infants and toddlers do not yet understand the cultural meaning of holiday customs. As new themes are developed, teachers can watch children's responses to new materials and activities and write down their descriptions of what children are exploring and experiencing. Around these observations, teachers can then build their teaching and learning goals, the vocabulary to accompany the theme, and the alterations that can be made in the activities in order to meet children's individual and special needs.

Theme: Getting to Know You

WHAT CHILDREN WILL EXPLORE AND EXPERIENCE

Identifying self, other children, and teacher by name and in pictures
Recognizing their own mirror image
Enjoying the active movement of their bodies
Listening to their own and others' voices

HOW TEACHERS CAN EXTEND AND EXPAND CHILDREN'S UNDERSTANDING AND SKILL

Labeling body parts
Using children's and teachers' names frequently and speaking slowly so children have an
    opportunity to repeat them; using names in songs
Giving names to dolls and stuffed animals
Calling attention to children's images in mirrors

OTHER CONCEPTS FOR TEACHERS TO DEMONSTRATE AND/OR TALK ABOUT

Possession—mine, yours, ours
Hiding and finding other children or oneself in mirror
Friendship and caring for friends; sharing and doing things together
Same/different
Concepts of gender (but not stereotypes)

VOCABULARY TO USE

you	yours	head	eyes	arms	boy
me	mine	hair	chin	hands	girl
I	his	ears	neck	feet	teacher
we	hers	nose	body	fingers	friend
him	her	mouth	legs	toes	mom/dad

SPECIAL CONSIDERATIONS FOR CHILDREN WITH SPECIAL NEEDS

Self-recognition is often delayed in children with mental retardation.
Frequent use of a child's name is helpful.
Children with sensory problems may need help with mirrors and voices.

Inclusive Child Care for Infants and Toddlers: Meeting Individual and Special Needs by Marion O'Brien © 1997 Paul H. Brookes Publishing Co., Baltimore.

Theme: Getting to Know You

Toy/Activity Type	Suggested Activities and Materials for This Theme
Building	Puppets Duplo people Fisher-Price play houses Toy cameras
House/doll	Baby dolls Dress up Birthday party (doesn't *have* to be anyone's birthday) Toy telephones Doll play
Active play **Outdoor play**	Dancing Interactive games (peekaboo, This Little Piggy, pat-a-cake, So Big) Animal sounds and movements Bubble chase Buzz-buzz Hide and seek
Sensory experiences, art, science, small-group activities	Collage of children's names "Read" the classroom photo album Take pictures of children See-through scarves Handprints and footprints Sunshiney faces Trace hands and feet Trace bodies Weigh and measure
Music	Sing songs using children's names Hokey-Pokey

Theme: Food

WHAT CHILDREN WILL EXPLORE AND EXPERIENCE

Doing things they usually watch adults do—cooking, shopping, and so forth
Experiencing pleasure in large-motor activity
Holding and manipulating toy foods, dishes, and pots and pans
Putting foods and pretend groceries in and taking them out of containers

HOW TEACHERS CAN EXTEND AND
EXPAND CHILDREN'S UNDERSTANDING AND SKILL

Labeling foods
Seeing, touching, and tasting real foods
Working together and having fun (e.g., cooking and serving, selling and buying)
Extending children's memory for mealtime routines and foods eaten
Cleaning up after cooking and eating

OTHER CONCEPTS FOR TEACHERS TO DEMONSTRATE AND/OR TALK ABOUT

Shape—foods come in many different shapes (e.g., fruit is often circular, pizza is cut in
   triangles, bread is square)
Same/different
Prepositional concepts—in, on, over, under, and so forth
Colors
Foods for good health—vegetables and fruits, milk
Table manners

VOCABULARY TO USE

stove	oven	hot	pan	pot	names of:
bowl	stir	cook	bake	pour	fruits,
serve	eat	drink	knife	fork	vegetables,
spoon	plate	cup	glass	dish	milk, juice

SPECIAL CONSIDERATIONS FOR CHILDREN WITH SPECIAL NEEDS

Children with digestive disorders or food allergies may have different experiences
   with foods than other children. Teachers must work to include these children in food-
   related activities while recognizing their individual responses and reactions to certain
   foods.

Inclusive Child Care for Infants and Toddlers: Meeting Individual and Special Needs by
Marion O'Brien © 1997 Paul H. Brookes Publishing Co., Baltimore.

Theme: Food

Toy/Activity Type		Suggested Activities and Materials for This Theme
Building		Stack plates and dishes Food puzzles Stack "sandwich" toys Toy barns and farm animals
House/doll		Plastic bowls, pots and pans, and pretend food Put groceries in sacks Feed baby dolls Make pretend pizza Restaurant Picnic or teddy bears' picnic Grocery store Pizza delivery
Active play Outdoor play		Exercises Hide (plastic food) and find Bean bag toss into grocery sacks and baskets
Sensory experiences, art, science, small-group activities		Contact paper collage of foods Play-Doh—make pancakes Textures of foods Wash dishes Pour water from pitcher into cups Visit the kitchen
Music		Bang on pots and pans with wooden spoons Old MacDonald Here We Go 'Round the Mulberry Bush

Theme: Ins and Outs

WHAT CHILDREN WILL EXPLORE AND EXPERIENCE

Putting things into, inside, over, and under other things; and taking (dumping) them out again

Filling and emptying containers

Putting their own body into, inside, over, under, and around other things

HOW TEACHERS CAN EXTEND AND EXPAND CHILDREN'S UNDERSTANDING AND SKILL

Using prepositional concepts of *in, out, over, under,* and *around*

Encouraging children's awareness of their bodies' movement in space

Guiding fine motor manipulation to ensure success

OTHER CONCEPTS FOR TEACHERS TO DEMONSTRATE AND/OR TALK ABOUT

Size—little things fit into bigger things

Shapes

Fits/does not fit

Full/empty

Hiding/finding

Open/closed

Inside/outside

VOCABULARY TO USE

in	out	empty	Where is (object label)?	inside
over	under	fit	ceiling	outside
up	down	open	floor	door
around	all gone	closed	full	window

SPECIAL CONSIDERATIONS FOR CHILDREN WITH SPECIAL NEEDS

Children with fine motor difficulties may need large containers and objects that are easy to grasp.

Children with movement or posture disorders need assistance putting their own bodies into containers and getting out again, but the experience is helpful for their motor control and coordination.

Inclusive Child Care for Infants and Toddlers: Meeting Individual and Special Needs by Marion O'Brien © 1997 Paul H. Brookes Publishing Co., Baltimore.

Theme: Ins and Outs

Toy/Activity Type	Suggested Activities and Materials for This Theme
Building	Nesting cups Shape sorters Cars, trucks, and garages from blocks Fisher-Price play house Puppets
House/doll	Dress up Hats, scarves, and blankets Plastic bowls, pots and pans, and pretend food Wrap baby dolls in blankets Grocery store Post office
Active play **Outdoor play**	Crates and boxes Go on a crawling "tour" Obstacle course Give rides in a laundry basket Bean bag toss Hula hoops Tunnel
Sensory experiences, art, science, small-group activities	Go for rides outdoors Wrap small toys in cloth and tape closed See-through scarves Paper bag puppets
Music	Go In and Out the Windows Where Is Thumbkin? Itsy-Bitsy Spider

Theme: Our Bodies

WHAT CHILDREN WILL EXPLORE AND EXPERIENCE

Becoming familiar with their own bodies—how their bodies feel and move and what they can do with them

Looking at others' bodies and seeing how they are similar to and different from their own bodies

Taking off and putting on clothes and using buttons, snaps, and laces

Looking at themselves in the mirror

HOW TEACHERS CAN EXTEND AND EXPAND CHILDREN'S UNDERSTANDING AND SKILL

Labeling body parts

Encouraging children's awareness of their bodies' movement in space

Giving simple directions (for things the children like to do) and following through to be sure children follow directions

Guiding fine motor manipulation

Having children do movement activities in front of a mirror

OTHER CONCEPTS FOR TEACHERS TO DEMONSTRATE AND/OR TALK ABOUT

Differences and similarities among people—size, color of skin, color and length of hair, faces, and different types of abilities

Taking care of our bodies—health, nutrition, and bathing and washing

VOCABULARY TO USE

head	eyes	feet	elbow	run	walk
hair	chin	toes	shoulder	hop	jump
ears	neck	arms	knee	skip	roll
nose	mouth	body	hands	crawl	spin

SPECIAL CONSIDERATIONS FOR CHILDREN WITH SPECIAL NEEDS

Children with motor disabilities may have difficulty performing some large motor activities. Activities should be geared so all children can have success.

Without emphasizing *disability*, this theme provides an opportunity to enhance children's understanding of how people are different.

Inclusive Child Care for Infants and Toddlers: Meeting Individual and Special Needs by Marion O'Brien © 1997 Paul H. Brookes Publishing Co., Baltimore.

Theme: Our Bodies

Toy/Activity Type		Suggested Activities and Materials for This Theme
Building		Plastic animals Puppets, finger puppets Tools Toy farms and farm animals Duplo people
House/doll		Mirrors Peekaboo with scarves and blankets Feeding baby dolls Toy telephones Doctor Hat store Shoe store Costume ball Doll play
Active play Outdoor play		Exercises—bend, jump, roll, and twirl Animal sounds and movements Dance Crawling races Roll and roll Walk in funny ways Wash baby dolls
Sensory experiences, art, science, small-group activities		Weigh and measure Contact paper collage of faces Fingerpaint Trace hands and feet Trace bodies
Music		Sing songs using children's names Hokey-Pokey

Theme: Animals

WHAT CHILDREN WILL EXPLORE AND EXPERIENCE

Holding and manipulating toy animals and examining eyes, legs, tails, and so forth
Seeing and touching live animals outdoors (if weather permits)
Seeing pictures of animals and comparing them with toys

**HOW TEACHERS CAN EXTEND AND
EXPAND CHILDREN'S UNDERSTANDING AND SKILL**

Labeling animals and body parts
Making animal sounds and imitating animal movements
Matching animals of similar type and matching pictures with toy animals
Comparing animals and people (e.g., body parts, movements)
Talking about children's pets and caring for them

OTHER CONCEPTS FOR TEACHERS TO DEMONSTRATE AND/OR TALK ABOUT

Size—animals come in sizes from tiny to huge
Same/different
Prepositional concepts—*in, on, over, under,* and so forth
Colors
Textures—furry versus smooth, soft versus hard, and so forth

VOCABULARY TO USE

names of animals, insects, dinosaurs, birds, fish, and so forth

legs	eyes	nose	barn	cage	crawl
body	wings	mouth	fence	gallop	walk
head	tail	farm	zoo	fly	swim

SPECIAL CONSIDERATIONS FOR CHILDREN WITH SPECIAL NEEDS

Children with allergies may make having a furry animal in the classroom impossible.
Children whose families have few resources may never have seen animals other than cats
   and dogs up close, or they may never have been to a zoo or a farm; thus, teachers
   must be sensitive to children's differences in knowledge and experience.

Inclusive Child Care for Infants and Toddlers: Meeting Individual and Special Needs by
Marion O'Brien © 1997 Paul H. Brookes Publishing Co., Baltimore.

Theme: Animals

Toy/Activity Type	Suggested Activities and Materials for This Theme
Building	Balancing bunnies Zoo animals and waffle blocks—make a zoo Stuffed animals and plastic crates Dinosaurs Toy barns and farm animals Duplo blocks—build animals Animal puzzles Animal puppets
House/doll	Stuffed animals Teddy bears' picnic Play dog and cat Tea party with stuffed animals Animal doctor Take stuffed animals for walks in strollers
Active play Outdoor play	Interactive games Animal sounds and movements Hide (toy animals) and find Go pretend fishing from the rocking boat Nature walk—look for birds and bugs Bean bag toss with Mickey Mouse or other target
Sensory experiences, art, science, small-group activities	Have animals visit the classroom for children to see and touch Contact paper collage with animal pictures Wash plastic animals Tell stories about animals Read books about animals
Music	Old MacDonald Itsy-Bitsy Spider Five Little Monkeys Baa Baa Black Sheep

Theme: All Around the House

WHAT CHILDREN WILL EXPLORE AND EXPERIENCE

Doing for themselves (in play) what they usually see adults doing
Experiencing water—how it feels, what soap does in water, what *wet* means
Sequencing a task (e.g., wash clothes, dry clothes, iron clothes, fold clothes)

HOW TEACHERS CAN EXTEND AND
EXPAND CHILDREN'S UNDERSTANDING AND SKILL

Encouraging pretend play at whatever level children can manage
Encouraging and enhancing small motor manipulation
Demonstrating folding (e.g., of scarves, blankets, bandanas, paper)
Talking about *wet* and *dry*

OTHER CONCEPTS FOR TEACHERS TO DEMONSTRATE AND/OR TALK ABOUT

Washing and soap
Labeling common household objects
Working together to complete a task and sharing and cooperation
Taking care of others

VOCABULARY TO USE

wash	clean	hammer	laundry	dust
scrub	dirty	pliers	washer	wax
rinse	wet	screwdriver	dryer	paint
vacuum	dry	tools	iron	brush
sweep	soapy	broom	mop	

SPECIAL CONSIDERATIONS FOR CHILDREN WITH SPECIAL NEEDS

Children with mental retardation have difficulty with pretend play and may need adaptations for exploration and manipulation of even ordinary household objects.
Some children may not enjoy water play if they are tactilely sensitive. Give them only a small amount of water or let them pour from container to container.

Inclusive Child Care for Infants and Toddlers: Meeting Individual and Special Needs by Marion O'Brien © 1997 Paul H. Brookes Publishing Co., Baltimore.

Theme: All Around the House

Toy/Activity Type		Suggested Activities and Materials for This Theme
Building		Tools (and workbench for toddlers) Fisher-Price play houses Any type of blocks—build houses and furniture
House/doll		Wash and sort pretend laundry Dress up Plastic bowls, pots, pans, wooden spoons, play food Make a "nest" for stuffed animals Put baby dolls to bed Wash dishes (no water except outside) Clean house Doll play
Active play Outdoor play		Hide household objects and find them Obstacle course Touch the ceiling, touch the floor Go on a crawling "tour" Give rides in a laundry basket Paint with water Wash windows Sweep the playground "Car" wash—bikes with big sponges Walk up stairs
Sensory experiences, art, science, small-group activities		Wash baby dolls Wash plastic animals Wash dishes Sponge painting
Music		Lullabies Here We Go 'Round the Mulberry Bush Go In and Out the Windows

Theme: The Doctor Is in

WHAT CHILDREN WILL EXPLORE AND EXPERIENCE

Taking care of others
Enjoying their bodies
Gaining control of their movements in space
Wearing special clothes and getting them on and off
Repeating in play routines and scripts what they have experienced in real life

HOW TEACHERS CAN EXTEND AND
EXPAND CHILDREN'S UNDERSTANDING AND SKILL

Helping children participate in pretend play
Labeling body parts
Talking about people who help—doctors, nurses, police, and firefighters
Encouraging children to talk about visits to the doctor to build children's narrative skills

OTHER CONCEPTS FOR TEACHERS TO TALK ABOUT

Health and ways to stay healthy
Caring for others and showing concern when others are sick or hurt
Self-awareness—teachers talking about times the children were sick
Feeling good

VOCABULARY TO USE

doctor	better	examine	weight	eyes
nurse	care	checkup	height	ears
sick	emergency	exercise	scale	throat
healthy	ambulance	help	measure	heart

SPECIAL CONSIDERATIONS FOR CHILDREN WITH SPECIAL NEEDS

Children with chronic health problems may have had negative experiences with doctors.
  Pretend play can help them feel in control, but teachers must be alert to their anxiety
  and fears.

Inclusive Child Care for Infants and Toddlers: Meeting Individual and Special Needs by
Marion O'Brien © 1997 Paul H. Brookes Publishing Co., Baltimore.

Theme: The Doctor Is in

Toy/Activity Type	Suggested Activities and Materials for This Theme
Building	Community helpers puzzles Flashlights Band-Aid boxes and small toys (opening and closing the boxes is a challenge to little fingers) Emergency vehicles and blocks to make garages
House/doll	Put baby dolls to bed Hats, scarves, and blankets Mirrors Cooking (healthful foods) Doctor and nurse Animal doctor
Active play Outdoor play	Exercises—bend, jump, roll, and twirl Push and pull Balance beam Take baby dolls to the doctor on bikes
Sensory experiences, art, science, small-group activities	Weighing and measuring children Wash baby dolls Flashlights
Music	Hokey-Pokey Head, Shoulders, Knees, and Toes If You're "Healthy" and You Know It . . .

Theme: Our Favorite Things

WHAT CHILDREN WILL EXPLORE AND EXPERIENCE

Seeing familiar things from home at school (but children may have difficulty sharing them!)
Finding pleasure in repetition of familiar, everyday routines
Learning to do new things with old, comfortable toys

HOW TEACHERS CAN EXTEND AND EXPAND CHILDREN'S UNDERSTANDING AND SKILL

Encouraging self-awareness—likes and dislike
Labeling colors
Talking about family members, home, pets, and experiences to help children build narrative skills

OTHER CONCEPTS FOR TEACHERS TO DEMONSTRATE AND/OR TALK ABOUT

Caring for family and friends
Sharing toys with friends
Playing together
Possession (e.g., mine, yours, ours)

VOCABULARY TO USE

mother	friend	house	love	mine
father	dog	home	like	yours
sister	cat	kitchen	best	his/hers
brother	bird	bedroom	favorite	ours
grandmother	fish	living room		
grandfather				

SPECIAL CONSIDERATIONS FOR CHILDREN WITH SPECIAL NEEDS

Some children may have disorganized family lives, live in single-parent homes, or may be living in a foster home or with relatives other than parents. The potential variety of family situations must be recognized and activities planned to suit the situations of all children, regardless of living situations.

Inclusive Child Care for Infants and Toddlers: Meeting Individual and Special Needs by Marion O'Brien © 1997 Paul H. Brookes Publishing Co., Baltimore.

Theme: Our Favorite Things

Toy/Activity Type		Suggested Activities and Materials for This Theme
Building		Duplo blocks with people Dinosaurs Soft foam blocks and a basket or crate to put them in Zoo animals and blocks Star builders Cars and trucks Everyone's favorite building toys (whatever the favorites are at the moment)
House/doll		Wrap baby dolls in blankets Toy telephones Dress up Put groceries in sacks Make pretend pizza Doll play Everyone's favorite house activity (whatever it is at the moment)
Active play **Outdoor play**		Bubble chase Hide and find anything Dance Obstacle course Rocking boat Sheet drag Bean bag toss Bowling Everyone's favorite game (whatever it is at the moment)
Sensory experiences, art, science, small-group activities		Favorite story books Bubbles Water play Contact paper collage with tissue paper, cotton balls Stickers Markers Everyone's favorite art project (whatever it is at the moment)
Music		If You're Happy and You Know It . . . Twinkle, Twinkle Little Star Itsy-Bitsy Spider Wheels on the Bus Five Little Monkeys Everyone's favorite songs (whatever the songs are at the moment)

Theme: Helping Others

WHAT CHILDREN WILL EXPLORE AND EXPERIENCE

Doing things cooperatively with others
Sequencing a task and taking turns to accomplish something
Playing games with and enjoying friends
Talking about everyday experiences

**HOW TEACHERS CAN EXTEND AND
EXPAND CHILDREN'S UNDERSTANDING AND SKILL**

Encouraging children's awareness of helping and being helped
Caring for friends and family
Encouraging giving and doing kind things—talking about how it feels good to help others
Turning activities into turn-taking exercises

OTHER CONCEPTS FOR TEACHERS TO DEMONSTRATE AND/OR TALK ABOUT

Words and signs for PLEASE, THANK YOU, YOU'RE WELCOME, HELP
All of the people who help the children all day long (e.g., parents, bus driver, teachers)
Helping others and cooperating to get things done
Sharing toys with friends

VOCABULARY TO USE

proud	hug	please	help
love	share	thank you	doctor
friend	give	you're welcome	nurse
cuddly	nice	server	mother
cooperate	think	driver	father

SPECIAL CONSIDERATIONS FOR CHILDREN WITH SPECIAL NEEDS

Children who have had difficult family lives may not be familiar with the concept of sharing or cooperation and may need a lot of support to let someone else go first when taking turns.
This theme presents a lot of opportunities for children to provide special help to those who have more severe disabilities.

Inclusive Child Care for Infants and Toddlers: Meeting Individual and Special Needs by Marion O'Brien © 1997 Paul H. Brookes Publishing Co., Baltimore.

Theme: Helping Others

Toy/Activity Type		Suggested Activities and Materials for This Theme
Building		Barns and farm animals Puppets, finger puppets Emergency vehicles Shape sorters
House/doll		Peekaboo with scarves and blankets Baby dolls Make "nests" for stuffed animals Animal doctor Restaurant cooks and servers Clean house Hat store, shoe store Beauty/barber shop Doctor and nurse
Active play Outdoor play		Balls—rolling and bouncing to each other Hide and find Interactive games Give rides in a laundry basket Pushing and pulling Bean bag toss Rocking boat Bowling Tunnel Work bench and tools
Sensory experiences, art, science, small-group activities		Play-Doh Make a group mural or collage Make paper bag puppets Watercolors—on paper or coffee filters Visit helpers (kitchen, office)
Music		If You're "Helping" and You Know It . . . Here We Go 'Round the Mulberry Bush Ring Around the Rosey Hokey-Pokey

Theme: How We Feel

WHAT CHILDREN WILL EXPLORE AND EXPERIENCE

Recognizing their emotions in a variety of different situations
Recognizing others' emotions and how they are similar to and different from their own
    emotions
Looking at themselves as they make faces in the mirror
Playing games with and enjoying friends
Sharing the classroom with families

HOW TEACHERS CAN EXTEND AND
EXPAND CHILDREN'S UNDERSTANDING AND SKILL

Encouraging children's awareness of themselves and their feelings
Labeling emotions and facial expressions
Caring for friends and family
Encouraging giving and doing kind things and talking about how it feels good to help
    others

OTHER CONCEPTS FOR TEACHERS TO DEMONSTRATE AND/OR TALK ABOUT

Using body language, gestures, and tone of voice to tell how someone feels
Having fun at parties and celebrations—surprise parties
Helping others and cooperating to get things done
Sharing toys with friends

VOCABULARY TO USE

happy	upset	proud	hug	please
sad	surprised	love	share	thank you
angry	scared	friend	give	you're welcome
mad	afraid	cuddly	nice	party
smile	frown	eyes	mouth	gift

SPECIAL CONSIDERATIONS FOR CHILDREN WITH SPECIAL NEEDS

Children with visual impairments may have difficulty recognizing facial expressions; teach-
    ers may need to focus on voice tone and body language.
Children with mental retardation and those who have experienced emotional stress may
    not display much emotion but still need to become aware of their feelings.

Inclusive Child Care for Infants and Toddlers: Meeting Individual and Special Needs by
Marion O'Brien © 1997 Paul H. Brookes Publishing Co., Baltimore.

Theme: How We Feel

Toy/Activity Type		Suggested Activities and Materials for This Theme
Building		Duplo people Books with pictures of people and people's faces Toy cameras Toy dinosaurs Musical instruments
House/doll		Mirrors Baby dolls Dress up Picnic Tea party Use puppets to tell fairy tales or recite nursery rhymes
Active play Outdoor play		Hide and find anything Interactive games Touch the ceiling, touch the floor Roll and roll Sheet drag Simon Says I Spy
Sensory experiences, art, science, small-group activities		Make collage of faces "Read" the classroom photo album Take pictures of children Stickers Listen to soft and loud sounds and voices Make a group mural of names and handprints Make sunshiney faces Mystery picture
Music		Sing songs using children's names Hokey-Pokey If You're Happy and You Know It . . . This Little Light of Mine ABCs

Theme: So Big

WHAT CHILDREN WILL EXPLORE AND EXPERIENCE

Becoming familiar with their bodies and where their bodies fit and don't fit (e.g., under things, inside boxes)
Learning relative sizes of similar objects
Putting things into containers—what fits and doesn't fit
Learning concepts of growth and change (e.g., not being a baby anymore; how beans grow)

HOW TEACHERS CAN EXTEND AND EXPAND CHILDREN'S UNDERSTANDING AND SKILL

Encouraging children's awareness of their bodies and how they are growing and changing—new things they can do
Using prepositional concepts of *in, under, over, above,* and so forth.
Talking about *big* and *little*
Visiting babies and talking about growing up

OTHER CONCEPTS FOR TEACHERS TO DEMONSTRATE AND/OR TALK ABOUT

Shapes
Fits/does not fit
Full/empty
Size differences among people
Body parts
Inside/outside

VOCABULARY TO USE

in	big	grow	height	dinosaur
over	little	change	inch	insect
up	tiny	baby	foot	elephant
around	huge	grown-up	ruler	giraffe
under	small	weight	scale	building

SPECIAL CONSIDERATIONS FOR CHILDREN WITH SPECIAL NEEDS

Children with motor disabilities will have difficulty with large motor movement activities and will need assistance to be successful.
Children with mental retardation will have difficulty grasping abstract concepts of size and will need concrete examples.

Inclusive Child Care for Infants and Toddlers: Meeting Individual and Special Needs by Marion O'Brien © 1997 Paul H. Brookes Publishing Co., Baltimore.

Theme: So Big

Toy/Activity Type		Suggested Activities and Materials for This Theme
Building		Puppets Duplo people Fisher-Price play houses Toy cameras Toy dinosaurs Pop beads and links Mega blocks and Duplos Stacking and nesting cups
House/doll		Mirrors Dress up Birthday party (it doesn't *have* to be anyone's birthday) Baby dolls Shoe store Hat store Beauty/barber shop
Active play Outdoor play		Obstacle course Crates and boxes Exercises—bend, jump, roll, and twirl Balls of different sizes Touch the ceiling, touch the floor Interactive games Tunnel Look UP! What do you see?
Sensory experiences, art, science, small-group activities		Weighing and measuring children Get out old classroom photo albums to see how children have changed Handprints and footprints Trace hands and feet Trace bodies
Music		Sing songs using children's names Hokey-Pokey Ring Around the Rosey

Theme: Things that Move

WHAT CHILDREN WILL EXPLORE AND EXPERIENCE

Becoming familiar with their bodies and how they move in space
Using wheels and learning how they make things easier to move
Pushing and pulling
Learning about trucks, traffic, and travel

HOW TEACHERS CAN EXTEND AND
EXPAND CHILDREN'S UNDERSTANDING AND SKILL

Encouraging children's awareness of their bodies and enjoyment of large motor activity
Using concepts of *fast, slow, ride, drive*
Looking at things moving in the water (e.g., tubs or pools outside, visit a fish tank)
Pointing out natural things that move outside—insects, birds, the wind

OTHER CONCEPTS FOR TEACHERS TO DEMONSTRATE AND/OR TALK ABOUT

Safety—crossing the street and wearing seat belts
Ways for people to move—trying different movements in front of a mirror
Ways animals move
Working together to make big things move

VOCABULARY TO USE

feet	run	walk	roll	airplane	wheels
toes	hop	crawl	spin	truck	turn
arms	skip	slide	fly	car	round
body	jump	swim	wings	bus	wind

SPECIAL CONSIDERATIONS FOR CHILDREN WITH SPECIAL NEEDS

Children with motor disabilities will have difficulty with large motor movement activities
    and will need assistance to be successful.
This theme presents an ideal opportunity to make a wheelchair a highly valued possession.
Children from low-income families may never have traveled; concepts of packing suitcases and going on a train or airplane will be unknown to them.

Inclusive Child Care for Infants and Toddlers: Meeting Individual and Special Needs by Marion O'Brien © 1997 Paul H. Brookes Publishing Co., Baltimore.

Theme: Things that Move

Toy/Activity Type		Suggested Activities and Materials for This Theme
Building		Transportation and gear puzzles Airplanes and helicopters Trucks and cars Emergency vehicles Tractors and farm animals Beads on wire
House/doll		Mirrors Play dog and cat Baby dolls Push-pull toys Grocery store—use shopping carts Dress up and go for a ride Make pizza and deliver it Take baby dolls or stuffed animals for stroller rides
Active play **Outdoor play**		Animal sounds and movements Balls—and all variations Bubble chase Crawling races Sheet drag Bike races Rocking boat Bowling Go on a walk outside to watch cars and trucks
Sensory experiences, art, science, small-group activities		Boats in tubs of water Crayons or markers—making circles (wheels) Bubbles Go for a stroller ride outdoors Paint with cars and trucks Paper plate coloring
Music		Wheels on the Bus Ring Around the Rosey Row, Row, Row Your Boat This Train Is Bound for Glory I've Been Working on the Railroad

Theme: Earth, Air, and Water

WHAT CHILDREN WILL EXPLORE AND EXPERIENCE

Contacting the natural world—plants, the earth, sand, trees, rocks
Getting dirty and being clean
Learning about water, water, and more water
Learning about the air and how we use it (e.g., breathing, blowing bubbles, inflating toys)

HOW TEACHERS CAN EXTEND AND
EXPAND CHILDREN'S UNDERSTANDING AND SKILL

Encouraging children's awareness of the world around them
Labeling the everyday—grass, roots, leaves, pebbles, cement, glass
Touching all types of surfaces—smooth, rough, sharp (but not too sharp), soft
Letting children experience the weather—sun, rain, snow, cold, hot

---

OTHER CONCEPTS FOR TEACHERS TO DEMONSTRATE AND/OR TALK ABOUT

Same/different
Colors and textures
Living and growing versus not living and growing
How plants grow
How dirt becomes mud
What soap does in water
How air dries our clothes (outside)
How ice melts

VOCABULARY TO USE

names of colors
names of plants, insects, birds, and animals in the outside play area

hard	smooth	bright	alive	sand	dirt
soft	shiny	wet	leaf	water	mud
rough	dark	slippery	grass		

SPECIAL CONSIDERATIONS FOR CHILDREN WITH SPECIAL NEEDS

Children with motor disabilities may need a lot of help being positioned so they can get in contact with the natural world, which may initially be uncomfortable and even unpleasant; let the child be the guide.
Children with allergies may need to stay on the playground.
Children with fine motor difficulties may especially enjoy water play.

Inclusive Child Care for Infants and Toddlers: Meeting Individual and Special Needs by Marion O'Brien © 1997 Paul H. Brookes Publishing Co., Baltimore.

Theme: Earth, Air, and Water

Toy/Activity Type	Suggested Activities and Materials for This Theme
Building	Cars and trucks Blocks of several kinds Toy farms and farm animals Flashlights Toy airplanes and helicopters
House/doll	Wash and fold pretend laundry Teddy bears' picnic Clean house Wash dishes Go camping On toddlers' pond
Active play Outdoor play	Bubble chase in the wind All types of water play Scarf dancing Sheet drag Parachute Nature walk
Sensory experiences, art, science, small-group activities	Water play—wash babies, wash animals Sand play Bubbles Plant seeds Water plants Watercolors Fingerpaints Shaving cream on tables
Music	Musical instruments Old MacDonald Here We Go 'Round the Mulberry Bush Itsy-Bitsy Spider

Theme: Senses

WHAT CHILDREN WILL EXPLORE AND EXPERIENCE

Becoming familiar with the sights, sounds, and textures of their world
Listening to their own and others' voices
Tasting and smelling
Being messy and then getting clean again

HOW TEACHERS CAN EXTEND AND
EXPAND CHILDREN'S UNDERSTANDING AND SKILL

Encouraging self-awareness
Labeling colors, textures, shapes, smells, tastes, and sounds
Describing concepts of size
Describing contours: rounded, smooth, and sharp

OTHER CONCEPTS FOR TEACHERS TO DEMONSTRATE AND/OR TALK ABOUT

Same/different
Hiding and finding
What tastes good and what doesn't
Listening
Loudness/quietness

VOCABULARY TO USE

eyes	smell	tongue	quiet	sweet	dark
ears	see	taste	soft	sour	whisper
fingers	hear	big	hard	yucky	shout
touch	mouth	little	rough	crunchy	sing
nose	teeth	loud	smooth	bright	names of colors

SPECIAL CONSIDERATIONS FOR CHILDREN WITH SPECIAL NEEDS

Children with sensory impairments will experience the activities in this theme differently
   from the other children. Teachers must be alert to their experiences, interpreting for the
   other children and helping them put their experience into words.
Children with digestive disorders or food allergies need to be watched carefully to be sure
   they do not eat foods as part of a tasting activity that they are not supposed to have.

Inclusive Child Care for Infants and Toddlers: Meeting Individual and Special Needs by
Marion O'Brien © 1997 Paul H. Brookes Publishing Co., Baltimore.

Theme: Senses

Toy/Activity Type		Suggested Activities and Materials for This Theme
Building		Puppets Duplo people Books with pictures of people and people's faces Toy cameras Squeeze toys with baskets or pails to put them in Flashlights
House/doll		Mirrors Telephones Dress up Hats, scarves, and blankets Feed baby dolls Beauty/barber shop Hat store Shoe store
Active play **Outdoor play**		Follow the leader (at making faces) Scarf dancing Interactive games Bubble chase Animal sounds and movements Exercises—bend, jump, roll, and twirl I Spy Buzz-buzz Washing windows
Sensory experiences, art, science, small-group activities		Contact paper collage (use shapes, textured pieces of cloth) Textures or texture blanket Play-Doh Stickers Listen to rattles, bells, musical toys Listen to soft and loud voices Listen to everyday sounds Make paper bag puppets Sponges in water Shaving cream on tables
Music		Musical instruments Pots, pans, and wooden spoons

Appendix B
Sample Play Activities
for Inclusive Infant and Toddler Care

Infants and toddlers learn constantly, and every event of their day offers potential for teaching. Nevertheless, high-quality child care for infants and toddlers requires that teachers also plan and organize learning experiences for children. The sample play activities described here provide examples of the ways in which a variety of play materials can be used for effective teaching of infants and toddlers. Creative teachers who are familiar with the individual characteristics of the children in their care will want to expand on the activities provided here and develop their own play and learning activities. Activity planning forms are provided for that purpose in Appendix C.

Appendix B is divided into three sections for each of the three types of play activities described in Chapter 5: Infant Play 1 Activities, Infant Play 2 Activities, and Toddler Play Activities. Although Infant Play 1 Activities are distinctly different in nature from the other two types of activities in that they are intended as brief individual interactions between a teacher and a child, rather than group play activities, the division of Infant Play 2 and Toddler Activities is somewhat arbitrary. Most of the Infant Play 2 Activities listed can be adapted for use with toddlers by making the activities more complicated and challenging. Similarly, many of the toddler activities, particularly those listed under the Building and Active Play categories, can be simplified for use with infants. Most activities have been listed in only one of these sections in order to avoid repetition. Teachers of infants are encouraged to browse through the toddler play activity descriptions, and teachers of toddlers are also encouraged to browse through the infant play activity descriptions, adapting ideas that appeal to them from any category.

INFANT PLAY 1 ACTIVITIES

This section includes a description of ways that teachers can play with babies by using the materials suggested on the Play 1 toy rotation list (see Figure 5.2 in Chapter 5). The teacher conducting Play 1 activities is also responsible for overseeing *all* of the children in the play area, ensuring their health and safety as well as encouraging their continuous involvement with toys. Therefore, this teacher must survey the entire area constantly in order to be aware of every child's location and actions. Rather than becoming involved in extended play with one or a few children, the teacher conducting Play 1 activities moves from one child to another child, interacting individually for a few minutes with each child and visually checking on all other children in between. New Play 1 toys are introduced into the play area every 15 minutes to provide variety in stimulation, to keep both children's and teachers' interest high, and to ensure that all toys are washed frequently.

In this appendix, ideas for use of the Play 1 materials are organized according to infants' degree of mobility (e.g., tiny babies, crawlers, walkers) because infants at different levels of motor development also typically vary in their understanding of objects and events. It is important for teachers to keep in mind that crawlers also enjoy doing the activities listed for tiny babies, and walkers also enjoy doing the activities listed for tiny babies and crawlers. Children with developmental delays or disabilities may be more advanced in their motor development than in their cognitive development or vice versa; therefore, teachers must observe individual children carefully to select the most effective way to use a Play 1 toy with each child. The suggestions provided here are only a starting point for the many ways responsive teachers can use Play 1 materials. A planning guide to help teachers develop new Play 1 activities appears in Appendix C.

SAMPLE INFANT PLAY 2 ACTIVITIES

This section of Appendix B includes a selection of thematically oriented activities that are described in Chapter 5 as Play 2 activities. These activities differ from those listed under Play 1 activities in that they are intended to involve a small group of children in joint play with a teacher. The teacher responsible for conducting Play 2 activities is not responsible for supervising the entire play area, which is a responsibility of the teacher conducting Play 1 activities. Therefore, Play 2 activities can usually involve more active and extended play, and the teacher can devote his or her full attention to the two or three children who are participating in the Play 2 activity.

Although Play 2 activities are intended to be fun for children and for teachers, they also provide excellent opportunities for infants to explore the world around them and gain new experiences with toys and other people. In order for Play 2 activities to be effective learning experiences for children, teachers responsible for these activities must think about them in advance and consider the possibilities each activity presents for teaching. Teachers' plans will not always be realized because sometimes children will guide the activity in ways the teacher never considered. However, it is necessary for responsive teachers to be prepared to capitalize on children's interest and involvement in Play 2 activities.

The descriptions of Play 2 activities included here suggest some of the ways infants may learn from involvement in the activities and also some of the concepts teachers can talk about while conducting the activities. The suggested learning goals for children are not always items one might find on a skill development chart, but rather are intended to expand teachers' ideas of the range of learning goals appropriate for infants and toddlers. As with Play 1 activities, the descriptions provided in this section represent only a small fraction of the possible play and learning activities that could be fit into a Play 2 framework. Teachers should be encouraged to modify or adapt these activities and develop many more of their own activities in response to the interests and abilities of the children in their care. A planning form for teachers' use is included in Appendix C.

SAMPLE TODDLER PLAY ACTIVITIES

The toddler play activities included in this section are organized based on the type of activity or the area in which the activity would typically be conducted: Building Area, House/Doll Area, Active Play Area and Outdoor, and Small Group. Suggested materials are listed for each activity, and it is most efficient if the materials for each activity are stored together in a plastic bin or storage box so that they can be brought to the classroom when needed and stored elsewhere when not in use. This type of organization requires duplicate copies of materials, however, which is not always practical. If activity materials are not stored together, one teacher can take time each afternoon to gather the next day's activity materials and bring them to the classroom.

Also included in the toddler activity descriptions are suggestions for the types of exploration toddlers are likely to do with the materials provided and the learning experiences that may be available to toddlers during the activity. These suggestions emphasize the limited experience toddlers have had with the world and the many possibilities that are available for learning from even the simplest materials or events. Play activities for toddlers do not have to result in obvious skill acquisition in order for teachers to be effective. An understanding of how the world works is built from many small experiences and insights, and these are the goals of toddler play, which is guided by responsive teachers.

Each activity description offers teachers some ideas for using the materials to get the activity started and how to expand on children's play, and the description also offers some suggestions of what to talk about with children during the activity to help build language skills. The ideas provided are far from exhaustive; toddler teachers will want to extend the suggestions, based on their own teaching skills and experiences with toddlers. A planning form for the development of new toddler activities and a weekly toddler activity schedule that can be used to plan classroom activities around a theme are included in Appendix C.

Infant Play 1 Activities

Activity or material	What teachers can do with TINY BABIES	What teachers can do with CRAWLERS[a]	What teachers can do with WALKERS[b]
Small balls	Give baby a ball to hold; if baby drops the ball, roll it back to baby and put it back in baby's hand.	Hand baby three balls, one at a time, observing what baby does after both hands are full.	Roll balls back and forth to baby.
	Hold balls in front of baby's face and encourage baby to visually track the ball from side to side and above baby's head.	Demonstrate dropping a ball into a container and encourage baby to imitate; then show baby how to dump the ball out.	Demonstrate gently throwing balls into a large crate or laundry basket; encourage baby to imitate.
	Encourage reaching by holding a ball out in front of baby or to baby's side.	Chase balls across the floor with baby.	Hide balls under cloths or cups; make the task increasingly more difficult as baby gets older.
Books	Read, read, read to baby.	Read, read, read to baby.	Read, read, read to baby.
	Let baby hold soft cloth or plastic books.	Have books that babies can explore and books that are for teachers to read to children; encourage children to understand the difference.	Play "Where's the _____?" by using simple labels that baby can find; encourage baby to point to pictures for teachers to label.
	Point to pictures or shapes and label them for baby.	Demonstrate turning the pages of baby's books; encourage baby to imitate.	Make up simple stories and rhymes about the pictures in baby's book; encourage baby to enjoy the sounds of language.

Infant Play 1 Activities

Activity or material	What teachers can do with TINY BABIES	What teachers can do with CRAWLERS[a]	What teachers can do with WALKERS[b]
Mega Blocks	Put baby on teacher's lap while teacher builds a tower with big blocks; encourage baby to reach for the tower and knock it over.	Demonstrate stacking one block on top of another; encourage baby to imitate. Sit baby on top of block, providing plenty of support.	Take turns with baby in stacking blocks until the tower is way above baby's head; help baby knock it down and make a big noise as it falls.
	Pub baby on stomach with blocks out in front; encourage baby to move forward and reach for the blocks.	Build a tower high enough for baby to use it as support for pulling to stand; help baby stand and cruise around the blocks.	Help baby climb onto a block and lift baby off as if baby is jumping—high up and then down.
	Play peekaboo by hiding teacher's face behind a block and then popping out—repeat several times to one side, then switch and watch baby's reaction.		Build a tunnel for baby to crawl through; when baby is inside, say, "Where's [baby's name]?" and show surprise when baby comes out.
Baby songs (use tapes or live music)	Sit facing baby (who can be on your lap, in an infant seat, or in a bouncer) and sing, using an animated face and exaggerated mouth movements to capture and hold baby's attention.	Use standard finger and hand motions or develop your own to accompany popular baby songs; encourage baby to imitate.	Encourage baby to move body in time with music; dance along with baby.
	Hold baby at arm's length in front of you, with feet touching the floor, and move baby to "dance" to the music.	As baby begins to make sounds with the music, imitate baby's sounds.	Respond to baby's requests for favorite songs to be repeated many times; babies need a lot of repetitions in order to know what to expect and to participate actively.
	Recite finger plays or sing songs, changing the tempo and pitch.	Demonstrate banging or tapping in time with the music; encourage baby to imitate.	Emphasize rhyming words or unusual sounds in songs or finger plays; encourage baby to imitate.

[a]Activities for crawlers can also include the activities listed for tiny babies.
[b]Activities for walkers can also include the activities listed for tiny babies and crawlers.

(continued)

Infant Play 1 Activities *(continued)*

Activity or material	What teachers can do with TINY BABIES	What teachers can do with CRAWLERS[a]	What teachers can do with WALKERS[b]
Chew and squeak toys (a large collection of rubber squeeze toys)	Hold toy in front of baby and make it squeak; encourage baby to reach and grasp toy. Encourage baby to practice getting objects to his or her mouth by giving baby a chew toy and guiding baby's hand to mouth. Use squeak toys to encourage visual following; when baby's attention wavers, squeak the toy to recapture baby's interest.	Use squeak toys as motivation for beginning crawlers by getting down on the floor about 3 feet in front of baby and holding a toy out toward baby, squeaking it to add interest. Hide a toy inside a cup or other container while baby watches; encourage baby to "search" for the toy. Demonstrate how to make toys squeak; help baby learn to squeeze or push down on toys to make noise.	With a lot of toys available, encourage older babies to give toys to younger babies; praise them exuberantly and use polite conventional expressions of "Please" and "Thank you" to accompany the exchanges. Wrap small toys in blankets or bandanas and set them in front of baby; encourage baby to unwrap the toy. Get out containers for toys and demonstrate in and out.
Toys with wheels	Roll small toys over baby's body, arms, and legs; watch baby's facial expression. Hold toy up in front of baby to encourage reaching; give baby the toy, even if the reaching is misdirected. With baby resting on back, place a wheeled toy on baby's chest or stomach; encourage baby to reach for and grasp the toy.	Make funny motor noises while rolling wheeled toys along the floor; encourage baby to imitate. Give baby a toy in each hand and watch what baby does. Push toy across floor in front of baby; encourage baby to chase toy.	Demonstrate rolling a wheeled toy down a ramp or incline; encourage baby to imitate. Sit facing baby and roll a toy back and forth between you and baby. Label the different types of trucks and cars and help baby sort them by type, size, shape, or color.

Infant Play 1 Activities

Activity or material	What teachers can do with TINY BABIES	What teachers can do with CRAWLERS[a]	What teachers can do with WALKERS[b]
Stacking rings	Put rings on baby's wrists and ankles and watch baby's reaction.	Look at baby through the center of a ring; encourage baby to imitate.	Roll rings across the floor; encourage baby to chase them and bring them back to you.
	Put a ring on your head and look at baby with a funny expression; let ring fall off and show surprise.	Demonstrate stacking rings on a post; encourage baby to imitate, providing guidance and help as needed.	Wrap rings in blankets or bandanas and set them in front of baby; encourage baby to unwrap the rings.
	Encourage baby to practice getting objects to mouth by giving baby a ring and guiding baby's hand to mouth.	Put a scarf or bandana through the center of a ring; encourage baby to pull it through all the way.	Help baby sort rings by size and color.
Toy telephones	Hold a small toy telephone or part of a telephone where baby can reach for it; let baby hold, touch, and taste the telephone.	Demonstrate how to dial or push buttons on the toy telephone; encourage baby to imitate.	Demonstrate greetings: "Hello," "Good-bye," "Hi," "How are you?"; practice "high fives"; encourage baby to imitate.
	Talk to baby on a toy telephone, using baby's name frequently; encourage baby to make babbling sounds in response.	Demonstrate how to hold the toy telephone receiver; encourage baby to imitate and to "talk" into the telephone.	Help baby match receivers and bodies of toy telephone by size and color.
	Use ringing or musical toy telephones to attract baby's attention to you, then smile, smile, smile.	Use the toy telephone activity to emphasize the names of all the babies, encouraging babies to look at each baby in turn as you use that baby's name.	Use the toy telephone for a "911" rescue operation; bring out the toy fire trucks and police vehicles.

[a]Activities for crawlers can also include the activities listed for tiny babies.
[b]Activities for walkers can also include the activities listed for tiny babies and crawlers.

(continued)

Infant Play 1 Activities *(continued)*

Activity or material	What teachers can do with TINY BABIES	What teachers can do with CRAWLERS[a]	What teachers can do with WALKERS[b]
Balancing bunnies	Give baby two copies of the same toy, one in each hand, and watch as baby compares them; encourage baby to bang them together at midline.	Give baby a bunny in each hand and watch what baby does when you offer baby a third bunny.	Demonstrate making hopping motions with bunnies; encourage baby to imitate.
	Hold a bunny in front of baby's face and encourage baby to visually track the bunny from side to side and above baby's head.	Demonstrate pulling two bunnies apart; place them loosely together again and encourage baby to imitate.	Wrap bunnies in blankets or bandanas and set them in front of baby; encourage baby to unwrap the bunnies.
	Encourage baby to practice getting objects to mouth by giving baby a bunny and guiding baby's hand to mouth.	Hide a bunny inside a cup or other container while baby watches; encourage baby to "search" for the bunny.	Demonstrate gently throwing bunnies into a large crate or laundry basket; encourage baby to imitate.
Large foam blocks (and other plastic-covered foam shapes)	With baby on teacher's lap, stack soft blocks on top of one another; encourage baby to reach for the tower and knock it over.	Demonstrate stacking blocks; encourage baby to imitate.	Take turns with baby in stacking blocks until the tower is above baby's head; help baby knock it down and build it back again.
	Give a big, soft block to hold; encourage baby to reach for the block if baby drops it.	Use a large foam shape as support for pulling to stand; help baby stand and cruise around the shape and practice letting go to sit down.	Help baby step up onto blocks or foam shapes, providing plenty of support and help; observe how baby handles the postural and balance adjustments.
	Play peekaboo by hiding teacher's face behind a block and then popping out—repeat several times to one side, then switch and watch baby's reaction.	Encourage baby to sit on blocks and pull to stand, using your hands as support.	Set up an obstacle course of blocks and demonstrate for baby how to walk around the blocks; encourage baby to imitate.

Infant Play 1 Activities

Activity or material	What teachers can do with TINY BABIES	What teachers can do with CRAWLERS[a]	What teachers can do with WALKERS[b]
Musical instruments	Sit baby on your lap, in an infant seat, or in a bouncer facing you and play a musical instrument (e.g., jingle bells, a harmonica, a marimba) to capture and hold baby's attention.	As baby begins to make sounds with the music, imitate baby's sounds.	Encourage baby to move body in time with music; dance along with baby.
	Put bells on baby's wrists or ankles and encourage baby to shake arms or legs to make music.	Demonstrate using a drum or other percussion instrument in time with taped music; encourage baby to imitate you.	Respond to baby's requests for favorite songs to be repeated many times; babies need a lot of repetition in order to know what to expect and to participate actively.
	Use finger plays or songs that are familiar and use musical instruments to accompany your singing; look directly at baby and smile!	Play different musical instruments behind baby's back; encourage baby to turn around and reach for the instruments.	Demonstrate how to play each instrument; encourage baby to imitate.
Animals and sounds (use plastic, rubber, and stuffed animals; books of animal pictures)	"Walk" toy animals over baby's body, arms, and legs; watch baby's facial expression.	Make animal sounds while moving animals along the floor; encourage baby to imitate.	Label the different kinds of animals and help baby sort them by type, size, shape, or color.
	With baby resting on back, place a toy animal on baby's chest or stomach; encourage baby to reach for and grasp the toy.	Give baby a different animal in each hand and then show baby another animal that matches one of the two animals baby is holding; watch what baby does.	While baby is standing, encourage baby to stoop to pick up an animal from the floor, then return to a stand; observe baby's balance and coordination.
	Facing baby, make animal sounds while holding the animal for baby to see; encourage baby to babble back at you and imitate baby's sounds.	Walk in imitation of various animals; be silly and encourage baby to chase after you.	Wrap animals in pieces of cloth and place them in front of baby; encourage baby to unwrap and find the animals.

[a]Activities for crawlers can also include the activities listed for tiny babies.
[b]Activities for walkers can also include the activities listed for tiny babies and crawlers.

(continued)

295

Infant Play 1 Activities *(continued)*

Activity or material	What teachers can do with TINY BABIES	What teachers can do with CRAWLERS[a]	What teachers can do with WALKERS[b]
Shapes and bowls (use plastic bowls and other containers and a variety of building toys in different shapes)	Hold a brightly colored shape in front of baby's face and encourage baby to visually track the shape from side to side and above baby's head.	Hand baby three shapes, one at a time, observing what baby does after both hands are full.	Demonstrate throwing balls into bowl from about a foot away; encourage baby to imitate.
	Put baby on your lap while you put shapes into bowls; encourage baby to reach for the shapes in the bowls.	Demonstrate dropping a shape into a bowl and encourage baby to imitate; show baby how to shake the bowl to make interesting sounds, then show how to dump the shapes out.	Demonstrate putting shapes into a shape sorter, using only circles unless baby is very skilled; encourage baby to imitate and master the task.
	Put a bowl on your head and look at baby with a funny expression; let bowl fall off and show surprise.	Put several shapes under an upside-down bowl while baby watches; encourage baby to pick up the bowl and find the shapes.	Help baby sort shapes by type, size, and color.
Photo albums	Take baby's picture with an instant camera; show baby picture of him- or herself and other babies.	"Read" the classroom photo album to baby, telling stories about the babies and what was happening when the pictures were taken.	Play "Where's _____?" using different babies' names and then pointing to the picture of the baby named and to the real baby in the classroom.
	Hold baby on your lap while looking at pictures with other babies.	Help baby turn pages of the photo album.	Give baby a toy camera and encourage baby to imitate teacher who is taking pictures with a real camera.
	Put pictures on a bulletin board for parents and others to see; hold baby up to pictures, pointing to and naming each baby.	Repeat babies' names and encourage baby to imitate or babble in return.	Hold baby's and teacher's pictures up beside a mirror; have baby look in mirror and look at pictures.

Infant Play 1 Activities

Activity or material	What teachers can do with TINY BABIES	What teachers can do with CRAWLERS[a]	What teachers can do with WALKERS[b]
Push-down/pop-up toys (use any enclosed tops that spin and jack-in-the-boxes)	Put baby on your lap while you make the toy move; encourage baby to reach for and touch the toy. With baby resting on back, place a large (but not heavy) toy on baby's chest or stomach; encourage baby to roll to knock the toy to the floor. Demonstrate for baby how to push a jack-in-the-box back into its box; help baby participate in pushing and closing the box.	Make a big production over the jack-in-the-box, being very dramatic about turning the handle and getting ready for the big surprise; then show exaggerated astonishment and joy when the puppet pops out—repeat until baby knows what to expect. Show baby how to push down on the top to make it move; demonstrate and encourage baby to imitate (give help as needed for success). Partially hide toys under blankets or behind your back; encourage baby to search for them.	Demonstrate how the jack-in-the-box works, letting baby explore the inside of the box as well as the puppet and the handle; encourage baby to make the toy work. Line up several tops and get them all working at once; laugh and giggle with baby and make "bets" about which one will stop first. Respond to baby's requests to continue making a particular toy work over and over; babies need a lot of repetition for mastery of events and actions.
Pull-apart/put together toys (use any type of construction toy that is easy to put together and pull apart)	Give baby two pieces of the building toy, one in each hand, and watch as baby compares them; encourage baby to bang them together at midline. Hold a brightly colored toy in front of baby's face and encourage baby to visually track the toy from side to side and above baby's head. Encourage baby to practice getting objects to mouth by giving baby a toy and guiding baby's hand to mouth.	Give baby a toy in each hand and watch what baby does when you offer baby a third toy. Demonstrate pulling two pieces of the toy apart; place them loosely together again and encourage baby to imitate. Hide a toy inside a cup or other container while baby watches; encourage baby to "search" for the toy.	Wrap toys in blankets or bandanas and set them in front of baby; encourage baby to unwrap the toys. Demonstrate how toys go together; set toys in front of baby and encourage baby to imitate, giving help as needed. Build a large construction with baby's help.

[a]Activities for crawlers can also include the activities listed for tiny babies.
[b]Activities for walkers can also include the activities listed for tiny babies and crawlers.

(continued)

Infant Play 1 Activities *(continued)*

Activity or material	What teachers can do with TINY BABIES	What teachers can do with CRAWLERS[a]	What teachers can do with WALKERS[b]
Large balls	With baby on your lap, play with a large ball, tossing it from hand to hand and throwing it into the air, then catching it again. Play peekaboo by hiding your face behind a large ball and then popping out—repeat several times to one side, then switch sides and watch baby's reaction. Let baby touch and feel the ball and push against it, then roll the ball back to within baby's reach.	Chase balls across the floor with baby. Using a very lightweight beach ball, throw ball so it bounces off baby's back; encourage baby to go get the ball. Sit baby on top of a large ball, holding baby tightly while rolling the ball from side to side and from back to front.	Roll ball back and forth with baby. Roll ball to the far end of the room; encourage baby to go get the ball and bring it back to you, then roll it again. Demonstrate gently throwing a large, lightweight ball into a round laundry basket (baby basketball); encourage baby to imitate.
Plastic blocks (use many different sizes and types of blocks mixed together)	Give baby two blocks of the same type, one in each hand, and watch as baby compares them; repeat with two very different blocks. Seat baby on your lap and stack blocks on top of one another; encourage baby to knock the tower down. Using a block, especially one that makes a sound when it is shaken, encourage baby's visual tracking—side-to-side, up and down, and in a circle.	Have baby hold a block in each hand and watch what baby does when you hold out a third and then a fourth block. Stack blocks into a tower, counting loudly, and let baby knock the tower over many times. Demonstrate dropping a block into a box or other container; have the baby retrieve the block and encourage imitation.	Help baby stack blocks to build a tower. Put blocks inside a paper bag and crumple the top to close the bag; encourage baby to open the bag and find the blocks. Make a train of blocks (stack two for the engine) and push the train along the floor, making "choo-choo" and whistle sounds.

Infant Play 1 Activities

Activity or material	What teachers can do with TINY BABIES	What teachers can do with CRAWLERS[a]	What teachers can do with WALKERS[b]
Rattles	Give baby a rattle to hold and shake; help baby shake the rattle to hear the sound. If baby drops rattle, put it back in baby's hand.

Shake a rattle out of the baby's view, to the side and back, and watch for baby to turn to the sound; if baby does not turn at first, call baby's name and then shake the rattle when baby looks.

Encourage reaching by holding a rattle out in front and to the side of baby and shaking it to attract baby's attention. | Give baby two different rattles and encourage baby to hit them together in a rhythm; encourage baby to hear the different sounds they make when hit against other surfaces.

For beginning crawlers, hold and shake a rattle about 3 feet in front of baby to encourage forward movement.

Use a rattle as accompaniment to a favorite song; encourage baby to rattle along with you. | Put a rattle or two inside a closed container and shake it to attract baby's interest; encourage baby to figure out how to get the container open (give help as needed).

While baby is standing, encourage baby to stoop to pick up a rattle and stand back up; put rattles in places where baby must bend and reach to get them so baby can practice balance and postural control.

Listen carefully to the different sounds different rattles make; encourage baby to listen with you. |

[a]Activities for crawlers can also include the activities listed for tiny babies.
[b]Activities for walkers can also include the activities listed for tiny babies and crawlers.

Infant Play 2 Activities

Building Activities

Activity	Materials needed	Teachers can talk about	TINY BABIES will explore and experience	CRAWLERS[a] will explore and experience	WALKERS[b] will explore and experience
All building toy activities	The building toy or toys listed on the activity plan for the day or week	Shapes, colors, sizes The names of the toys What the children are doing with the materials What teachers are doing	Looking, reaching, touching toys Holding a toy in their hands Tasting the toys Watching other children Putting toys on their heads or balancing them on the tops of their hands or arms	Pulling pieces of toys apart Knocking down towers or other constructions, or watching them fall Banging pieces of toys together and banging them on other surfaces to hear the different sounds they make Beginning sorting—first by size, then shape, then color Giving and receiving toys—lots of "thank you's"—first with teachers, then with other children	Putting pieces of toys together (with lots of teacher help) Helping teachers build towers or other constructions Putting toy pieces into baskets, boxes, or bins; dumping them out again; putting them in again

Suggested building toys for infants: cars and trucks, Duplos with people, finger puppets, foam blocks, plastic animals, pop beads, shape sorters, stacking and nesting toys, star builders, waffle blocks.

[a]Activities for crawlers can also include the activities listed for tiny babies.
[b]Activities for walkers can also include the activities listed for tiny babies and crawlers.

House/Doll Activities

Activity	Materials needed	Teachers can talk about	TINY BABIES will explore and experience	CRAWLERS[a] will explore and experience	WALKERS[b] will explore and experience
Baby dolls **variation: stuffed animals**	Various sizes and types of baby dolls Doll clothes Doll furniture	Babies, body parts, clothes, caring, giving What children do with the dolls What teachers are doing	Touching babies Looking at eyes Feeling babies' hair, hands, and feet Watching other children	Holding babies Hugging and kissing babies Moving babies' arms and legs Opening and closing babies' eyes	Carrying babies Helping teachers dress babies Imitating teachers' pretend care of babies
Dress up **variation: hats and shoes**	Clothes and accessories of all kinds: shoes, hats, neckties, aprons, gowns, purses A wall-mounted mirror	Textures and colors of clothes The names of the types of clothing children are look at, touching, or wearing How beautiful the children look! On and off What children are doing What teachers are doing	The feel of different types of fabric in their hands, stroking their arms or legs, or on their faces Looking at themselves in the mirror Peekaboo with teachers who cover their heads with clothing items Wearing hats and taking them off	Looking in the mirror to see how wearing different hats makes them look different Choosing their own clothing item Giving away clothes to younger babies	Walking in grown-up shoes Putting hats on teachers Practicing some simple dressing skills, with teachers' help

[a]Activities for crawlers can also include the activities listed for tiny babies.
[b]Activities for walkers can also include the activities listed for tiny babies and crawlers.

(continued)

House/Doll Activities *(continued)*

Activity	Materials needed	Teachers can talk about	TINY BABIES will explore and experience	CRAWLERS^a will explore and experience	WALKERS^b will explore and experience
Hats, scarves, and blankets **variation: peekaboo with scarves and blankets**	A big box of adult- and child-size hats Scarves, bandanas, doll blankets A mirror	Hats, heads, hair, scarves, clothes, neck, on, off What children are doing with the hats and scarves What teachers are doing	Holding hats and scarves, feeling the different textures The feel of scarves on their cheeks, arms, legs Watching other children	Wearing hats and look-ing at themselves in the mirror Wrapping scarves around themselves Having teachers wrap and tie scarves around their heads Putting scarves on top of toys	Wrapping scarves around small toys Waving scarves in time to music
Make a "nest" for stuffed animals	A variety of stuffed ani-mal toys Pillows and blankets A beanbag chair	Cozy, warm, safe, comfortable, soft, pillows, nest Names of the animals Children's names What children are doing What teachers are doing	Being in the "nest" with the stuffed animals Reaching for and hold-ing stuffed animals Rolling on and off pillows Watching the other children	Helping to stack pillows and blankets to make a "nest" Putting animals in the "nest" Crawling into the "nest"	Bringing other toys for the "nest" Taking the "nest" apart and putting it together again Walking on pillows Climbing into and out of a beanbag chair Pretending to sleep and then waking up Imitating teachers' singing of lullabies "Helping" teachers read bedtime stories to the stuffed animals

House/Doll Activities

Activity	Materials needed	Teachers can talk about	TINY BABIES will explore and experience	CRAWLERS[a] will explore and experience	WALKERS[b] will explore and experience
Plastic bowls, pots and pans, and pretend food	Plastic kitchen and serving equipment of various sizes, colors, and textures For food, use plastic play food or small construction toys that will fit into the bowls and pans	Cooking, foods, how things taste Label the pots, pans, and serving equipment Sizes, shapes, and colors of materials What children are doing with the equipment and food What teachers are doing	Looking at, touching, and holding toys Having bowls put on their heads and getting them off The sounds of play food inside bowls or pans when they are shaken	Putting food into bowls or pans and especially dumping it out again Banging bowls or pans together and against other surfaces in the classroom and listening to the different sounds they can make	Carrying the pots and pans around the classroom Following teachers' lead, pretending to cook food and serving it in bowls Giving food to younger babies Pretending to eat
Putting groceries into sacks	Pretend food Food containers that have been emptied and cleaned (e.g., cereal boxes, salt containers, plastic water bottles, milk cartons) Paper grocery sacks	The names of grocery items, foods, sections of the grocery store In and out as items are placed into and taken out of sacks What the children are doing with the groceries and sacks What teachers are doing	Looking, reaching, and touching grocery items; holding grocery sacks The sound of paper sacks as they are opened and crumpled Watching other children	Putting grocery items into sacks Dumping grocery items out of sacks Putting other toys into sacks	Carrying sack with one or two items in it from one end of the classroom to another With teachers' help, taking turns filling a grocery sack Stacking grocery items to make a tower; knocking it down

[a]Activities for crawlers can also include the activities listed for tiny babies.
[b]Activities for walkers can also include the activities listed for tiny babies and crawlers.

(continued)

House/Doll Activities (continued)

Activity	Materials needed	Teachers can talk about	TINY BABIES will explore and experience	CRAWLERS[a] will explore and experience	WALKERS[b] will explore and experience
Tea party **variations:** birthday party; have a party for stuffed animals	Teapots, cups, saucers, pitchers, small plates A small tablecloth to spread on the floor Napkins Stuffed animals to join the party Party hats	Parties, birthdays, setting the table Pouring, sipping, drinking, making tea, birthday cakes Labeling cups, saucers, plates, pitchers, teapot Simple directions What children are doing What teachers are doing	Looking at, touching, holding, and tasting teacups and small pitchers Banging two cups together at midline Reaching for toys held out in front of them and above their heads Putting their hands inside cups and pitchers	Crawling on and looking under the tablecloth Putting fingers through the handles of cups and pitchers Wearing cups as hats Singing "Happy Birthday" after a fashion Finding cups or toys the teacher has wrapped in napkins or partially hidden under upside-down cups	Sorting cups, saucers, plates, pitchers Stacking cups and plates on top of each other, then knocking them down Sitting around the tablecloth and, following the teacher's lead, sipping tea Finding hidden objects under cups or pitchers or under the tablecloth
Telephones	A lot of different sizes and types of play and real telephones	Ringing, talking, greetings (e.g., Hello, Goodbye, How are you?) Use children's names by "calling" each one in turn Listening to sounds and voices What children are doing What teachers are doing	Holding and touching the telephones Hearing their names as they are "called" on the telephone Listening to musical or ringing telephones Watching other children	Dialing the telephones Holding the telephones up to their heads in imitation of teachers Banging telephones together to hear the sounds they make	Saying the names of other children Imitating teachers' words of greeting Matching up parts of telephones by size and color Carrying telephones around the classroom

House/Doll Activities

Activity	Materials needed	Teachers can talk about	TINY BABIES will explore and experience	CRAWLERS[a] will explore and experience	WALKERS[b] will explore and experience
Wash and sort laundry	Bandanas, blankets, handkerchiefs, napkins, doll clothes, and other small cloth items Laundry baskets	Label the items being washed Clean and dirty clothes Wash, dry, iron, fold, stack, sort What the children are doing What teachers are doing	Looking at, touching, and holding pretend laundry Reaching for items held out in front of them and above their heads Playing peekaboo with teachers Watching other children	Putting laundry items into laundry baskets, dumping them out again With teachers' help, "sorting" laundry Crawling into laundry baskets Getting a ride inside laundry baskets Putting other toys into laundry baskets	Imitating teachers' folding of blankets, napkins, handkerchiefs Putting laundry items on their heads Climbing into and out of laundry baskets Giving younger babies rides in laundry baskets (with teachers' help) Helping teachers "wash" the laundry
Wrap babies in blankets **variations:** **put babies to bed;** **feed babies**	Various sizes and types of baby dolls Scarves, bandanas, and blankets for wrapping babies Doll furniture Plastic spoons and cups	Babies, body parts, blankets, warm, cold, cover, sleep, nap What children do with the dolls and with the blankets What teachers are doing	Touching babies and touching the scarves and blankets Looking through sheer scarves Watching other children	Holding and cuddling babies Wrapping scarves or blankets around babies Looking through sheer scarves Wearing scarves on their heads Covering babies with blankets and bandanas	Wrapping and then rocking babies to sleep Pretending to sing to babies, with teachers' help Patting babies gently to help them sleep

[a] Activities for crawlers can also include the activities listed for tiny babies.

[b] Activities for walkers can also include the activities listed for tiny babies and crawlers.

Active Play and Outdoor Activities

Activity	Materials needed	Teachers can talk about	TINY BABIES will explore and experience	CRAWLERS[a] will explore and experience	WALKERS[b] will explore and experience
Balls **variation: chase the ball**	A variety of balls of different sizes, shapes, and textures	Balls, round, roll, throw, soft Games played with balls Taking turns and playing together What the children are doing What teachers are doing	Looking at and reaching for balls held out in front, to the side, or above the baby's head Holding small balls Feeling the different textures on texture balls Watching other children	Rolling balls back and forth with the teacher and other children Throwing balls forward Getting on top of big balls Watching teachers blow up beach balls—and helping	Kicking balls Rolling balls down a wedge or ramp Throwing balls up in the air (only lightweight balls)
Bubble chase	Homemade or commercial bubble solution Wands	B-B-B-Bubbles—encourage babies to make a "Bu" sound Describe what bubbles do: float, pop, shine, go up, come down What children are doing What teachers are doing	Watching bubbles float above them Reaching for bubbles The feel of bubbles on their skin and bursting bubbles that touch them Watching other children	Chasing after bubbles as they float downward Waving at bubbles above them Imitating teachers' mouth movements as they blow bubbles	Reaching for bubbles above their heads Stepping on bubbles on the floor

Active Play and Outdoor Activities

Activity	Materials needed	Teachers can talk about	TINY BABIES will explore and experience	CRAWLERS[a] will explore and experience	WALKERS[b] will explore and experience
Crates and boxes **variation: pushing and pulling**	Plastic crates, such as those used for milk, or storage crates Cardboard boxes	In and out Boxes, crates, climbing, sitting, standing Pulling, pushing, forward, backward What children are doing What teachers are doing	Being inside a box or crate, with teacher present Getting a ride in the box or crate Watching other children	Crawling inside a box or crate Using the box as support to pull to stand Cruising around the box or crate Putting other toys inside the box or crate; reaching in to get them out again	Standing inside a box or crate Turning the box or crate over and climbing on top of it (with teacher's help) Sitting on an upside-down box or crate Pushing and pulling a box or crate around the room
Crawling races	A softly carpeted floor Plastic-covered foam mats	Body parts and body movements Speed, fast, slow, forward, backward	Teachers can place young babies on mats on their stomachs and help them push forward by providing support behind their feet; place an attractive toy out of reach in front of them to encourage movement and reaching	Teachers can get out in front of two or three crawling babies and hold out an attractive toy, encouraging children to come to the teachers (have extra toys available for each child) Teachers can move in a circle in front of crawling children to encourage them to turn and bend as they crawl	Teachers can encourage walkers to crawl and walk backward, to walk on "all fours," and to duck-walk to develop balance and movement skills

[a]Activities for crawlers can also include the activities listed for tiny babies.
[b]Activities for walkers can also include the activities listed for tiny babies and crawlers.

(continued)

Active Play and Outdoor Activities *(continued)*

Activity	Materials needed	Teachers can talk about	TINY BABIES will explore and experience	CRAWLERS[a] will explore and experience	WALKERS[b] will explore and experience
Dancing **variation: scarf dancing**	Music Dolls and stuffed animals, if desired A variety of soft and sheer scarves	Body parts, body movements Tempo of the music Words to the songs Children's names What children are doing What teachers are doing	Dancing with a teacher Listening to the music Watching other children Touching and holding scarves Looking through sheer scarves	Moving arms and body in time with the music Singing along Waving scarves in time with the music	Dancing Holding other children's and teachers' hands in a circle to dance
Exercises **variation: stretch**	Softly carpeted floor Exercise mats or quilted blankets A full-length mirror is a great addition	Body parts and body movements Simple directions and help to children to follow them What children are doing What teachers are doing	Make sure baby's arms and legs are free to move (not tightly wrapped or in restrictive clothing) Teachers can move baby's arms and legs, stretching them out, then bending them up to baby's body; repeat several times Gently massage baby's body, arms, and legs Hold baby upright to put some weight on legs Bounce baby on lap	Imitating teachers' movements of arms and legs, stretching then flexing Teachers can help babies do one or two sit-ups, push-ups, and other exercises in teachers' own routines	Joining teachings in doing jumping jacks Jumping (most babies will bend their knees and bring their bodies up but not get their feet off the ground) Walking on a taped line on the floor (or a low balance beam)

308

Active Play and Outdoor Activities

Activity	Materials needed	Teachers can talk about	TINY BABIES will explore and experience	CRAWLERS[a] will explore and experience	WALKERS[b] will explore and experience
Go on a (crawling) "tour"— visit every corner of the classroom	No materials needed— just teacher imagination and enthusiasm	Everything you see and do Describe what children are doing and what they are looking at	"Touring" with a teacher; going to areas of the classroom or building babies do not normally see	Following a teacher— and sometimes having a teacher follow them—as they crawl around the room When no babies are sleeping, crawl into the sleep area (being sure the floor is completely safe) Crawl into the diapering area to get a new view of a place where children are normally carried	Look into, and under, and around everything in the room Put small toys or parts of toys in different corners of the room and "collect" them while touring

[a]Activities for crawlers can also include the activities listed for tiny babies.
[b]Activities for walkers can also include the activities listed for tiny babies and crawlers.

(continued)

Active Play and Outdoor Activities *(continued)*

Activity	Materials needed	Teachers can talk about	TINY BABIES will explore and experience	CRAWLERS[a] will explore and experience	WALKERS[b] will explore and experience
Hide and find	Small toys Objects to hide the toys under (e.g., bandanas, cups, boxes)	Labels for the toys Play "Where's the _____? Here it is!" All gone In, out, under What the children are doing What teachers are doing	Touching and holding the toys and containers Reaching for toys held out to the side, above, and in front of them Putting hands into cups and boxes	Finding partially hidden objects, especially if the children watch the teacher hide the objects Playing peekaboo Putting toys into cups and boxes and dumping them out	Finding an object hidden under a cup or box Finding an object under one of two cups, after watching the teacher hide the object Hide and seek—child turns away while teacher "hides" object in plain view in another part of the room, then child searches for object Hiding objects for teachers to find
Interactive games: peekaboo, This Little Piggy, So Big, pat-a-cake	No materials needed, although new teachers might want to have a book of baby games and finger plays handy for reference	The back-and-forth turn taking of verbal games; give babies plenty of time to reply and participate Repeat games at least 8 or 10 times so babies have time to anticipate and take part	Listening to the sounds of teachers' voices and the rhymes and rhythms of the games Being the focus of the teacher's attention when it's their turn to play Watching other children	Learning the body movements that go with each game Asking (nonverbally) for repeats of their favorites Imitating teachers and other children	Learning the words and sounds that go with each game Initiating games by making the sounds or signs that go with the game Taking turns with other children

Active Play and Outdoor Activities

Activity	Materials needed	Teachers can talk about	TINY BABIES will explore and experience	CRAWLERS[a] will explore and experience	WALKERS[b] will explore and experience
Obstacle course	Plastic-covered foam mats and shapes (large blocks, wedges, and tunnels) set up to create a path for children	Body parts and body movements Children's names Use simple directions and guide children to follow them What children are doing What teachers are doing	Moving through the obstacle course in the arms of a teacher Watching other children	Crawling on a variety of different surfaces Finding new ways to get from one place to another Using foam shapes as supports to pull up to stand and cruise	Practicing balance by walking on different surfaces and angles Pushing foam shapes into different configurations Taking turns, with teachers' help Rolling balls or cars down slopes
Play dog and cat variation: **animal sounds and movement**	No materials are needed, but stuffed dogs and cats (or other animals) are helpful to involve the youngest infants	Dogs and cats, the sounds they make, how they walk The names of the children's and teachers' pets How people treat their pets Body parts What children are doing What teachers are doing	Watching and listening to teachers and other children Holding and touching stuffed animals if available	Imitating the teachers as they bark and meow Imitating the teachers as they walk on four legs like a dog or cat	Following the teachers' lead in pretending to be dogs or cats Doing dog or cat "tricks" (e.g., sitting up, rolling over)

[a]Activities for crawlers can also include the activities listed for tiny babies.
[b]Activities for walkers can also include the activities listed for tiny babies and crawlers.

(continued)

Active Play and Outdoor Activities *(continued)*

Activity	Materials needed	Teachers can talk about	TINY BABIES will explore and experience	CRAWLERS[a] will explore and experience	WALKERS[b] will explore and experience
Push and pull toys	A variety of different toys with wheels, including some that make interesting sounds	Wheels, things that go, turning, round, stop, fast, slow Pushing and pulling Motor noises, imitating sounds of trucks, cars, and other toys What children are doing What teachers are doing	Sounds of toys and other people Feel of wheels on their arms and legs Touching, reaching for, and holding toys Scooting forward after a toy that moves	Crawling along, pulling a toy by a string held in one hand Sitting and pushing toys with feet Examining the wheels of toys and how they work Putting fingers inside small openings in toys (with supervision) Using large push toys to practice supported walking	Walking and pushing a toy at the same time Walking and pulling a toy at the same time Rolling two-wheel toys together so they crash into each other Rolling toys with wheels down a ramp or slope
Rolling and rolling	A softly carpeted floor A variety of mats of different textures and surfaces make for a more interesting activity Dolls and stuffed animals, if desired	Body parts Movement: rolling over, crawling, upside down The feel of the surfaces children are rolling on What children are doing What teachers are doing	With teachers' help, rolling from stomach to back, then from back to stomach Reaching for an attractive toy placed out to the side to encourage children to roll over and get the toy	Rolling all the way over—stomach to back to stomach Rolling into someone else who is also rolling Watching other children roll	Rolling for distance: all the way across the room Having a rolling "race" Rolling down a slope (on a soft climber, for example) Rolling dolls or stuffed animals

312

Active Play and Outdoor Activities

Activity	Materials needed	Teachers can talk about	TINY BABIES will explore and experience	CRAWLERS[a] will explore and experience	WALKERS[b] will explore and experience
Sheet drag **variation: give rides in a laundry basket**	A bedsheet—put one or more children on one end of the sheet and pull it gently forward across the floor	Body movement The feel of being moved through space Speed, fast, slow, stop, go What children are doing and looking at What teachers are doing	Being gently moved across the floor; the vestibular stimulation of unusual movement Watching and listening to other children	Learning to make postural adjustments in response to movement; the feeling of being off balance as the sheet starts and stops Crawling under the sheet	Taking turns with other children (with teachers' help) Helping a teacher pull the sheet Wrapping up in the sheet
Touch the ceiling; touch the floor	No materials needed	Up, down, floor, ceiling, wall, room, window, vent, high, low What children are doing What teachers are doing with the children	The feeling of being lifted high above other children and then lowered (gently) back down Watching people and things from a new and different viewpoint Watching other children go up and down	Reaching for and touching the ceiling, the walls, decorations hung from the ceiling, and air vents (if clean enough) Being suspended upside down so they can touch the floor with their hands only, and touch the ceiling with their (bare) feet	Indicating to the teacher (by sounds or gestures) whether and when they want to go up or down Taking a doll or stuffed animal with them and making the doll touch the ceiling, touch the floor

[a]Activities for crawlers can also include the activities listed for tiny babies.
[b]Activities for walkers can also include the activities listed for tiny babies and crawlers.

Art/Sensory Experiences

Activity	Materials needed	Teachers can talk about	TINY BABIES will explore and experience	CRAWLERS[a] will explore and experience	WALKERS[b] will explore and experience
Bubbles	Commercial or home-made bubble solution, wands and bubble blowers (for teachers only)	Bubbles, blow, float, pretty, pop What children are seeing as the bubbles float in the air What children do and what the teachers are doing	Watching the bubbles Feeling a bubble that is blown to fall on their arm or leg Watching other children	Chasing after bubbles that land on the floor Waving at bubbles as they float down Tasting bubbles	Stepping on bubbles that land on the floor Trying to catch bubbles that are floating near them Trying to blow bubbles (with wand held by teacher)
Collage	Clear contact paper fastened with masking tape to a wall or a flat surface like a tabletop Shapes, pictures, yarn pieces—anything—to stick to the contact paper	Sticky Pictures, shapes, colors, and so forth What children do and what their facial expressions suggest they are thinking	The feel of sticky contact paper Watching other children Touching and holding collage objects or pictures	Seeing objects or pictures stick to the contact paper, then taking them off again Seeing that objects stick to the contact paper but not to other things	Cooperating with other children and the teacher Selecting pictures or objects to put on the collage Rearranging objects or pictures on the collage

314

Art/Sensory Experiences

Activity	Materials needed	Teachers can talk about	TINY BABIES will explore and experience	CRAWLERS[a] will explore and experience	WALKERS[b] will explore and experience
Crayons or markers	Washable, nontoxic crayons or markers Blank paper A hard surface for children to work on (e.g., table, lap desk, clipboard)	Paper, markers Colors What children are doing What teachers are doing	Watching other children Holding paper	Making marks on paper (and other surfaces) Making marks on their own hands Tearing and crumpling paper	The difference between scribbling and making vertical or horizontal strokes How different size and color markers make different marks on paper
Flashlights	Good-quality flashlights with strong batteries A cloth diaper or receiving blanket	Light, dark, switch, on, off, under, through What the children are seeing when the flashlight is shining on something What teachers are doing with the flashlights	Seeing the light go on and off Looking at the light as it shines through a thin cloth Watching the light beam move across the ceiling, along the floor, up and down the walls	Trying to switch the flashlight on and off Finding "hidden" objects inside boxes, using the flashlight Chasing the light beam across the floor	Holding and shining the flashlight themselves (with careful supervision so as not to shine it in other babies' faces) Turning the flashlight on and off Looking at the flashlight beam through a thin cloth, through the teacher's hands, and through their own hands

[a]Activities for crawlers can also include the activities listed for tiny babies.

[b]Activities for walkers can also include the activities listed for tiny babies and crawlers.

(continued)

Art/Sensory Experiences *(continued)*

Activity	Materials needed	Teachers can talk about	TINY BABIES will explore and experience	CRAWLERS[a] will explore and experience	WALKERS[b] will explore and experience
Going for rides out- doors	Strollers or wagons with lots of padding Enough teachers so each one is responsible for only two babies	Everything you see, everyone passed on the ride Weather, temperature, buildings, grass, trees, flowers, wind What the children are doing and looking at What teachers are doing	The change of scenery Fresh air and sunshine (or clouds) Stop frequently to get down to babies' level and talk with them about what they see; let them touch the nat- ural world around them	When you stop, let the children crawl or sit in a safe, grassy area In fall, give children leaves to hold or crumple In spring and summer, visit flower beds In winter, give each child a small pailful of snow	The experience of walk- ing outdoors where sur- faces are not smooth and grass tickles your feet and legs Watching bugs Waving at people and saying "Hi" when peo- ple pass by
Listen to rat- tles, bells, musical toys	A collection of toys that make noise, some dif- ferent-sounding bells, wind-up musical toys, other instruments	Loud, soft, quiet, ring, whisper, shout, buzz, ears, sounds What children do and what teachers do with the toys and bells Imitate the sounds of the toys and bells	Hearing the sounds and turning their heads to find the source of the sounds	Holding on to toys with handles, making bells ring by batting and shaking them	Imitating sounds, imitat- ing teachers making sounds Listening for very quiet sounds Finding hidden toys that make sounds

316

Art/Sensory Experiences

Activity	Materials needed	Teachers can talk about	TINY BABIES will explore and experience	CRAWLERS[a] will explore and experience	WALKERS[b] will explore and experience
Listen to the sounds of people doing things **variation: listen to everyday sounds**	No materials—just take a baby from one place to another where people are doing things: fixing food, writing, singing, talking on the telephone No materials—take a baby from one place to another where something makes noise: a clock that ticks, a radio, keys that rattle, a refrigerator, or a washer or dryer	What you and the baby can hear Loud, soft, voice, quiet, sing, noisy, ring, telephone, pencil, paper What the child is looking at What the other person is doing	Being carried and held Watching other people Listening to teacher describe and imitate the sounds	Imitating sounds along with you Seeing new faces and places and viewing things from a different angle	Walking to new places, with a little help Watching people do things (e.g., cook, type, make a phone call, vacuum)
Playdough **variation: make pancakes with Play-Doh**	Commercial Play-doh or homemade play-dough A protected hard surface (e.g., low table, flat surface covering the carpet)	Squishy, squeeze, roll, flatten Round, ball, flat, pancake Describe what children are doing and looking at What teacher is doing with the Play-Doh	Watching and listening to other children Touching Play-Doh	How Play-Doh feels when you squeeze it, poke it, and push it together between your hands	Imitating the teacher's actions in rolling Play-Doh into a ball and flattening it into a pancake How different colors of Play-Doh combine

[a]Activities for crawlers can also include the activities listed for tiny babies.

[b]Activities for walkers can also include the activities listed for tiny babies and crawlers.

(continued)

317

Art/Sensory Experiences *(continued)*

Activity	Materials needed	Teachers can talk about	TINY BABIES will explore and experience	CRAWLERS[a] will explore and experience	WALKERS[b] will explore and experience
"Read" the classroom photo album	Pictures of children, families, and teachers in a photo album or looseleaf book	Children's names Teachers' names Names of family members and pets in pictures	Looking at pictures Touching pages in books Hearing their own names and the names of familiar people	Seeing pictures of themselves—now and when they were younger Matching up pictures with names of familiar people Turning pages of books	Pointing to pictures of people they know Pointing to pictures to ask teachers to label people or things
See-through scarves	A variety of sheer scarves A supply of small toys and dolls to "hide"	Look, find, hide, see, soft, scarf, fold, wrap Play peekaboo Describe what things look like through the scarf What the children are doing and looking at What teachers are doing	The feel of the scarves on their hands, legs, tummies, and faces Holding a scarf Watching the other children	Pulling the scarves off of the teacher's head when playing peekaboo "Finding" toys hidden under the scarves (but still visible) Crawling on the scarves Looking through the scarves	Putting scarves over their own heads for peekaboo "Hiding" toys under the scarves and "finding" them again Waving the scarves to music in a version of a scarf dance Crumpling up the scarves and putting them into things, including their own pockets Walking on the scarves

Art/Sensory Experiences

Activity	Materials needed	Teachers can talk about	TINY BABIES will explore and experience	CRAWLERS[a] will explore and experience	WALKERS[b] will explore and experience
Soft and loud	No materials needed—just voices	Whisper, shout, loud, soft, quiet, noisy, sing, yodel, hiss, sssh Talk in rhymes, sing, and use children's names Make B-B-B and P-P-P sounds Imitate children's sounds	The change in pitch and volume as your voice goes from a whisper to a (controlled) shout and back again Hearing you imitate the sounds they make The back-and-forth turn taking of "conversation"	A chance to practice being very quiet and very loud (briefly) Listening to the teacher's play with words and sounds and imitating sounds	A chance to whisper and shout a few words Joining in songs Listening to rhymes and repeating parts of them
Squeeze toys	A variety of toys that make squeaking noises when squeezed	Imitate sounds Squeeze, push, fist, squeak What children are doing with the toys What teachers are doing	Listening to the sounds and locating the source of the sounds Watching other children Reaching for toys held in front of them	Chasing after squeeze toys pushed out in front of them Banging on the toys to make noise Putting the toys into and out of boxes or bins	Standing on toys to make them squeak Filling bins or buckets with the toys and dumping them out Holding and squeezing the toys
Stickers	A supply of stickers Plain paper in different colors	Sticky, glue On and off Paper, pictures What the children are doing	Watching other children Holding paper (tasting it, too!)	Putting a sticker on the paper and then trying to get it back Getting a sticker stuck on their fingers	Crumpling paper Putting stickers on themselves

[a]Activities for crawlers can also include the activities listed for tiny babies.
[b]Activities for walkers can also include the activities listed for tiny babies and crawlers.

(continued)

Art/Sensory Experiences *(continued)*

Activity	Materials needed	Teachers can talk about	TINY BABIES will explore and experience	CRAWLERS[a] will explore and experience	WALKERS[b] will explore and experience
Take pictures of children	A camera, preferably one that produces instant pictures Toy cameras for children so they can imitate teachers	Children's names Posing for pictures, saying "cheese" Camera, film, flash, pictures, photographs, album What teachers are doing	Watching other children Looking at pictures Touching, holding, and tasting books (plastic or cardboard books, not those with photos in them)	Imitating teachers' use of a camera Posing Looking at pictures of themselves	Saying "cheese" Helping teachers put photos in album Comparing pictures of themselves when they were younger with pictures taken today
textures **variations: texture blanket** **textures of foods**	Small pieces of cloth of different textures Blankets or quilts made of cloth of different textures Real fruits and vegetables	Soft, smooth, rough, fuzzy, furry, bumpy, hard How each piece of cloth feels when you touch it What children are doing What teachers are doing	The feel of different textures rubbed gently across their arms, legs, tummies, and in their hands Lying on the textured blanket Holding and touching the fruits and vegetables	Crumpling and folding the cloth pieces Putting the cloth pieces into and out of a bag or box Crawling across the textured blanket Rolling the fruits and vegetables	Smoothing out the cloth and using it to cover toys Folding the cloth and wrapping toys in it Stepping on pieces of cloth of different textures Walking on the textured blanket Labeling the fruits and vegetables Sorting by food type and color

Art/Sensory Experiences

Activity	Materials needed	Teachers can talk about	TINY BABIES will explore and experience	CRAWLERS[a] will explore and experience	WALKERS[b] will explore and experience
Water play **variations:** **washing dishes;** **washing plastic animals**	(Outdoors or in a tile-floored area) A tub of water A small amount of soapsuds Large paintbrushes Some small toys that float; some toys that sink Use plastic dishes and sponges; have a dish drainer handy Use plastic animals	Water, soap, wet, cry, sink, float, drip, splash, pour What children do and what happens to the water when they touch it or drop things into it	Watching and listening to the other children The feel and sound of water What wet feels and tastes like	Making splashes Stirring up bubbles in the water Putting toys into and taking them out of the water	Pour water from one container to another Scrubbing toys with sponges Drying toys

[a]Activities for crawlers can also include the activities listed for tiny babies.

[b]Activities for walkers can also include the activities listed for tiny babies and crawlers.

Toddler Play Activities

Building Area Activities

Activity	Materials needed	What children will explore and experience	What teachers can do	What teachers can talk about
All building toy activities	The building toy or toys listed on the day's schedule (Teachers should be encouraged to use combinations of building toys in a single activity and to get out a second type of building toy as needed to keep children's interest high and extend children's play creatively)	Manipulating the objects and seeing how they fit together or stack How the toys feel (e.g., hard, soft, rounded, square) and taste Cooperating with teachers and other children to build something (and knock it down) Pleasure in mastery of a difficult task as they learn to pull pieces apart, fit puzzle pieces correctly, and finally build structures Lining pieces up Turn taking and working toward a shared goal with others	Begin by stacking or putting toys together and talking animatedly about what you are doing. Follow children's lead in continuing the activity, focusing on what they are interested in experiencing and exploring. Some construction toys have small holes in them—children will explore these holes with their fingers; if toys are squeezable, air may come out of those holes when toys are squeezed. Older children will create more elaborate towers that should be protected from the younger ones; teachers can build structures for younger children to knock down and help older ones build towers.	The materials — labeling, using a lot of specific verbs to describe children's actions Colors, shapes, sizes Use imagination to describe what children construct; have them use the materials (especially animals, vehicles) in ways that imitate familiar daily routines for the children Use parallel talk and self-talk to describe children's and your own activity

Building Area Activities

Activity	Materials needed	What children will explore and experience	What teachers can do	What teachers can talk about
Barns and animals	Barns and silos Fence sections Animals Tractors and trucks	Opening and closing barn doors; taking top off of silo and putting it back Putting small toys inside the barn and inside the silo; taking them out again Rolling tractors and trucks on floor and into barn Holding animals Comparing similarities and differences among animals Making animal sounds	Match similar animals and point out that even different looking ones can be labeled with the same name. Help children fill and dump toys, using the silo. Build fence around animals to make a barnyard. Encourage cooperative play among children—give them roles to play (e.g., one is the farmer on the tractor, one is herding the cows, one is feeding the chickens).	Animals, body parts, what farms are like, what people do on farms, how barns are used All animals Make animal sounds Talk about *in and out, fill and dump* Talk about what animals eat
Cameras	Toy cameras—enough for all children	Looking through a small hole at the world Imitating adult activities—all children have had their pictures taken Pressing the button to make a click Pretending to pose for pictures—saying "cheese"	Encourage children to take pictures of specific other children—there's nothing to share, but they will feel as though they have done something nice for the other child. Give children practice in following simple directions (e.g., "Take a picture of the baby").	Cameras, pictures Talk about things they can see through the viewfinder, or hold out objects (label them) so the children can look at them

Suggested building toys for toddlers: airplanes and helicopters, barns and farm animals, beads on wire frames, car and trucks, dinosaurs, Duplos with people, emergency vehicles, finger puppets, hand puppets, large cardboard blocks, links, Mega blocks, plastic tools and tool-bench, pop beads, puzzles, shape sorters, soft foam blocks, stacking and nesting toys, star builders, waffle blocks, wooden blocks, zoo animals.

(continued)

Building Area Activities *(continued)*

Activity	Materials needed	What children will explore and experience	What teachers can do	What teachers can talk about
Fisher-Price houses and people	Houses Furniture Vehicles People and animals	Different rooms in houses Opening doors in the houses Setting up furniture—putting things where they want them (making choices) Putting cars in the garage Moving people around the house Practicing daily routines in miniature	Get out several houses and lots of furniture and people. Talk animatedly about playing house and what the people are doing or where you are putting the furniture. As children gather, let them take the lead in directing the activity. Encourage children to take the pretend people through daily routines (e.g., "What happens next?") to encourage narrative skill. Suggest one child's play family invite another child's play family to come for a visit.	Label the rooms in a house, label furniture, and give names to people. Talk about which furniture belongs in which rooms. Talk about everyday routines. Encourage polite "pretend" conversation.

House/Doll Area Activities

Activity	Materials needed	What children will explore and experience	What teachers can do	What teachers can talk about
Beauty/ barber shop	Brushes and large-toothed combs	Pretending to wash their own and others' (or dolls') hair	Bring out a large bin of hair supplies and begin talking about washing hair, fixing hair, brushing and combing hair.	Times when children have had their hair washed, brushed, combed, and cut
	Mirrors	Manipulating the materials		Different hairstyles—short hair, long hair, curly hair, straight hair, blonde, and brunette
	Hair dryer (electric cord removed)	Putting barrettes and bows in one another's hair and the teacher's hair	Demonstrate the steps in washing, rinsing, and drying hair.	The materials
	Beauty/barber products (e.g., empty shampoo and hair spray containers)	Looking at themselves in the mirror	Show children how to use barrettes and bows.	How it feels to have hair brushed, combed, washed, and cut (it doesn't hurt)
	Hair rollers	Touching each other's hair and the teacher's hair	Follow children's lead, expanding on what they find interesting about the materials.	Use self-talk and parallel talk
	Barrettes and bows	Practicing brushing and combing their own hair		
	Hair ribbons	What a brush and comb feel like in their hand, on their arms or legs, and against their face	(Be sure to wash all these materials thoroughly after each use—perhaps have two separate sets of materials so the same activity can be repeated in a day.)	
	Dolls with hair			

(continued)

House/Doll Area Activities *(continued)*

Activity	Materials needed	What children will explore and experience	What teachers can do	What teachers can talk about
Birthday party **variation: tea party**	Tablecloth Dishes Party hats and whistles Tea sets: teapots, cups and saucers, pitchers, and cream and sugar A fancy tablecloth Stuffed animals or dolls Dress-up clothes	The experience of a party—with no stress! Setting a "table" Singing "Happy Birthday" Playing party games Serving food to other children; pretending to eat	Begin the activity by getting out party materials and announcing, "Let's have a birthday party!" Singing "Happy Birthday" also usually draws a crowd. Help children set the table with plastic tableware. Bring out play food to the party. Have children "wrap" presents, using cloth or newspaper, and give them to friends.	Use children's names frequently in singing "Happy Birthday" Birthday parties teachers have attended; birthdays teachers remember Gifts, presents, giving, sharing, surprises, friends, fun, games, singing Party items: cake, candles, lemonade, juice, treats Use self-talk and parallel talk

House/Doll Area Activities

Activity	Materials needed	What children will explore and experience	What teachers can do	What teachers can talk about
Camping	Backpacks Canteens Flashlights Camping supplies Easy-to-set-up tents Dishes and food	Putting things into their backpacks and taking them out again Turning flashlights on and off and shining them all around the room Getting under a tent Pretending to do daily activities in a different setting: sleeping in a tent and having meals outdoors Cooperating with others to set up a camping site Going on a hike with friends	Get out backpacks and talk about going on a hike and setting up camp. As children gather, give each child a backpack and have them pack up some food for the trip. Organize a hike around the room, then stop and set up camp. Pretend it's night, turn on flashlights, go to bed in the tents; then it's morning—get up and get breakfast. Follow children's lead as the level of pretend play involved will be appropriate only for the oldest children; younger ones will enjoy the manipulation of materials and watching your activities and the others' activities.	Camping, hiking, woods, outdoors, tents, campers, backpacks Times you have been camping; times the children and their families have been camping or hiking What a tent is, what it's like to be in a tent when the wind blows, when it rains Label backpacks, flashlights, tents, and food items Use parallel talk and self-talk

(continued)

House/Doll Area Activities *(continued)*

Activity	Materials needed	What children will explore and experience	What teachers can do	What teachers can talk about
Cleaning house	Child-size brooms, mops, and dustpan Dust cloths Aprons Feather dusters	Using child-size versions of adult tools Imitating everyday actions of adults Wearing aprons Working together to get the classroom clean Motor activity of sweeping, mopping, and dusting	Get out the cleaning supplies and go to work, talking enthusiastically about what the teacher is doing. As children gather, give each child a task, using simple directions and helping the children follow your directions. Give children something special to wear: an apron, hat, and tool belt. Encourage joint play and cooperative activity in cleaning the room. Help children learn to give away toys by encouraging them to trade cleaning equipment and take turns.	Labeling the cleaning equipment Clean versus dirty, dust, dirt, sweeping, mopping, shiny, new, bright How good it is to have a clean house

House/Doll Area Activities

Activity	Materials needed	What children will explore and experience	What teachers can do	What teachers can talk about
Cooking variation: **making pizza**	Play food (and small building toys, such as links or pop beads, to serve as food)	Imitating activities they see parents and other adults do all of the time	Get out the cooking equipment and begin to bake a batch of cookies or make mashed potatoes, talking enthusiastically about what you are doing.	Foods the children are familiar with; labeling the play food items and giving labels to pretend foods the children cook
	Stove and oven plus some portable stovetops	Putting food into containers and taking it out again		
	Pots and pans	Putting pots and pans into the oven; placing them on the stove	As children gather, let each child choose a pot or pan and some food to cook.	Meals teachers and children have shared together
	Baking pans, muffin tins, and cookie sheets			The oven and stove are hot; food is hot (blow on it), juice is cold
	Plastic bowls and wooden spoons	Serving other children and teachers and giving food to other children	Encourage some children to sit at the table and be served by others, giving children practice in offering toys to others.	Use parallel talk and self-talk
	Dishes and serving utensils	Taking turns with other children as the cook	Cooperation in preparing a meal or making a cake.	

(continued)

House/Doll Area Activities (continued)

Activity	Materials needed	What children will explore and experience	What teachers can do	What teachers can talk about
Doctor **variation: animal doctor**	Child-size doctor kits Extra stethoscopes Doll beds and dolls Hospital dress-up clothes Band-Aids Child-size cots Use stuffed animals as "patients"	Manipulating the materials in the doctor kits Listening to their own and others' hearts with stethoscopes Caring for others Opening real Band-Aids and putting them on themselves or others Remembering their own doctor visits and imitating things that happened then Taking pretend roles—doctor, nurse, mom or dad, patient, or child	Bring out the doctor kits and other materials and talk about how one of the dolls (or children) doesn't feel well and needs a doctor. Let children initially define their own roles, but encourage them to switch roles and take turns being doctor and patient. Develop a scenario and repeat it, with small variations, several times so children can begin to pick up the "script." Demonstrate how to (pretend) take temperatures, blood pressure, listen to heart rate, take a pulse, check reflexes, look into ears, put Band-Aids on, and give "shots." Emphasize similarities between children (e.g., "Doro and Leslie are both wearing doctor coats"). Encourage children to give things to one another and to take turns with materials.	Visits to the doctor that teachers have made; visits children have made What usually happens at the doctor's office (e.g., first you check in, then you wait, then you talk to the nurse, then the doctor) Why people go to the doctor (e.g., for checkups, to stay healthy, when they are sick) What a hospital is and why people go to the hospital—if there are children with chronic illnesses who have been in the hospital a lot, this can include their experiences Label the materials in the doctor kits and the actions you and the children do with them Label body parts Use parallel talk and self-talk

House/Doll Area Activities

Activity	Materials needed	What children will explore and experience	What teachers can do	What teachers can talk about
Doll play	Dolls or stuffed animals The materials needed for a specific "script": getting babies up in the morning, feeding babies, having a nap, and taking babies for walks	Imitation of routine events that happen in their daily lives Repetition of familiar routines that build shared knowledge among toddlers, allowing them to expand their social play repertoire The beginnings of pretense and role taking Caring (pretend) for another person	Get out dolls and other materials and begin a script, talking through the sequence of events that accompanies that script. As children come to the area, encourage them to imitate part of the script. As children become involved with the dolls, teachers can follow children's lead, imitating their actions and extending them to enhance children's play.	Talk in detail about each step in the script, reminding children of times they have lived through the activity: getting up, eating, napping, and going for a walk. Leave gaps in the script for children to fill in, or make "mistakes" so children can correct you. Use a lot of parallel talk and self-talk so children can connect your words with the actions that are so familiar to them.

(continued)

House/Doll Area Activities *(continued)*

Activity	Materials needed	What children will explore and experience	What teachers can do	What teachers can talk about
Dress up **variation: costume ball**	Clothes of all kinds: shoes, hats, neckties, aprons, gowns, purses, and leftover Halloween costumes A wall-mounted mirror When children are dressed up, play music and have everyone dance	Practice in dressing themselves How different they look in different clothing Feeling grown-up by wearing grown-up clothes Feeling attractive and well dressed Playing with real adult belongings Having fun	Open the dress-up closet or bring out the containers of dress-up clothes, talking animatedly about dressing up. Let children choose their own items—girls can wear men's hats; boys can wear women's nightgowns. Encourage exploration of mirror images.	Labeling the clothing items Textures, colors Buttons, ties, snaps How wonderful the children look in their new clothes—you cannot give too many compliments! Emphasize similarities between children (e.g., "Both Mark and Amy are wearing baseball caps!") Use parallel talk and self-talk

House/Doll Area Activities

Activity	Materials needed	What children will explore and experience	What teachers can do	What teachers can talk about
Grocery store	Play food	Imitating everyday activities of adults	Get out grocery items, baskets, and carts and put grocery items around area, talking about the grocery store and the different sections of a grocery store.	Label grocery items, foods, and sections of the grocery store
	Empty containers, such as cereal boxes, salt shakers, plastic water bottles, and milk cartons	Putting grocery items into carts, bags, or baskets and taking them out again		Talk about shopping, the routine of going to the grocery store, walking up and down the aisles, and standing in line at the checkout counter
	Cash registers	Cooperating to fill baskets and then have their "purchases" added up	As children gather, let their interest and exploration guide the activity.	
	Play money			How the wheels turn on the grocery carts
variations: post office	Grocery carts, baskets, and sacks	Taking turns at different roles—shopper cashier	Help children learn to use the cash registers.	Times the teacher has been grocery shopping, or the times children have been shopping
	Envelopes of all different sizes	Sealing envelopes, writing on them, and putting stamps and stickers on them	Encourage joint "shopping" and turn taking.	
	Used office paper			
	Stickers, tape, crayons, markers	Putting "mail" in mailboxes	Have children take dolls or stuffed animals shopping with them—let them ride in the cart.	
	Play mailbox	Delivering mail		
restaurant	Play food	Taking orders from other children and teachers	Practice instruction following—"Please get me the Rice Krispies."	
	Dishes, trays	Cooking and serving food		
	Materials and menus from local restaurants	Running a drive-in restaurant	Follow a basic routine, with slight variations, so children can learn the "script."	
	Cash registers	Taking turns at different roles: server, diner, cook, and cashier		
	Aprons			

(continued)

House/Doll Area Activities *(continued)*

Activity	Materials needed	What children will explore and experience	What teachers can do	What teachers can talk about
Laundry	Child-size washer and dryer, if available	Imitating familiar adult routines	Bring out the laundry equipment and a good supply of blankets, clothes, and other items.	Doing laundry; what the steps are in doing laundry
	Child-size iron and ironing board or table	Opening and closing the doors to the washer and dryer	Have at least three laundry baskets to avoid conflicts.	How good it is to have clean clothes
	Bandanas, blankets, cloth napkins, sheets, doll clothes, and anything that can be "washed"	Putting clothes into and out of machines and laundry baskets	Begin by talking animatedly about doing laundry and all of the steps involved; how nice it is to have clean clothes, and how good they smell.	Putting clothes in and taking them out (of washer, dryer, laundry basket)
	Laundry baskets	Folding and unfolding		
	Empty laundry detergent containers	Pretending to iron clothes	As children gather, follow their lead and elaborate on what they find interesting about the materials.	
		Climbing into and out of the laundry baskets, turning the baskets upside down on their heads, and putting dolls and other toys in the laundry baskets		

House/Doll Area Activities

Activity	Materials needed	What children will explore and experience	What teachers can do	What teachers can talk about
Picnic	Blankets, large sheets, napkins, or tablecloth "Picnic" basket Plastic food Dishes and plastic tableware	Putting food into the basket and taking it out Spreading blankets or cloth on the floor Setting places for the picnic	Begin the activity by packing up several picnic baskets with food, dishes, and napkins and talking animatedly about what is going to happen.	What a picnic is—eating outdoors, sitting on the ground Label the foods, dishes, and tableware
variation: teddy bears' picnic	Stuffed animals	Giving food to one another	As children gather, have them help collect food and dishes for the picnic. Lay out a cloth on the floor, with children's help. Demonstrate setting a "table" for eating. Encourage children to give food to each other. Pretend to eat. Chase away pretend bugs. Sing "Teddy Bears' Picnic."	Times you have been on picnics; times the children have been on picnics; times the class has eaten outdoors Weather—what is good picnic weather and what is not What foods taste like Polite requests (e.g., "Please pass the tomato") Use parallel talk and self-talk

(continued)

House/Doll Area Activities (continued)

Activity	Materials needed	What children will explore and experience	What teachers can do	What teachers can talk about
Pizza delivery	Pizza pans Play pizza Spatula Plastic baskets Dishes Dolls and stuffed animals	Imitating activities they have seen adults do at home and in restaurants Manipulating the materials: cutting pizza, scooping it up, and putting it on plates Serving other people (and dolls) and giving pizza slices to other children Cooperating to "make" pizza and deliver it to other children	Get out enough materials. (e.g., plates, pizza slices, pans) so all children can participate. Begin by talking about how good pizza is and how much fun it is to make. As children gather, give each child a pan and a piece of pizza; encourage joint play and cooperation in making the pizza. When pizza comes out of the oven, suggest delivery targets (e.g., "Give this piece to Katie") to give children practice in giving things to others.	Ingredients that make up pizza How pizza tastes Times you have eaten pizza; times children have eaten pizza Pizza is hot, the oven is hot Describe what children are doing and what the teacher is doing (parallel talk and self-talk)

House/Doll Area Activities

Activity	Materials needed	What children will explore and experience	What teachers can do	What teachers can talk about
Scarves and blankets **variation:** **scarf dancing**	Lots and lots of filmy scarves, bandanas, and doll-size blankets Play dance music and encourage children to wave their scarves as they dance	The feel of different fabric textures How the world looks through a sheer scarf Playing peekaboo Hiding objects and finding them again Folding and unfolding Covering dolls, stuffed animals, or other toys Crumpling up scarves and putting them in their pockets	Get out the scarves, bandanas, and blankets and talk animatedly about playing peekaboo or hide-and-seek. Follow the children's lead as to what is interesting to them about the materials. Cover your own head with a scarf or blanket and say, "Where's [teacher's name]?"—let children pull the scarf off your head. Cover children's heads—for younger or more timid children, cover only part-way—and do the same. Have children cover parts of their body—"Where's Karen's leg?"—and uncover them—"There it is!" Have children cover dolls or other toys and find them.	The textures of different scarves and blankets—soft, rough, silky, fuzzy Colors, sizes How you can see through some scarves and not others How things look through a pink or a blue scarf The children's name—"Where's Zeke?"—then lock around as if you can't find him, letting the other children tell you where he is Use parallel talk and self-talk

(continued)

House/Doll Area Activities *(continued)*

Activity	Materials needed	What children will explore and experience	What teachers can do	What teachers can talk about
Shoe store	A variety of shoes	Arranging items for display in the store	Get out the items for sale and the cash registers and begin setting up the store, talking about what you are doing.	Label items in the store
	Shoe boxes	Trying on the clothes		Talk about shopping, buying clothes, and going to stores
	Cash registers	Looking at themselves in the mirror	As children gather, let their interest and exploration guide the activity—young toddlers will explore the materials, whereas older ones may be able to participate in simple role play.	Put items into boxes, cover with lids, and let children "find" what's inside, showing surprise when they open the boxes
	Play money	Putting items into boxes, bags, or shopping baskets, then taking them out again		
variations: **hat store** **pet store**	Purses			
	Replace shoes with hats	Taking turns at various roles (with a lot of teacher help): customer, sales, or cashier		Use parallel talk and self-talk
	Have stuffed animals as pets			
Toddlers' pond	A piece of blue fabric or a blue sheet	Imagining they are at a pond	Get out the "pond" and talk animatedly about ponds and water and animals.	Water, splash, deep, shallow, wet, dry
	Stuffed and plastic animals, especially frogs, ducks, fish, and turtles	Pretending to swim	As children gather, take them to the edge of the pond and then have them wade into the pond, lie down and swim, and walk across the pond on the lily pads.	The animals that live in or near ponds; what they do, what they eat, the sounds they make, how they move
	Toy boats	Jumping from one "lily pad" to another and taking turns doing it		Sing songs related to water and ponds: Row, Row, Row Your Boat, Five Green and Speckled Frogs, and so forth
	Green circles as lily pads for walking across the pond	Making the animals move and make noises	Bring out animals and describe how different types of animals live in and near ponds.	
		Pretending to be animals or fish		Use parallel talk and self-talk
		Singing songs		

338

Active Play Area and Outdoor Activities

Activity	Materials needed	What children will explore and experience	What teachers can do	What teachers can talk about
Animal sounds and movements	Teacher energy and enthusiasm Pictures of zoo or farm animals to help children connect the sounds with the animals A full-length mirror is a nice addition	Listening to and making animal noises Imitating the teacher and other children Active and creative body movement Looking at pictures of animals Watching themselves move in funny ways in the mirror	Encourage several children to make the same animal sounds. Organize a parade of animals. Point to children's image in the mirror so they can see themselves doing funny things. Do the same animal sounds and movements over several times—it often takes toddlers several tries to catch on.	Make up songs or chants to fit each animal (e.g., "I'm a duck, duck, duck—When I walk like this . . .") Label body parts that are distinguishing features of animals—giraffe with long neck, four legs for lots of animals, and wings for a duck Talk about sizes of animals, how they feel, and where they live Talk about how people and animals are the same and different Sing Old MacDonald and other animal songs

(continued)

Active Play Area and Outdoor Activities *(continued)*

Activity	Materials needed	What children will explore and experience	What teachers can do	What teachers can talk about
Balance beam	A wooden balance beam, not very high, or strips of wide masking tape on the floor	Balancing on the beam Taking turns with other children Helping others by holding their hand while they walk across the beam Walking with one foot on and one foot off the beam Crawling on the beam Sitting on the beam Standing on one foot Jumping over the beam	Get out the balance beam or put down tape (have one or more children help) and begin to walk on the beam yourself, talking animatedly about what you are doing and how exciting it is. Put a soft mat at one end of the beam for children to jump onto (can pretend they are jumping into a pool). Have children put beanbags on their heads while they walk along the beam to increase challenge of balancing. Encourage children to take turns—play Follow-the-Leader. **Note:** Have children walk on the balance beam in bare feet—socks are too slippery.	Walking, standing, crawling, sitting, balance, straight up, on, off, forward, backward, jumping, hopping Describe what children are doing, using active verbs Emphasize turn taking and children's names

Active Play Area and Outdoor Activities

Activity	Materials needed	What children will explore and experience	What teachers can do	What teachers can talk about
Balls	Lots of balls of different sizes and shapes Foam wedges to roll balls down Plastic crates for targets	What different types of balls do—footballs do not roll like other balls, for example Practice throwing, rolling, and kicking How different balls feel—some are soft, some are heavy, some can be blown up (beach balls), some fit in your hand, and some you can sit on	Get out the balls and the crowd will come running! Encourage children with less physical skill to sit with the teacher and roll a ball back and forth with another child.	Rolling, throwing, kicking Round Colors of the balls Big, little, soft, hard
Beanbag toss	Beanbags A target, such as, a stand-up cardboard picture with holes cut in it, plastic crates or cardboard boxes, grocery bags, or hula hoops	Throwing beanbags and (maybe) hitting a target How beanbags feel in your hands and under your feet Taking turns throwing at a target	Get out the beanbags and one or more targets, and begin to play. As children arrive, give them each several beanbags and show them what you are doing. Follow the children's lead and match the activity to their abilities. Encourage children to hand beanbags to one another, to teach the concept of giving.	The colors, sizes, and shapes of beanbags *In and out, under and over, up and down* Throwing, tossing, hitting something, missing Taking turns

(continued)

Active Play Area and Outdoor Activities *(continued)*

Activity	Materials needed	What children will explore and experience	What teachers can do	What teachers can talk about
Bowling	Bowling pins Balls	Be prepared for this activity to look nothing like the bowling alley you are used to! Toddlers will explore the bowling pins in their own way—by holding, rolling, touching, tasting, and banging Playing with balls Playing cooperatively—rolling balls back and forth (with teacher's help)	Set up a few bowling pins in several different places around the area. As children gather, give each one a ball and help them roll the ball toward the pins. Show children how to kick the pins to knock them down. Let older children work at setting the pins up (it's harder than you think!). Follow the children's lead to determine what they find interesting and exciting about the materials—do not try to impose a "right" way to play with these toys.	Bowling, balls, rolling, falling down, setting up Make lots of noises when bowling pins get knocked over Talk about times you have been bowling and what a bowling alley is like Use parallel talk and self-talk

Active Play Area and Outdoor Activities

Activity	Materials needed	What children will explore and experience	What teachers can do	What teachers can talk about
Bubble chase	Homemade or commercial bubble solution Wands	Running and trying to catch bubbles—eye–hand coordination The sight of bubbles floating in the air Practice at blowing very lightly to produce bubbles (with teacher's help) Having fun—bubbles always get smiles and laughter!	Begin the activity by blowing bubbles and talking about what the bubbles are doing and what they look like. As children gather to watch and chase the bubbles, follow their lead as to what is interesting and exciting for them. Encourage children to touch and pop bubbles and also to let some fall to the floor and pop on their own. Encourage children to take turns popping the bubbles. Help children lean to blow their own bubbles.	B-B-B-B-Bubbles—give children practice with the "B" sound Size, color of bubbles What bubbles do: float, pop, shine, go up, come down Use parallel talk and self-talk

(continued)

Active Play Area and Outdoor Activities (*continued*)

Activity	Materials needed	What children will explore and experience	What teachers can do	What teachers can talk about
Buzz-buzz	No materials needed	Active and creative movement in imitation of the teacher Making buzzing noises Involvement in a group activity Having fun and being silly with an adult	Sit beside one or more toddlers and quietly explain you are the queen bee and they are your helpers in the hive. With the toddlers accompanying you, go around the room making buzzing sounds and flapping your wings. Make frequent stops around the room to land on a flower (perhaps another toddler!) and taste the nectar. Demonstrate flying slowly, then speeding up; close to the ground, then up high; being loud, then whispering and tiptoeing. Turn the "bees" into airplanes or helicopters, or into great big or little tiny birds.	Lots of BUZZ sounds Talk about flowers, insects, bees, honey, wings, and flying Describe the speed of flying and whether you are high or low Use children's names frequently as you buzz by them

Active Play Area and Outdoor Activities

Activity	Materials needed	What children will explore and experience	What teachers can do	What teachers can talk about
Gas station	Bikes (foot-powered) Doll strollers or shopping carts Gas pumps Cash registers	Riding bikes—using their own power to move them The wheels or the bikes—let toddlers turn the bikes upside down to examine the wheels Pushing wheeled toys Making motor noises Feeling the hose on the gas pump	Get materials out with children's help and talk about trips to the gas station and all the things that happen there. Help children learn to push themselves forward on the bikes (most go backwards first!). Be the gas station attendant—demonstrate washing windows, checking the oil, and filling the tires with air. Encourage children to take turns using the gas pumps. Have children give each other rides (those who have trouble with this can give rides to dolls or stuffed animals as a first step).	Driving, fast, slow, cars and trucks, full, empty, stop, go, wheels, going around, going on trips Talk about times you have been to the gas station Talk about riding in cars and on buses Talk about car seats

(continued)

345

Active Play Area and Outdoor Activities *(continued)*

Activity	Materials needed	What children will explore and experience	What teachers can do	What teachers can talk about
Hula hoops	Enough hula hoops for every child (and the teacher) Beanbags (to toss into the circle)	Large motor coordination The feel of a hula hoop Holding and carrying such a large thing How the hula hoop rolls What a circle is	Bring in the hula hoops (have one or more children help) and begin doing something fun with one of them, talking animatedly about what you are doing. Follow children's lead to see what they are interested in; do not have preconceived ideas about how the hula hoops should be used. Show children how the hula hoops will roll across the room. Demonstrate a beanbag toss into the center of a hula hoop; hold a hoop upright so children can throw bean-bags through it. Use the hula hoop as the center for a Ring Around the Rosey game. Make hula hoops into an obstacle course.	Round, hoop, roll, circle Describe what you are doing with the hula hoops and what the children are doing Emphasize similarities among children in what they are doing Encourage turn taking and cooperative play

Active Play Area and Outdoor Activities

Activity	Materials needed	What children will explore and experience	What teachers can do	What teachers can talk about
Marching band	Musical instruments Hats	Playing instruments, making "music," walking in time to music Cooperating with one another in a band Marching with other children and teachers Taking turns using different instruments	Get out the instruments and children will come running. Encourage participating children to sit as you give each one an instrument (repeated practice for several consecutive days at sitting before getting an instrument will be effective). Once all children have instruments, help each one, as needed, make the instrument work (do not require children to continue sitting after they have an instrument but to come back and sit down if they want a new one). Organize a parade around the classroom and outside.	Music, bands, labels for instruments, the sounds they make Tempo, fast, slow, loud, soft, quiet, noisy, boom, squeak Encourage children to listen to the sounds of different instruments (perhaps as the teacher plays them first)

(continued)

Active Play Area and Outdoor Activities *(continued)*

Activity	Materials needed	What children will explore and experience	What teachers can do	What teachers can talk about
Obstacle course	Mats and wedges Large foam blocks Pillows	Active movement of their bodies in space Practice in balancing and being off balance Imitating one another's actions Sharing a fun experience with other children	Set up mats and wedges in an arrangement that provides a lot of space for children to climb and crawl without running into one another too frequently. Surround the structure with more mats and/or pillows to ensure safety. Have children help set up. Talk enthusiastically about what you are doing. Encourage children to play Follow-the-Leader. Show children how to do somersaults, climb up to the top (not too high), and jump off onto a mat.	Use parallel talk to describe what the children are doing and experiencing Use the children's names frequently Point out when they are imitating each other or doing similar things to encourage joint play

Active Play Area and Outdoor Activities

Activity	Materials needed	What children will explore and experience	What teachers can do	What teachers can talk about
Rocking boats	One large or at least two small rocking boats	Vestibular stimulation and practice in balancing as the boats rock	Bring the boats into the classroom, and the children will gather!	Talk about boats and water and fishing and where you might go in a boat
		Making the boat rock while riding in it, and while outside the boat	Help children climb into the boat and get seated before the boat begins to rock.	Use parallel talk to describe what children are doing, using active and descriptive verbs
		Cooperating with other children to make the boats rock	Support children whose balance reactions are not well developed so they can stay upright as the boat rocks.	Give simple directions that children can understand and follow
		Pretending they are in a real boat and there is water beneath them	Have children take turns riding in the boat—match up those who like a "wild" ride with those who prefer calm seas.	Talk about turn taking
		Climbing into and out of the boat	Pretend to be on a lake with fish in it.	Emphasize children's cooperative efforts: "Mary and Chris have made the boat rock together"
			Sing boat songs: Row, row, row . . . The oars on the boat go back and forth	

(continued)

349

Active Play Area and Outdoor Activities (continued)

Activity	Materials needed	What children will explore and experience	What teachers can do	What teachers can talk about
Tunnel	A collapsible tunnel, preferably one with an opening in the center so children are always within a teacher's reach Balls	Crawling inside a tunnel Taking turns going through the tunnel Darkness (somewhat) inside the tunnel How the tunnel feels from inside and from outside Feeling another person going through the tunnel	Bring in the tunnel and have children help open it up. A teacher can stay at one end and have the children crawl toward him or her. The teacher can pretend to be a lion or tiger, and growl at children as they come through. Roll balls through the tunnel and have children chase the balls. Pull the tunnel around in a circle while one or two children are inside it. Pretend the tunnel is a tent. Be careful of the number of children in the tunnel at one time and keep the movement of children orderly—lots of supervision is needed.	Inside and outside Going *through* the tunnel Use parallel talk to describe in detail what children are doing, using active and descriptive verbs Emphasize similarities between children: "Danny and Jason are both in the tunnel!" Talk about turn taking

Active Play Area and Outdoor Activities

Activity	Materials needed	What children will explore and experience	What teachers can do	What teachers can talk about
Washing windows	Sponges Spray bottles containing clear water Cloth dish towels or wash-cloths (easier for toddlers to handle than paper towels)	Participating in routine adult activities—things they've seen their parents do at home Working together to get the windows "clean" Motor activity or reaching and scrubbing	Get out the materials and talk animatedly about how much fun it is to wash windows. Give each participating child his or her own spray bottle and help each child learn to spray by squeezing the handle. Show children how to wipe the water off the window. Emphasize turn taking and cooperation—pair up children so that one sprays and the other wipes, then reverse roles.	Windows and what you can see out of them Workers and how important it is to keep things clean How cooperation works to get jobs done easier and better Point out how children help each other

Small Group Activities
(Art, Science, Sensory Experiences)

Activity	Materials needed	What children will explore and experience	What teachers can do	What teachers can talk about
Collage, using Contact paper	Clear Contact paper, fastened with masking tape to a table or wall with the sticky side out Pictures or objects to place on the collage, such as magazine pictures to match the week's theme, cotton balls, ribbons, small toys, small pieces of colored tissue paper or cellophane, and cut-out shapes	Sticking pictures or objects onto the Contact paper and then taking them off again—this collage is a "work in progress," not a finished product Working together on a project Looking at their collage when it is displayed in the classroom	Get the Contact paper ready before children come to the area. Have pictures cut out ahead of time, or have objects ready so each child has a supply of his or her own. As children gather, let their interest guide the activity.	Sticky, pictures, designs Label the pictures or objects the children place on the collage Describe what children are doing Talk about what a wonderful collage they are making together

352

Small Group Activities

Activity	Materials needed	What children will explore and experience	What teachers can do	What teachers can talk about
Fingerpaint handprints	Fingerpaints Fingerpaint paper Construction paper	The feel of fingerpaints on their hands and fingers Following simple directions, with teachers' help The shape of their hands Working together with other children to make a mural of handprints	Prepare fingerpaints and fasten paper to table that is covered with newspaper. Demonstrate putting hands in paint and making a handprint. Encourage children to explore the paint; be patient with those who do not like messy play.	Colors, the feel of the paint (e.g., squishy, soft, gooey, messy) Different sizes of hands Right hand compared with left hand Fingers, thumbs, palm, fist, wrist, fingernails, knuckles Use self-talk and parallel talk
Mystery picture	White paper Black paint—tempera (thinned) Paint brushes (long-handled, large brushes are best) White crayons Newspaper to protect tables	Use of paint brushes and crayons Experience with paper Following simple directions Seeing a design appear—like magic!	Give each child a piece of paper and a white crayon and let them draw with the crayon on the paper. They won't see anything, so this needs to go quickly. Younger children may need to have the teacher make a design for them. Demonstrate for the children how to paint with black paint on the paper—the picture will "mysteriously" appear.	Paint, brushes, crayons, paper, pictures What the children see happening as they paint over the design with black paint That they are seeing the crayon marks underneath the paint

(continued)

Small Group Activities (continued)

Activity	Materials needed	What children will explore and experience	What teachers can do	What teachers can talk about
Painting with cars and trucks	Small vehicles Tempera paint in shallow containers Construction paper Smocks or t-shirts to protect children's clothes Newspaper to protect table tops	Seeing marks left by the wheels dipped in paint The motor activity of rolling cars and trucks on paper Imitating each other	Place shallow containers of paint in the center of the table. Demonstrate dipping the wheels of a car or truck into the paint and then rolling it on the paper. Let children use several different colors of paint, trading vehicles with one another.	
Paper bag puppets	Small paper bags (lunch bag size) Prepared features (e.g., eyes, mouths, bows, glasses, noses, baseball hats) Yarn for hair Glue	The feel of glue and how it works Trying to move features after they have been glued Facial features Opening the paper bag and putting their hands inside How yarn feels	Give each child a paper bag and a variety of facial features. Put a small plateful of glue on the table where two or three children can reach it. Most children will need help with the glue at first, but let them explore it once they have been shown how it is used. Do not have a model for children to copy—let them create their own "faces." Demonstrate the use of puppets—putting bag on your hand and making puppet talk.	Facial features, faces, expressions Count eyes, ears, noses, and mouths on the children's faces Have a mirror handy so children can look at their own faces Glue, sticky, stuck, messy, yuck

354

Small Group Activities

Activity	Materials needed	What children will explore and experience	What teachers can do	What teachers can talk about
Play-Doh	Homemade or commercial Play-Doh—a small amount for each child Cookie cutters	How the Play-Doh feels in their hands Squashing the Play-Doh, rolling it between their hands Using cookie cutters and pushing down; then seeing the shapes they make	Set out a small amount of Play-Doh for each child and some for the teacher. Demonstrate flattening out the Play-Doh to make pancakes or pizza. Demonstrate rolling the Play-Doh into a ball—a basketball or apple. Demonstrate using cookie cutters to make shapes.	Shapes, colors, flat, round, circle, squeeze, squish, bang, push What they are doing with their Play-Doh—what you are making What the children's creations look like—be creative!
Pouring water from pitcher into cups	A sink or large dishpan for each child—or outdoor space Pitchers and cups Water	How water "works" How to tip a pitcher to pour water How to tell when a cup is full	Give each child a small pitcher of water and some cups. Demonstrate pouring. Let children drink the water they pour—give fresh water to each child. If outdoors, have children pour water from pitcher onto plants.	Water, wet, dry, pour, drink, cup, pitcher, juice, milk Pouring drinks at mealtime Use parallel talk and self-talk

(continued)

Small Group Activities *(continued)*

Activity	Materials needed	What children will explore and experience	What teachers can do	What teachers can talk about
Puzzles	A selection of puzzles for children of different ability levels (Using the same set of puzzles throughout an entire week builds mastery)	Mastering a challenging task Persisting at solving a problem Following simple directions Recognition of shapes Manipulating small toys	Select a puzzle for each child that presents a challenge but is not impossible. Demonstrate for a child who is unfamiliar with puzzles. Help and guide children so they are successful, but do not solve the puzzle for them. Let children enjoy the pleasure of repeating the same puzzle several times before getting out a more difficult or less familiar puzzle.	The pictures or shapes of the puzzle What children are doing with the puzzle pieces and simple instructions, following through as needed so the child understands the direction
Shaving cream	Cans of shaving cream Children in smocks (or swimsuits outside) to protect their clothes	The feel of shaving cream on their hands Making shapes out of shaving cream Making a mess without getting into trouble Having fun	Spread the shaving cream on tables or on tablecloths on top of tables. Let children explore and experience the shaving cream any way they want (but prevent them from tasting). If children are reluctant to get messy, give them a small dab of shaving cream to feel—do not insist that all children participate.	Smooth, creamy, mushy, goopy, sliding, squeeze, goop, messy What children are doing and what they are feeling The shapes they make with the shaving cream

Small Group Activities *(continued)*

Activity	Materials needed	What children will explore and experience	What teachers can do	What teachers can talk about
Sunshiney faces **variation: glue children's pictures in the center of the sun face**	Paper plates Circles cut from yellow construction paper (prepared in advance) Strips of yellow and orange construction paper for rays of sun (prepared in advance) Glue Crayons Newspaper to cover tables	Glue—what it feels like, how it is used Handling paper and crayons Crumpling paper Tearing paper Following simple directions	Demonstrate for children how to glue circles in center of plates—but do not insist that children do it the "right" way. Have children color on the yellow face (or directly on the plate). Help the older children glue strips of paper to the outside of the plate to make rays for	Glue, paper, crayons, plates, sun, yellow, faces, summer, warmth, sunglasses, round, circle, roll, wheels Sticky, stuck, messy, yuck The colors the children are using Use parallel talk and self-talk

(continued)

Small Group Activities (continued)

Activity	Materials needed	What children will explore and experience	What teachers can do	What teachers can talk about
Tracing hands and feet	Paper Crayons Pencil or marker for teacher to trace child's hands and feet	Seeing a copy of their own hands and feet Following directions Imitating other children	As a child stands on a piece of paper or places hands on a piece of paper, the teacher traces around them; the child can then color in the outline (or just use crayons on the paper).	Hands, feet, fingers, toes Simple directions that they can follow (e.g., "put your hand here. Hold it still please") Big, small
variation: tracing bodies	Large sheets of paper big enough for child to lie on Markers for teachers to use in tracing Crayons for children	The feel of a pencil or marker around their hands and feet Manipulating crayons to make marks on paper	Point out similarities and differences across different children—and comparison with teachers.	

358

Small Group Activities

Activity	Materials needed	What children will explore and experience	What teachers can do	What teachers can talk about
Washing plastic animals **variations:** wash babies; wash dishes; use sponges in the water instead of toys	Large bowls or dishpans about half-full of water with a little soap added Plastic animals Towels	The experience of water—how it feels, what it does, what things do when dropped in water Feeling of responsibility for taking care of their toys Participation in a regular adult routine	Demonstrate washing and drying toys. Have children work in pairs, helping each other, and switching roles frequently. Pretend animals are drinking water. Some children are timid about getting themselves wet at first; they should be given a chance to try the water on their own terms.	Washing, water, wet, dry, bath, soap, clean, dirty Body parts of the animals Baths, times children have had baths—make it fun and exciting Use parallel talk and self-talk
Watercolors **variation:** use food coloring in a small amount of water; paint on paper towels or coffee filters	Watercolor paints Paper Water in small cups or bowls Brushes (long-handled, large brushes are best) Smocks or t-shirts to protect children's clothes	Colors and mixing colors What a brush is used for, how it feels, how to hold it Making marks on paper	Give each child a piece of white paper and a brush. Two children can share paints and a cup of water. Demonstrate dipping brush into water, then into paint, then onto paper—then let children experiment.	Colors, brightness, mixing colors, brushes, water, paint, paper What the children are doing and what their pictures look like Similarities between children in what they are doing Compliment children who are sharing paints

(continued)

Small Group Activities (*continued*)

Activity	Materials needed	What children will explore and experience	What teachers can do	What teachers can talk about
Weighing and measuring	An accurate scale A tape measure or wall-mounted measuring stick	Concepts of size, growth, and change Repeating a routine that is familiar to them from the doctor's office in another (perhaps less stressful) context Following simple directions	Bring the scale and measuring tape into the classroom, or take children in small groups to another room for weighing and measuring. Encourage children to bring dolls or stuffed animals or other toys to be weighed and measured.	Size, big, little, height, weight, long, short, growing, So Big!, older, age Similarities between children—pairing up those who are the same height or weight or age Use self-talk and parallel talk

Appendix C

Planning Forms for Infant and Toddler Play

Building a curriculum for inclusive infant-toddler care programs involves advance planning by directors and teachers. Play activities should be *fun* for children and teachers. In addition to having fun, however, teachers of infants and toddlers should have teaching and learning goals in mind when they present play activities to children. Some of these goals will be focused on basic concepts or skills that are applicable to all of the children in the group. Others will be most appropriate for a specific age or ability level. Finally, in an early intervention program, it is important to incorporate individual outcomes desired for children with special needs into activity planning. The play activity planning forms included in this appendix provide an outline for teachers and curriculum planners to use in identifying the learning opportunities inherent in materials and activities that are enjoyable and attractive to young children.

Play 1 Activity: _____

What teachers can do with:

TINY BABIES

CRAWLERS

WALKERS

Play 2 Activity: _____ Type: _____

Materials needed:

_____

What teachers can talk about:

_____

What TINY BABIES will explore and experience:

_____

What CRAWLERS will explore and experience:

_____

What WALKERS will explore and experience:

_____

Variations on the activity:

Inclusive Child Care for Infants and Toddlers: Meeting Individual and Special Needs by Marion O'Brien © 1997 Paul H. Brookes Publishing Co., Baltimore.

Activity: _____ Area: _____

Preparation needed:

_____

Other materials:

_____

What to do:

_____

Variations on the activity:

_____

What children will explore and experience during this activity:

_____

What teachers can talk about:

_____

Accommodations for children with special needs:

_____

Inclusive Child Care for Infants and Toddlers: Meeting Individual and Special Needs by Marion O'Brien © 1997 Paul H. Brookes Publishing Co., Baltimore.

TODDLER PLAY ACTIVITIES

Building Toy Area

Week of: _____

Theme: _____

	MONDAY	TUESDAY	WEDNESDAY	THURSDAY	FRIDAY
A					
B					
C					
D					

House/Doll Area

	MONDAY	TUESDAY	WEDNESDAY	THURSDAY	FRIDAY
A					
B					
C					
D					

Active Play Area

	MONDAY	TUESDAY	WEDNESDAY	THURSDAY	FRIDAY
A					
B					
C					
D					

(continued)

Inclusive Child Care for Infants and Toddlers: Meeting Individual and Special Needs by Marion O'Brien © 1997 Paul H. Brookes Publishing Co., Baltimore.

	MONDAY	TUESDAY	WEDNESDAY	THURSDAY	FRIDAY
Small Group					
Music					
Stories					

Outdoor Play

	MONDAY	TUESDAY	WEDNESDAY	THURSDAY	FRIDAY
A					
B					
C					

Alternate Play Activities for Rain/Snow/Cold

	MONDAY	TUESDAY	WEDNESDAY	THURSDAY	FRIDAY
A					
B					
C					

Inclusive Child Care for Infants and Toddlers: Meeting Individual and Special Needs by Marion O'Brien © 1997 Paul H. Brookes Publishing Co., Baltimore.

Appendix D

Recording Forms
for Inclusive Infant-Toddler Care

Quality care for infants and toddlers demands careful attention to record keeping. Because children cannot report to parents everything that happened to them during the day, teachers must be sure that parents receive a full record of their children's day. Parents of infants need to know how their babies are eating, when they last slept, and what their overall disposition was each day. Once toddlers begin the process of toilet training, parents want to be kept up-to-date on their children's progress. Thus, much of the information recorded on the forms included in this appendix should be transferred to the Take-Home Report (see Figure 3.1) for parents' information.

Record keeping is even more important when children have special needs. Children's health and well-being may depend on knowing how much and when they ate or slept and how often they had a wet diaper. Accurate records of medication dosages and times administered can be vital, as well as teachers' observations of changes in children's appearance or behavior.

The forms included in this appendix are useful but uncomplicated ways of keeping track of basic care routines for infants and toddlers. When a child care center has accurate and complete records, parents gain confidence in the quality of care provided, and communication among teachers and between teachers and parents is easier. (Teachers may need to make extra photocopies of each form in order to accommodate the number of children in their classroom). Recent records should be maintained in the classroom for easy reference; after about 3 months, records can be transferred to storage where they should be kept for several years.

Date: _____

Infant Feeding Record

Child's name							
Breakfast Formula or milk, cereal, and fruit and/or vegetable	Time: Foods and Amounts Caregiver's Initials:	Time: Foods and Amounts Caregiver's Initials:	Time: Foods and Amounts Caregiver's Initials:	Time: Foods and Amounts Caregiver's Initials:	Time: Foods and Amounts Caregiver's Initials:	Time: Foods and Amounts Caregiver's Initials:	Time: Foods and Amounts Caregiver's Initials:
Lunch Formula or milk, fruit and/or vegetable, cereal, and/or meat, poultry, or cheese	Time: Foods and Amounts Caregiver's Initials:	Time: Foods and Amounts Caregiver's Initials:	Time: Foods and Amounts Caregiver's Initials:	Time: Foods and Amounts Caregiver's Initials:	Time: Foods and Amounts Caregiver's Initials:	Time: Foods and Amounts Caregiver's Initials:	Time: Foods and Amounts Caregiver's Initials:

(continued)

Infant Feeding Record   *(continued)*

Date: _____

Child's name						
Snack	Time:	Time:	Time:	Time:	Time:	Time:
Formula, milk, or juice, and bread or crackers	Foods and Amounts	Foods and Amounts	Foods and Amounts	Foods and Amounts	Foods and Amounts	Foods and Amounts
	Caregiver's Initials:	Caregiver's Initials:	Caregiver's Initials:	Caregiver's Initials:	Caregiver's Initials:	Caregiver's Initials:
Snack	Time:	Time:	Time:	Time:	Time:	Time:
Formula, milk, or juice, and bread or crackers	Foods and Amounts	Foods and Amounts	Foods and Amounts	Foods and Amounts	Foods and Amounts	Foods and Amounts
	Caregiver's Initials:	Caregiver's Initials:	Caregiver's Initials:	Caregiver's Initials:	Caregiver's Initials:	Caregiver's Initials:

Inclusive Child Care for Infants and Toddlers: Meeting Individual and Special Needs by Marion O'Brien © 1997 Paul H. Brookes Publishing Co., Baltimore.

Health Check Record   Week: _____

Child's name	Day checked (circle one)	✔ (if OK)	Problems, general disposition, and action
	M T W TH F		
	M T W TH F		
	M T W TH F		
	M T W TH F		
	M T W TH F		
	M T W TH F		
	M T W TH F		
	M T W TH F		

Inclusive Child Care for Infants and Toddlers: Meeting Individual and Special Needs by Marion O'Brien © 1997 Paul H. Brookes Publishing Co., Baltimore.

Infant Diapering and Sleep Record

Date: _____

Child's name									
7:00									
7:15									
7:30									
7:45									
8:00									
8:15									
8:30									
8:45									
9:00									
9:15									
9:30									
9:45									
10:00									
10:15									
10:30									
10:45									
11:00									
11:15									
11:30									
11:45									
12:00									
12:15									

(continued)

Directions: Record for each child each hour: **D** if dry; **W** if wet; **BM** if soiled; **S** during any 15-minute period child is asleep.

Inclusive Child Care for Infants and Toddlers: Meeting Individual and Special Needs by Marion O'Brien © 1997 Paul H. Brookes Publishing Co., Baltimore.

Infant Diapering and Sleep Record (*continued*)

Date: _____

Child's name									
12:30									
12:45									
1:00									
1:15									
1:30									
1:45									
2:00									
2:15									
2:30									
2:45									
3:00									
3:15									
3:30									
3:45									
4:00									
4:15									
4:30									
4:45									
5:00									
5:15									
5:30									
5:45									

Directions: Record for each child each hour: **D** if dry; **W** if wet; **BM** if soiled; **S** during any 15-minute period child is asleep.

Inclusive Child Care for Infants and Toddlers: Meeting Individual and Special Needs by Marion O'Brien © 1997 Paul H. Brookes Publishing Co., Baltimore.

Toddler Diapering/Toilet Record

For the Week of: _____

CHILD	MONDAY			TUESDAY			WEDNESDAY			THURSDAY			FRIDAY			NEW STAGE?

Directions: Record for each child at each toileting time: **D** if dry, **W** if wet, or **BM** if soiled: slash; and then **0** if child did not sit on the potty seat, **N** if child sat but did not go, **W** if child wet while on the potty seat, or **BM** if child did a bowel movement while on the potty seat.

Inclusive Child Care for Infants and Toddlers: Meeting Individual and Special Needs by Marion O'Brien © 1997 Paul H. Brookes Publishing Co., Baltimore.

PLEASE RECORD TIMES EACH DAY

Daily Attendance Record

Date: _____

Child's name	Time in	Time out	Special instructions

Record each child's name and time if child leaves and returns to classroom:

Child's name	Time out	Time in	Where?

Inclusive Child Care for Infants and Toddlers: Meeting Individual and Special Needs by Marion O'Brien © 1997 Paul H. Brookes Publishing Co., Baltimore.

Day: _____ Date: _____ $\mathcal{FYI}$

Record any information about children, staff, and events. Also record any reminders for other supervisors, bus riders, family services coordinators, or directors.

Children's health/medications:

Schedule/telephone number changes for parents:

Teacher/staff issues:

Mealtime/kitchen/food issues:

Bus issues and information for bus riders:

Other information, concerns, or unusual events:

Inclusive Child Care for Infants and Toddlers: Meeting Individual and Special Needs by Marion O'Brien © 1997 Paul H. Brookes Publishing Co., Baltimore.

Medication Request Form

Child: _____

Prescription number: _____

Time last given: _____

Day and Date: _____

Type of medication: _____

Parent signature: _____

PARENTS: Please fill in times and exact amounts of medication to be given.

TIME	AMOUNT

STAFF: Please fill in your name and the time the child was given the medication.

STAFF GIVING MEDICATION	TIME GIVEN

Inclusive Child Care for Infants and Toddlers: Meeting Individual and Special Needs by Marion O'Brien
© 1997 Paul H. Brookes Publishing Co., Baltimore.

Index

Page numbers followed by "t" denote tables; those followed by "f" denote figures.

LINCOLN CHRISTIAN UNIVERSITY

LaVergne, TN USA
02 March 2010
174708LV00004B/29/A